BLACKSTONE'S GUIDE TO

The Sanctions and Anti-Money Laundering Act 2018

BLACKSTONE'S GUIDE TO

The Sanctions and Anti-Money Laundering Act 2018

Hugo D. Lodge

OXFORD
UNIVERSITY PRESS

OXFORD
UNIVERSITY PRESS

Great Clarendon Street, Oxford, OX2 6DP,
United Kingdom

Oxford University Press is a department of the University of Oxford.
It furthers the University's objective of excellence in research, scholarship,
and education by publishing worldwide. Oxford is a registered trade mark of
Oxford University Press in the UK and in certain other countries

First Edition published in 2020

Impression: 1

Published in the United States of America by Oxford University Press
198 Madison Avenue, New York, NY 10016, United States of America

British Library Cataloguing in Publication Data
Data available

Library of Congress Control Number: 2020936085

ISBN 978–0–19–884477–8

Printed in Great Britain by
Ashford Colour Press Ltd, Gosport, Hampshire

Foreword

Without the 2018 Act, the UK would be in a state of paralysis. Its sanctions and anti-money laundering (AML) regimes would have no mechanism for keeping pace with fast-changing events.

The Brexit debate did not dwell on the implications for sanctions and AML regimes in the UK. Nevertheless, the UK had come to depend on the EU as providing the mechanisms for imposing sanctions, and for providing the conduit for international standards in AML to be brought into English law.

The Guide deals concisely with the major changes introduced by the 2018 Act. The UK's overarching sanctions scheme has been amended in five key respects. First, the potential scope of UK sanctions has been considerably broadened. HM Government can now impose sanctions regulations considered 'appropriate' for a diverse range of purposes. In particular, the *Magnitsky* amendment was a late change to the Act, allowing the UK to impose sanctions on those who commit gross human rights violations. Second, HM Government now has the power to designate persons not only by name but also by description, in situations where it is impractical to identify by name all designated persons. Third, the process of challenge by designated persons in the UK courts has been strictly defined and subjected to greater control. The 2018 Act prevents designated persons from immediately challenging regulations before the courts; they must first request either variation or revocation of the designation from the Secretary of State. Fourth, the 2018 Act includes a broad licensing power. Fifth, the obligation to report information to the authorities in respect of financial sanctions is extended to a far greater range of natural and legal persons. These are important changes.

This is an insightful and practical Guide to the new law. Practitioners will particularly appreciate its clear focus on the core new power in Section 1 (Chapter 2), financial sanctions including asset freezes (Chapter 3), requests for ministerial review (Chapter 8), and subsequent challenge in the courts (Chapter 9). Finally, in Chapter 13, there is a useful review of changes made to UK AML immediately before Brexit. Hugo Lodge draws on his experience of twenty years at the London Bar, his recent work at the Financial Conduct Authority, private practice offshore, and being instrumental in the establishment of the Cayman Attorneys Regulation Authority. I commend this excellent book which provides sure-footed guidance and much needed clarity for the uncertain days ahead.

David Perry QC
6 KBW College Hill

Preface

Not only is the 2018 Act necessary to preserve the UK's sanctions post-Brexit, it also provides scope for divergence from the EU. HM Government has indicated an appetite to go further and faster than the EU in tackling the perpetrators of human rights abuses.

Also, in the detail of the Post-Brexit Russia sanctions there are early signs of the UK adopting a subtly different approach from the EU in its treatment of certain Russian-owned entities.[1] Further, the Prime Minister was urged in January 2020 to take unilateral action against Iran in respect of the detention of Nanzanin Zaghari-Ratcliffe.[2] In the same month, the UK Chancellor of the Exchequer warned there would be 'divergence' from the EU trade rules post-Brexit.[3] These may be further early signs of a willingness on the part of the UK to take a different path from the EU. The 2018 Act provides a mechanism for divergence.

This Guide examines the broad new powers of UK ministers in the sanctions field, and precisely how designated persons can seek review of them, and ultimately bring judicial challenges.

As for anti-money laundering, no doubt the UK will continue to look to the Financial Action Task Force (FATF) standards. However, there is a new margin of discretion in the 2018 Act for the UK post-Brexit to depart from the EU approach. Compliance practitioners will wish to keep a close eye on possible areas of future divergence, explored in this Guide. The final section of the book includes a review of the last EU-driven reforms to UK AML law, implementation of the Fifth Money Laundering Directive(5MLD).[4]

In this book, each section of the 2018 Act is considered in sequence, but practitioners may wish to focus on the new core power for the UK to make its own sanctions post-Brexit, found in Section 1 (Chapter 2), financial sanctions including asset freezes (Chapter 3), requests for ministerial review (Chapter 8), and subsequent challenge in the courts (Chapter 9). Current UK sanctions against Russia,[5] which came into effect on Brexit day, are used as a case study throughout the Guide.

---

[1] Guidance notes to that regime issued by the Office of Financial Sanctions Implementation (OFSI) allude to divergence in terms (emphasis added): 'This means that the securities of subsidiaries incorporated or established in the UK are not subject to these prohibitions. *This differs from the EU sanctions regime.*' See Appendix 5 to this Guide.

[2] https://www.bbc.com/news/uk-51216013.

[3] https://www.bbc.com/news/uk-politics-51161808.

[4] Directive (EU) 2018/843, available at: https://eur-lex.europa.eu/legal-content/EN/TXT/?uri=CELEX:32018L0843.

[5] See Appendices 4 and 5 to this Guide.

Potentially controversial topics for divergence in anti-money laundering policy are considered in Chapter 13.

The author is grateful to his former colleagues Rachel Cundall and Jack Carter for research and help in drafting the early chapters of this Guide. Though all three are experienced regulators, the views expressed in this Guide are solely those of the author. Any errors which remain are his alone. Finally, the author is ever thankful to his inspirational parents.

The law is stated as at 1 March 2020.

Contents

TABLE OF CASES xv

TABLE OF LEGISLATION xvii

1. INTRODUCTION

A. Transition, Controversy, and Divergence 1.01
1. Transition 1.01
2. The Purpose of Sanctions and Recent Controversy 1.11
3. Future Divergence in UK Sanctions 1.17

B. Context of the 2018 Act 1.30
1. Overview of Pre-Brexit Sanctions Regime 1.30
2. HM Government Departments and Agencies with a Sanctions Role 1.40
3. International Assessment of UK Sanctions and AML Schemes 1.45
4. Legislative History: Controversial Passage of the 2018 Act 1.55
5. Overview of the 2018 Act: Reform of Existing UK Sanctions Scheme 1.69
6. The Comparative Picture: Sanctions Schemes Amongst the EU's Neighbours 1.70
7. The New AML Powers in the 2018 Act 1.75
8. The Scope of the Book 1.78

2. POWER TO MAKE, AMEND, AND SUSPEND SANCTIONS

A. Core Power and Additional Requirements 2.01
1. Overview 2.01
2. Passage of the Bill: Additions to the Core Power 2.02
3. Core Power to Make Sanctions Regulations: Section 1 2.07
4. Human Rights Violations: *Magnitsky* 2.17
5. Additional Requirements: Section 2 2.25
6. Temporary Powers in Relation to Existing EU Sanctions Lists 2.30

B. Powers to Suspend, Revoke, and Amend Sanctions Regulations 2.37
1. Suspension of Prohibitions and Requirements 2.37
2. Revocation and Amendment of Regulations under Section 1 2.39
3. Amending the Type of Sanctions 2.42

C. Guidance, Reporting, and 'Future-proofing' 2.44
1. Guidance 2.44
2. Report in Respect of Offences in Regulations 2.47
3. 'Future-proofing' the Sanctions Scheme 2.49

3. FINANCIAL SANCTIONS
A. Overview of Financial Sanctions 3.01
1. Types of Financial Sanctions and New Methods of Implementation 3.01
2. Territorial Application of Financial Sanctions 3.11
3. Broad Interpretation of Financial Sanctions 3.18
4. Asset Freezes: Pre-Brexit Context 3.21
B. Asset Freezing under the 2018 Act 3.31
C. Definitions of Key Terms in Financial Sanctions 3.36
1. Source of Definitions 3.36
2. Dealing 3.37
3. Freezing 3.39
4. Funds, Economic Resources, and Goods 3.42
5. Financial Services and Financial Products 3.46
D. Ownership and Control 3.50
1. Avoiding an Overly Narrow Approach to Sanctions Compliance 3.50
2. Defining Ownership and Control 3.52
3. Minority Interests 3.56
4. Joint Interests 3.58

4. TRADE SANCTIONS
A. Distinctions from Arms Embargoes 4.01
B. Purpose of Trade Sanctions 4.04
C. Scope of Trade Sanctions 4.08
1. Export 4.08
2. Import 4.11
3. Key Definitions and Concepts 4.13
4. Trade Sanctions in Relation to Other UK Laws 4.23

5. IMMIGRATION SANCTIONS
A. Travel Bans 5.01
B. Exemptions 5.05
C. Section 48 Immigration Appeals 5.12

6. AIRCRAFT AND SHIPPING
A. Aircraft 6.01
B. Shipping 6.09
1. Controlling the Movement of Ships 6.09
2. Procedure for Dealing with Goods Seized from Ships 6.17
3. Revocation and Review in Relation to Ships 6.19

7. DESIGNATED PERSONS AND DESIGNATION POWERS
A. Designated Persons: OFSI Lists 7.01
1. Publicly Available Lists 7.01

2. Implementation of Sanctions without Delay 7.11
3. Proscription under the Terrorism Act 2000 7.13

B. Designation of Persons: Powers under the 2018 Act 7.17
1. Context and Key Provisions 7.17
2. Section 11: Designation of a Person by Name under a Designation Power 7.23
3. Section 12: Designation of Persons by Description under a Designation Power 7.31
4. Section 13: Persons Named by or under UN Security Council Resolutions 7.35

8. REVIEW BY APPROPRIATE MINISTER

A. Power to Vary or Revoke Designation 8.01
1. Overview 8.01
2. Section 22: Power to Vary or Revoke a Designation Made under Regulations 8.04

B. Right to Request Variation or Revocation of Designation 8.07
1. The Core Right to Request Variation or Revocation of Designation 8.07
2. The New Regulations on Sanctions Review Procedure 8.12
3. Requests in Relation to Temporary EU Lists 8.32
4. Right of a UN-named Person to Request a Review 8.36

C. Periodic and Other Reviews 8.37
1. Periodic Review of Certain Designations 8.37
2. Review by Appropriate Minister of Regulations under Section 1 8.38
3. Independent Review of Regulations with Counter-terrorism Purpose 8.42
4. Periodic Reports on Exercise of Section 1 Power 8.44

9. COURT REVIEW OF DECISIONS

A. Overview of Court Review 9.01

B. Availability of Court Review in the 2018 Act 9.10

C. Preliminary Matters 9.12

D. Closed Material Procedures 9.16

E. Disclosure 9.21

F. Case Law: Grounds for Challenge 9.25

G. Damages 9.37

10. LICENCES AND EXEMPTIONS

A. Overview 10.01

B. Exceptions and Licences 10.04
1. Exceptions 10.04
2. Licences 10.08
3. Immigration Exceptions 10.11

C. Protection for Compliance 10.12

D. Guidance 10.14
1. Crediting Frozen Accounts 10.15

2. Protection for Non-designated Independent Persons 10.16
3. Ring-fencing 10.17
4. OFSI Licensing Review and Non-retrospectivity 10.18
5. Licensing Grounds: UK Regimes 10.20
6. Licensing Grounds: Other Domestic Regimes 10.21
7. General Licences 10.23
8. Applying for a Licence 10.34
9. Submitting an Application 10.38
10. Counter-terrorism Regimes 10.41

11. ENFORCEMENT

A. Enforcement under the 2018 Act 11.01
1. The Mechanism for Imposing Fines 11.01
2. Overview of 2018 Amendments 11.03
3. Detailed Guidance from OFSI 11.08

B. International Assessment 11.14

12. INFORMATION AND REPORTING OBLIGATIONS

A. Overview of Existing Obligations 12.01

B. Section 16: Information 12.04

C. Guidance on Reporting Obligations 12.09

13. ANTI-MONEY LAUNDERING

A. Anti-money Laundering Powers in the UK Post-Brexit 13.01
1. Overview of the Amendments Made by the 2018 Act 13.01
2. Pre-Brexit AML Regime under EU Law 13.05
3. The Impact of the 2018 Act on AML in the UK 13.12
4. The Core AML Power: Section 49 13.15
5. AML Topics on Which Further Regulations May Issue 13.18

B. Anti-money Laundering in British Overseas Territories 13.40
1. The Statutory Scheme 13.40
2. Commentary 13.44

C. AML Update 2020: The Implementation of '5MLD' 13.48
1. Extension of Scope of Regulations: Tax Advisers, Letting Agents, and Art Dealers 13.51
2. Further Requirements for Policies, Controls, and Procedures (Regulation 19) 13.55
3. Extended Training Requirements (Regulation 24) 13.58
4. Supervisors Approving Individuals (Regulation 26) 13.59
5. Customer Due Diligence (Regulation 27 and Regulation 28) 13.62
6. Change to Dealing with Discrepancies on Registers (Under Regulation 30A) 13.66
7. Changes to Enhanced Due Diligence (Chapter 2, 2017 MLRs) 13.73
8. Trust Registration 13.81
9. E-money Thresholds for CDD 13.82

10. Duty to Respond to Information Requests: Accounts and Safe-deposit Boxes 13.83
11. Crypto Registration with FCA 13.84

APPENDICES

Appendix 1 Sanctions and Anti-Money Laundering Act 2018 115
Appendix 2 The Sanctions Review Procedure (EU Exit) Regulations 2018 175
Appendix 3 The Sanctions and Anti-Money Laundering Act 2018 (Commencement. 1) Regulations 2018 179
Appendix 4 Russia (Sanctions) (EU Exit) Regulations 2019 181
Appendix 5 Guidance for the financial and investment restrictions in Russia 245
Appendix 6 Extracts from the Policing and Crime Act 2017 253
Appendix 7 Guidance: How to prove and verify someone's identity 265
Appendix 8 Office of Financial Sanction Implementation: Financial Sanctions 299
INDEX 303

Table of Cases

A v SSHD [2005] 2 AC 68 . . . . . 9.31, 9.34
Anns v Merton LBC [1978] AC 728 . . . . . 9.26
Bank Mellat v HM Treasury I [2013] UKSC 38. . . . . 9.19, 9.23, 9.36
Bank Mellat I—2 [2013] UKSC 39 . . . . . 9.27, 9.30
Bank Mellat II [2014] EWHC 3631 . . . . . 9.22, 9.24
C v HM Treasury [2016] EWHC 2039 . . . . . 9.32
Caparo Industries PLC v Dickman [1990] 2 AC 605. . . . . 9.37
Europaisch-Iranische Handelsbank AG v Council of the European Union, Case C-585/13 P 3.20
R (Actis SA) v SSCLG [2007] EWHC 344 . . . . . 9.21
R (Bredenkamp) v SSFCA [2013] EWHC 2480 (Admin) 9.21
R (Greenfield) v SSHD [2005] UKHL 14 . . . . . 9.39
R (Morgan Grenfell & Co Ltd) v Inland Revenue Commissioners [2002] UKHL 21; [2003] 1 AC 563 . . . . . 8.31
R (on the application of Medway Council) v Secretary of State for Transport [2002] EWHC 2516. . . . . . 9.12
R v. Forsyth; R v. Mabey [2011] UKSC 9 . . . . . 1.31
Race Relations Board v Charter [1973] AC 868, 901F-G. 8.40
Ridge v Baldwin [1946] AC 40 . . . . . 2.35
Roberts v Hopwood [1925] AC 578 . . . . . 8.05
Rooke's Case (1598) 5 Co Rep 99b 2.26
Safa Nicu Sepahan Co. v Council of the European Union, Case C-45/15 P. 3.20
SSHD v AF (No 3) [2010] 2 AC 269. . . . . . 9.22
SSHD v CC and CF [2012] EWHC 2837. . . . . . 9.34
SSHD v MB [2006] EWCA Civ 1140. . . . . . 9.35
Stradling v Morgan (1560) 1 P 199 . . . . . 8.31
Tariq v Home Office [2012] 1 AC 452. . . . . . 9.24
Three Rivers DC v Bank of England (No. 3) [2001] UKHL 16 . . . . . 9.38
Van Gend en Loos v Nederlandse Administratie der Belastingen (Case 26/62); [1963] ECR 1; [1970] CMLR 1 . . . . . 1.33
Videocon Global Limited (1) Videocon Industries Limited (2) v Goldman Sachs International [2016] EWCA Civ 130. . . . . . 8.08
Westminster City Council v Croyalgrange Ltd 83 Cr. App. R. 155 . . . . . 3.25
Westminster Corporation v London North Western Railway [1905] AC 426. . . . . . 2.26

Table of Legislation

Statutes

Anti-Terrorism, Crime and Security Act 2001 (ATCSA 2001) 1.38, 10.22, 11.11, 13.17
British Nationality Act 1981
Sch 6 . . . . 13.43
Counter-Terrorism Act 2008 (CTA 2008) 1.38, 9.14, 9.16, 9.17, 9.19, 9.27, 10.22, 11.11
s 63 . . . . 9.22
Companies Act 2006
Pt 21A 13.42
s 86 . . . . 8.13
Crime and Courts Act 2013 . . . . 11.05
Criminal Finances Act 2017 (c. 22) 2.23, 3.05
s 13 . . . . 1.59
s 13(3) 2.19
s 13(4) 2.19
s 58(1)(6) 2.19
Customs and Excise Management Act 1979 . . . . 4.24, 11.04
European Communities Act 1972 (ECA) 1.05, 13.14
s 2(1) 1.09, 1.33, 13.01
s 2(2) 1.33, 13.08
European Union (Withdrawal) Act 2018 . . . . 1.36, 2.30, 13.14
s 2 . . . . 13.12
s 2(1) 13.03, 13.12, 13.21
s 7 . . . . 13.12, 13.21
s 7(1) 13.03
European Union (Withdrawal Agreement) Act 2020
s 1A 1.05, 1.18
s 1A(3)(a) 1.22
Export Control Act 2002 . . . . 1.39, 4.21
s 11(3) 4.28
Extradition Act 2003
Pt 1 . . . . 8.08
Financial Services (Banking Reform) Act 2013 . . . . 10.17
Human Rights Act 1998
s 8 . . . . 9.39
Immigration Act 1971 . . . . 1.39
s 8B 5.01, 5.02–5.04, 5.15
Immigration Act 2016 (c. 19)
s 76 . . . . 5.01
Immigration and Asylum Act 1999 (c. 33)
s 8 . . . . 5.01
Import, Export and Customs Powers (Defence) Act 1939
s 8(1)(a) 4.28
Justice and Security Act 2013 (JSA 2013)
s 6 . . . . 9.20
Policing and Crime Act 2017 . . . . 1.39, 11.08, 11.09, 11.11
Pt 8 . . . . 11.05
s 146 . . . . 11.01
ss 152–155 . . . . 1.31, 3.02
s 154 . . . . 7.11
s 155 . . . . 7.11
Proceeds of Crime Act 2002 (POCA 2002) 12.01, 12.10, 13.17
Pt 5 . . . . 2.23
Pt 7 . . . . 12.01, 13.35
s 41 . . . . 3.05
s 241A 2.18, 2.19
Sanctions and Anti-Money Laundering Act 2018 (c. 13) 1.01–1.03, 1.06, 1.07, 1.08, 1.10, 1.12, 1.16, 1.17, 1.27, 1.32, 1.36, 1.55, 1.56, 1.61, 1.68, 1.75, 1.80, 2.01, 2.11, 2.12, 2.16, 2.17, 2.23, 3.05, 3.20, 3.27, 3.36, 3.41, 3.48, 3.50, 4.23, 5.11, 5.14, 6.11, 7.01, 7.02, 7.11, 7.16, 9.01, 9.03, 9.04, 9.06, 9.09, 10.02, 10.17, 10.21, 12.01, 12.03, 12.06, 12.09, 13.13, 13.23, 13.24, 13.44, 13.45, 13.47, 13.48
Pt 1 . . . . 2.42

Pt 2 . . . . .1.76
Ch 1 . . . . .2.42
Ch 2 . . . . .7.22
Ch 4 . . . . .7.22
s 1 . . . . .2.07, 2.30, 2.31, 2.39, 2.45, 4.10, 4.11, 4.13, 4.17, 4.18, 4.20, 4.21, 7.23, 8.01, 8.04, 8.14, 8.38, 10.03, 12.07
s 1(1) 2.09, 2.42
s 1(2) 2.09, 2.42
s 1(2)(a)–(i) 2.25, 2.27
s 1(2)(f) 1.59
s 1(3) 1.30, 2.14, 6.13
s 1(5) 2.15
s 1(5)(a) 3.03
s 1(5)(c) 4.08
s 1(5)(d) 6.01
s 1(5)(e) 6.10
s 1(7) 2.18
s 1(8) 2.09
s 1(9) 2.07
s 2 . . . . .1.57, 2.06, 2.14
s 2(1) 1.10, 2.25
s 2(2) 2.26
s 2(3) 2.27
s 2(4) 2.27, 2.41
s 2(5) 2.28
s 3 . . . . 2.15, 3.03, 3.31, 7.18
ss 3–7 . . . . .2.49
s 3(1) 3.35
s 3(1)(a) 3.03, 3.31
s 3(1)(b) 3.32
s 3(1)(c) 3.32
s 3(1)(d) 3.33
s 3(1)(g) 3.34
s 3(2) 3.34
s 3(3) 3.35
s 4 . . . . 2.15, 5.01
s 5 . . . . 2.15, 4.05
s 5(1) 4.09
s 5(2) 4.10
s 6 . . . . 2.15, 6.02
s 6(1)(a) 6.02
s 6(1)(b) 6.03
s 6(1)(e) 6.06
s 6(3) 6.04
s 6(4) 6.08
s 6(5) 6.07
s 6(6) 6.05
s 6(8) 6.01
s 6(9) 6.01
s 7 . . . . 2.15, 6.10
s 7(3) 6.14
s 7(4) 6.15
s 7(5) 6.16
s 7(8) 6.12
s 8 . . . . .2.15, 2.42, 2.49
s 9 . . . . .3.31, 4.10, 7.19
ss 9–13 . . . . .7.18
s 10 . . . . 7.21, 7.28
s 11 . . . . .2.32, 7.20, 7.31
s 11(2) 7.24, 7.33
s 11(2)(b) 7.27
s 11(2)(b)(ii) 1.58
s 11(3) 7.29
s 11(7)–(9) 1.58
s 12 . . . . 2.32, 7.20
s 12(3) 7.31
s 12(4) 7.31
s 12(5) 7.33
s 13 . . . . 7.20, 7.35
s 13(2) 7.35
s 13(3) 7.35
s 14 . . . . .6.13
s 15 . . . . .5.05, 10.04, 10.11
s 15(2)(a) 10.04
s 15(2)(b) 10.08
s 15(3) 10.09
s 15(6) 10.11
s 16 . . . . 12.04, 12.08
s 16(1)(a)(ii) 12.07
s 17 . . . . 6.18, 11.03
s 17(3) 11.03
s 17(4)–(6) 11.04
s 17(8) 11.04
s 17(9) 11.05
s 18 . . . . 1.57, 2.48
s 18(2) 2.48
s 19 . . . . 1.28, 6.18
s 19(4) 6.18
s 20 . . . . 1.28, 6.18
s 21 . . . . .1.28

s 21(1)–(3) 1.28
s 22 . . . . . 8.05
s 22(1) 8.04, 8.05
s 22(2) 8.04
s 22(3) 8.05
s 22(4) 8.05
s 23 . . . . . 8.07, 8.09, 8.10, 8.14, 8.17, 8.18, 8.36, 9.10
s 23(1) 8.07
s 23(2) 8.10
s 24 . . . . . 8.37, 9.10
s 24(4) 8.37
s 25 . . . . . 8.07, 8.14, 8.17, 8.18, 8.35, 8.36, 9.10
s 26 . . . . . 6.19
s 27 . . . . . 6.20, 8.14, 8.17, 8.18, 8.28, 9.10
s 28 . . . . . 9.10
s 28(2) 6.23
s 29 . . . . . 5.24, 8.14, 8.17, 8.18, 8.28, 9.10
s 29(3) 5.25
s 30 . . . . . 1.57, 8.38
s 30(2) 8.38, 8.41
s 30(3) 8.39
s 30(7) 8.38
s 31 . . . . . 8.43
s 31(4) 8.42
s 31(5)(b) 8.42
s 32 . . . . . 8.44
s 32(1)(b) 8.44
s 32(3) 8.44
s 33 . . . . . 1.58, 8.08, 8.12, 8.34
s 34 . . . . . 1.05, 2.30, 8.32
s 34(1)(a) 2.31
s 34(1)(b) 2.31
s 34(3) 2.31
s 34(3)(a) 8.32
s 34(4) 2.31
s 34(5) 2.30
s 35 . . . . . 1.05, 2.32, 8.32
s 35(1) 8.33
s 35(1)(b) 2.33
s 35(2) 2.34, 8.33
s 35(3) 8.33
s 35(3)–(7) 2.32
s 36 . . . . . 8.32, 9.10
s 36(2) 8.32
s 37 . . . . . 8.35, 9.10
s 38 . . . . . 8.01, 8.09, 9.10, 9.11, 9.18
s 38(3) 9.15
s 39 . . . . . 1.05, 9.39
s 39(2) 9.37
s 40 . . . . . 9.16, 9.18, 9.20
s 41 . . . . . 6.17
s 42 . . . . . 2.37
s 42(3) 2.38
s 43(1) 2.45
s 43(2) 2.45
s 44 . . . . . 10.12
s 45 . . . . . 2.39
s 45(2)(a) 2.40
s 45(2)(b) 2.40
s 45(5) 2.40
s 46 . . . . . 2.41
s 47 . . . . . 2.42, 2.43, 2.49
s 47(1)(b) 2.42
s 48 . . . . . 5.15, 5.16
s 48(4) 5.12
s 49 . . . . . 13.15, 13.19, 13.20, 13.25, 13.27, 13.32–13.34, 13.36–13.38
s 49(2) 13.15
s 49(3) 13.17
s 50 . . . . . 13.31
s 51 . . . . . 1.53, 1.60, 1.77, 13.04, 13.31, 13.40, 13.41
s 51(2) 13.42
s 51(7) 13.42
s 55 . . . . . 2.15
s 60 . . . . . 3.03, 3.31
s 60(1) 3.42
s 60(2) 3.44
s 60(3) 3.39
s 60(4) 3.39
s 61 . . . . . 3.03, 3.33
s 61(1) 3.46
s 61(2) 3.47
s 62(6) 4.10
Sch 1 . . . . . 2.15, 4.05
  Pt 1 . . . . . 4.09, 4.25
  para 2 . . . . . 4.10
  para 3 . . . . . 4.11, 4.28
  para 4 . . . . . 4.13
  para 5 . . . . . 4.13

para 6 . . . . .4.14
para 7 . . . . .4.14
para 8 . . . . .4.15
para 9 . . . . .4.15
para 10 . . . . .4.15
paras 11–14. . . . . .4.17
para 13 . . . . .4.17
para 14 . . . . .4.17
para 15 . . . . .4.18
para 16 . . . . .4.19
paras 17–20. . . . . .4.20
paras 21–23. . . . . .4.21
para 21 . . . . .4.21
para 22 . . . . .4.21
para 23 . . . . .4.21
para 24 . . . . .4.22
para 25 . . . . .4.22
para 26 . . . . .4.22
para 27 . . . . .4.24
para 28 . . . . .4.24
para 29 . . . . 4.25, 4.26
para 30 . . . . .4.26
para 31 . . . . .4.27
para 32 . . . . .4.28
para 33 . . . . .4.28
para 34 . . . . .4.28
para 35(a) 4.15
para 35(b) 4.12
para 37 . . . . .4.13
para 38 . . . . .4.29
Sch 2 . . . . 1.76, 13.15, 13.20,
13.25, 13.38, 13.39
Pt 2. . . . . .13.02
para 1 . . . . .13.21
paras 2–17. . . . . .13.21
para 2(1) .13.25
para 2(2) .13.26
para 3 . . . . .13.27
para 4 . . . . .13.28
para 5 . . . . .13.30
para 6 . . . . .13.31
paras 7–14. . . . . .13.32
para 15 . . . . 13.33, 13.34
para 18 . . . . .13.34
para 22 . . . . .13.36
para 23(1) 13.37
para 23(1)(b). 13.37
para 24 . . . . 13.22, 13.38
Sch 3 . . . . 5.03, 11.07
Senior Courts Act 1981 . . . . .9.37
s 31 . . . . .9.15
Serious Crime Act 2007 . . . . .11.05
Serious Organised Crime and Police
Act 2005
Pt 2, Ch 1 . . . . .11.04
Special Immigration Appeals Commission
Act 1997 . . . . .1.69
Terrorism Act 2000 . . . . .13.17
Sch 2 . . . . 7.13, 7.34
Terrorism Act 2006 . . . . 1.69, 7.13
s 22 . . . . .7.34
s 36 . . . . .8.43
Terrorist Asset-Freezing etc. Act 2010
(TAFA 2010). 1.38, 8.43, 9.14,
9.17, 10.22, 13.17
Pt 1 . . . . .1.32
s 26 . . . . .9.32
s 40 . . . . .3.30
United Nations Act 1946
s 1(1). 1.31
Value Added Tax Act 1994. . . . . .13.54

Statutory Instruments

Andrey Lugovoy and Dmitri Kovtun
Freezing Order 2018, SI 2018/60 . . . 1.21
Civil Procedure Rules (CPR) 9.14
Pt 18 . . . . .9.21
Pt 22
PD 22. . . . . .8.21
Pt 54 . . . . .9.15
Pt 79 . . . . .9.17
r 79.17 . . . . .9.17
r 79.18 . . . . .9.17
r 79.22 . . . . .9.17
r 79.25 . . . . .9.17
Pt 82 . . . . .9.20
International Tax Compliance Regulations
2015, SI 2015/878, amended by
SI 2017/598 . . . . .13.62
Landsbanki Freezing Order 2008,
SI 2008/2668 . . . . .1.21

Money Laundering and Terrorist Financing (Amendment) Regulations 2019, SI 2019/1511 . . . . 13.50
reg 4(1)(b)(j) .13.84
reg 4(1)(b)(k). 13.84
reg 4(2) 13.51
reg 4(3) 13.52
reg 4(4) 13.52
reg 4(6) 13.54
reg 5(1)(c) 13.62
reg 5(2) 13.63
reg 5(2)(b) 13.63
reg 5(2)(c) 13.65
Money Laundering Regulations 2007, SI 2007/2157 . . . . . .1.09, 13.07, 13.08
Money Laundering, Terrorist Financing and Transfer of Funds (Information on the Payer) Regulations 2017, SI 2017/692 . . . . . . 8.15, 12.01, 13.08, 13.14, 13.19, 13.21, 13.27, 13.34, 13.36, 13.37, 13.38, 13.50
Pt 3 . . . . 13.29, 13.62
Pt 5A. 13.83
Pt 8 . . . . .13.30
reg 8 . . . . .13.23
reg 16 . . . . .13.25
reg 17 . . . . .13.25
reg 17(2) 13.26
reg 18 . . . . .13.25
reg 18(2)(b) 13.26
reg 19(4)(a) 13.55
reg 19(4)(c) 13.55
reg 20(1)(b) 13.55
reg 20(4)(a) 13.55
reg 21 . . . . .13.29
reg 24 . . . . .13.58
reg 24(1)(a) 13.58
reg 26 . . . . .13.60
reg 28 . . . . .13.63
reg 28(3) 13.63
reg 28(8) 13.64
reg 30A 13.67
reg 30A(3) .13.69
reg 33 . . . . .13.73
reg 33(1)(b) 13.77
reg 33(3A) .13.80
reg 38 . . . . .13.82
Sch 1 . . . . .1.65
Russia (Sanctions) (EU Exit) Regulations 2019, SI 2019/855 . . . . .3.54
Pt 5 . . . . .10.05
Pt 8 . . . . .12.04
Pt 9 . . . . .12.02
reg 5 . . . . .5.04
reg 6(2) 7.24
reg 6(2)(d) .7.32
reg 6(3) 7.25
reg 9 . . . . .7.28
reg 11(4) 3.38
reg 11(5) 3.37
regs 12–15. .3.41
reg 15 . . . . .3.29
reg 20 . . . . .5.04
reg 21(2) 4.10
reg 22 . . . . .4.07
reg 56(2) 10.13
reg 57 . . . . .6.09
regs 64–68. .10.10
reg 69 . . . . 5.09, 10.11
reg 70 . . . . .12.05
reg 71 . . . . .12.05
reg 72 . . . . 12.05, 12.06
reg 77 . . . . .12.07
reg 78 . . . . .12.08
Sanctions Review Procedure (EU Exit) Regulations 2018, SI 2018/1269 . . . . 8.12, 8.34
reg 2 . . . . .8.13
reg 3 . . . . 8.14, 8.34
reg 4 . . . . .8.15
reg 4(3) 8.16
reg 4(4) 8.17
reg 4(5) 8.18, 8.20
reg 4(6) 8.20
reg 4(7) 8.23
reg 4(8) 8.23
reg 5 . . . . .8.25
reg 6 . . . . .8.26
reg 7 . . . . 8.08, 8.27
reg 8 . . . . .8.28
reg 9 . . . . 8.30, 8.31
Serious Crime Prevention Orders 11.05

The Al-Qaida (Asset-Freezing) (Amendment) Regulations 2016, SI 2016/937 .... 13.17
Unregistered Companies Regulations 2009, SI 2009/2436 ....13.68

Other Legislation

Cayman Islands

Proceeds of Crime Law
s 2 ....13.23

Switzerland

Federal Act on the Implementation of International Sanctions, 2003 .....1.71

United States

Magnitsky Act 2012.................1.59
Patriot Act 2001
s 319 ....3.11

European Legislation

Directives

Directive 2005/60/EC..............13.07
Directive 2006/126/EC..............8.15
Directive (EU) 2015/849.......1.09, 13.03, 13.05, 13.07, 13.21, 13.27, 13.66
Art 9.2.........................13.77
Directive (EU) 2018/843... 1.09, 1.75, 1.80, 13.03, 13.09–13.11, 13.14, 13.31, 13.40, 13.48, 13.49, 13.85

Regulations

Regulation (EC) 2271/96.............1.13
Regulation (EC) 2252/2004...........8.15
Regulation (EU) 2014/910...........13.65
Regulation (EU) 2015/847............1.09

Treaties & Conventions

European Convention on Human Rights 5.12, 7.28
Art 6 ....9.19, 9.23
Art 8 ....9.30
Protocol 1
Art 1 ....9.30
Refugee Convention.................5.15
UN Charter 2.08, 8.36
Ch VII, Art 41..............1.31, 2.09
Withdrawal Agreement 1.07, 12.09
Art 126 ....1.07
Art 127 ....1.07, 1.18
Art 127(6).......................1.07
Art 129(6) 1.22, 1.24
Art 132 ....1.07

1

INTRODUCTION

A. Transition, Controversy, and Divergence	1.01
1. Transition	1.01
2. The Purpose of Sanctions and Recent Controversy	1.11
3. Future Divergence in UK Sanctions	1.17
B. Context of the 2018 Act	1.30
1. Overview of Pre-Brexit Sanctions Regime	1.30
2. HM Government Departments and Agencies with a Sanctions Role	1.40
3. International Assessment of UK Sanctions and AML Schemes	1.45
4. Legislative History: Controversial Passage of the 2018 Act	1.55
5. Overview of the 2018 Act: Reform of Existing UK Sanctions Scheme	1.69
6. The Comparative Picture: Sanctions Schemes Amongst the EU's Neighbours	1.70
7. The New AML Powers in the 2018 Act	1.75
8. The Scope of the Book	1.78

A. TRANSITION, CONTROVERSY, AND DIVERGENCE

1. Transition

Without the Sanctions and Anti-Money Laundering Act 2018 ('the 2018 Act'),[1] the UK would not meet its international obligations post Brexit.[2] Further, the 2018 Act gives the UK the means to take a different course from the EU on sanctions policy. Early signs are that the UK is determined to diverge, at least in respect of freezing the assets of Russian citizens, amongst others, whom the UK holds responsible for human rights abuses.[3] 1.01

[1] The Sanctions and Anti-Money Laundering Act 2018 (c. 13) received Royal Assent on 23 May 2018, at Appendix 1 of this Guide.

[2] As set out in HM Government's White Paper, *Public consultation on the United Kingdom's future legal framework for imposing and implementing sanctions* (Cm 9408).

[3] The UK's Foreign Secretary stated this intention in January 2020: https://www.ft.com/content/38cd4b7e-32fd-11ea-a329-0bcf87a328f2.

The UK prior to Brexit was dependent on the EU to provide a mechanism for the UK to discharge its sanctions duties as a United Nations (UN) signatory.

1.02 Whilst it was an EU member, the UK contributed and adhered to the EU's Common Foreign and Security Policy (CFSP), which encompassed targeted financial sanctions. Absent the 2018 Act, the UK would in future lack the means to impose its own sanctions independently of the UN, in all but the most limited counter-terrorist arenas.

1.03 Nor, after the transition period, could the UK amend its existing Money Laundering Regulations (MLRs), absent the 2018 Act. Without this new legislation, as David Perry QC concludes in the Foreword to this Guide, there would be paralysis.

1.04 To understand the scale of current UK sanctions regimes, around 2,000 entities and individuals are the target of such sanctions. Terrorist groups such as Al Qaida and Da'esh are targeted, and country-specific regimes subsist in respect of Iran, Russia, and North Korea (DPRK).

1.05 As for transition, in addition to a general transition period for Brexit,[4] so, in the arena of sanctions, temporary powers enable the UK Government to amend existing EU sanctions lists.[5] However, this interim power is limited to adding or removing the names of designated persons to existing EU lists. It would be wholly inadequate in isolation, being quickly overtaken by events post-transition.

1.06 Therefore, post-transition, a central purpose of the 2018 Act will be to enable the UK to continue to implement UN sanctions regimes and, additionally, to deploy its own sanctions to meet domestic national security and UK foreign policy objectives. The early signs of divergence are considered in detail below, at section A.3.

1.07 However, it is important to note that during the transition period, the UK will continue to be bound by EU sanctions.[6] Moreover, the default position is that UN and EU sanctions will continue to be implemented in the UK through EU law during the transition period.[7] The latest guidance from the Office of Financial Sanctions Implementation (OFSI)[8] states:

---

[4] Section 1A of the European Union (Withdrawal Agreement) Act 2020 (Withdrawal Act), given Royal Assent on 23 January 2020, states that despite the repeal of the 1972 Act on 'exit day': '[t]he European Communities Act 1972, as it has effect in domestic law or the law of a relevant territory immediately before exit day, continues to have effect in domestic law... on and after exit day so far as provided by subsections (3) to (5).'

The 1972 Act therefore continues to have effect until 11pm on 31 December 2020 unless otherwise stated by the UK Government, per section 39 Withdrawal Act.

[5] By sections 34 and 35 of the 2018 Act.

[6] Per the Withdrawal Agreement, the UK has entered into a transition period, which will continue until 31 December 2020: see Article 126, with the technical if unlikely possibility of extension for up to two further years, by Article 132. Article 127 of the Withdrawal Agreement envisages that EU law will continue to apply until the end of the Transition Period, and references to Member States in the EU sanctions regime shall include the UK, by Article 127(6). The Withdrawal Agreement was ratified on 29 January 2020.

[7] OFSI issued Guidance in January 2020, Chapter 5 of which is reproduced at Appendix 8 to this Guide.

[8] ibid.

During the transition period, the government can also bring into force autonomous UK sanctions regimes through [the 2018 Act]. [The 2018 Act] gives the UK the power to impose, update and lift sanctions after leaving the EU. However, most sanctions regimes, for which regulations have been laid under the Sanctions Act, will not come into force fully until 1 January 2021.

Aside from sanctions, after transition the UK will have lost its EU mechanism for making regulations for the purposes of anti-money laundering (AML) and counter the financing of terrorism (CFT). The 2018 Act also bridges this legislative gap, considered in detail in Chapter 13 of this Guide. 1.08

To develop the detailed historical context, before Brexit, the UK relied on the European Communities Act (ECA) 1972[9] to transpose EU Directives on AML and CFT. Ultimately these Directives were driven by standards and guidance from the Financial Action Task Force (FATF). Such powers were used in June 2017 to transpose the Fourth EU Money Laundering Directive and associated Funds Transfer Regulation, which provided a wholesale revision of the UK's 2007 Money Laundering Regulations (MLRs) with even greater focus on adoption of a risk-based approach (RBA). The transposition of the Fifth Money Laundering Directive (5MLD) is considered in Chapter 13 of this Guide. 1.09

Although section 2(1) of the European Union (Withdrawal) Act 2018[10] preserved the UK's AML/CTF regime as at 31 January 2020, the UK will continue to need a power to make, amend, and repeal relevant regulations by secondary legislation. The lack of a power would in future prevent the UK updating that regime to address matters including emerging risks and updated international standards. Hence the 2018 Act is necessary not just in respect of sanctions, but across the wider AML sphere. 1.10

2. The Purpose of Sanctions and Recent Controversy

Charles Proctor identifies[11] a fundamental shift in the use of sanctions in the modern era. Until the 1980s, a serious diplomatic rift might have led to severance of financial and commercial links with a government and all the people in its territory, Proctor gives the example of Argentina and the Falklands conflict of 1982. By contrast, the modern approach is to target political leaders and their associates, rather than the population at large, so that sanctions bite on individuals with personal involvement in current affairs. 1.11

[9] Section 2(1) ECA: 'All such rights, powers, liabilities, obligations and restrictions from time to time created or arising by or under the Treaties, and all such remedies and procedures from time to time provided for by or under the Treaties, as in accordance with the Treaties are without further enactment to be given legal effect or used in the United Kingdom shall be recognised and available in law, and be enforced . . .'

[10] Section 2(1) EU(W)A 2018: 'EU-derived domestic legislation, as it has effect in domestic law immediately before exit day, continues to have effect in domestic law on and after exit day.'

[11] Charles Proctor, *The Law and Practice of International Banking* (2nd edn, OUP 2015) Part F at 47.10 et seq.

1.12 HM Government's current approach is as per the Explanatory Note[12] to the 2018 Act: 'Sanctions are an important foreign policy and national security tool. They are restrictive measures which are designed to be temporary and can be used to coerce a change in behaviour, to constrain behaviour, or to communicate a clear political message to other countries or persons.' Prior to Brexit the main three drivers of UK sanctions have been the UN, the EU, and 'domestic' UK counter-terrorism priorities.

1.13 There are times when the sanctions regimes of apparent allies can conflict, most notably with the recent US antipathy to trade with Cuba and Iran. When the US government withdrew from the Joint Committee Plan of Action (JCPOA) in 2018, the President of the European Commission moved to amend the Blocking Regulation.[13] Its aim is to protect businesses from the extra-territorial effects of sanctions adopted by third countries, in this case the US. In such circumstances, a company may find itself in breach of US sanctions, with relatively little comfort from EU blocking provisions,[14] as they may be denied access to the US financial system.

1.14 In other contexts, the UN Security Council chooses not to act (especially when prevented from doing so by a Russian or Chinese veto), but cooperation between the EU and the US, with the support of others, including Canada, Australia, Switzerland, and Norway, has led to sanctions in any event. Recent examples include Syria,[15] and enhancing UN sanctions with additional autonomous measures, for example in respect of North Korea.[16]

1.15 As for the scale of sanctions in force, the UK currently implements a little over thirty sanctions regimes. The Office of Financial Sanctions Implementation (OFSI)[17] maintains central lists of designated persons and provides regular email updates to any interested subscriber. This number includes country-specific sanctions regimes, as mentioned most notably in relation to Russia, Iran, and North Korea. Other sanctions regimes implemented by the UK target Da'esh,[18] Al Qaida, and terrorist groups. Pursuant to the Syria and North Korea sanctions regimes alone, the UK has designated over 500 individuals and entities who are considered a threat to international peace and security. In total there are at any one time in the region of 2,000 individuals and entities subject to sanctions implemented by the UK.

1.16 The Explanatory Note to the 2018 Act claims on behalf of HM Government that 'Sanctions can have a real impact, as shown in the key role they played in bringing Iran to the negotiating table and securing agreement to place robust safeguards on its nuclear programme.' The counterpoint to this is that sanctions regimes can only

[12] http://www.legislation.gov.uk/ukpga/2018/13/pdfs/ukpgaen_20180013_en.pdf.

[13] Regulation 2271/96.

[14] https://ec.europa.eu/fpi/what-we-do/updated-blocking-statute-support-iran-nuclear-deal_en.

[15] https://www.gov.uk/guidance/sanctions-on-syria.

[16] https://www.gov.uk/government/publications/financial-sanctions-north-korea-democratic-peoples-republic-of-korea.

[17] https://www.gov.uk/government/organisations/office-of-financial-sanctions-implementation.

[18] https://www.gov.uk/government/collections/uk-sanctions-on-isil-daesh-and-al-qaida.

be effective if adopted consistently, and the US approach in respect of sanctions against Iran has been less than consistent:[19] see, as mentioned above, its withdrawal from the JCPOA.[20]

3. Future Divergence in UK Sanctions

The 2018 Act creates the potential for the UK sanctions and AML regimes to diverge from those of EU Members; there have been early differences in respect of the Russia Sanctions regime (see below), and statements from the UK Foreign Secretary show an appetite for substantial divergence in respect of human rights abuses.[21] 1.17

As a starting point, per Article 127 of the Withdrawal Agreement and section 1A of the Withdrawal Act, EU law will continue to apply in the UK until the end of the transition period, unless otherwise stated by HM Government. Thus, the UK will continue to be bound by existing EU sanctions legislation, as well as newly issued and updated regulations and decisions published by the Council of the European Union in relation to sanctions during the transition period.[22] Potential for divergence after that period remains. 1.18

By contrast, the broader UK AML scheme is less susceptible to the political priorities of the day, and all European countries will ultimately continue to be driven by the standards and guidance from FATF[23] (its secretariat is based at the Organisation for Economic Co-operation and Development (OECD) in Paris). Signatories are held through 'mutual evaluation' to a common set of standards,[24] and seek convergence around them. 1.19

There was an early glimmer of a divergent approach in the new UK's sanctions against Russia (see Appendix 4 to this Guide). Guidance notes[25] to that regime issued by OFSI allude to divergence in terms (emphasis added): 'This means that the securities of subsidiaries incorporated or established in the UK are not subject to these prohibitions. *This differs from the EU sanctions regime.*' 1.20

Whether the UK has the appetite to diverge substantially and consistently from the EU in respect of sanctions policy has been moot.[26] The UK should be reluctant to deploy unilateral financial sanctions. The guiding principle must be that sanctions are most effective when imposed by many actors on the international stage. Recent examples of highly targeted action against such actors are the *Landsbanki* 1.21

[19] https://www.telegraph.co.uk/news/2018/08/06/america-dismisses-eu-blocking-statute-iran-sanctions-finally/.

[20] http://knowledge.freshfields.com/en/Global/r/3759/us_withdrawal_from_the_iran_deal__what_happens_now.

[21] https://www.ft.com/content/38cd4b7e-32fd-11ea-a329-0bcf87a328f2.

[22] See section A.1 of this Chapter of the Guide for a discussion of the transition period.

[23] http://www.fatf-gafi.org/.

[24] http://www.fatf-gafi.org/publications/fatfrecommendations/documents/fatf-recommendations.html.

[25] Appendix 5 to this Guide.

[26] The analysis in this Chapter of the Guide draws heavily on examples from http://researchbriefings.files.parliament.uk/documents/CBP-8402/CBP-8402.pdf by Ben Smith.

Freezing Order 2008[27] issued against specified Icelandic financial institutions linked with the financial crisis, and the *Andrey Lugovoy and Dmitri Kovtun Freezing Order 2018*[28] against the suspected Russian assassins of Alexander Litvinenko.[29]

1.22 Whether or not there is a sustained appetite for divergence, the mechanism exists.[30] HM Government has pledged to coordinate UK and EU sanctions even if it is outside of the EU's Common Foreign and Security Policy (CFSP), whilst expressly reserving the option of diverging if it is in the vital national interest and reasons are given.[31]

1.23 The UK has pledged to consult the EU, if not always comply. HM Government's July 2018 White Paper *Legislating for the Withdrawal Agreement between the United Kingdom and the European Union* said:[32] 'The UK and the EU will maintain regular dialogue and consultation on foreign, security and defence policy, and the consultation mechanisms agreed for CFSP during the implementation period will be an important part of maintaining our ongoing effective cooperation, including on sanctions policy.'

1.24 Even where the vital national interest exception is invoked,[33] Article 129(6) of the Withdrawal Agreement states that in 'a spirit of mutual solidarity, the United Kingdom shall refrain from any action likely to conflict with or impede Union action based on that decision, and the Member States shall respect the position of the United Kingdom'. Nothing in this pledge indicates that the UK would not be prepared to go further than an EU sanctions regime; it would not conflict with or impede an EU decision for the UK to impose more stringent conditions on a target of particular interest to the UK or threat to its national interest. This is the basis of the UK's indications that they will lead a 'crackdown on human rights abusers'.[34]

1.25 Aside from European considerations, trans-Atlantic alliances are in flux. The US has diverged in sanctions policy from the EU in respect of Iran and Cuba, as discussed above. Any rise of nationalist and protectionist agendas may be a challenge to the cooperation which makes international sanctions effective.

1.26 Post-Brexit, much will depend on the extent to which the UK chooses to ally itself with the EU or the US, as and when the two diverge on sanctions policy. The US is

---

[27] https://www.legislation.gov.uk/uksi/2008/2668/pdfs/uksi_20082668_en.pdf.

[28] http://www.legislation.gov.uk/uksi/2018/60/pdfs/uksi_20180060_en.pdf.

[29] https://www.theguardian.com/world/2016/jan/19/alexander-litvinenko-the-man-who-solved-his-own-murder.

[30] In respect of CFSP decisions, but not those arising under other Treaties. The UK cannot diverge from UN Security Council Resolutions.

[31] Section 1A(3)(a) of the Withdrawal Act provides that on or after 31 January 2020, HM Government has the discretion to exclude certain things from the definition of 'the Treaties' and 'the EU Treaties' in the 1972 Act, which might include CFSP decisions. Further, Article 129(6) of the Withdrawal Agreement states that, following CFSP decisions made after 31 January 2020, the UK may 'make a formal declaration to the High Representative of the Union for Foreign Affairs and Security Policy, indicating that, for vital and stated reasons of national policy, in those exceptional cases it will not apply the decision'.

[32] At para. 102.

[33] See n. 31 in this Chapter.

[34] https://www.ft.com/content/38cd4b7e-32fd-11ea-a329-0bcf87a328f2.

more punitive in respect of Iran. The UK has reportedly taken a more sympathetic approach to Iran during the coronavirus outbreak.[35] By contrast, in a demonstration of unity of purpose, the US had been quick to impose a fresh round of sanctions against Russian targets following the poisoning of the Skripals in Salisbury during March 2018.

Whatever the level of divergence, Tom Keatinge, Director of the Royal United Services Institute (RUSI), argues that the UK's influential role in sanctions will be diminished post the 2018 Act: 1.27

> while Brexit may provide a sense of independence, the UK's ability to design sanctions that vary to any significant degree from those imposed by the EU will be limited. True, the significant role played by the UK as one of the leading global financial centres means that financial sanctions imposed unilaterally by the UK will still carry weight. However, this approach will certainly add complication for financial institutions seeking to comply with what may be divergent sanctions policies of the EU and the UK (as is already the case with discrepancies between the EU and the US over Iran).

Finally, it appears that on the face of the 2018 Act, it could not be used to implement so-called secondary (or 'extra-territorial') sanctions[36] on behalf of the UK, as the US does in relation to non-US entities who enter into transactions with US sanctions targets outside US jurisdiction. The limit of extra-territoriality is cast by section 21 of the 2018 Act, to include UK persons (legal and natural)[37] anywhere in the world (but not other persons) and to any person's conduct which takes place within the UK (borders and waters).[38] 1.28

Early divergence in sanctions policy has placed the UK mid-Atlantic: more hawkish than the EU on human rights abuses, more dove-like than the US on Iran. 1.29

B. CONTEXT OF THE 2018 ACT

1. Overview of Pre-Brexit Sanctions Regime

The 2018 Act maintains the basic differentiation of sanctions: financial, trade, immigration, and those in relation to shipping/aircraft.[39] The EU had provided the conduit for almost all sanctions pre-Brexit, counter-terrorism being a recent exception, analysed below. 1.30

Stepping back from the domestic picture, the UN imposes financial sanctions and requires its signatory Member States to implement them through Resolutions passed by the Security Council under Article 41 Chapter VII of the UN Charter.[40] 1.31

[35] Ibid.

[36] Although there are extra-territorial powers in relation to the stopping and boarding of ships, see sections 19 and 20 of the 2018 Act.

[37] Section 21(2) and (3) of the 2018 Act.

[38] Section 21 (1) of the 2018 Act,

[39] Section 1(3) of the 2018 Act.

[40] https://www.un.org/sc/suborg/en/sanctions/information.

Section 1(1) United Nations Act 1946[41] provided powers for the UK Government to implement UN sanctions through Order in Council.[42] In the counter-terrorism sphere however, in early 2011 the UK Supreme Court ruled that the 1946 Act could not be lawfully used to apply asset freezes: *R v. Forsyth; R v. Mabey* [2011] UKSC 9.

1.32 This decision led to the passing of the Terrorist Asset-Freezing Act 2010. Part 1 of the 2010 Act, dealing with terrorist asset-freezing, is repealed by the 2018 Act.

1.33 The EU implements all financial sanctions imposed by the UN, through EU regulations. Under the European Communities Act 1972 pre-Brexit these regulations had direct effect[43] in the UK, as they continue to do in each EU Member State.

1.34 Also, the EU can also impose its own financial sanctions, sometimes referred to as 'EU autonomous' sanctions. These are also implemented through regulations which have direct effect in all EU Member States.[44]

1.35 Prior to Brexit, the UK passed statutory instruments (UK regulations) to supplement EU laws having direct effect, namely to:

- impose penalties for breaches of EU regulations;
- obtain, provide, and use information relating to the operation of these regulations.

1.36 Returning to the short-term focus, the European Union (Withdrawal) Act 2018 froze sanctions regimes and designations in effect as at 31 January 2020, the date of the UK's withdrawal from the EU. Crucially, there would be no post-transition power for frozen sanctions to be amended to keep pace with events. Absent the 2018 Act, the UK would therefore be unable to add, change, or remove sanctions regimes in response to UN requirements or in furtherance of other foreign policy or national security objectives.

1.37 The UK also needed new powers to implement those sanctions which do not emanate from the UN, otherwise it will be unable to cooperate with international allies, using sanctions as a foreign policy and national security tool for objectives which have not passed the Security Council.

1.38 Aside from this EU mechanism, as mentioned, in certain circumstances connected with the threat of terrorism, the UK previously had the power to impose its own financial sanctions and restrictions under narrowly defined circumstances pursuant to the following legislation (collectively the 'domestic regimes'):

[41] http://www.legislation.gov.uk/ukpga/1946/45/pdfs/ukpga_19460045_en.pdf.

[42] Since 1 April 2017, UN and EU financial sanctions have automatic effect in domestic law by virtue of sections 152 to 155 of the Policing and Crime Act 2017: see Appendix 6 to this Guide. The effect is temporary until substantive regulations come into force, or thirty days pass, per regulation 152.

[43] The principle of 'direct effect' was established by the ECJ in *Van Gend en Loos v Nederlandse Administratie der Belastingen* (Case 26/62); [1963] ECR 1; [1970] CMLR 1. Section 2(1) ECA is set out at above footnote x. Criminal sanctions for non-compliance with EU sanctions were introduced by the UK under section 2(2) of that Act.

[44] More about the work of the EU in relation to financial sanctions is found on their website: https://eeas.europa.eu/headquarters/headquarters-homepage/423/sanctions-policy_en>.

- Terrorist Asset-Freezing etc. Act 2010 (TAFA 2010);
- Counter-Terrorism Act 2008 (CTA 2008);
- Anti-Terrorism, Crime and Security Act 2001 (ATCSA 2001).

Crucially, these powers are not wide-ranging enough to allow the UK to proceed post-Brexit, without the 2018 Act. This is because they are restricted to the counter-terrorism sphere.

As for broader context, other pre-2018 Act legislation relating to sanctions includes the Immigration Act 1971. Under this legislation there is automatic physical exclusion for individuals from the UK who are subject to UN or EU travel bans. Also, the Export Control Act 2002 enables trade sanctions to be implemented. The Policing and Crime Act 2017 allowed UN sanctions to be implemented without delay and amended measures used to enforce financial sanctions, considered in detail in Chapter 3 of this Guide. 1.39

2. HM Government Departments and Agencies with a Sanctions Role

Several UK Government departments and agencies will continue to have roles in its sanctions regime post-Brexit. 1.40

The Foreign & Commonwealth Office (FCO) negotiates all international sanctions. 1.41

As for financial sanctions, such as asset-freezing orders, HM Treasury (HMT) is the UK's competent authority for implementation, through its OFSI.[45] HMT also makes designations under UK domestic regimes and can impose monetary penalties for breaches of such sanctions. Financial sanctions are dealt with in Chapter 3 of this Guide. The National Crime Agency (NCA) investigates alleged breaches of financial sanctions. There is an important distinction to be drawn here between reporting obligations which overlap. Sending a suspicious activity report (SAR) to the NCA does not absolve an entity of its duty to report a suspected sanctions breach to OFSI.[46] 1.42

Turning to trade, the Department for International Trade (DIT), through its agency the Export Control Organisation (ECO), has the role of implementing trade sanctions and embargos, detailed at Chapter 4 of the Guide. HM Revenue & Customs (HMRC) enforces breaches of trade sanctions. 1.43

As for immigration sanctions, the Home Office (HO) implements travel bans, dealt with at Chapter 5 of this Guide. 1.44

3. International Assessment of UK Sanctions and AML Schemes

In December 2018, FATF was broadly positive in its Mutual Evaluation Report (MER)[47] of the parts of the sanctions regime for which the UK had been responsible. 1.45

---

[45] https://www.gov.uk/government/organisations/office-of-financial-sanctions-implementation.

[46] Discussed in more detail in Chapter 12 of this Guide.

[47] FATF, Mutual Evaluation Report December 2018: https://www.fatf-gafi.org/media/fatf/documents/reports/mer4/MER-United-Kingdom-2018.pdf. All quoted extracts in this section of the Guide are taken from this MER.

1.46 The FATF MER executive summary stated that the UK 'has been a leader in designating terrorists at the UN and EU level, and takes a leading role promoting effective global implementation of proliferation-related TFS [targeted financial sanctions]'.

1.47 FATF was impressed that the UK has frozen assets and other funds pursuant to its [nuclear] proliferation financing sanctions programme, and taken steps to increase the overall effectiveness of its targeted financial sanctions regime, including through the creation of the OFSI and the strengthening of penalties for breaching TFS.

1.48 FATF suggested that 'minor improvements are required in relation to applying penalties for sanctions breaches, ensuring consistent application of TFS and communicating designations immediately'.

1.49 As for the broader assessment of the domestic AML regime, there was praise[48] at a general level for the UK's 'robust understanding of its money laundering/terrorist financing (ML/TF) risks which is reflected in its public national risk assessments (NRAs)'. Recent developments, and the potential for divergence between the UK and EU, are looked at in more detail in Chapter 13 of this Guide.

1.50 Turning to enforcement, FATF was impressed by the way in which the UK 'proactively investigates, prosecutes and convicts a range of TF activity, in line with its identified risks in this area'. The latest available statistics for the UK are 7,900 investigations, 2,000 prosecutions, and 1,400 convictions annually for 'standalone' ML or where ML is the 'principal offence'. However, FATF sought to look beyond these headline figures to focus on high-end ML. 'High-end money laundering' is defined in the 2017 National Risk Assessment[49] as the laundering of large amounts of criminal funds (often the proceeds of serious fraud or overseas corruption) through the UK financial and professional services sectors. FATF noted that although investigations of these offences have increased:

> These cases generally take years to progress to prosecution and conviction and limited statistics are available on high-end ML investigations, prosecutions and convictions prior to its prioritisation in 2014. As a result, it is not yet clear whether the level prosecutions and convictions of high-end ML is fully consistent with the UK's threats.

1.51 As for beneficial ownership, FATF found that the 'UK is a global leader in promoting corporate transparency and has a good understanding of the ML/TF risks posed by legal persons and arrangements'. Whilst Beneficial Ownership (BO) information on trusts is available to the competent authorities through a registry maintained by HMRC[50] (of trusts with tax consequences in the UK), FATF found that the register itself 'is not yet fully populated'.

---

[48] https://www.fatf-gafi.org/media/fatf/documents/reports/mer4/MER-United-Kingdom-2018.pdf.

[49] https://assets.publishing.service.gov.uk/government/uploads/system/uploads/attachment_data/file/655198/National_risk_assessment_of_money_laundering_and_terrorist_financing_2017_pdf_web.pdf.

[50] https://www.gov.uk/guidance/register-your-clients-estate.

In respect of People with Significant Control (PSC) of companies, typically someone with 25 per cent or more of shares or voting rights, the register is maintained by Companies House.[51] As for legal persons, basic and beneficial ownership information is freely and immediately available to the public and all competent authorities through a central public register. Here FATF found room for improvement in that 'this information is not verified for accuracy which limits its reliability'. 1.52

Section 51 of the 2018 Act, requiring the governments of British Overseas Territories (BOTs) to introduce 'publicly accessible' registers of BO of companies by the end of 2020, since extended to 2023,[52] is also considered in more detail at Chapter 13 of the Guide. The alternative, adopted in the Cayman Islands, is to have a verified accurate register, accessible at short notice online by law enforcement and competent authorities.[53] 1.53

Both registers are distinct from the public register of BO of foreign companies investing in the UK property market, which has been delayed until at least the Summer of 2019, to the frustration of Transparency International[54] and others. 1.54

4. Legislative History: Controversial Passage of the 2018 Act

Although the 2018 Act is a necessary piece of legislation, without which the post-Brexit UK would be powerless to keep its sanctions and AML regimes up to date, its passage proved controversial. 1.55

A point of contention was the use of 'Henry VIII' powers afforded to ministers under the 2018 Act. Such powers enable ministers to 'amend or repeal provisions in an Act of Parliament using secondary legislation',[55] subject to a lower degree of Parliamentary scrutiny than primary legislation. Examples explored in this Guide include the creation of new criminal offences, and the power to amend existing money laundering regulations. The Law Society (of England and Wales) and others submitted that primary legislation would be more appropriate in these fields.[56] 1.56

HM Government acceded to a series of concessions during the passage of the Bill. It was amended to require ministers to meet additional requirements when creating new sanctions (becoming section 2 of the 2018 Act) and when creating new criminal offences (enacted as section 18). A clause was also inserted to the Bill (becoming section 30) compelling ministers to review annually any new regulations relating to the creation of new sanctions. 1.57

[51] https://www.gov.uk/government/news/people-with-significant-control-psc-who-controls-your-company.

[52] https://www.caymancompass.com/2018/12/23/fco-beneficial-ownership-register-to-be-made-public-by-2023/.

[53] http://www.tia.gov.ky/pdf/AEOI_News_&_Updates.pdf.

[54] https://www.transparency.org.uk/press-releases/ti-uk-disappointed-government-to-miss-own-deadline-on-revealing-true-owners-of-companies-buying-uk-property/.

[55] https://www.parliament.uk/site-information/glossary/henry-viii-clauses/.

[56] The Law Society submission to the House of Commons Public Bill Committee (see: https://publications.parliament.uk/pa/cm201719/cmpublic/sanctions/memo/SAMLB05.pdf).

1.58 Criticism was also levelled at the potential infringements of due process for 'designated persons'. HM Government, persuaded by Lords Pannick and Judge, made a number of amendments to address these concerns including to: (1) ensure a designated person is entitled to a statement of the reasons why they have been designated (see section 11 (7)–(9) of the Act); (2) ensure ministers exercise the power to designate persons only to the extent it is proportionate to do so (see section 11 (2)(b)(ii)); and (3) enhance the procedure on how ministers handle requests for designations to be reviewed (see section 33).

1.59 A further amendment to the Bill was the introduction of a '*Magnitsky*' clause. The provision[57] allows ministers to make sanctions regulations against those who have committed an abuse of human rights.[58] This follows a similar provision in the 2017 Criminal Finance Act that allows ministers to freeze the assets of international human rights violators in the UK.[59] Both provisions (in keeping with legislation elsewhere such as the United States' 2012 Magnitsky Act itself) followed the case of the Russian auditor accountant Sergei Magnitsky, who was killed having revealed an alleged fraud involving the Russian tax authorities.

1.60 Another high-profile addition to the Bill was the mandate to British Overseas Territories (BOTs) by section 51 to create a public register of beneficial owners by the end of 2020. The timetable has since been revised, to 2023,[60] and is considered in Chapter 13 of this Guide.

1.61 The Public Bill Committee received a variety of submissions in relation to what became the 2018 Act. Both the Government of the British Virgin Islands and the International Financial Centres Forum argued that the Bill should not require a public register of beneficial ownership for BOTs, citing the potential constitutional and economic consequences of such a provision. Transparency International UK and Global Witness argued in favour of its adoption. Both viewpoints were united in submissions which called for HM Government to hasten its efforts to adopt a public register of the beneficial owners of overseas entities owning UK property, while Global Witness also argued a public register should be created for the beneficial owners of UK-connected trusts. The UK's Companies House and company formation were also identified as areas of concern for Transparency International UK and Global Witness (as well as e-filing). They both requested that HM Government increase resources allocated to Companies House and enhance AML supervision of company formation.

---

[57] Section 1(2)(f) of the 2018 Act.

[58] https://hansard.parliament.uk/Lords/2018-05-21/debates/26FDB218-927C-44F8-8053-55DCE6B22A16/SanctionsAndAnti-MoneyLaunderingBill(HL)#contribution-14BB15AD-8842-4F43-A846-87D41203B44A.

[59] See section 13 Criminal Finances Act 2017, and for an explanation of Unexplained Wealth Orders generally, Hugo Lodge, *Criminal Finances Act 2017: A Guide to the New Law* (The Law Society Publishing 2017) chapter 6.

[60] https://www.caymancompass.com/2018/12/23/fco-beneficial-ownership-register-to-be-made-public-by-2023/.

As mentioned above, The Law Society of England and Wales raised several concerns, notably in relation to the breadth of ministerial powers afforded in the Act and in respect of access to justice and due process. 1.62

Professor Prem Sikka launched a wide-ranging attack on the UK's current AML regime, with criticism reserved for company formation and the regulatory system. 1.63

UK Finance asked for guidance to be issued alongside the new sanction regimes created by the Act, a new domestic licensing regime to be included in the Act, that the UK 'Nexus' to be more clearly defined, and for there to be more clarity on information reporting obligations. 1.64

The Solicitors Regulation Authority (SRA) took the opportunity to explain its role as part of UK's anti-money laundering regime, as a professional body supervisor listed on Schedule 1 of the 2017 MLRs. 1.65

Amnesty International UK called for the Bill to ensure that brass-plate companies (e.g. shell companies used by arms exporters) can be tackled by enforcement agencies. Transparency International UK recommended that all TCSPs authorized by Companies House should have an AML supervisor, called for a draft bill creating a public register for beneficial owners of UK property, and added further weight to calls for BOTs to create publicly accessible registers of the ultimate beneficial owners (UBOs) of companies. 1.66

Global Witness argued that the UK Companies House needs more resources and clear responsibility for ensuring companies comply with the register and investigating and prosecuting those that do not. They too called for public registers to be created relating to BOs of UK-connected trusts, BOs of UK properties that are created by overseas companies, and Company BOs in UK's Overseas Territories. 1.67

Against this backdrop, the 2018 Act was passed. 1.68

5. Overview of the 2018 Act: Reform of Existing UK Sanctions Scheme

The UK's overarching sanctions scheme has been amended in five key respects: 1.69

- The potential scope of UK sanctions has been considerably broadened. As discussed in Chapter 2 of this Guide, HM Government can now impose sanctions regulations considered 'appropriate' for a diverse range of purposes. These include those made to comply with a UN obligation or any other international obligation; for the prevention of terrorism; in the interests of national or international peace and security; or, most broadly of all, to further a UK foreign policy objective. Further, the *Magnitsky* amendment was a late change to the then Bill, allowing the UK to impose sanctions on those who commit gross human rights violations. The scope of the UK sanctions regime is therefore wider post-Brexit, given UK sanctions will not effectively need approval by the twenty-seven other EU Member States in the future.
- HM Government has the new power to designate persons not only by name but also by description, in situations where it is impractical to identify by name all designated persons; see Chapter 7 of this Guide. The description, however, must

be sufficiently precise that a reasonable person would be able to identify individuals falling within the designation. There is an analogy here with the powers of proscription in the Terrorism Act 2006.[61]

- The process of challenge in the Courts has been defined and subjected to greater control. As discussed in Chapter 9 of this Guide, the 2018 Act prevents designated persons from immediately challenging regulations before the courts; they must first request either variation or revocation of the designation from the Secretary of State. Only after ministerial refusal may a designated person seek judicial review of a sanctions-related decision. If the judicial review is successful, the HM Government will only be liable for damages if it is found to have acted negligently or in bad faith. A closed court procedure may be used in cases where individuals have been designated based on sensitive intelligence material. There are analogies here with the special counsel procedure used in closed court hearings initiated under the Special Immigration Appeals Commission Act 1997.[62]
- The 2018 Act includes a broad licensing power. HM Government has confirmed that it intends to issue general licences for issues that are urgent; that could not be foreseen at the time of the drafting of the sanctions regulations, or need to be time-limited. The US Department of Treasury takes a similar approach through its Office of Foreign Assets Control (OFAC).[63] Licensing is discussed in detail in Chapter 10 of this Guide.
- The obligation to report information to the authorities in respect of financial sanctions is extended to a far greater range of natural and legal persons. As detailed in Chapter 12 of this Guide, from 8 August 2017 UK financial sanctions regulations required relevant businesses and professionals (e.g. financial institutions, lawyers, and accountants) to report to OFSI when they know or suspect a breach of financial sanctions. Failing to do so is a criminal offence. The 2018 Act allows for such sanctions-reporting obligations to be extended now to apply to any individual or firm. This broader power reflects existing reporting obligations provided for under EU law, breach of which was not a criminal offence under domestic law pre-Brexit.

6. The Comparative Picture: Sanctions Schemes Amongst the EU's Neighbours

1.70 This section of the Guide provides context in looking at the recent sanctions policy of key neighbours to the UK, and how the EU has responded to potential divergence.

[61] For an explanation see Alun Jones, Rupert Bowers, and Hugo D. Lodge, *Blackstone's Guide to the Terrorism Act 2006* (OUP 2006) chapter 6.

[62] https://publications.parliament.uk/pa/cm200405/cmselect/cmconst/323/32307.htm.

[63] https://www.treasury.gov/about/organizational-structure/offices/pages/office-of-foreign-assets-control.aspx.

Switzerland, historically neutral, has adopted legislation[64] allowing it to impose sanctions regimes emanating from the EU, or the OSCE, to further compliance with international law or respect for human rights. 1.71

The nature and extent of Swiss alignment with EU sanctions is made on a case-by-case, fact-sensitive basis. There is a hint of frustration in the European Council's comment in 2017: 1.72

> The [European] Council encourages Switzerland to remain close and consistent in the application of the restrictive measures including preventing their circumvention. The Council invites Switzerland to maintain and further improve its alignment with the EU's restrictive measures in respect of actions undermining or threatening the territorial integrity, sovereignty and independence of Ukraine, and in view of Russia's actions destabilising the situation in Ukraine.

As discussed in the previous paragraphs of this Guide, the UK is taking a slightly different approach from the EU in respect of sanctions against Russia. 1.73

Similarly, Norway adopted laws in 2001 allowing it to impose EU restrictive measures on a piecemeal basis. Whilst the EU implemented a full range of economic measures against Russia following its interference in Ukraine, the UN Security Council became effectively paralysed with exercise of the Russian veto as permanent member. Public discourse in Norway focused on the propriety of Norway enforcing EU sanctions, about which it had no say or influence. Ultimately, Norway elected to implement the sanctions in August 2014, with the then Norwegian foreign minister clarifying:[65] 1.74

> The Government [of Norway] will align itself with the EU's new restrictive measures against Russia. Since the start of the crisis in Ukraine, Norway has stood united with the EU and other like-minded countries in responding to Russia's violations of international law. We will do so this time as well.

7. The New AML Powers in the 2018 Act

Though the bulk of the 2018 Act is concerned with implementation of a new sanctions scheme for the UK, Chapter 13 of this Guide deals in detail with the important changes to the broader AML suite of UK powers and regulations, and an overview of the recent developments in 5MLD. 1.75

Part 2 and Schedule 2 of the 2018 Act provide the powers for HM Government to continue to make provision in relation to AML, specifically: the detection, investigation, or prevention of money laundering or terrorist financing or the implementation of FATF standards. Previously the mechanism had been to transpose EU Money Laundering Directives into secondary legislation. Post-Brexit that avenue is closed. 1.76

---

64 Federal Act on the Implementation of International Sanctions, 2003.

65 'Norway to implement new restrictive measures against Russia', Norwegian Ministry of Foreign Affairs press release, 11 August 2014.

1.77 A controversial addition to the 2018 Act was the mandate[66] to British Overseas Territories (BOTs) to implement registers of beneficial ownership, originally by the end of 2020.[67] BOTs is a designation which excludes the Isle of Man, Jersey, and Guernsey, whilst the British Virgin Islands and Cayman Islands are included. This is also discussed in more detail in Chapter 13 of this Guide.

8. The Scope of the Book

1.78 In common with its predecessors in the series, this Blackstone's Guide introduces a new piece of legislation and discusses its likely effects. It would be difficult to explain and understand these without first considering some context provided by the current statutory scheme. As for targeted sanctions, most emphasis in the Guide is placed on financial and trade sanctions. By contrast, a detailed treatment of each discrete area of UK law in which sanctions operate, e.g. immigration or shipping, is beyond the scope of this book.

1.79 As the intended audience for the Guide includes practitioners, the book draws heavily on existing financial sanctions guidance[68] from OFSI, seeking to anticipate how it will be affected by the new post-Brexit regime.

1.80 Another focus of this Guide is recent changes to the AML regime of the UK, in the light of 5MLD and the 2018 Act.[69]

---

[66] Section 51 of the 2018 Act.

[67] The timetable has changed; see Chapter 13 for detail.

[68] https://assets.publishing.service.gov.uk/government/uploads/system/uploads/attachment_data/file/685308/financial_sanctions_guidance_march_2018_final.pdf.

[69] See Chapter 13 of this Guide.

2

POWER TO MAKE, AMEND, AND SUSPEND SANCTIONS

A. Core Power and Additional Requirements 2.01
1. Overview 2.01
2. Passage of the Bill: Additions to the Core Power 2.02
3. Core Power to Make Sanctions Regulations: Section 1 2.07
4. Human Rights Violations: *Magnitsky* 2.17
5. Additional Requirements: Section 2 2.25
6. Temporary Powers in Relation to Existing EU Sanctions Lists 2.30

B. Powers to Suspend, Revoke, and Amend Sanctions Regulations 2.37
1. Suspension of Prohibitions and Requirements 2.37
2. Revocation and Amendment of Regulations under Section 1 2.39
3. Amending the Type of Sanctions 2.42

C. Guidance, Reporting, and 'Future-proofing' 2.44
1. Guidance 2.44
2. Report in Respect of Offences in Regulations 2.47
3. 'Future-proofing' the Sanctions Scheme 2.49

A. CORE POWER AND ADDITIONAL REQUIREMENTS

1. Overview

The potential scope of UK sanctions has been considerably broadened by the 2018 Act. HM Government can now impose sanctions regulations considered 'appropriate' for a diverse range of purposes. These include those made to comply with a UN obligation or any other international obligation, for the prevention of terrorism, in the interests of national or international peace and security or, most broadly of all, to further a UK foreign policy objective. Further, the *Magnitsky* amendment was a late change to the Act, allowing the UK to impose sanctions on people who 2.01

commit gross human rights violations. The scope of the UK sanctions regime is therefore wider post-Brexit, given UK sanctions will not effectively need approval by the twenty-seven other EU Member States in the future.

2. Passage of the Bill: Additions to the Core Power

2.02 This section of the Guide demonstrates the extent to which the core power was widened during the passage of the Bill; for the current position see the following passage of this Guide below, at section A.3.

2.03 The 2018 Bill began its report stage in the House of Lords on 15 January 2018. Amendment here fundamentally extended HM Government's powers. Additions were made to the definition of 'discretionary purposes' for which sanctions could be promulgated.

2.04 By way of context, the Bill originally provided that the appropriate Minister may impose sanctions regulations in three circumstances: for the purposes of compliance with a UN obligation; for the purposes of compliance with any other international obligation, or; for one of the discretionary purposes set out in the Bill.

2.05 As to the last of these categories, the Bill, as originally introduced, was restricted to four discretionary purposes for which sanctions could be imposed. These were:

i. for furthering the prevention of terrorism, in the United Kingdom or elsewhere;

ii. if the sanctions are in the interests of national security;

iii. if the sanctions are in the interests of international peace and security, or

iv. for furthering a foreign policy objective of the government of the United Kingdom.

The Lords amendment extended the scheme by adding four more discretionary purposes to this list. These additional purposes are:

v. to promote the resolution of armed conflicts or the protection of civilians in conflict zones;

vi. to promote compliance with international humanitarian and human rights law;

vii. to contribute to multilateral efforts to prevent the spread and use of weapons and materials of mass destruction, or

viii. to promote respect for human rights, democracy, the rule of law and good governance.

2.06 The relevant sections only passed with yet further additions to the list, and are dealt within the following paragraphs. The field in which the UK is now competent to impose sanctions was broadened considerably during the passage of the Bill. The broadest areas of discretion are subject to additional requirements placed on the Minister; see section 2 of the 2018 Act.

3. Core Power to Make Sanctions Regulations: Section 1

Section 1 gives effect to the central purpose of this part of the 2018 Act. It empowers an appropriate Minister to make regulations imposing sanctions. An 'appropriate Minister' is defined[1] as the 'Secretary of State' and 'the Treasury'. 2.07

This power allows the UK to continue to comply with its international obligations as a signatory to the UN Charter, and to use sanctions to meet its own broad foreign policy and national security objectives after exiting the EU. The pre-Brexit scheme it replaced is set out in Chapter 1 of this Guide. 2.08

New sanctions may now be made where the appropriate Minister considers it appropriate for the following purposes:[2] 2.09

a. complying with a United Nations obligation;[3]
b. complying with any other international obligation, which would include obligations arising from UK membership of other international organizations, for example the Organization for Security and Co-operation in Europe (OSCE), as well as other international treaties or agreements which may fall within section 1(8); or
c. for discretionary purposes which:[4]
    i. further the prevention of terrorism in the UK or elsewhere;
    ii. are in the interests of national security;
    iii. are in the interests of international peace and security;
    iv. promote the resolution of armed conflicts or the protection of civilians in conflict zones;
    v. provide accountability for, or be a deterrent to, gross violations of human rights, or otherwise promote compliance with international human rights law or respect for human rights (the *Magnitsky* amendment);
    vi. promote compliance with international humanitarian law;
    vii. contribute to multilateral efforts to prevent the spread and use of weapons and materials of mass destruction;
    viii. promote respect for democracy, the rule of law and good governance; or
    ix. further a foreign policy objective.

The categories in which the UK ministers are now competent to make sanctions is therefore broad. The human rights amendments follow the *Magnitsky* case, discussed in Chapter 1 of this Guide, and the following section A.4. 2.10

---

[1] Section 1(9) of the 2018 Act and see Chapter 1, section A.2 of this Guide for a discussion of which Departments of State are concerned in the UK sanctions scheme.

[2] By section 1(1) of the 2018 Act.

[3] The UN imposes financial sanctions and requires its signatory Member States, including the UK, to implement them through Resolutions passed by the Security Council, under Article 41, Chapter VII of the UN Charter.

[4] By section 1(2) of the 2018 Act.

2.11 The last of these, 'furthering a policy objective', is wide in ambit. By way of illustration, the FCO website in early 2019 displayed major priorities (Brexit, chemical weapons in Syria and Salisbury, marine protection) but also the then Prime Minister recalling 'I've met boy and girl Scouts and Guides here in Kenya' adding that she wanted to encourage such ambition. Promoting the Scouts in Africa is therefore a foreign policy objective, albeit a minor one, within the meaning of the 2018 Act. There is no threshold in the Act, but Ministers and public bodies must not act irrationally.

2.12 The penultimate sub-category of 'good governance' again seems to cast the net wide. The UN has said the following:[5]

> Good governance has 8 major characteristics. It is participatory, consensus oriented, accountable, transparent, responsive, effective and efficient, equitable and inclusive and follows the rule of law. It assures that corruption is minimized, the views of minorities are taken into account and that the voices of the most vulnerable in society are heard in decision-making. It is also responsive to the present and future needs of society.

It may be thought that every government in history has had the potential for improvement in at least one of these eight categories. Yet, furthering this modest end would be a legitimate target for sanctions under the 2018 Act.

2.13 The limiting factors will be practical, on this broad legal definition. There would not in practice be the impetus to impose sanctions on a country for denigrating the Scouts or Guides. Also, sanctions are only ever effective if adopted internationally by allies. Trivial causes would not attract wide international support. Nevertheless, the law here is couched in terms which afford ministers a wide discretion.

2.14 One potential brake on this wide discretion is found in section 1(3): sanctions regulations made by the appropriate Minister must set out the purpose for which they are made (subsection (3)). There are further requirements for regulations made for a purpose which is not compliance with a UN or other international obligation, detailed in section 2, see below.

2.15 By section 1(5) the different overall categories of sanctions are laid out. These are regulations which do one or more of the following:[6]

(a) impose financial sanctions (see section 3 of the 2018 Act), Chapter 3 of this Guide;

(b) impose immigration sanctions (see section 4), Chapter 5 of this Guide;

(c) impose trade sanctions (see section 5 and Schedule 1), Chapter 4 of this Guide;

(d) impose aircraft sanctions (see section 6), Chapter 6 of this Guide;

(e) impose shipping sanctions (see section 7), Chapter 6 of this Guide;

(f) impose sanctions within section 8 (other sanctions for purposes of UN obligations);

---

[5] https://www.unescap.org/sites/default/files/good-governance.pdf.

[6] With references to sections and Schedules of the 2018 Act, and to Chapters of this Guide.

(g) make supplemental provision in connection with any provision of the regulations or other regulations made under this section.

Parliamentary procedures applying to sanctions regulations depends on their content (see section 55).

Though the overarching categories of subject matter for UK sanctions remains the same post-Brexit and the 2018 Act, now the UK is promulgating its own sanctions, rather than relying on the direct effect of EU sanctions regulations. The UK had always retained certain powers in relation to counter terror sanctions, it had previously relied on Orders in Council to implement UN sanctions (see Chapter 1 of this Guide). 2.16

4. Human Rights Violations: *Magnitsky*

This is the '*Magnitsky*' amendment, discussed in Chapter 1 of this Guide, and the area in which there have been early signs of divergence between the UK and EU. The UK's Foreign Secretary has indicated an appetite to use the 2018 Act to reportedly 'crack down on human rights abusers' based in Russia and elsewhere.[7] He stated, 'Our shared mission in the world is not confined to trade and security—it's also a joint mission to serve as a force for good'. 2.17

The new power is found in section 1(7) of the 2018 Act, which defines 'gross violation of human rights as: 2.18

Conduct which constitutes, or is connected with, the commission of a gross human rights abuse or violation; and whether conduct constitutes or is connected with the commission of such an abuse or violation is to be determined in accordance with section 241A of the Proceeds of Crime Act 2002.

The definition imported from section 241A of the Proceeds of Crime Act 2002 (POCA 2002) is comprehensive and wide-ranging; it was inserted by the Criminal Finances Act 2017,[8] and is set out in full here as it does not appear in any part of the 2018 Act or its Explanatory Note (commentary follows): 2.19

(1) Conduct constitutes the commission of a gross human rights abuse or violation if each of the following three conditions is met.
(2) The first condition is that—
 (a) the conduct constitutes the torture of a person who has sought—
  (i) to expose illegal activity carried out by a public official or a person acting in an official capacity, or
  (ii) to obtain, exercise, defend or promote human rights and fundamental freedoms, or
 (b) the conduct otherwise involves the cruel, inhuman or degrading treatment or punishment of such a person.

[7] https://www.ft.com/content/38cd4b7e-32fd-11ea-a329-0bcf87a328f2.

[8] Section 241A POCA 2002 was inserted by Criminal Finances Act (CFA) 2017 (c. 22), ss 13(3), 58(1)(6) (with s. 13(4)). For commentary on CFA 2017 generally, see Hugo Daniel Lodge, *Criminal Finances Act 2017: A Guide to the New Law* (Law Society Publishing 2017).

(3) The second condition is that the conduct is carried out in consequence of that person having sought to do anything falling within subsection (2)(a)(i) or (ii).
(4) The third condition is that the conduct is carried out—
 (a) by a public official, or a person acting in an official capacity, in the performance or purported performance of his or her official duties, or
 (b) by a person not falling within paragraph (a) at the instigation or with the consent or acquiescence—
  (i) of a public official, or
  (ii) of a person acting in an official capacity,
  who in instigating the conduct, or in consenting to or acquiescing in it, is acting in the performance or purported performance of his or her official duties.
(5) Conduct is connected with the commission of a gross human rights abuse or violation if it is conduct by a person that involves—
 (a) acting as an agent for another in connection with activities relating to conduct constituting the commission of a gross human rights abuse or violation,
 (b) directing, or sponsoring, such activities,
 (c) profiting from such activities, or
 (d) materially assisting such activities.
(6) Conduct that involves the intentional infliction of severe pain or suffering on another person is conduct that constitutes torture for the purposes of subsection (2)(a).
(7) It is immaterial whether the pain or suffering is physical or mental and whether it is caused by an act or omission.
(8) The cases in which a person materially assists activities for the purposes of subsection (5)(d) include those where the person—
 (a) provides goods or services in support of the carrying out of the activities, or
 (b) otherwise provides any financial or technological support in connection with their carrying out.

2.20 The essential elements of the definition are that 'gross human rights abuses' comprise torture, inhuman, cruel, or degrading treatment of a person, on the grounds that he or she has been 'obtaining, exercising, defending or promoting' human rights or have been seeking to expose such abuses or illegal behaviour (possibly as a whistle-blower) when committed by a public official.

2.21 'Torture' is further defined as 'intentional infliction of severe pain or suffering on another person' and it is immaterial if that pain is mental or physical, and it does not matter whether it is caused by act or omission. It is difficult to conceive of intentional infliction of pain by omission; possibly it would include the case of a leading politician deliberately failing to respond to a natural disaster if it affected a minority population which had been vocal opponents of the regime.

2.22 Activity by any person connected with any such gross human rights conduct is also caught. The definition here includes providing goods and services in support of the abuses, e.g. feeding and transporting soldiers sent to summarily execute a campaigning journalist.

2.23 Thus, the new sanctions scheme under the 2018 Act is the mirror of the reforms made by CFA 2017, which brought gross human rights abuses within the scope of POCA 2002. Specifically, under the amended Part 5 of POCA 2002 there can now be civil recovery of the (financial or material) proceeds of such behaviour by public officials. There is a symbolic element this reform of POCA 2002, as such persecution may not result in financial profit. The sanctions corollary may be more effective.

This amendment has allowed the UK to take a more proactive approach in using targeted financial sanctions against those who violate human rights; it will be interesting to see if this is the first step on a divergent path or whether the EU follows suit. 2.24

5. Additional Requirements: Section 2

The test in the original Bill was for the Minister to determine merely whether or not a particular sanction was 'appropriate'. Lords Pannick and Judge supported amendments which were passed, adding additional requirements to the promulgation of sanctions for a 'discretionary purpose'. This is defined[9] as a purpose which is not compliance with a UN obligation nor other international obligation but is one of the wider discretionary purposes within section 1(2) (a) to (i), from the prevention of terrorism through to the promotion of respect for democracy, the rule of law, and good governance. 2.25

The Minister must determine that there are 'good reasons' to pursue the purpose of the regulations, he or she must determine that the imposition of sanctions is a 'reasonable course of action for that purpose'.[10] This is an additional requirement of internal consideration to be undertaken by the Minister, presumably on the advice of officials. It is unclear what this adds in practice to the public law duty[11] of a Minister of the Crown to act reasonably, with the prospect of being judicially reviewed for taking an unreasonable course. As Michael Fordham QC states in his Judicial Review Handbook,[12] 'Unreasonableness is a recognised ground for judicial review. But it runs deeper, rooted in strong common law resistance to unreasonableness. That is why, for example, Courts strive to avoid statutory interpretations which are unreasonable and an affront to justice and good sense.' It is difficult to see how the 2018 Act even adds anything to the sixteenth-century principle in *Rooke's Case* (1598) 5 Co Rep 99b, per Lord Coke: 2.26

> notwithstanding that the words of the commission give the authority to the commissioners to do according to their discretions, yet their proceedings ought to be limited and bound with the rule of reason and law.

This internal requirement of determination is strengthened by a further external requirement that the appropriate Minister must lay before Parliament, at the time that the regulations (or draft regulations) are laid, a report which addresses the requirements detailed in this section,[13] namely: 2.27

---

[9] Section 2(1) of the 2018 Act.
[10] Section 2(2) of the 2018 Act.
[11] *Westminster Corporation v London North Western Railway* [1905] AC 426, 430.
[12] Fifth Edition, 7.7.
[13] Section 2(4) of the 2018 Act.

(a) why the Minister considers that carrying out that purpose would meet one or more of the discretionary purposes in paragraphs (a) to (i) of section 1(2), from prevention of terrorism through to good governance etc.
(b) why the Minister considers that there are good reasons to pursue that purpose, and
(c) why the Minister considers that the imposition of sanctions (defined[14] as prohibitions and requirements imposed for the stated purposes) is a reasonable course of action for that purpose.

2.28 The Minister is not compelled to disclose anything which might damage national security or international relations.[15] A different test may apply at the later stage of review by a Court, when rulings in recent high-profile coroner's/terrorism inquests have emphasized the need for the government to show the Court sensitive material, if not all the parties.

2.29 This additional Parliamentary scrutiny of discretionary sanctions does not apply to the temporary power for the Minister to add names to an existing EU sanctions list. Subject to the ultimate safeguard that temporary is defined as 'two years' when such power will cease to apply.

6. Temporary Powers in Relation to Existing EU Sanctions Lists

2.30 Later in the scheme of the 2018 Act, at Chapter 3, section 34, there are temporary powers in relation to EU sanctions lists. Though the definition of 'temporary' was a vexed one in relation to the 'Irish backstop' throughout Brexit negotiations, here it is defined as a two-year period.[16] They enable alterations to be made to any EU sanctions regimes retained by the EU (Withdrawal) Act 2018 and which have not been supplanted by a UK sanctions regime contained in regulations made under section 1 of the 2018 Act. The rationale for this is to ensure that EU sanctions regimes can be updated for a short period post-Brexit, until they are replaced by UK regimes.

2.31 The powers are limited to enabling Ministers to add or remove names[17] from lists (defined as any Annex, instrument, or other document,[18] or EU Council regulation[19]) of persons who are designated due to their inclusion in a list attached to an EU instrument. They do not enable the substantive sanctions in retained EU law to be amended. Any such provision would require new regulations under section 1 of the 2018 Act. There is no limit to the amount of times the same individual person can be added to or removed from a list[20] under these temporary powers, within the two-year interim period.

2.32 Section 35 of the 2018 Act sets out the conditions for adding a person's name to an EU sanctions list (except UN named persons). The conditions are a mirror of the

[14] Section 2(3) of the 2018 Act.
[15] Section 2(5) of the 2018 Act.
[16] Section 34(5) of the 2018 Act.
[17] Section 34(3) of the 2018 Act.
[18] Section 34(1)(a) of the 2018 Act.
[19] Section 34(1)(b) of the 2018 Act.
[20] Section 34(4) of the 2018 Act.

conditions for designation of persons under sections 11 and 12 of the Act. However, instead of having regard to the provisions in UK regulations, the Minister must have regard to the purposes of the EU legislation (as set out in section 35(3) to (7)).

For a Minister to treat a person as if they had been added to an EU sanctions list, the Minister must consider it 'appropriate' to do so, reflecting the domestic test, this time having regard to the purpose of the EU legislation, and to the likely significant effects of the designation on the person, as far as known.[21] 2.33

The focus of this power is to extend or change the number of persons who are caught by sanctions targeting a particular activity, rather than extend the range of activities covered. The test of whether a new person is involved in the existing activity is at section 35(2): 2.34

'an involved person' means a person who—
(a) is or has been involved in an activity which is specified, by regulations made by an appropriate Minister, in relation to the list in question,
(b) is owned or controlled directly or indirectly by a person who is or has been so involved,
(c) is acting on behalf of or at the direction of a person who is or has been so involved, or
(d) is a member of, or associated with, a person who is or has been so involved.

The Minister must inform the newly designated person of their designation as soon as reasonably practicable, including a statement of reasons for the designation, which conforms with UK public law standards. Knowing the fact of a designation and the reasons for it is requires in order that a false, mistaken, or unfair designation may be challenged. Common law has long safeguarded Natural Justice and basic fairness. *Ridge v Baldwin* [1946] AC 40, 113–14: 2.35

the essential requirements of natural justice at least include that before someone is condemned, he is to have an opportunity of defending himself, and in order that he may do so that he is made aware of the charges or allegations or suggestions which he has to meet.

However, there is no need for a designated person to be notified *in advance* of any designation coming into effect, which notification would be a serious impediment to the efficacy of any such sanction.

The rights of challenge by designated persons under these temporary powers are dealt with at Chapters 8 and 9 of this Guide. 2.36

B. POWERS TO SUSPEND, REVOKE, AND AMEND SANCTIONS REGULATIONS

1. Suspension of Prohibitions and Requirements

As for suspension, section 42 permits sanctions regulations, or at a more granular level restrictions within sanctions regulations, to be suspended for a period of time. 2.37

[21] Section 35(1)(b) of the 2018 Act.

They are held in abeyance, i.e. they would remain on the statute book but not be binding within the UK. This allows the UK Government flexibility in circumstances where sanctions might need to be temporarily lifted or changed, but where it is not be appropriate to revoke sanctions regulations completely. For example, if a state which was subject to sanctions has provided satisfactory evidence of putting its nuclear capability beyond use this may warrant sanctions being suspended to 'reward' that compliant behaviour. Or if there were a restriction on transporting nuclear material this may need to be temporarily lifted in order to take agreed steps so that the material can be made safe. A Minister could suspend the regulations but still retain the ability, should the state in question revert to its previous behaviour or fail to meet a specified condition, to apply the regulations again effectively and without delay.

2.38 The period of any suspension can, by section 42(3), 'be expressed in any way', including a period which begins or ends when a specified condition is met. Such a condition might be that a recent expansionist state puts its military equipment beyond use, or that a state subject to sanctions must allow freedom of movement of a minority group from a refugee camp to a particular city. Alternatively, the suspension could be expressed as applying for six months from when the weapons are put beyond use, or in the latter example, starting forthwith and ending when all the refugees have reached the city, at which point the sanction will be revoked, see below.

2. Revocation and Amendment of Regulations under Section 1

2.39 As for revocation, section 45 provides for the revocation or amendment of regulations made under section 1 of the 2018 Act. This is expressed in terms of a clarification that section 1 contains the inherent power to make new regulations in respect of the same subject matter.

2.40 Unsurprisingly, if regulations are amended, they must continue to be appropriate for their stated purpose.[22] Save in cases where they are made for the purposes of compliance with a UN or other international obligation, the Minister must also consider that there are good reasons to pursue the stated purpose of the regulations and that the imposition of sanctions is a reasonable course of action for that purpose.[23] Where the stated purpose of a sanction is compliance with a UN or international obligation, section 45(5) also enables references to UN obligations to be updated.

2.41 Again, unsurprisingly, there is still a requirement to lay a report before Parliament in the case of an amendment to sanctions for discretionary purposes: section 46 is the mirror of section 2(4).Otherwise the safeguards could be easily circumvented.

[22] Section 45(2)(a) of the 2018 Act.
[23] Section 45(2)(b) of the 2018 Act.

3. Amending the Type of Sanctions

Section 47 allows an appropriate Minister to amend Part 1 of the 2018 Act through regulations to add different types of prohibitions and requirements not yet listed within Chapter 1 of the 2018 Act, apart from section 8: financial, immigration, trade, aircraft, and shipping. However, this power can only be used for types of sanctions that the UK is or has been under a UN or other international obligation to impose.[24] It does not enable any modification to be made to the purposes for which sanctions can be made, i.e. it does not permit an amendment to the list of purposes (such as prevention of terrorism to promoting good governance etc.) at sections 1(1) and 1(2). 2.42

In this way, section 47 is intended to future-proof the 2018 Act against a fast-changing sanctions sphere. It enables new sanctions measures agreed internationally to be brought within the scope of the 2018 Act. For example, if technological advances result in commercial space travel, the monetization of a person's DNA or the holding of crypto/ virtual assets/currency in an unanticipated form, section 47 would allow restrictions to be introduced without the need for further primary legislation. Such regulations must follow the draft affirmative procedure. 2.43

C. GUIDANCE, REPORTING, AND 'FUTURE-PROOFING'

1. Guidance

A recent example of detailed Office of Financial Sanctions Implementation (OFSI) Guidance, in respect of UK sanctions against Russia post-Brexit, can be found at Appendix 5 to this Guide. 2.44

Section 43(1) imposes a duty on an appropriate Minister who makes sanctions regulations under section 1 of the 2018 Act to issue guidance about the prohibitions and requirements imposed by those sanctions regulations. The guidance, by section 43(2) may include best practice for compliance with sanctions, details about enforcement, and details of relevant exceptions, where the prohibitions and requirements do not apply. 2.45

The requirement on the Minster to issue guidance is mandatory, but some of the contents (such as examples of best practice) are not. At present OFSI maintains guidance online as to current UK sanctions regimes.[25] 2.46

2. Report in Respect of Offences in Regulations

Historically, Parliament has been reluctant to allow new criminal offences to be created by secondary legislation, though in the second half of the twentieth century 2.47

[24] Section 47(1)(b) of the 2018 Act.

[25]. e.g. the long-standing measures in respect of Iraq can be found at https://www.gov.uk/government/publications/financial-sanctions-iraq.

approximately 90 per cent of criminal offences were brought into being through statutory instrument.[26] The Law Commission has described the decision about whether or not to create a criminal offence as, 'a law-creating step of great (arguably, of something approaching constitutional) significance'.[27]

2.48 As a safeguard, section 18 of the 2018 Act therefore requires that where regulations made under section 1 include criminal offences, a report identifying the offences, and giving the Minister's good reasons for creating them, and for setting any maximum terms of imprisonment that apply to them, must be laid before Parliament by section 18(2).

3. 'Future-proofing' the Sanctions Scheme

2.49 Earlier in the scheme of the 2018 Act, section 8 enables appropriate Ministers to implement other forms of sanctions not specifically mentioned in sections 3 to 7, which are required in order to comply with UN obligations. This will enable HM Government to continue to uphold the UK's international law obligations in the event that the UN requires the imposition of a prohibition or requirement not otherwise contained within sections 3 to 7, i.e. outside the overarching categories of financial, immigration, trade, aircraft, and shipping. It therefore 'future-proofs' the 2018 Act against the development of new types of sanctions by the UN Security Council, and therefore has the same rationale as section 47.

---

[26] *Legal Studies*, University of Glasgow research paper: http://eprints.gla.ac.uk/143568/13/143568.pdf.

[27] Law Commission Criminal Liability in Regulatory Contexts (Consultation Paper No. 195, 2010) at para. 1.49.

3
FINANCIAL SANCTIONS

A. Overview of Financial Sanctions	3.01
1. Types of Financial Sanctions and New Methods of Implementation	3.01
2. Territorial Application of Financial Sanctions	3.11
3. Broad Interpretation of Financial Sanctions	3.18
4. Asset Freezes: Pre-Brexit Context	3.21
B. Asset Freezing under the 2018 Act	3.31
C. Definitions of Key Terms in Financial Sanctions	3.36
1. Source of Definitions	3.36
2. Dealing	3.37
3. Freezing	3.39
4. Funds, Economic Resources, and Goods	3.42
5. Financial Services and Financial Products	3.46
D. Ownership and Control	3.50
1. Avoiding an Overly Narrow Approach to Sanctions Compliance	3.50
2. Defining Ownership and Control	3.52
3. Minority Interests	3.56
4. Joint Interests	3.58

A. OVERVIEW OF FINANCIAL SANCTIONS

1. Types of Financial Sanctions and New Methods of Implementation

Recent UK practice has seen the development of financial sanctions in the form of asset freezes, restrictions on access to financial services and assets, and at its most draconian, directions to cease all manner of business. 3.01

Prior to Brexit, the mechanism for implementing financial sanctions was[1] that sections 152 to 155 of the Policing and Crime Act[2] 2017 automatically imported UN and EU financial sanctions into domestic UK law. 3.02

[1] Since 1 April 2017.

[2] At Appendix 6 to this Guide.

3.03 The 2018 Act changes this. By way of overview, the core power for UK ministers to promulgate financial sanctions, including asset freezes, is by section 1(5)(a) to 'impose financial sanctions'. The detailed powers are found at section 3 of the Act, including 3(1)(a) in respect of 'freezing funds or economic resources'. Key definitions at the heart of these new powers are found at sections 60 and 61 of the 2018 Act.

3.04 Targeted asset freezes will continue to apply to named individuals, entities, and bodies. Freezes restrict access to funds and economic resources. A person subject to an asset freeze will be listed on the Office of Financial Sanctions Implementation (OFSI)'s consolidated list.[3] There is a second list of entities subject to capital market restrictions.

3.05 It is important to note that these asset freezes apply under targeted financial sanctions regimes, following the process of designation by a Minister. This is to be distinguished from other asset freezing measures in the UK, available under the Proceeds of Crime Act 2002 (POCA 2002). By section 41 POCA 2002, a restraint[4] application may be made by certain state agencies at any time following the commencement of the criminal investigation, and at any stage of the criminal proceedings. Note the subject of such a POCA 2002 freeze must be subject to criminal investigation by police or other agency, or prosecution in the courts, whereas sanctions targets are simply designated by a Minister. By way of further distinction, the Criminal Finances Act 2017 (CFA 2017) introduced interim freezing orders by way of further amendment to POCA 2002, for cases where the UK state is seeking an Unexplained Wealth Order (UWO).[5] Whilst there is no need for a criminal investigation or prosecution in the case of interim freezing orders (UWOs are sought from the High Court), that process involves presentation of evidence to a judicial authority, rather than Executive designation as in the case of sanctions under the 2018 Act.

3.06 Turning to consider other forms of financial sanction, restrictions on access to financial markets and services can apply to named individuals, entities and bodies, specified groups, or entire sectors. Guidance to current UK sanctions against Russia is in these terms:[6]

> The names of designated persons are not included in the Regulations, but instead will appear on the administrative list on gov.uk. This enables immediate publication following a decision to make or amend a designation, limiting the opportunity for designated persons to remove assets from the UK.

3.07 To date UK financial sanctions have taken the form of:

i) investment bans;
ii) restrictions on access to capital markets;

---

[3] https://www.gov.uk/government/publications/financial-sanctions-consolidated-list-of-targets/consolidated-list-of-targets.

[4] A useful summary of the five preconditions for a restraint order is found at https://www.cps.gov.uk/legal-guidance/proceeds-crime, Chapter 2.

[5] For a full analysis of Unexplained Wealth Orders, see Hugo Daniel Lodge, *Criminal Finances Act 2017: A Guide to the New Law* (The Law Society 2017) chapter 6.

[6] See Appendix 5 to this Guide, p. 246 of this Guide.

iii) directions to cease banking relationships and activities;
iv) requirements to notify or seek authorization prior to certain payments being made or received;
v) restrictions on the provision of financial, insurance, brokering, or advisory services or other financial assistance.

Directions to cease all business will specify the type of business and can apply to a specific person, group, sector, or country. 3.08

In this respect, the UK system is becoming more redolent of the US approach to financial sanctions, with recent use of blanket country or region-specific measures. 3.09

Again, by way of example, current sanctions against Russia are illustrative. The Guidance to that sanctions regime states:[7] 3.10

> Under the Regulations, it is prohibited to, directly or indirectly, extend a participation, or acquire any ownership interest, in land located in Crimea. The same restrictions also apply when it comes to acquiring any ownership interest in an entity which has a place of business located in Crimea (a 'relevant entity').

Here UK sanctions apply to whole sectors (land ownership and ownership of corporate vehicles) in an entire region (Autonomous Republic of Crimea and the City of Sevastopol).

2. Territorial Application of Financial Sanctions

Pre-Brexit, the UK and EU refrained from adopting sanctions laws with exorbitant extra-territorial effect. Antonios Tzanakopolous observes[8] that '[t]he EU and UK policy, however, is not reciprocated by other countries, notably by the US.' He points to section 319 of the USA Patriot Act 2001 which provides that for the purposes of forfeiture, if funds are in a foreign bank and that bank has an interbank account in the US with a covered financial institution, 'the funds shall be deemed to have been deposited into the interbank account in the United States'. 3.11

A safe rule of thumb is that once listed in the US, the sanction applies to everyone in the world. 3.12

On a more detailed analysis, EU financial sanctions (including those implementing UN sanctions) continue to apply post-Brexit within the geographical territory of the EU, and beyond that to all EU persons, wherever they are in the world. 3.13

Similarly, UK financial sanctions apply within the territory of the UK and to all UK persons, wherever they are in the world. There are extensions (by Orders in Council) to British Overseas Territories such that a mirror approach is taken in those jurisdictions. By way of example, the Financial Reporting Authority in the Cayman 3.14

[7] Appendix 5 to this Guide, p. 248 of this Guide.

[8] Antonios Tzanakopolous, 'UK Sanctions Regimes' in William Blair, Richard Brent, and Tom Grant (eds), *Banks and Financial Crime: The International Law of Tainted Money* (2nd edn, OUP 2017) at 9.25.

Islands maintains and distributes mirror regimes to the OFSI consolidated list in the UK. Cayman sanctions apply to those doing business in or from the Islands, and to Cayman nationals wherever they are in the world.

3.15 Therefore, all individuals and legal entities who are within, or who undertake activities within the UK's territory, must comply with the UK financial sanctions that are in force. All UK nationals and UK legal entities established under UK law, including their branches, must also comply with UK financial sanctions that are in force, irrespective of where their activities take place.

3.16 Likewise, all nationals of all EU states and legal entities established under EU law must continue to comply with the EU financial sanctions that are in force, irrespective of where their activities take place.

3.17 In short, once a sanction is listed in the US, it is prudent to begin with the assumption that everyone must comply. The situation is more nuanced with UK and EU regimes, with their more conservative approaches to extra-territoriality.

3. Broad Interpretation of Financial Sanctions

3.18 OFSI interprets prohibitions widely; this is consistent with the way in which the EU courts and other member states proceed. According to their published guidance, whilst they will not seek to draw in activities that clearly fall outside of a prohibition, OFSI will consider a wide range of actions when assessing if a breach of financial sanctions has taken place.

3.19 By way of counter-balance, as an integral part of HM Treasury, OFSI is subject to the challenge of judicial review of administrative action. A public body must not act in a capricious, unreasonable, irrational, or improper manner (see Chapter 9 of this Guide).

3.20 The new mechanisms under the 2018 Act for challenge to designation by seeking ministerial review, and then review by the courts, are dealt with in detail at Chapters 8 and 9 of this Guide.[9]

4. Asset Freezes: Pre-Brexit Context

3.21 The most common form of financial sanction had been an asset freeze; under such a sanction it is generally prohibited from:

- dealing with the frozen funds or economic resources, belonging to or owned, held or controlled by a designated person;
- making funds or economic resources available, directly or indirectly, to, or for the benefit of, a designated person;

[9] For an example of successful challenge by a designated person see *Safa Nicu Sepahan Co. v Council of the European Union*, Case C-45/15 P. By contrast for one of many unsuccessful challenges see *Europaisch-Iranische Handelsbank AG v Council of the European Union*, Case C-585/13 P.

- engaging in actions that, directly or indirectly, circumvent the financial sanctions prohibitions.

Anyone who becomes aware that they are dealing with a person or assets subject to financial sanctions has duties to 'freeze and report'.[10] These are immediate obligations, in contrast with the US system which has a grace period in certain circumstances.

Under the UK system, funds and economic resources are to be frozen immediately by the person in possession or control of them. An asset freeze does not involve a change in ownership of the frozen funds or economic resources, nor are they confiscated or transferred to OFSI or another arm of the State for safekeeping. 3.22

A person who either knows or has 'reasonable cause to suspect' that they are in possession or control of, or are otherwise dealing with, the funds or economic resources of a designated person must immediately:[11] 3.23

- freeze them;
- not deal with them or make them available to, or for the benefit of, the designated person, unless:
  - there is an exemption in the legislation that can be relied on
  - there is a licence from OFSI (or relevant authority, such as the Governor in a British Overseas Territory);
- report them to OFSI (or relevant body, e.g. the FRA in the Cayman Islands).

As for basic definitions, 'reasonable cause to suspect' appears to be an objective test in that it asks whether there were factual circumstances from which an honest and reasonable person should have inferred knowledge or formed the suspicion. Inclusion of 'honesty' in the objective test imports a subjective element, blurring the precision of the test. It is clear that 'willful blindness' does not amount to a defence under general principles of English criminal law. 3.24

A jury can impute actual knowledge on evidence that the defendant had a suspicion but 'shut his eyes to the obvious or refrained from inquiry because he suspected the truth but did not want to have his suspicion confirmed' (as per *Westminster City Council v Croyalgrange Ltd* 83 Cr. App. R. 155, per Lord Bridge). 3.25

The willful blindness doctrine is helpfully adapted to a modern and international context by ACAMS:[12] 3.26

Willful Blindness: Legal principle that operates in money laundering cases in the U.S. and is defined by courts as the 'deliberate avoidance of knowledge of the facts' or 'purposeful

[10] The mantra is a theme throughout OFSI publications.

[11] Again, the basic formulation of 'freeze, don't deal, report' is restated by OFSI at paragraph 7 here: https://assets.publishing.service.gov.uk/government/uploads/system/uploads/attachment_data/file/804021/Travelex_monetary_penalty.pdf.

[12] https://www.acams.org/aml-glossary/index-w/.

indifference.' Courts have held that willful blindness is the equivalent of actual knowledge of the illegal source of funds or of the intentions of a customer in a money laundering transaction.

3.27 The recent Guidance provides a general formula which is expected to underpin regimes under the 2018 Act: if funds are made available (directly or indirectly) to a designated person, or economic resources are made available (directly or indirectly) that would likely be exchanged, or used in exchange, for funds, goods, or services, this may constitute a criminal offence.

3.28 Similarly, the Guidance predicts, if funds or economic resources are made available for the benefit of a designated person and they obtain, or are able to obtain, a 'significant financial benefit', this may constitute a criminal offence. In this case, 'financial benefit' includes the discharge, in whole or in part, of a financial obligation for which the designated person is wholly or partly responsible.

3.29 In the context of post-Brexit UK sanctions against Russia (Appendix 4 to this Guide) the provision creating the criminal offence for breach (making funds available) is in these terms:

> Making funds available for benefit of designated person
>
> 13.—(1) A person ('P') must not make funds available to any person for the benefit of a designated person if P knows, or has reasonable cause to suspect, that P is making the funds so available ...
>
> ...
>
> (3) A person who contravenes the prohibition in paragraph (1) commits an offence.
> (4) For the purposes of this regulation—
> (a) funds are made available for the benefit of a designated person only if that person thereby obtains, or is able to obtain, a significant financial benefit, and
> (b) 'financial benefit' includes the discharge (or partial discharge) of a financial obligation for which the designated person is wholly or partly responsible.

Mirror provisions appear in the Russia regime in respect of making economic resources available (by its regulation 15).

3.30 For TAFA 2010, there may be additional restrictions on the provision of financial services (see Chapter 2 of this Guide and Section 40 of TAFA 2010).

B. ASSET FREEZING UNDER THE 2018 ACT

3.31 Considering more closely how the scheme of the 2018 Act relates to asset freezing, as mentioned, section 3 sets out the broad range of financial sanctions that can be imposed including asset freezes.[13] The core power derived from subsection (1)(a)

[13] Section 3(1)(a) of the 2018 Act.

enables the UK government post-Brexit to subject a designated person[14] to an asset freeze. As discussed above, asset freezing means that it is generally prohibited to deal with the funds or economic resources, belonging to or owned, held, or controlled by a designated person. This would limit a designated person's ability to deal with any economic resource or funds they currently own, hold, or control. The terms 'funds', 'economic resources' and 'freeze' are defined in section 60 of the 2018 Act.

Wide powers appear at subsections (1)(b) and (c) enabling HM Government 3.32 to prevent financial services from being provided to, or being procured from, prescribed persons (including designated persons). The UK may impose wider financial restrictions, including prohibitions on access to finance and capital markets. This may include, but is not limited to, prohibiting the supply of financial services to certain markets, or sections of markets (e.g. real estate agents in Crimea), or preventing the transfer of funds to a country, region, or sector (e.g. prohibition on buying land in the City of Sevastopol). An example of this is the sectoral measures currently in place aimed at limiting access to EU capital markets for Russian State-owned financial institutions. The post-Brexit sanctions against Russia are set out at Appendix 4 to this Guide (with associated guidance at Appendix 5). The term 'financial services' is also defined in section 61.

By subsection (1)(d), HM Government may prohibit funds and economic 3.33 resources being made available to, or for the benefit of, prescribed persons (including designated persons). This provision also forms part of an asset freeze. 'Financial products' are also defined in section 61.

Further, subsections (1)(g) and (2) enable the government to place restrictions 3.34 on owning, controlling, or having a prescribed interest in, or commencing or maintaining commercial relationships with, prescribed persons (including designated persons). These powers enable the UK Government to put in place the wide range of sanctions previously implemented via EU legislation. Though, as seen in the Guidance[15] on current sanctions against Russia, subtle differences may emerge between the current approach of the UK and the former emphasis of the EU regimes.

Finally, subsection (3) provides that the powers in subsection (1) include the abil- 3.35 ity to prohibit funds, economic resources, or financial services being made available, received, procured, or provided, either directly or indirectly to, from, or by a designated person. These terms are widely couched, to maximize the scope of ministerial discretion.

[14] By section 9 of the 2018 Act.

[15] See Appendix 5 to this Guide at p. 247 of this Guide, where the UK is taking a different approach in respect of the securities of subsidiaries incorporated in the UK.

C. DEFINITIONS OF KEY TERMS IN FINANCIAL SANCTIONS

1. Source of Definitions

3.36 Asset freezes have a broad reach due to the wide definitions of key terms adopted in the new legislation and guidance. Definitions in the 2018 Act are considered below, in the light of the most recent guidance published by HMT.[16]

2. Dealing

3.37 'Dealing with economic resources' generally means using the economic resources to obtain funds, goods, or services in any way, including, but not limited to, by selling, hiring, or mortgaging them. The everyday use by a designated person of their own economic resources for personal consumption is not prohibited. A recent particularization of this is seen in the post-Brexit UK sanctions against Russia, as follows:[17]

> a person 'deals with' economic resources if the person— (a) exchanges the economic resources for funds, goods or services, or (b) uses the economic resources in exchange for funds, goods or services (whether by pledging them as security or otherwise).

3.38 'Dealing with funds' has a recent iteration[18] in that:

> a person "deals with" funds if the person—
>
> (a) uses, alters, moves, transfers or allows access to the funds, (b) deals with the funds in any other way that would result in any change in volume, amount, location, ownership, possession, character or destination, or (c) makes any other change, including portfolio management, that would enable use of the funds.

3. Freezing

3.39 As for the freezing of funds, section 60(3) of the 2018 Act defines 'freezing' for these purposes. Freezing funds prevents the designated person from dealing with funds in any way, including for example moving funds (for example from one account to another), changing their worth or ownership, or any use whatsoever.

3.40 Further, subsection (4) explains the application of 'freezing' to economic resources which fall outside of the definition of funds, such as property or other assets. It prevents these goods from being 'dealt with'.

3.41 Regulations made under the 2018 Act, by way of new sanctions regimes, will define what is meant by 'making available' funds and economic resources, e.g.

---

[16] Post-EU Exit Guide to Financial Sanctions (Published 1 February, updated 25 October 2019) https://www.gov.uk/government/publications/post-eu-exit-financial-sanctions-general-guidance.

[17] Appendix 4 to this Guide, regulation 11(5).

[18] Appendix 4, regulation 11(4).

regulations 12 to 15 inclusive of the recent sanctions against Russia (see Appendix 4 to this Guide).

4. Funds, Economic Resources, and Goods

As for defining 'funds', section 60(1) of the 2018 Act defines them as financial assets and benefits of any kind. It sets out a list of examples; this list is not exhaustive, and any form of financial assets which do not appear on the list will still be subject to sanctions if they are a financial asset or benefit to the designated person. By targeting 'funds' as defined here in such broad terms, the HM government intends sanctions can effectively stem a designated person's revenue stream or access to assets. 3.42

To attempt a comprehensive definition, 'Funds' therefore means financial assets and benefits of every kind, including but not limited to: 3.43

- cash, cheques, claims on money, drafts, money orders, and other payment instruments;
- deposits with financial institutions or other entities, balances on accounts, debts, and debt obligations;
- publicly- and privately-traded securities and debt instruments, including stocks and shares, certificates representing securities, bonds, notes, warrants, debentures, and derivatives contracts;
- interest, dividends, or other income on or value accruing from or generated by assets;
- credit, right of set-off, guarantees, performance bonds, or other financial commitments,
- letters of credit, bills of lading, bills of sale;
- documents showing evidence of an interest in funds or financial resources.

Turning to consider 'economic resources', section 60 (2) of the 2018 Act defines the term, providing HM Government with an even wider power to restrict access to any type of asset which would not be covered under 'funds'. Guidance[19] states that economic resources therefore means assets of every kind—tangible or intangible, movable or immovable—which are not funds, but may be used to obtain funds, goods, or services. 3.44

Finally, 'goods' generally means items, materials, and equipment. The recent UK sanctions against Russia[20] impose restrictions on military goods (Chapter 2 in the regime), dual-use goods (Chapter 3), and energy related goods, i.e. those linked to oil exploration and production (Chapter 4). Infrastructure related goods are restricted by Chapter 5 of the new regime, in so far as they could be used in Crimea. 3.45

---

[19] Ibid.

[20] See Appendix 4 to this Guide.

5. Financial Services and Financial Products

3.46 Moving to consider services and products, section 61 (1) of the 2018 Act begins to define 'financial services' as any service of a financial nature, which is less than illuminating. More helpfully, it then sets out a non-exhaustive list of examples; and any forms of financial service which do not appear on the list will still be subject to sanctions if they are utilized to move funds which are subject to sanctions or to move, transfer, or increase the wealth of the designated person or associated entities. The following are financial services within the scope of the 2018 Act:

(a) insurance-related services consisting of—
- (i) direct life assurance;
- (ii) direct insurance other than life assurance;
- (iii) reinsurance and retrocession;
- (iv) insurance intermediation, such as brokerage and agency;
- (v) services auxiliary to insurance, such as consultancy, actuarial, risk assessment and claim settlement services;

(b) banking and other financial services consisting of—
- (i) accepting deposits and other repayable funds;
- (ii) lending (including consumer credit, mortgage credit, factoring and financing of commercial transactions);
- (iii) financial leasing;
- (iv) payment and money transmission services (including credit, charge and debit cards, travellers' cheques, and bankers' drafts);
- (v) providing guarantees or commitments;
- (vi) financial trading (as defined in subsection (2));
- (vii) participating in issues of any kind of securities (including underwriting and placement as an agent, whether publicly or privately) and providing services related to such issues;
- (viii) money brokering;
- (ix) asset management, such as cash or portfolio management, all forms of collective investment management, pension fund management, custodial, depository and trust services;
- (x) settlement and clearing services for financial assets (including securities, derivative products, and other negotiable instruments);
- (xi) providing or transferring financial information, and financial data processing or related software (but only by suppliers of other financial services);
- (xii) providing advisory and other auxiliary financial services in respect of any activity listed in sub-paragraphs (i) to (xi) (including credit reference and analysis, investment and portfolio research and advice, advice on acquisitions and on corporate restructuring and strategy).

In the above definition, 'financial trading' means, by section 61(2), trading on one's own account or for account of customers, whether on an investment exchange, in an over-the-counter market, or otherwise, in financial products. 3.47

Guidance on the recent sanctions against Russia[21] explains the focus on preventing designated persons from processing payments including, with emphasis added to illustrate an acceptance by OFSI of further divergence from the EU: 'credit, charge and debit cards, travellers' cheques and bankers' drafts. *This differs from the EU sanctions regime.*' In the 2018 Act 'Financial products' are defined by reference to a number of different types of financial product, including transferable securities and money market instruments. 3.48

The other priority of the new Russia sanctions regime is 'transferable securities or money-market instruments'. The Russia sanctions regulations[22] prohibit dealing with, directly or indirectly, a transferable security or money market instrument if it has a maturity exceeding thirty days and was issued after 1 August 2014 by five named Russian banks and non-UK entities owned by those banks. Similar restrictions are set out in respect of six Russian corporate entities (Appendix 5 to this Guide, p 3, first column). Again, there is an interesting disparity here between the UK and EU approach to UK incorporated subsidiaries of targeted Russian companies. 3.49

D. OWNERSHIP AND CONTROL

1. Avoiding an Overly Narrow Approach to Sanctions Compliance

There is obvious danger inherent in adopting an overly narrow approach to sanctions compliance, given the wide net cast by the 2018 Act. For compliance professionals and advisers, it will not suffice simply to check a list of customers and counter-parties against the OFSI Consolidated List. This is because the *assets* of a designated person may be subject to an asset freeze, and there is no consolidated list of assets (for obvious practical reasons—such a list would be immense and impossible to maintain.) 3.50

Thus, if a person or entity is designated, their name will be recorded on the consolidated list, as discussed. By contrast, an asset freeze and some financial services restrictions will apply to entities (meaning a body of persons corporate or unincorporated, or any organization or association or combination of persons) that are owned or controlled, directly or indirectly, by a designated person. Those entities may well not be designated in their own right, so their names will not necessarily appear on the consolidated list. However, those entities are similarly subject to financial sanctions. There is just as much a prohibition on dealing with their assets and complying with the obligations to 'freeze and report'. 3.51

[21] Appendix 5.
[22] Ibid.

2. Defining Ownership and Control

3.52 According to Guidance issued[23] pre-Brexit, an entity is owned or controlled directly or indirectly by a designated person in each of the following circumstances:

- The designated person holds (directly or indirectly) more than 50 per cent of the shares or voting rights in an entity;
- The designated person has the right (directly or indirectly) to appoint or remove a majority of the board of directors of the entity; or
- It is reasonable to expect that the designated person would be able to ensure the affairs of the entity are conducted in accordance with the person's wishes. This could, for example, include:
  - Appointing, solely by exercising voting rights, a majority of the members of the administrative, management or supervisory bodies of an entity, who have held office during the present and previous financial year;
  - Controlling alone, under an agreement with other shareholders in or members of an entity, a majority of shareholders' or members' voting rights in that entity;
  - Having the right to exercise a dominant influence over an entity, under an agreement entered into with that entity, or to a provision in its Memorandum or Articles of Association, where the law governing that entity permits its being subject to such agreement or provision;
  - Having the right to exercise a dominant influence referred to in the point above, without being the holder of that right (including by means of a front company);
  - Having the ability to direct another entity in accordance with the designated person's wishes. This can be through any means, directly or indirectly. For example, it is possible that a designated person may have control or use of another person's bank accounts or economic resources and may be using them to circumvent financial sanctions.

3.53 If any of the above criteria are met, and the person who owns or controls the entity is also a designated person, then financial sanctions will also apply to that entity in its entirety (meaning these assets should also be frozen). This is because the prohibitions on making funds or economic resources available directly or indirectly to a designated person, also prohibit making them available to an entity who is owned or controlled, directly or indirectly, by the designated person.

3.54 A recent and detailed example of this two-stage test is found in the post-Brexit UK sanctions regime in respect of Russia.[24] To determine whether a corporation subject to that regime, targeting Russian state-owned financial institutions, ('C') is owned or controlled, directly or indirectly, by a natural person ('P') the first condition is either that P:

---

[23] Ibid.

[24] See Appendix 4 to this Guide, The Russia (Sanctions) (EU Exit) Regulations 2019, paragraph 7.

(a) holds directly or indirectly more than 50% of the shares in C,

or (b) holds directly or indirectly more than 50% of the voting rights in C,

or (c) holds the right directly or indirectly to appoint or remove a majority of the board of directors of C...

... The second condition is that it is reasonable, having regard to all the circumstances, to expect that P would (if P chose to) be able, in most cases or in significant respects, by whatever means and whether directly or indirectly, to achieve the result that affairs of C are conducted in accordance with P's wishes.

HM Government, via OFSI, has stated at public meetings that it will look to designate owned or controlled entities/individuals in their own right where possible. However, this is no reason to adopt an overly narrow approach to sanctions compliance, the consequences of non-compliance are serious (see Chapter 11 of this Guide). 3.55

3. Minority Interests

If a designated person has a minority interest in another entity, this does not necessarily mean that financial sanctions also apply to them as the ownership and control criterion may not have been met. It will be necessary to consider whether a designated person is effectively in control e.g. because the affairs of the entity are conducted in accordance with the designated person's wishes. If they are, then the ownership and control criterion will be satisfied. 3.56

Attention is also needed as to any changes in the percentage interest held by the designated person, in case it increases to greater than 50 per cent (or they obtain a majority interest) at which point financial sanctions will also apply to that entity. 3.57

4. Joint Interests

For the purposes of the asset freeze a designated person will be taken to own funds/economic resources even if they are owned jointly with another person, or where the designated person only owns part of them. Additionally, a designated person is taken to own funds/economic resources where the designated person's ownership consists of any interest (whether legal or equitable). 3.58

If two or more persons hold shares or rights jointly, each of them will be treated as owning those shares or rights. This also applies to joint arrangements where all holders of shares or rights exercise their rights jointly. In this case, all parties subject to the joint arrangement are considered as owning those shares or rights. 3.59

4

TRADE SANCTIONS

A. Distinctions from Arms Embargoes	4.01
B. Purpose of Trade Sanctions	4.04
C. Scope of Trade Sanctions	4.08
1. Export	4.08
2. Import	4.11
3. Key Definitions and Concepts	4.13
4. Trade Sanctions in Relation to Other UK Laws	4.23

A. DISTINCTIONS FROM ARMS EMBARGOES

4.01 In the UK, trade sanctions should be distinguished from arms embargoes. The latter comprise a ban on the export of military arms and related material, e.g. ammunition, weapons, and other military goods. Thus, embargoes relate to all goods and technologies on a 'UK military list'.[1] Certain similar goods though not listed may also require a licence either under 'military end-use controls' or 'weapons of mass destruction' end-use controls.

4.02 The list includes a broad range of guns, though not those firing blanks or 'dummy' ammunition as well as (see ML4 on the list): 'Bombs, torpedoes, rockets, missiles, other explosive devices and charges, and related equipment and accessories'. There are current entries on the list for robots, lasers, aircraft, and spacecraft, as well as civilian 'drones'. As for chemical weapons there are full definitions provided of chemical agents, 'biological agents', toxic chemicals and mixtures containing such agents or chemicals, 'riot control agents', radioactive materials, related equipment, components, and materials. ML9 on the list fully defines restricted 'Vessels' of war, special naval equipment, accessories, components, and other surface 'vessels'.

4.03 The list runs to twenty-eight pages and fuller consideration is beyond the scope of this Guide. Suffice it to say that the Military List is broad in its definition and

[1] The consolidated military list is maintained here: https://www.gov.uk/government/publications/uk-strategic-export-control-lists-the-consolidated-list-of-strategic-military-and-dual-use-items-that-require-export-authorisation.

encompasses weapons and vehicles which would be used by an army, navy, or air force. It expressly includes certain para-military and police equipment, e.g. for countering riots.

B. PURPOSE OF TRADE SANCTIONS

As distinct from arms embargoes, trade sanctions are used to prevent a greater variety of activities relating to target countries, specific sectors within those countries, or designated persons. Trade sanctions cover the export, import, movement, and transfer of goods and technology, and the provision and procurement of services, beyond the narrow military list of goods and technologies. Trade sanctions also cover investment and company ownership. The post-Brexit Russia sanctions regime[2] is summarized in its own Guidance[3] thus (emphasis added): 4.04

> Under the Regulations, it is prohibited to, directly or indirectly, extend a participation, or acquire any ownership interest, in land located in Crimea. *The same restrictions also apply when it comes to acquiring any ownership interest in an entity which has a place of business located in Crimea (a 'relevant entity').*

By way of overview, the bulk of the provisions in the 2018 Act relating to trade sanctions are found in Schedule 1. These are given force by section 5 of that Act. 4.05

Further, the threefold contrast between arms embargoes, trade sanctions, and those financial sanctions (see Chapter 3 of this Guide) which are applicable to importers and exporters is helpfully demonstrated in recent OFSI guidance.[4] 4.06

A blurring of these categories is seen in the current UK trade sanctions against Russia under which[5] 'The export of military goods to, or for use in, Russia is prohibited.' 4.07

C. SCOPE OF TRADE SANCTIONS

1. Export

The core power to create new trade sanctions is found in section 1(5)(c) of the 2018 Act. 4.08

Such regimes may[6] impose restrictions for one of the purposes set out in Part 1 of Schedule 1, which details the types of trade sanctions that can be imposed, against whom they can lie, and their effect. 4.09

---

[2] At Appendix 4 to this Guide.

[3] Appendix 5, p. 248 of this Guide.

[4] https://assets.publishing.service.gov.uk/government/uploads/system/uploads/attachment_data/file/706182/FAQ_guidance_for_the_import_and_export_sector.pdf.

[5] See Appendix 4 to this Guide, Chapter 2, regulations 22 et seq.

[6] By section 5(1) 2018 Act.

4.10 Paragraph 2 of that Schedule deals with the export of specified goods, given force by section 5(2) of the 2018 Act. Regulations may provide for the prevention of exports to, or for the benefit of, prescribed countries. Also, trade sanctions may be made in relation to exports to, or for the benefit of, three categories of persons. These three groups cover:

a. designated persons (see section 9 of the 2018 Act);
b. persons 'connected with a country' prescribed in the regulations. Section 62(6) specifies that sanctions regimes under section 1 are free to define the nature of the connection between the persons and the prescribed country. This category could capture all persons connected to a country in a specified way with each regime. This is something of a blank cheque for Ministerial discretion, as drafted. Current sanctions against Russia have four criteria for connection (emphasis added):[7]
   - an individual who is, or an association or combination of individuals who are, ordinarily *resident* in Russia,
   - an individual who is, or an association or combination of individuals who are, *located* in Russia,
   - a person, other than an individual, which is *incorporated or constituted* under the law of Russia, or
   - a person, other than an individual, which is *domiciled* in Russia.
c. a prescribed description of persons connected with a prescribed country. Again, section 62(6) specifies that those promulgating regulations have discretion to set out the nature of the connection between prescribed descriptions of people and the prescribed country. As before, this category could also capture groups of persons connected to a country in the specified way. For example, a regulation could specify the prescribed description of persons as 'military commanders at or above the rank of General' and the connection could be 'currently residing in or present in the jurisdiction, whether retired or serving in a public or private capacity'.

2. Import

4.11 Moving from the export side to look at imports, paragraph 3 of Schedule 1 refers. Sanctions regimes issued under section 1 of the 2018 Act may prohibit the import of goods either originating from or consigned from a prescribed country. This may include goods originating in a prescribed country though they are routed via a third country and vice versa.

4.12 'Origin' is defined in paragraph 35(b) of Schedule 1 such that goods will be held to originate in a country including where they are produced or manufactured there.

[7] Appendix 4 to this Guide, Chapter 1, regulation 21(2).

3. Key Definitions and Concepts

In terms of the purposes to which new section 1 regimes can apply, paragraph 4 deals with movement of specified goods outside the UK. Paragraph 5 relates to the transfer of specified technology, whom it may benefit, and where they may be based (N.B. this is not limited to the UK). Technology in this case is defined in paragraph 37 and includes both information and software. 4.13

By paragraphs 6 and 7, sanctions regulations can prevent specified goods or technology from being made available or acquired. 'Making available' includes situations other than export and extends beyond the UK to prescribed countries and specified ships. This definition would cover a gift, delivery, or disposal of goods and technology. 4.14

'Acquisition' is defined in paragraph 35(a) in broad terms including purchase, lease, borrowing, or acceptance of a gift. 4.15

Paragraphs 8 and 9 focus on sanctions which would include restrictions from making land available. Military activities are in the sights of paragraph 10. 4.16

The provision of services (as opposed to goods) are at the core of paragraphs 11 to 14, and new sanction regimes may prohibit all or some services being provided. paragraphs 13 and 14 state that section 1 regulations may restrict services that are connected to other sanctions prohibitions or connected to particular projects, industries, sectors, infrastructure, aircraft, ships, services, or other activities. This legislation is widely couched, to provide maximum scope for the Executive to act. 4.17

Vessels are the subject matter of paragraph 15. It provides that sanctions regulations under section 1 can place restrictions on goods, technology, and services connected with vessels that are designated under UN Security Council resolutions. 4.18

As for fine or antique art, paragraph 16 provides that sanctions regulations can deal with objects of cultural interest; they can be identified specifically by name (e.g. 'the artefacts known as the Parthenon or Elgin Marbles') or by description ('any sculptures made by Phidias or his assistants, except those still physically located in Greece'). 4.19

The focus of paragraphs 17 to 20 is to set out how goods, services, and technology can be described in section 1 sanctions regulations. Those promulgating sanctions may choose to refer to goods by information recorded on them (e.g. a label on the back of a painting), or the use or purpose to which goods may be put, or their place of origin. 4.20

Paragraphs 21 to 23 provide that new section 1 regulations may include cross-references to other legislation and lists. This includes references to orders made under the Export Control Act 2002 (paragraph 21), to EU lists (paragraph 22) and to other technical lists, including those related to the UK's UN obligations (paragraph 23). 4.21

As for ships and aircraft (see Chapter 6 of this Guide), paragraphs 24 and 25 clarify that the movement of vehicles, ships, and aircraft under their own power may be counted as exports or imports. Finally, paragraph 26 enables vessels to be described by reference to a UN instrument. The theme here is to provide flexibility in allowing Ministers to adhere to the UK's international obligations. 4.22

4. Trade Sanctions in Relation to Other UK Laws

4.23 In the year to May 2010, more than 700 new criminal offences were created, 75 per cent of them by secondary legislation.[8] The 2018 Act continues this tradition, of allowing Ministers rather than the legislature to increase the scope and effect of criminal statutes.

4.24 By way of modification to the criminal law, paragraph 27 (Schedule 1, 2018 Act) allows regulations to modify, up to a maximum of ten years, the period of imprisonment in relation to offences under the Customs and Excise Management Act 1979 (CEMA). Paragraph 28 enables sanctions regulations to modify provisions of CEMA that apply in relation to the enforcement of prohibitions or requirements contained in sanctions regulations.

4.25 As for proportionality, paragraph 29 specifies that regulations made under Part 1 of Schedule 1 may not have the effect of prohibiting or regulating certain specified activities, unless the interference by the regulations in the freedom to carry on the activity in question is necessary (and no more than necessary).

4.26 There is a test of necessity by paragraph 30, which states that it is for the appropriate Minister to determine that any interference in any of the activities described in paragraph 29 is necessary, in light of the circumstances prevailing at the time, having considered the reasons for seeking to control the activity in question and the need to respect the freedom to carry on the activity.

4.27 Paragraph 31 specifies that references to goods, technology, land, or services being moved, made available, acquired, provided, procured, or received are reference to those things being done directly or indirectly.

4.28 Further definition is provided by paragraphs 32 and 33, which define 'export' and 'import' for the purposes of the Schedule and specify that goods moved between the Isle of Man and the United Kingdom are not to be regarded as exports or imports. The Isle of Man forms part of a joint customs area with the United Kingdom. This is in line with section 11(3) of the Export Control Act 2002 and section 8(1)(a) of the Import, Export and Customs Powers (Defence) Act 1939. Paragraph 34 specifies that goods imported into the Isle of Man in contravention of a prohibition, where a corresponding prohibition applies to the import of goods of that kind to the UK pursuant to a purpose mentioned in paragraph 3, may be regarded as imported if they are subsequently moved from the Isle of Man to the United Kingdom.

4.29 Finally, paragraph 38 clarifies that references to services in Schedule 1 may include financial services.

[8] Jonathan Sumption, *Trials of the State* (Profile Books Ltd. 2019) 5.

5
IMMIGRATION SANCTIONS

A. Travel Bans	5.01
B. Exemptions	5.05
C. Section 48 Immigration Appeals	5.12

A. TRAVEL BANS

Section 4 of the 2018 Act provides for travel bans post-Brexit. Individuals subject to travel bans are classified as 'excluded persons' within the meaning of section 8B of the Immigration Act 1971 (IA 1971).[1] The banning mechanism is that section 8B IA 1971 provides that such an excluded person must be refused leave to enter or leave to remain in the UK. Any leave that this person already holds is cancelled, and any exemption from immigration control ceases to have effect. 5.01

Travel bans are used to restrict the movement of designated persons and those said to be associated with regimes or groups, including terrorist groups, whose behaviour is considered unacceptable by the international community. Prior to Brexit section 8B IA 1971 provided for an international travel ban made either by the UN Security Council or the EU to be enforceable by the UK. Unless an exemption applies a person who is subject to a travel ban was prevented from entering the UK. 5.02

The 2018 Act (see Schedule 3) amends section 8B IA 1971 to accommodate UK autonomous sanctions regimes, as well as making provision for retained EU travel bans after the UK has left the EU. 5.03

The current sanctions against Russia[2] demonstrate the standard form in which UK regimes post-Brexit will deal with travel bans, at sanction Regulation 20: 'A person who is designated under regulation 5 for the purposes of this regulation is an excluded person for the purposes of section 8B of the Immigration Act 1971.' 5.04

---

[1] As amended by the Immigration and Asylum Act 1999 (c. 33) section 8 and the Immigration Act 2016 (c. 19) section 76.

[2] Appendix 4 to this Guide.

B. EXEMPTIONS

5.05 The 2018 Act provides, by section 15, a power to exempt individuals or a group of individuals from the effects of a travel ban. This provides Executive flexibility to mitigate the effects of a travel ban either in specific prescribed circumstances, or on a case-by-case basis, for example, to allow an individual to travel to attend an international conference convened by an intergovernmental organization. This can be done either through an exception in the regulations or as directed later by the Secretary of State.

5.06 The UK Government has stated that the exceptions provision will be used in circumstances that are either foreseeable or have been agreed with international partners in advance, for example, for humanitarian or religious reasons, to take part in peace talks, or to give evidence at a trial. The exceptions provision may also be used where there is an international law obligation, for example if the UK is hosting an international inter-governmental organization or an international conference convened under the auspices of the UN.

5.07 OFSI has issued detailed FAQs[3] for charities and other non-governmental organizations (NGOs), including how to apply for 'humanitarian' licences.

5.08 Unlike an exception, a direction would be a flexible mechanism, which could contain conditions, be granted subject to certain criteria, be of a finite duration, and be subsequently varied, revoked, or suspended. This would allow the Minister to direct that an individual be exempt from the effects of a travel ban in circumstances which were either not foreseeable at the time that the sanctions regulations were created or were not agreed with international partners at the time the sanctions regime was negotiated.

5.09 Directions under the post-Brexit sanctions regime against Russia can be issued under regulation 69[4] in the following terms:

> (2) A direction under this regulation—
>
> (a) may contain conditions.
>
> (b) must be of a defined duration (and that duration may be expressed in any way, including, for example, being expressed in a way such that the direction ceases to have effect on, or within a specified period after, the occurrence of a specified event).
>
> (3) The Secretary of State may vary, revoke or suspend a direction under this regulation at any time.

An individual to whom an exception or direction applied would be given either temporary admission if outside the jurisdiction, or bail in a custody/detention case. Also available would be a form of leave for a specified period to allow them entry.

---

[3] See https://assets.publishing.service.gov.uk/government/uploads/system/uploads/attachment_data/file/653168/OFSI_Charity_FAQ_web.pdf.

[4] Appendix 4 to this Guide.

There will not be the same discretion for the UN designations, as there is an international obligation to implement them which subsists. The process for an exemption to a UN designation will remain the same as pre-Brexit. HM Government will consider any request for an exemption to a travel ban on a case-by-case basis. If HM Government agrees that a person should be allowed to travel to the UK it will apply to the UN for an exemption. 5.10

In relation to activity carried out for the purposes of national security or for the prevention or detection of serious crime, the 2018 Act allows for exceptions to prohibitions in the regulations. The aim is to ensure that UK sanctions legislation does not inhibit legitimate behaviour. 5.11

C. SECTION 48 IMMIGRATION APPEALS

By section 48(4) of the 2018 Act, there is a power for the Secretary of State to make further regulations providing for immigration appeals. The imposition of a travel ban on a designated person, whether that person is identified by name or by description, has consequences for his or her immigration status. Those who are already in the UK will lose the right to remain here and may be subject to removal from the jurisdiction. As a result, the designated person may seek to claim asylum or humanitarian protection or claim that removal will breach their human rights under the ECHR. Those who become designated persons whilst outside the UK will be refused entry if they seek to travel here. They too may claim that this breaches their human rights. 5.12

Such 'immigration claims' are usually decided by the Secretary of State for the Home Department ('Home Secretary'). Bringing an asylum claim has certain consequences under the Immigration Acts, such as the ability to access financial support. A decision on an immigration claim by the Home Secretary may give rise to a right of appeal before the Immigration and Asylum Chamber of the First Tier Tribunal ('The Tribunal'), a specialist body with expertise in deciding such claims. 5.13

HM Government has stated that it recognizes that the proper decision maker in respect of an immigration claim is the Home Secretary, and the proper venue for deciding an appeal related to an immigration claim is the Tribunal. However, there is an overlap between these immigration claims and claims that can be made under the review and challenge mechanisms in the 2018 Act. 5.14

Section 48 therefore gives a power to the Secretary of State to make regulations setting out the mechanisms by which the immigration consequences of sanctions will be considered. These regulations will ensure that immigration claims are sent to the Home Secretary for decision and appeals against such decisions are made to the Tribunal for resolution. This process is intended to ensure that UK's immigration obligations under both ECHR and the Refugee Convention (as defined in section 8B IA 1971) will continue to be dealt with by those parts of government 5.15

and Her Majesty's Courts and Tribunals Service that are best equipped to deal with them.

5.16 Further, the section 48 power enables any consequential amendments to legislation, including primary legislation, that such provisions require. Regulations made by the Home Secretary under the section 48 power will use the draft-affirmative procedure.

6

AIRCRAFT AND SHIPPING

A. Aircraft 6.01
B. Shipping 6.09
1. Controlling the Movement of Ships 6.09
2. Procedure for Dealing with Goods Seized from Ships 6.17
3. Revocation and Review in Relation to Ships 6.19

A. AIRCRAFT

The core power to impose aircraft sanctions is found in section 1(5)(d) of the 2018 Act. Aircraft caught by the 2018 Act include drones and space-ships, but they must be civilian not military. Section 6(9) refers. Foreign police helicopters and aircraft could be subject to sanctions. Further, there is a broad definition of the geography of the UK for the purposes of this part of the Act, to include its territorial sea (section 6(8)). 6.01

Detailed provisions (under section 6 of the 2018 Act) enable HM Government to impose sanctions against aircraft, by way of either prohibitions or requirements. These powers would, for example, permit the Secretary of State to make directions controlling the movement of an aircraft within the UK (if it were being transported on a ground-based vehicle, or on a civilian vessel within its waters) and flying in the airspace over the UK (see section 6(1)(a)). 6.02

Directions made under the Act could also require a disqualified aircraft to remain in the UK once landed or, if in flight somewhere in the world, to not overfly the UK (section 6(1)(b)). Similarly, a direction can be given for an aircraft to leave UK airspace. 6.03

Such directions can be given, pursuant to section 6(3), by the Secretary of State to the Civil Aviation Authority (CAA), who have responsibility for air traffic control, to a licensee who is providing air traffic services, or to an airport operator in relation to a disqualified aircraft. Any one of these bodies will also have the authority to direct aircraft operators or pilots in command of disqualified aircraft for the same purposes. 6.04

Disqualified aircraft are, by section 6(6), those registered in, or originating from, a prescribed (sanctioned) country, as well as aircraft which are owned, chartered, 6.05

or operated by designated persons or persons connected with a prescribed country. Aircraft sanctions will allow the government to control the movement of disqualified aircraft in line with its existing sanctions obligations. For example, there is currently a prohibition against aircraft operated by North Korea or aircraft originating from North Korea from overflying the UK. Aircraft sanctions will also enable relevant UK permits to be denied to such aircraft which would prevent them from using UK airports.

6.06 The 2018 Act also allows regulations to be made by the Minister which would prevent UK persons registering an aircraft in a prescribed country which is subject to sanctions (section 6(1)(e). Regulations may also make it an offence to own, charter, or operate an aircraft which is registered in a prescribed country.

6.07 Directions can also be given to a British-controlled aircraft, preventing the aircraft from overflying or landing in a prescribed country, by section 6(5).

6.08 The 2018 Act also provides the power for the Secretary of State prevent the registration of aircraft and a power to direct the CAA to remove an aircraft from the UK aircraft register (section 6(4)) where it has been identified that a designated person holds an interest in that aircraft or where an aircraft has been chartered by demise to a designated person.

B. SHIPPING

1. Controlling the Movement of Ships

6.09 A typical example of a shipping sanction is seen in the current UK regime against Russia, where the Minister may now ban British cruise ships from entering a Crimean port. Regulation 57 of that regime[1] provides:

> (4) A Crimean ports direction—
>
> (a) may be given to any master or pilot of a British ship which is a cruise ship, or to masters and pilots of British ships which are cruise ships generally;
>
> (b) may be of indefinite duration or a defined duration.

6.10 The core power to impose these and any other shipping sanctions is now section 1(5)(e) of the 2018 Act. Section 7 contains the detailed powers to control the movement of disqualified, designated or specified ships to prevent such ships from entering UK waters. If they have already done so, there is the power to require such ships to leave, or to be detained whilst enforcement action is taken against them.

6.11 As for the key definitions, vessels may be subject to sanctions if they are either disqualified (see below) or if they are specified by a UK Minister under the 2018 Act.

6.12 Disqualified ships are, by section 7(8), those which are registered in, fly the flag of, or originate from a prescribed (sanctioned) country. They can also be ships which

[1] Appendix 4 to this Guide.

are owned (wholly or partially), controlled, chartered, operated, or crewed (wholly or partially) by designated persons, or persons connected with a prescribed country. A designated ship is one which has been designated by the UN. A specified ship is one which has been specified by the appropriate Minister.

Provisions relating to the UK Minister specifying ships are set out at section 14. The test is whether the Minister: 6.13

(a) has reasonable grounds to suspect that the ship is, has been, or is likely to be, involved in an activity specified in the regulations, and
(b) considers that it is appropriate for that ship to be specified, having regard to the purpose of the regulations as stated under section 1(3).

The Secretary of State may give directions, by section 7(3) to the master or pilot of a ship or direct the relevant harbour authority to give such a direction. These directions can include, but are not limited to, directing a ship to leave the UK, to go to a specified harbour, or not to enter the UK's territorial sea and waters. 6.14

Section 7(4) allows for ships to be refused registration on the UK Ship Register on the basis that a designated person or persons connected with a prescribed country hold an interest in them, or because it has been specified by an appropriate Minister. If a vessel is already on the UK Ship Register, this section provides it to be removed if those circumstances arise. 6.15

The Secretary of State can also issue directions to a British ship anywhere in the world, in order to prevent it from entering a country in which relevant sanctions are in force, by section 7(5). This is the power behind the example above, banning cruise ships from docking in Crimea. 6.16

2. Procedure for Dealing with Goods Seized from Ships

Section 41 of the 2018 provides a power for the Minister to make further detailed regulations setting out how goods seized from ships are to be dealt with. 6.17

By section 19[2] of the 2018 Act the enforcement of regulations (see section 17) may be used to confer wide powers to, inter alia:[3] 6.18

(a) stop a ship;
(b) board a ship;
(c) require any person found on a ship boarded by virtue of this section to provide information or produce documents;
(d) inspect and copy such documents or information;
(e) stop any person found on such a ship and search that person for—
    (i) prohibited goods, or
    (ii) any thing that might be used to cause physical injury or damage to property or to endanger the safety of any ship;

...

[2] And see section 20 for non-UK conduct.
[3] Per section 19(4) of the 2018 Act.

3. Revocation and Review in Relation to Ships

6.19 Section 26 of the 2018 Act provides the Minister with the power to revoke specification of ship at any time. If at any time the Minister considers that the required conditions are not met in respect of a ship specification, the Minister must revoke the specification.

6.20 By section 27, there is a right to request revocation of specification of ship at any time while a ship specification has effect. Any person affected by it may request the Minister to revoke the specification.

6.21 Where a person has made a request under this section in respect of a specification, no further request may be made under this section by that person or any other person in respect of that specification unless the grounds on which the further request is made are or include that there is a significant matter which has not previously been considered by the Minister.

6.22 On a request under this section the Minister must decide whether to revoke the specification or to take no action with respect to it.

6.23 Further, there is provision for periodic review where ships are specified. For the purposes of this section (by section 28(2)) each of the following is a 'review period'—

(a) the period of 3 years beginning with the date when the regulations are made, and
(b) each period of 3 years that begins with the date of completion of a review under this section of specifications made under the regulations.

6.24 In respect of a UN-designated ship there is a distinct right to request review by section 29 of the 2018 Act. Any person affected by such a sanction may request the Secretary of State to use the Secretary of State's 'best endeavours' to secure that a ship so designated ceases to be designated for any purposes of the Resolution.

6.25 In a mirror of the domestic-focused provision, where a person has made a request under this section in respect of the designation of a ship, no further request may be made under this section by that person or any other person in respect of that designation unless the grounds on which the further request is made are or include that there is a significant matter which has not previously been considered by the Secretary of State, by section 29(3).

7
DESIGNATED PERSONS AND DESIGNATION POWERS

A. Designated Persons: OFSI Lists 7.01
1. Publicly Available Lists 7.01
2. Implementation of Sanctions without Delay 7.11
3. Proscription under the Terrorism Act 2000 7.13

B. Designation of Persons: Powers under the 2018 Act 7.17
1. Context and Key Provisions 7.17
2. Section 11: Designation of a Person by Name under a Designation Power 7.23
3. Section 12: Designation of Persons by Description under a Designation Power 7.31
4. Section 13: Persons Named by or under UN Security Council Resolutions 7.35

A. DESIGNATED PERSONS: OFSI LISTS

1. Publicly Available Lists

At the heart of the 2018 Act, is the process by which UK Ministers can designate who is subject to targeted financial sanctions post-Brexit. OFSI at HM Treasury maintains two publicly available lists of those subject to financial sanctions. The first is a list of all the targets of asset-freezing sanctions. This is a list comprised of the names of designated persons. A second list sets out restrictions on access to capital markets, and is focused on Russian subjects, following actions to destabilize Ukraine. 7.01

The first, 'consolidated list' is published and updated at https://www.gov.uk/government/publications/financial-sanctions-consolidated-list-of-targets. 7.02

This comprises a current schedule of all asset-freeze targets listed under UK autonomous financial sanctions legislation and UN sanctions. In the immediate aftermath of Brexit, some entries on the list relate to those retained from EU law. As time passes, UK under the 2018 Act will replace those EU remnants (see by way of example at Appendix 4 and 5 to this Guide, the new regime and guidance in respect 7.03

of Russia). The individuals and entities listed are known collectively as 'designated persons'. OFSI publishes the consolidated list online and sends regular email update alerts to assist businesses and individuals comply with UK financial sanctions. The list is further adopted and disseminated in British Overseas Territories, e.g. by the Financial Reporting Authority in the Cayman Islands.

7.04 OFSI has stated that its target is to update its consolidated list within one working day for all new UN and UK listings coming into force in the UK, and within three working days for all other amendments.

7.05 By way of practical advice, any person who has been delisted but whose name remains on the consolidated list is encouraged to email OFSI (ofsi@hmtreasury.gov.uk) with evidence of delisting.

7.06 The consolidated list contains a range of information to assist in the identification of designated persons. For an individual natural person this may include:

- aliases
- date of birth
- passport details
- nationality
- last known address
- employment or role.

If the name of an individual or entity ('A') being dealt with by another person ('B') matches one or more entries on the consolidated list, this is known as a 'name match'. However, this does not necessarily mean that A is the same person as the one on the list. If B is satisfied that this is the case, a match in name only, B need not need to take further action.

7.07 Some people have commonly occurring names. By way of illustration, if B is a solicitor dealing with a childhood prodigy singer called Thomas Jones in Wales, B may have no concern about an apparent match with someone of an identical name on the consolidated list, if that other Thomas Jones is 60 years old and employed in a munitions factory in Syria. The name is not unusual.

7.08 By contrast, if the individual or entity B is dealing with matches all the information on the consolidated list, this is likely to be a 'target match'. If, having consulted the consolidated list, B is still unsure on whether B has a target match for A, B should contact OFSI for assistance by email.[1]

7.09 The second list maintained by OFSI is of entities subject to capital market restrictions: it is found here:

https://www.gov.uk/government/publications/financial-sanctions-consolidated-list-of-targets/ukraine-list-of-persons-subject-to-restrictive-measures-in-view-of-russias-actions-destabilising-the-situation-in-ukraine.

[1] ofsi@hmtreasury.gov.uk.

OFSI maintains this separate list of entities subject to specific capital market restrictions. It is worth noting that these entities are not contained on the consolidated list. For the original source of information on the restrictions that apply to these entities please see the Ukraine (Sovereignty and Territorial Integrity) regime page.[2] The post-Brexit measures and Guidance are contained in this book.[3] 7.10

2. Implementation of Sanctions without Delay

There has been a requirement for implementation of UN financial sanctions 'without delay' since 1 April 2017. Namely, prior to Brexit all new UN listings took effect in UK law for either (i) a period of thirty days; or (ii) until the EU lists the Designated Person (within that thirty-day window), whichever was the shorter (see sections 154 and 155 of the Policing and Crime Act 2017, at Appendix 6 to this Guide). Since the date of Brexit, where listings are made under a new UN Security Council Resolution, they have effect in UK law via regulations made under the 2018 Act. 7.11

The FCO will continue to publicize UN listings. OFSI will add all those subject to financial sanctions to the consolidated list.[4] OFSI publishes notices describing changes to financial sanctions.[5] OFSI notifies its subscribers by email whenever a new notice is published.[6] 7.12

3. Proscription under the Terrorism Act 2000

By way of context, an organization may be proscribed ('banned') under Schedule 2 of the Terrorism Act 2000 if the Home Secretary believes it is involved in terrorism and it is proportionate to do so. The Terrorism Act 2006 expanded these powers to ban organizations if the Home Secretary believes they are in fact a proscribed organization acting under a different name.[7] 7.13

Because proscription involves different restrictions, and because not all proscribed organizations are subject to financial sanctions, the list of proscribed organizations is not included in OFSI's consolidated list. 7.14

The list of proscribed organizations is maintained by the Home Office and can be found on GOV.UK.[8] 7.15

Banning organizations by description rather than name was the forerunner of provisions in the 2018 Act to designate sanctions targets in the same way. 7.16

---

[2] https://www.gov.uk/government/publications/financial-sanctions-ukraine-sovereignty-and-territorial-integrity.

[3] Appendices 4 and 5 to this Guide.

[4] For more information see: http://www.legislation.gov.uk/uksi/2017/478/contents/made

[5] https://www.gov.uk/government/collections/financial-sanctions-regime-specific-consolidated-lists-and-releases.

[6] https://public. govdelivery.com/accounts/UKHMTREAS/subscriber/new.

[7] See Alun Jones, Rupert Bowers, and Hugo D. Lodge, *Blackstone's Guide to the Terrorism Act 2006* (OUP 2006) Chapter 6, 'Proscription'.

[8] https://www.gov.uk/government/publications/proscribed-terror-groups-or-organisations.

B. DESIGNATION OF PERSONS: POWERS UNDER THE 2018 ACT

1. Context and Key Provisions

7.17 By way of context, there are currently around 2,000 designated persons under existing UK sanctions regimes. Common examples include people involved in supporting the Syrian regime or those assisting in the pursuit of nuclear, ballistic, and weapons of mass destruction programmes in North Korea.[9]

7.18 The Minister may designate a person to be the subject of sanctions by the core powers under sections 9 to 13 of the 2018 Act. These provisions empower the Minister to delegate persons to be held individually subject to sanctions measures such as asset freezes (see section 3 of the 2018 Act and Chapter 3 of this Guide).

7.19 Section 9 defines the term 'designated persons'. Such persons can include individual natural persons, along with a body of persons which includes companies and other entities that have legal personality, as well as associations or groups of persons.

7.20 Persons can be designated by an appropriate Minister either by name (see discussion of section 11 in section B.2 of this Chapter) or description (see discussion of section 12 in section B.3 of this Chapter) which is analogous to banning terrorist organizations by description, discussed in the previous segment. There is a separate procedure for the designation of those named in UN Security Council resolutions (see discussion of section 13 in section B.4 of this Chapter).

7.21 By section 10, Ministers are empowered to set out in regulations how designation powers are to be exercised, including requirements for notification and publicity. Regulations must place an obligation on the appropriate Minister to take such steps as are reasonably practicable to inform designated persons of their designation, though there is no need for a designated person to be notified in advance of any designation coming into effect. To do so might defeat the object of targeted financial sanctions to freeze assets, instead allowing resources to be dissipated.

7.22 These designation provisions must be considered alongside provisions in Chapter 2 of the 2018 Act, which require Ministers to undertake regular reviews of sanctions and give designated persons the right to reassessment, and Chapter 4, which enable designated persons to have access to review in the courts. Designation is the first stage, which may be subject to review by the Minister and/or court.

2. Section 11: Designation of a Person by Name under a Designation Power

7.23 This section empowers an appropriate Minister to designate a person by name, such that the person will become the subject of a sanctions regime made under section 1 of the 2018 Act.

[9] As mentioned, the Russia sanctions guidance is set out at Appendix 5.

The Minister may only designate a person where the Minister has[10] reasonable grounds to suspect the person is involved in, or connected to, an activity set out in the regulations for a particular sanctions regime ('an involved person') and considers that it is appropriate to designate that person. In respect of UK sanctions regime against Russia, by its regulation 6(2)[11] such a person: 7.24

(a) is or has been involved in destabilising Ukraine or undermining or threatening the territorial integrity, sovereignty or independence of Ukraine,
(b) is owned or controlled directly or indirectly ... by a person who is or has been so involved,
(c) is acting on behalf of or at the direction of a person who is or has been so involved, or
(d) is a member of, or associated with, a person who is or has been so involved.

More detailed guidance is given, see sanctions regulation 6(3) as to what is meant by destabilizing, etc. Ukraine, namely that: 7.25

the person is responsible for, engaging in, providing support for, or promoting any policy or action which destabilises Ukraine or undermines or threatens the territorial integrity, sovereignty or independence of Ukraine; (b) the person provides financial services, or makes available funds, economic resources, goods or technology that could contribute to destabilising Ukraine or undermining or threatening the territorial integrity, sovereignty or independence of Ukraine; (c) the person provides financial services, or makes available funds, economic resources, goods or technology, to— (i) a person who is responsible for a policy or action which falls within paragraph (a), or (ii) a person who provides financial services, or makes available funds, economic resources, goods or technology, as mentioned in sub-paragraph (b); (d) the person obstructs the work of international organisations in Ukraine; (e) the person conducts business with a separatist group in the Donbas region; (f) the person is a relevant person trading or operating in Crimea; or (g) the person assists with the contravention of a relevant provision.

The aim is to give a UK Minister clear direction (e.g. naming the Donbas separatists) but also a wide margin of flexibility. The definition illustrates the difficult with seeking to enshrine in legislation a detailed framework for the exercise of Executive discretion. To return to an earlier example, would letting down the tyres of a coach containing visiting Cub Scouts count as 'obstructing the work of international organisations'? Secondary legislation is being promulgated here at a level of granular detail which is little more than a list of policy objectives. Its integrity and purpose as law is questionable. 7.26

The Minister must have regard[12] to the purpose of the sanctions regime as set out in the regulations and to the likely significant effects of the designation on the person, as far as known. 7.27

When a person has been designated by name, the notification required by section 10 must include a brief statement of reasons. This is in recognition of both public law concepts of natural justice and Human Rights under the European Convention. However, the Minister does not have to disclose anything which might damage national security or international relations, the prevention or 7.28

[10] By section 11(2) of the 2018 Act.
[11] Appendix 4 to this Guide.
[12] By section 11(2)(b) of the 2018 Act.

detection of serious crime, or the interests of justice. Information can be disclosed on a confidential basis.[13]

7.29 An 'involved person' could[14] include an individual, group, or organization involved in an activity, or a person controlled by them, someone acting on their behalf, or an associated person.

7.30 Again, under the current Russia sanctions regime, its Guidance explains:[15]

> The names of designated persons are not included in the Regulations, but instead will appear on the administrative list on gov.uk. This enables immediate publication following a decision to make or amend a designation, limiting the opportunity for designated persons to remove assets from the UK.

3. Section 12: Designation of Persons by Description under a Designation Power

7.31 This is a mirror provision to section 11 but provides for circumstances where an appropriate Minister designates persons by description rather than by name. This power can only be exercised when it is not practicable for the Minister to identify by name all the persons falling within the description,[16] though it remains to be seen how this is interpreted. By way of safeguard, the description must be[17] sufficiently precise that a reasonable person would know whether any person falls within it.

7.32 An example under the current Russia sanctions regulations (see Appendix 4 to this Guide at sanctions regulation 6(2)(d)) would be that the Minister may be able to identify a group of people who are threatening the territorial integrity of Ukraine and may designate that any member of that group is therefore subject to sanctions. If, by way of fictitious illustration, that group called itself 'Sevastopol Freedom Fighters (SFF)', a UK Minister would not have to name each member (this would be difficult without access to SFF's membership records) but could designate the whole group.

7.33 In addition, the same restrictions apply[18] as to designations under section 11(2).

7.34 Nevertheless, this is a broad extension of Executive power, which carries potential threats to individual liberty. The danger is that a whole group is targeted without proper consideration. If the total membership of a group cannot be quantified, how can a judgement be made about each of its members, some unknown? With an avowed terror organization, a UK Minister may have no doubt at all. However, there will be other very different groups who contain a range of members, e.g. the rump of a Communist Party in a former Soviet Republic. Much will depend on Ministerial discretion and judgement. As mentioned, this use of proscribing by description is

---

[13] See for example regulation 9 in the Russia regime at Appendix 4 to this Guide.

[14] By section 11(3) of the 2018 Act.

[15] Appendix 5 to this Guide, p. 246 of this Guide.

[16] See section 12(4) of the 2018 Act.

[17] By virtue of section 12(3) of the 2018 Act.

[18] By section 12(5) of the 2018 Act.

the continuation of a trend seen in the Terrorism Act 2006, where pursuant to section 22 of that Act, the Secretary of State may treat organizations as proscribed when they do not appear on the list in Schedule 2 to the 2000 Act.

4. Section 13: Persons Named by or under UN Security Council Resolutions

Section 13 bites where the UK has an obligation under international law to designate persons who are named on a UN list. In these cases, the regulations made under the 2018 Act must provide that the persons named on a UN list are designated persons. Sections 13(2) and (3) enable the regulations to refer to the UN list without having to duplicate that list in UK regulations. 7.35

8

REVIEW BY APPROPRIATE MINISTER

A. Power to Vary or Revoke Designation 8.01
 1. Overview 8.01
 2. Section 22: Power to Vary or Revoke a Designation Made under Regulations 8.04
B. Right to Request Variation or Revocation of Designation 8.07
 1. The Core Right to Request Variation or Revocation of Designation 8.07
 2. The New Regulations on Sanctions Review Procedure 8.12
 3. Requests in Relation to Temporary EU Lists 8.32
 4. Right of a UN-named Person to Request a Review 8.36
C. Periodic and Other Reviews 8.37
 1. Periodic Review of Certain Designations 8.37
 2. Review by Appropriate Minister of Regulations under Section 1 8.38
 3. Independent Review of Regulations with Counter-terrorism Purpose 8.42
 4. Periodic Reports on Exercise of Section 1 Power 8.44

A. POWER TO VARY OR REVOKE DESIGNATION

1. Overview

8.01 The 2018 Act introduces a strictly controlled ministerial review mechanism. The Act prevents[1] designated persons from immediately challenging section 1 regulations before the courts, by way of judicial review. Rather, they must first request either variation or revocation of the designation from the appropriate Minister (at the Treasury or Secretary of State level). Only after that initial stage may a designated person seek judicial review of a sanctions-related decision; see Chapter 9 of this Guide. Thus, those who are subject to financial sanctions can challenge their listing, but financial sanctions will remain in place while the challenge or request is being considered.

[1] Section 38 of the 2018 Act.

It is important to note that there is a different procedure for those names within UN sanctions, see section B.4 of this Chapter of the Guide. 8.02

Ministers must react to requests for variation and revocation, but they must also comply with periodic reviews, as per section C of this Chapter of the Guide. 8.03

2. Section 22: Power to Vary or Revoke a Designation Made under Regulations

The same appropriate Minister[2] who made a designation under section 1 of the 2018 Act has the power[3] to revoke or vary that designation. Plainly such revocation has the effect that the designated person in question would no longer be subject to the restrictions set out in the relevant section 1 sanctions regulations. 8.04

As for variation, the Explanatory Notes[4] state: '[v]arying a designation would allow the Minister to adjust a designation to match any change in the situation, for example updating the information used to identify an individual as new information comes to light.' Section 22 therefore permits the appropriate Minister to vary or revoke a designation at their discretion. Notwithstanding the political underpinning of sanctions, a Minister of the Crown is still subject to public law principles. In any subsequent court review of this ministerial review stage of the process, the evidence and advice (suitably redacted) offered by officials to the Minister may become disclosable, under the duty of candour: see Chapter 9 of this Guide. Basic reasonableness permeates administrative law. Per Lord Wrenbury, *Roberts v Hopwood* [1925] AC 578, 613, stating that a decision-maker 'must, by use of his reason, ascertain and follow the course which reason directs. He must act reasonably.' By contrast, section 22(3) is mandatory in that it obliges Ministers to use this power to revoke a designation, 'If at any time the Minister considers that the required conditions are not met'. The sub-section bites where the required conditions of the relevant designation power are not met in respect of the designation.[5] Such review may follow actions taken by persons to seek reassessment of their designation, or under HM Government's own periodic review of designations, as set out below. Sanctions of their nature should be temporary expressions of political disapproval. Thus, the section 22 power is vital. 8.05

Variation and revocation in respect of ships is dealt with in Chapter 6 of this Guide. 8.06

[2] Section 22(1) of the 2018 Act states that it must be the 'appropriate Minister who made that delegation', though plainly this refers to the office and its incumbent rather than the individual politician who personally made the decision, so that one Secretary of State may review his or her predecessor's decision if there has been a 'reshuffle' or change of government.

[3] By section 22(2) of the 2018 Act.

[4] Ibid.

[5] Section 22(4) of the 2018 Act.

B. RIGHT TO REQUEST VARIATION OR REVOCATION OF DESIGNATION

1. The Core Right to Request Variation or Revocation of Designation

8.07 Section 23 of the 2018 Act gives designated persons the right to ask[6] HM Government to revoke or vary their designation, 'At any time while a relevant designation has effect',[7] for example where a person believes he has been misidentified or considers the designation does not meet the necessary evidential standard. This is an internal administrative challenge which leads to a reassessment of a designation by the Minister on the advice and information provided by officials and is designed to allow access to speedy redress. It will be interesting to see how many Ministerial reviews are 'successful' from the viewpoint of the designated person. Misidentification may be more readily conceded than failure to meet the evidential test.[8]

N.B. section 23 does not apply to designations that are made as a result of a UN obligation—separate provision is made for this in section 25 which is explained below at section B.4 of this Chapter.

8.08 The appropriate Minister has a duty to consider these requests as soon as reasonably practicable, though as further specified in section 33,[9] time does not run until the Minister 'has receipt … of the information needed for making the decision'. In the context of Extradition cases the courts have taken a robust approach to the definition of producing the subject of a European Arrest warrant before a court 'as soon as practicable',[10] but in that case the liberty of the detained individual is more directly infringed. By contrast, in commercial cases the courts do not construe the phrase 'as soon as reasonably practicable' as making time of the essence: *Videocon Global Limited (1) Videocon Industries Limited (2) v Goldman Sachs International* [2016] EWCA Civ 130.

8.09 The Minister may take the decision to use the section 23 power to vary or revoke a designation or may choose to take no such action so that the designation remains in force. To reiterate, designated persons need to follow this procedure before bringing any challenge in the courts, per section 38.

8.10 Once such a request has been considered once under section 23, the Minister is not required to reconsider any further requests from the same person,[11] 'unless the

[6] Though presumably in the absence of such an explicit 'right to request', the designated person could in any event have written to the Minister and sought judicial review of any response within the usual three-month time limit. Pre-Brexit a designated person had to choose whom to petition in writing: the UN focal point for delisting, or the FCO to petition the UN in respect of the same; for EU listings, the General Secretariat of the Council of the European Union; for UK listings, The Treasury Solicitor. Section 23 is a welcome streamlining.

[7] Section 23(1) of the 2018 Act.

[8] See Appendix 7 to this Guide for HM Government's own best practice on establishing identity.

[9] This safeguard is reiterated in Regulation 7 of the Sanctions Review Procedure (EU Exit) Regulations 2018 (2018 No. 1269).

[10] Under Extradition Act 2003, Part 1, detained persons must appear before an appropriate judge as soon as practicable, a matter of the next available court sitting day rather than several days or weeks.

[11] Section 23(2) of the 2018 Act.

grounds on which the further request is made are or include that there is a significant matter which has not previously been considered by the Minister'. The stated purpose of this restriction[12] is to guard against vexatious repetition of requests. There is an analogy here with the principle that repeated bail applications cannot be made in criminal proceedings absent a change of circumstances. In a variety of other cases, both civil and criminal appellate courts would want to know the reason why any 'fresh evidence' was not available at an earlier hearing and refuse permission to appeal absent a robust justification. By contrast there is no explicit requirement in section 23 of the 2018 Act that a fresh application should state the reason why the any new matter was not raised at the initial application. There can be little advantage in the designated person withholding any meritorious point from the first application. It appears there is no bar to subsequently raising a new point even if it should have been included first time. Again, the context may be a ministerial reluctance to admit all but the most glaring misidentifications. As for HM Government's own best practice on establishing proof of identity, see Appendix 7 to this Guide.

Request for variation and revocation in relation to ships is dealt with in detail in Chapter 6 of this Guide. 8.11

2. The New Regulations on Sanctions Review Procedure

Three pages of straightforward requirements have been issued by the Minister of State at FCO as of 27 November 2018, under section 33 of the 2018 Act. The regulations[13] reproduced at Appendix 2 of this Guide set out the procedures applying to the ministerial review and reassessment mechanisms in the Act. They were stated to come into force on 7 January 2019, and therefore took effect as at the date of Brexit. 8.12

Regulation 2 defines which 'address' persons must provide, depending on their natural or legal status. In relation to an individual, this means the address where that individual usually resides; in relation to a UK company it means the address of the registered office;[14] in relation to a non-UK incorporated company it means the address of its principal place of business in its country of incorporation or, if applicable, its registered office; finally, there is a catch-all in relation to an unincorporated body, organization, association, or combination of persons: it means the address of their main place of business or activity. 8.13

Regulation 3 sets out the different types of request for ministerial review under post-Brexit sanctions regimes (i.e. regulations made under section 1 of the 2018 Act) to which these procedural rules apply: 8.14

(a) section 23 of the 2018 Act (core right to request variation or revocation of designation);

(b) section 25 (right of UN-named person to request review);

[12] Explanatory Notes to the 2018 Act.

[13] Sanctions Review Procedure (EU Exit) Regulations 2018 (2018 No. 1269), the Explanatory Notes to which are frankly unnecessary.

[14] That a company is required to have under section 86 of the Companies Act 2006(b).

(c) section 27 (right to request revocation of specification of ship);

(d) section 29 (UN-designated ship: right to request review).

8.15 Regulation 4 sets out the content of the request, required by a designated person. The request must be made in writing in English. It must include the requester's—

(a) name;

(b) address;

(c) correspondence address, if different; and

(d) proof of identity,[15] if the requester is an individual.

Reliable proof of identity (with a score of 3 under the latest guidance[16]) is found in a range of documents which include the following:

- passports that meet the International Civil Aviation Organisation (ICAO) specifications for machine-readable travel documents;
- identity cards from an EU or European Economic Area (EEA) country that follow the Council Regulation (EC) No 2252/2004 standards;
- UK photocard driving licences;
- EU or EEA driving licences that follow the European Directive 2006/126/EC;
- a Northern Ireland electoral identity card;
- a US passport card.

The highest level (with a score of 4) of proof of identity is found in:

- biometric passports that meet the ICAO specifications for e-passports;
- identity cards from an EU or EEA country that follow the Council Regulation (EC) No 2252/2004 standards and contain biometric information;

a UK biometric residence permit.

8.16 As for intermediaries applying on behalf of designated persons, by regulation 4(3) where a person is acting on behalf of the requester, that person must provide confirmation of authority to act on behalf of the requester.

8.17 The person applying, whether it is the designated person or an intermediary, must specify[17] whether the application is for: a variation under section 23; revocation under section 23; review under section 25; revocation under section 27; review under section 29 of the 2018 Act.

[15] Various levels of simplified, standard, and enhanced due diligence exist in international standards from FATF. Pre-Brexit the 2017 Money Laundering Regulations were the most recent general iteration in the UK. Proof of identity is established in diverse ways to differing standards by HM Government. For recent detailed guidance see 17 December 2019 'Identity proofing and verification of an individual' at Appendix 7 to this Guide.

[16] Ibid.

[17] Regulation 4(4).

The person applying must give reasons for the application and explain:[18] where the request is for a variation under section 23 of the 2018 Act, why the designation should be varied and what variation is requested; where the request is for revocation under section 23, why the designation should be revoked; where the request is for review under section 25, why the requester's name should be removed from the relevant UN list; where the request is for revocation under section 27, how the requester is affected by the ship specification and why the specification should be revoked; where the request is for review under section 29, how the requester is affected by the designation and why the designation should cease. 8.18

There is no prescribed word limit for these explanations. It would doubtless assist the requester to keep submissions clear, concise, and tied closely to the evidence provided, see below. 8.19

By regulation 4(6), a request must include 'relevant evidence of the explanation provided under paragraph (5), where such evidence is available to the requester'. The corollary appears to be that evidence which is not available should be alluded to, along with the reasons for its non-availability. As a public body the appropriate Minister, and HM Government, are under a duty to comply with basic fairness, natural justice, and reasonableness.[19] If a document is in the possession of HM Government but not accessible to the applicant, it should be requested in writing. 8.20

As to the form of evidence, this is still at pre-court stage though there is an element of formality. The 'evidence' will have more weight if it complies with Practice Direction 22[20] on Civil Procedure Rules (CPR) Part 22 which states the following: 8.21

> **2.1** The form of the statement of truth verifying a statement of case, a response, an application notice or a notice of objections should be as follows:
>
> '[I believe] [the (claimant or as may be) believes] that the facts stated in this [name document being verified] are true.'
>
> **2.2** The form of the statement of truth verifying a witness statement should be as follows:
>
> 'I believe that the facts stated in this witness statement are true.'

Some modification will be required. If the designated person is signing a witness statement then plainly 2.2 above applies. If another document is being 'produced' by a witness statement then 2.1 should be used, and the word claimant could be substituted by 'applicant' or 'requester'. This is a new procedural area and the three-page Regulations do not provide this level of detail. 8.22

By Regulation 4(7), where a request includes any evidence which is not in English, the request must include a translation of that evidence into English, and the translation must: include a signed declaration by the translator that the translation is an accurate translation of the evidence; include the date of the translation and the full name and contact details of the translator. 8.23

---

[18] Regulation 4(5).

[19] See *Roberts v Hopwood* [1925] AC 578, 613.

[20] See https://www.justice.gov.uk/courts/procedure-rules/civil/rules/part22/pd_part22.

8.24 Where this is not the first request a designated person has made, by Regulation 4(8) it is categorized as a 'further request', and so the further request 'must explain what the significant matter giving rise to the further request is, and why it is significant'. It would also be prudent to set out why the information was not available at the time of the initial request.

8.25 As for the practicalities of where to send the request, by Regulation 5 it must be made electronically to sanctions.reassessment@fco.gov.uk. In a case 'where it is not reasonably practicable for the requester to make a request electronically', a request may be submitted in hard copy to Sanctions Unit, Foreign and Commonwealth Office, King Charles Street, London SW1A 2AH. It is difficult to imagine a case in which it would not be practicable for most persons to send an email, perhaps if the individual was unrepresented and imprisoned, or in the case of someone forbidden by order or bail condition from using the internet.

8.26 Turning to consider the next stages of the process, Regulation 6 enables the Minister to seek further information in relation to the request. The requester must provide any such further information, where such information is available to the requester, 'as soon as reasonably practicable'. There will be little motive for delay on the part of the requesting person, though the phrase is ambiguous.

8.27 Regulation 7 confirms that a decision must be made by the appropriate Minister, again 'as soon as reasonably practicable', after the appropriate Minister has received the information necessary to make a decision

8.28 The decision, having been made, must then be notified by the appropriate Minister to the requester or intermediary, by Regulations 8. The Minister must inform the requester in writing of the decision on the request and the reasons for it, 'as soon as reasonably practicable after' the decision is made. This is a further and separate period from time allowed for the decision to be made. Where the decision is in relation to a request under section 27 of the 2018 Act (right to request revocation of specification of ship) or section 29 (UN designated ship: right to request review), the Minister may also inform any person affected by the ship specification or designation of the decision and the reasons for it.

8.29 Matters may be withheld from the reasons given where the Minister considers that they should be excluded on the following grounds: in the interests of national security or international relations; for reasons connected with the prevention or detection of serious crime in the United Kingdom or elsewhere; or in the interests of justice.

8.30 By Regulation 9, the appropriate Minister may take steps to publicize the decision on a request, and the reasons for it. Again, matters may be excluded from the published reasons where the Minister considers that they should be excluded on the above grounds.

8.31 'International relations' is a broad category; for example UK Governments have been criticized for a reticence in challenging the Kingdom of Saudi Arabia. It will be interesting to see how Regulation 9 is interpreted by Ministers. In addition to the basic reasonableness and natural justice points made above, there is a public law duty to avoid startling/unreasonable statutory interpretation. In *R (Morgan Grenfell & Co*

Ltd) v Inland Revenue Commissioners[21] at 8 per Lord Hoffmann, 'the courts will ordinarily construe general words in a statute, although literally capable of having some startling or unreasonable consequence ... as not having been intended to do so'.[22]

3. Requests in Relation to Temporary EU Lists

During the temporary two-year period (see sections 34 and 35 of the 2018 Act) section 36 enables persons who are designated under a retained EU sanctions list to make a request to be removed from that list. Application must be made (section 36(2)) to the appropriate Minister who made the decision (in a section 34(3)(a) case or else to any an appropriate Minister). 8.32

Such a request must plainly be granted where the conditions of section 35(1) are not met, namely that the appropriate Minister does not have reasonable grounds to suspect the designated person is an 'involved person' (see sections 35(2) and (3)) or does not consider it appropriate for the person to be designated. It seems unlikely that a Minister would add a name to an existing EU list during the interim period, only to remove it on these grounds. 8.33

The decision must be made as soon as reasonably practicable[23] after the appropriate Minister receives the necessary information to make the decision, and the person who made the request must be informed as soon as reasonably practicable after the decision is made. N.B. the 'new' procedural regulations[24] do not apply to requests for ministerial review under interim EU lists, by Regulation 3. 8.34

Section 37 provides that where a person is on a retained EU sanctions list by virtue of a UN Security Council resolution, the procedure for seeking removal from that list reflects the procedure in section 25; namely, that they can only make a request to the appropriate Minister to use best endeavours to remove their name from the relevant UN list, see section B.4 of this Chapter. This section reflects the position that the UK is under a binding obligation[25] in international law to designate the person, and the obligation persists until the designation is lifted by the UN. 8.35

4. Right of a UN-named Person to Request a Review

Under section 25 of the 2018 Act, a designated person who has been named in order for the UK to comply with a UN resolution may request that the appropriate Minister use their 'best endeavours' to persuade the UN to remove them from the relevant UN instrument. The appropriate Minister must decide whether or not to comply with this request. Once a request has been made, further requests cannot be made unless there is a significant new matter (similar to the provision under section 23). 8.36

[21] [2002] UKHL 21 [2003] 1 AC 563.

[22] The principle is older, traced back to Lord Hobhouse in *Stradling v Morgan* (1560) 1 P 199 at 44.

[23] Although, see discussion of section 33 in sections B.1 and B.2 of this Chapter.

[24] Sanctions Review Procedure (EU Exit) Regulations 2018 (2018 No. 1269).

[25] As signatory to the UN Charter, see Chapter 1 of this Guide for discussion.

This section again reflects the fact that the UK is under a binding obligation in international law as signatory to the UN Charter to designate the person, and the obligation persists unless and until the designation is removed by the UN.

C. PERIODIC AND OTHER REVIEWS

1. Periodic Review of Certain Designations

8.37 At the level of individual designated persons, section 24 of the 2018 Act requires the government to reconsider every designation which is in force within a maximum of three years[26] since either the regime was established, or the last review. In theory the section permits reviews to be carried out against a shorter time frame if, in the unlikely event, that is desired. The aim is to ensure that the information against all designated persons is regularly reviewed, and that sanctions which are supposed to be temporary in their nature sanctions do not roll on indefinitely. In practice, this will require an administrative reassessment of the evidence used to designate a person, in each case. Presumably Ministers will act on briefing notes, summaries, and advice prepared by their officials.

2. Review by Appropriate Minister of Regulations under Section 1

8.38 At the higher level of each sanctions regime, section 30 of the 2018 Act requires that, on an annual basis,[27] the appropriate Minister must consider whether sanctions regulations under section 1 are still 'appropriate' for their specified purposes.[28]

8.39 As for sanctions regulations which are made for a purpose other than compliance with UN obligations (or other international obligations), the Minister must also consider whether there are good reasons to pursue that purpose and whether sanctions are a reasonable course of action for that purpose.[29] Again, given the supposedly temporary nature of sanctions, this is aimed at ensuring that each regime only remains in place for as long as it serves a valid purpose.

8.40 This exercise is more of a political review of the regime, focused on the question of whether it is contributing to its intended purpose, rather than a review of the evidence supporting each designation. There is an overlap here between public law, world politics, and domestic government administration. The courts have deprecated the description 'quasi-judicial' saying it is 'apt to confuse rather than clarify; though it may legitimately be used to denote a twilight area and to signify to which of the neighbouring areas the situation in the question is more akin'.[30] Though high politics plays its part in annual reviews, the points made earlier in this Chapter

[26] Section 24(4) of the 2018 Act.
[27] Section 30(7) of the 2018 Act.
[28] Section 30(2) of the 2018 Act.
[29] Section 30(3) of the 2018 Act.
[30] *Race Relations Board v Charter* [1973] AC 868, 901F-G per Lord Simon.

about a Minister of the Crown being held to standards of basic fairness must apply. In practice the reviews will not lead to the addition of any regimes, merely their subtraction. It seems unlikely that this section will be the subject of litigation.[31]

The appropriate Minister who has carried out the review is required to lay before Parliament a written report outlining the conclusions of the review.[32] 8.41

3. Independent Review of Regulations with Counter-terrorism Purpose

The independent reviewer will by 31 January each calendar year[33] notify the Minister and/ or HM Treasury of intended reviews for that year. Reviews 'must be completed during that calendar year or as soon as reasonably practicable after the end of it'.[34] 8.42

Section 31 of the 2018 Act requires, per the Explanatory Note:[35] 8.43

> the appointment of an independent reviewer to conduct reviews of sanctions regulations which impose asset freezes or similar financial sanctions, where the regulations are made for purposes relating to the prevention of terrorism and they have been referred to the independent reviewer by the Secretary of State or the Treasury for review. It is intended to replicate the role of the independent reviewer appointed under the Terrorist Asset Freezing etc. Act 2010, which is abolished by the 2018 Act.

Independent review of anti-terror measures was first consolidated by Part 3, section 36 of the Terrorism Act 2006. The independent reviewer was obliged to lay a report before Parliament annually.[36]

4. Periodic Reports on Exercise of Section 1 Power

As the Explanatory Note states in respect of section 32, the 2018 Act, 8.44

> A report under this section must identify regulations made for the purpose of providing accountability for or being a deterrent to gross human rights violations. It must also specify any recommendations made by a Parliamentary Committee for the use of that power in relation to such violations and include any government response.

This is a safeguard which monitors, on an annual basis,[37] the extent to which sanctions regimes targeted at 'a relevant human rights purpose' are being both introduced and revoked.[38] The intention here is for the Legislature to hold the Executive to account to ensure pursuit of such abuses.

---

[31] Perhaps, if an organization such as Amnesty International or Transparency International could show they had standing in a cause.

[32] Section 30(2) of the 2018 Act.

[33] Section 31(4) of the 2018 Act.

[34] Section 31(5)(b) of the 2018 Act.

[35] Ibid.

[36] See Alun Jones, Rupert Bowers, and Hugo D. Lodge, *Blackstone's Guide to the Terrorism Act 2006* (OUP 2006) chapter 10.

[37] Section 32(3) of the 2018 Act.

[38] Section 32 (1)(b) of the 2018 Act.

9

COURT REVIEW OF DECISIONS

A.	Overview of Court Review	9.01
B.	Availability of Court Review in the 2018 Act	9.10
C.	Preliminary Matters	9.12
D.	Closed Material Procedures	9.16
E.	Disclosure	9.21
F.	Case Law: Grounds for Challenge	9.25
G.	Damages	9.37

A. OVERVIEW OF COURT REVIEW

9.01 Prior to the 2018 Act, most sanctions in force in the UK derived from EU law, including sanctions decided at UN level but implemented by EU regulations. Prior to Brexit, UK courts frequently took the view that the correct venue for challenging sanctions was therefore elsewhere, e.g. the EU Courts.

9.02 Post-Brexit the position is made clear; there is no remedy available in the UK courts for challenge to UN sanctions, and challenge in the EU Courts falls away as EU regulations no longer have effect per se. However, previous UK jurisprudence will remain relevant on preliminary issues (disclosure, injunctions, etc.) as will case law on unilateral UK sanctions, and challenges based on Human Rights arguments.

9.03 The 2018 Act provides a tightly controlled court review mechanism. Designated persons are prevented from immediately challenging regulations before the courts. Rather, they must first request either variation or revocation of the designation from the Minister.

9.04 Only after that stage may a designated person seek judicial review of a decision under the 2018 Act. In the event that court challenge is successful, HM Government will only be liable for damages if it is found to have acted negligently or in bad faith.

9.05 Also, of note, a 'closed' court procedure may be used in cases where individuals have been designated based on 'sensitive' intelligence material.

9.06 A fundamental distinction is that the 2018 Act does not allow court review for those targets designated by the United Nations. HM Government's position is that decisions of the UN Security Council are binding on the UK, as a matter of international treaty obligation. A domestic court could not derogate from such commitments.

One of the UN's sanctions regimes contains an appeal process, via the Ombudsperson[1] to the ISIL (Da'esh) and Al-Qaida Sanctions Committee, set up by UN Security Council Resolution 1904 (2009). In all other UN regimes, there is no similar redress for a designated person. 9.07

For all other UN listings, a request should be sent to the UN focal point for delisting. More information about the focal point is available on the UN's website.[2] 9.08

Nevertheless, under the 2018 Act, it seems likely that UK courts will have significant influence on UK sanctions policy. The case load of judicial review applications before the courts fell to around 4,000 in 2016. It is not just the Administrative Court which may see an upturn, claimants and defendants can appeal to the Court of Appeal (Civil Division) and ultimately to the Supreme Court. 9.09

B. AVAILABILITY OF COURT REVIEW IN THE 2018 ACT

Section 38 of the 2018 Act ensures that 'an appropriate person'[3] who does not agree with a decision made under Part 1 of the Act has a route to challenge a government decision in the courts. These decisions include: 9.10

a. an administrative reassessment of a UK designation, under section 23;
b. a UK government review of a UK designation, under section 24;
c. an administrative reassessment of a UN designation, under section 25;
d. an administrative reassessment of a retained EU designation, under section 36 or 37;
e. an administrative reassessment of a UK-specified ship, under section 27;
f. a UK government review of a UK-specified ship, under section 28; or
g. an administrative reassessment of a UN-specified ship, under section 29.

When considering an application brought under section 38, the courts will apply the principles of judicial review. There is no reason to think that the previous case law on preliminary matters and unilateral UK sanctions will be disregarded. 9.11

C. PRELIMINARY MATTERS

As for judicial review generally, courts in the UK will not decline from adjudicating on a decision merely because it has been taken in respect of a nationally important 9.12

[1] https://www.un.org/sc/suborg/en/node/189.

[2] https://www.un.org/sc/suborg/en/sanctions/delisting.

[3] Discussed in section C of this Chapter.

policy pursued by a Minister who is also accountable to Parliament. One such high profile example was the challenge to the decision to exclude Gatwick Airport from proposals to expand airport capacity in England.[4]

9.13 The most salient preliminary point, as mentioned, is that if a designated person seeks a revocation or variation of their listing, they must apply for this through the mechanism provided for in the relevant sections on Ministerial Review in the first instance, before they are able to access the redress through the courts. The stated aim of this restrictive provision is, per the Explanatory Note, to help ensure that, 'quick redress is available to the designated person and seeks to minimize unnecessary litigation, on the part of both the designated person and the government'. It is moot whether a wrongly designated individual will appreciate that aim.

9.14 The primary venue for domestic challenge to UK sanctions designations will be the Administrative Court, though the Commercial Court hears cases for damages claims brought following successful challenges to sanctions. Civil Procedure Rules (CPR) will apply substantive sanctions challenges; these are periodically updated. Prior to the coming into force of the 2018 Act, the two statutes dealing with unilateral UK sanctions were the Counter-Terrorism Act 2008 (CTA 2008) and the Terrorist Asset Freezing etc. Act 2010 (TAFA 2010). Case law on those statutes is still relevant and considered below.

9.15 In judicial review cases generally, an applicant must have 'sufficient interest'[5] or 'standing', previously *locus standi.* For Court Review under the 2018 Act, the definition of an 'appropriate person' is found at section 38(3):

> (3) 'The appropriate person' means—
> (a) in relation to a decision within subsection (1)(a), the person named by the designation or, where the designation is of persons of a specified description, any person of that description;
> (b) in relation to a decision within subsection (1)(b) or (d), any person affected by the decision;
> (c) in relation to a decision within subsection (1)(c), the person who made the request.

D. CLOSED MATERIAL PROCEDURES

9.16 Section 40 of the 2018 Act sets out that that the closed material procedures (CMP) provided for in the Counter-Terrorism Act 2008 may be used in respect of legal challenges under the 2018 Act. The effect is that HM Government may apply to the court for sensitive material to be disclosed only to special advocates and the court, i.e. not the applicant, on the basis of this being in the public interest. HM Government is able to use sensitive information to support the imposition of sanctions on persons without the additional requirement of more open disclosure of such material.

---

[4] *R (on the application of Medway Council) v Secretary of State for Transport* [2002] EWHC 2516.

[5] The test for CPR Pt 54 judicial review is set out in section 31, Senior Courts Act 1981.

Such procedures have been developed in the CPR to deal with challenges under both CTA 2008 and TAFA 2010. Part 79 CPR is most relevant, including provision to: modify the general rules of evidence and disclosure;[6] applications by HM Treasury to withhold certain evidence;[7] appointment of special advocates, as counsel who review evidence but do not share it with their applicant client;[8] and the use of closed hearings from which the public are excluded.[9] 9.17

Section 40 of the 2018 Act also sets out how, on the first occasion that the Lord Chancellor makes rules of court (which set out the court's procedure) about the use of the closed material procedure in relation to challenges under section 38, the Lord Chancellor must consult the relevant heads of the judiciary in England and Wales, and in Northern Ireland. In Scotland, the power to make rules of court resides in the Court of Session, and this section makes no provision in respect of those rules. 9.18

The use of CMP in hearings challenging sanctions under CTA 2008 was considered in *Bank Mellat v HM Treasury I*.[10] Lord Neuberger confirmed that CMP are not in principle incompatible with Article 6 ECHR (Right to a fair hearing) but that such restrictions must be set out in statute, as they are not permitted at common law. 9.19

Beyond the narrow scope of section 40 of the 2018 Act, expressly referring to CMP, section 6 of the Justice and Security Act 2013 (JSA 2013) allows for CMP in civil proceedings. Part 82 CPR refers. In summary, applicants challenging designation under the 2018 Act may not find they are in possession of all the material used by the Minister in making his original decision. The restriction in respect of such disclosure may be significant and requires further consideration. 9.20

E. DISCLOSURE

Judicial Review proceedings in the Administrative Court generally have a more restrictive approach to disclosure than the Chancery or Queen's Bench Divisions,[11] though exceptions can be made where 'disclosure appears to be necessary in order to resolve the matter fairly and justly'.[12] A similar approach will be taken by the courts to CPR Part 18 Requests for Further Information. 9.21

A major restriction will arise in cases where the relevant public body asserts that material is being withheld on the grounds of national security. *Bank Mellat II*[13] saw an application under section 63 CTA 2008, where HMT sought to rely upon material it refused to disclose to the claimant bank. The approach in a leading control 9.22

[6] CPR 79.22.
[7] CPR 79.25.
[8] CPR 79.18.
[9] CPR 79.17.
[10] [2013] UKSC 38.
[11] See *R (Actis SA) v SSCLG* [2007] EWHC 344.
[12] *R (Bredenkamp) v SSFCA* [2013] EWHC 2480 (Admin).
[13] [2014] EWHC 3631.

orders case[14] was followed: namely that the applicant must be given sufficient information about the allegations against him to enable him to give effective instructions to his legal counsel.

9.23 Lord Neuberger MR went further, on appeal in *Bank Mellat I*,[15] holding that in all cases to which Article 6 ECHR applies, there are irreducible minimum rights which, again, required the disclosure of sufficient information about the evidential case against the person to enable him to give effective instructions.

9.24 In *Bank Mellat II* Collins J revisited the authority of *Tariq v Home Office*[16] in which the Supreme Court stated that the test for disclosure depended on the nature and weight of the circumstances on each side of the application, and that civil claims were not in the same category as deprivation of liberty cases. Collins J emphasized that even a bank could suffer utterly damaging effects on its ability to function, and that this should be taken into account in determining the level of necessary disclosure.

F. CASE LAW: GROUNDS FOR CHALLENGE

9.25 The basis for challenging designations will be the usual grounds for judicial review: illegality, irrationality, or procedural impropriety.

9.26 An unhelpful distinction emerged from the case of *Anns v Merton LBC*[17] where Lord Wilberforce drew a distinction between policy aspects of a public body's functions and operational ones, stating that a duty of care was more likely to arise in the latter. This has not prevented judicial scrutiny of sanctions.

9.27 *Bank Mellat I—2*[18] is the leading case on challenge to unilateral sanctions against an Iranian bank under CTA 2008. Both substantive and procedural grounds were argued before the Supreme Court. Lord Sumption set the scene by saying that nuclear non-proliferation was an important public interest and that HM Treasury should be 'allowed a large margin of judgement' and that 'This is pre-eminently a matter for the executive'. However, there was no reason in principle why the UK courts would refuse to entertain judicial review of such sanctions.

9.28 Case law from both EU and UK courts discloses two distinct grounds of substantive challenge: basis and proportionality.

9.29 One mode of challenge is to attack the *basis* for the sanctions designation. What were the reasons and were they rationale? What was the factual matrix on which the decision rests, and did the decision-maker err on those facts? Could there have been further investigation by law enforcement or other authorities?

14 *SSHD v AF (No 3)* [2010] 2 AC 269.
15 [2013] UKSC 38.
16 [2012] 1 AC 452.
17 [1978] AC 728.
18 [2013] UKSC 39.

The other was to attach the substance of a decision to impose sanctions is to challenge the *proportionality* of a particular sanctions regime. Such arguments will be based on ECHR rights such as the right to family life,[19] or the right to property.[20] *Bank Mellat I -2* held that proportionality depends on a careful analysis of the underlying facts to determine: 9.30

1) Whether its objective is sufficiently important to justify the limitation of a fundamental right;
2) Whether it is rationally connected to the objective;
3) Whether a less intrusive measure could have been used;
4) Whether having regard to these factors, and weighing the severity of any consequences, a fair balance has been struck between the rights of the community and the rights of the individual subject of sanctions.

Further, the majority held that the analysis in *A v SSHD*[21] had application here, and that the issue of discrimination was relevant to the question of proportionality. HMT had failed to justify why this particular bank had been singled out for sanctions. The arbitrary nature of the decision was disproportionate. 9.31

The first case to be decided on designation under section 26 TAFA 2010 was *C v HM Treasury* [2016] EWHC 2039. 9.32

Mr. Justice Cranston held that HM Treasury bore three burdens to discharge before making a designation: 9.33

1) HM Treasury must have a reasonable belief that the person is or has been involved in terrorist activity;
2) HM Treasury must consider it necessary for the purposes connected with protecting members of the pubic from terrorism that financial sanctions should be so applied;
3) If both are met, HM Treasury has a discretion to designate (such that this is a power not a duty).

As for 'reasonable belief', he held that the authority of *SSHD v CC and CF*[22] had helpful dictum in that the test does not require proof of underlying facts on the civil standard of a balance of probabilities. Regard was had to the test of Laws LJ in *A v SSH,* that 'Belief is a state of mind by which the person in question thinks that X is the case. Suspicion is a state of mind by which the person in question thinks that X may be the case.' 9.34

As for 'necessity' of financial sanctions, he held that the test in *SSHD v MB*[23] applied. The plain need for the measure must be seen in the context of proportionality. 9.35

[19] Article 8 ECHR.
[20] Article 1 ECHR, Protocol 1.
[21] [2005] 2 AC 68.
[22] [2012] EWHC 2837.
[23] [2006] EWCA Civ 1140.

9.36 Aside from challenges on substantive grounds, judicial review may be pursued on *procedural* grounds. The rights to make representations on a designation decision and the right to effective judicial protection will be key. It will not be the case that there is a right to prior consultation in every circumstance. *Bank Mellat I* is authority that the entity must have been targeted for a good reason, and that principles of fairness and good administration will apply.

G. DAMAGES

9.37 By section 39(2) of the 2018 Act, where a court would otherwise have the power to award damages (for example, by virtue of the Senior Courts Act 1981 for England and Wales), it may not do so unless the court considers that the use of the power under challenge amounts to committing the tort of negligence[24] (or for Scotland, that there has been negligence), or there has been bad faith. This approach is comparable with the current law on awards of damages in sanctions cases within the EU.

9.38 The finding of a court that a public authority had breached a ground of judicial review would not in any event automatically result in compensation at common law: 'Illegality without more does not give a cause of action' per *Three Rivers DC v Bank of England (No. 3).*[25]

9.39 However, section 39 is a significant restriction on the jurisprudence which developed under section 8 of the Human Rights Act 1998 (HRA 1998).[26]

[24] A seminal three-fold classification of negligence is seen in *Caparo Industries PLC v Dickman* [1990] 2 AC 605 at 617–18.

[25] [2001] UKHL 16.

[26] See in particular *R (Greenfield) v SSHD* [2005] UKHL 14.

10

LICENCES AND EXEMPTIONS

A. Overview	10.01
B. Exceptions and Licences	10.04
1. Exceptions	10.04
2. Licences	10.08
3. Immigration Exceptions	10.11
C. Protection for Compliance	10.12
D. Guidance	10.14
1. Crediting Frozen Accounts	10.15
2. Protection for Non-designated Independent Persons	10.16
3. Ring-fencing	10.17
4. OFSI Licensing Review and Non-retrospectivity	10.18
5. Licensing Grounds: UK Regimes	10.20
6. Licensing Grounds: Other Domestic Regimes	10.21
7. General Licences	10.23
8. Applying for a Licence	10.34
9. Submitting an Application	10.38
10. Counter-terrorism Regimes	10.41

A. OVERVIEW

In the sanctions context, a 'licence' is a written authorization from the Office of Financial Sanctions Implementation (OFSI) permitting an otherwise prohibited act. By contrast, an 'exception' to a prohibition applies automatically in certain defined circumstances as set out in the regulations and does not require a licence from OFSI. 10.01

The 2018 Act includes a broad licensing power. HM Government has confirmed that it intends to issue general licences for issues that are urgent; i.e. those which could not be foreseen at the time of the drafting of the sanctions regulations; or need to be time-limited. A general licence may be issued where HM Government introduces an unrelated financial services policy that would otherwise be hindered by sanctions law and does not contradict the policy intent of the particular sanctions regime. 10.02

10.03 Specific exceptions and licensing powers will be contained in the text of the sanctions regulations themselves, made under section 1 of the 2018 Act, which will allow transactions and activity which would otherwise be prohibited to take place in particular circumstances. To continue working through the example of the current UK sanctions against Russia, its Guidance helpfully summarizes the position on both exceptions and licenses, detailed in the next section of this Chapter.

B. EXCEPTIONS AND LICENCES

1. Exceptions

10.04 The key provision on exceptions is section 15 of the 2018 Act, which enables Ministers to disapply the effect of sanctions in particular circumstances. Section 15(2)(a) enables regulations to provide for exceptions to any prohibition or requirement imposed by regulations. Such an exception may be used in the following ways:

a. to enable interest or other earnings on accounts to accrue, provided that any such interest, other earnings and payments will also be frozen;
b. to enable financial or credit institutions in the UK to credit frozen accounts where they receive funds transferred to the account of a sanctioned person, entity or body, provided that any credits to such accounts will also be frozen;
c. to enable the export of, and associated technical assistance for, equipment used by peacekeeping missions.

10.05 Taking the example of the regime in respect of Russia: as for the restriction on providing loan or credit arrangements to eleven named corporations (and their non-UK subsidiaries), detailed exceptions are provided in terms:[1]

Exceptions

The prohibitions outlined above in relation to loans and credit arrangements are not breached if any of the following are granted:

- A relevant loan which makes funds available for a non-restricted trade. 'Non-restricted trade' refers to any trade that is not prohibited under Part 5 of the Regulations.
- A relevant loan that makes emergency funds available to meet applicable solvency or liquidity criteria for a relevant subsidiary, as defined in the Regulations.
- A relevant loan consisting of a drawdown or disbursement made under an arrangement that was entered in to before 15th September 2014, as detailed in the Regulations'

10.06 The purpose of these exceptions is to mitigate the effect unvarnished sanctions would have entities beyond the scope of the corporations on the lists (other trades and subsidiaries) and, in its third limb, recognizing that loans predating the year of Russian annexation of Crimea should also be out of scope.

[1] See Russia (Sanctions) (EU Exit) Regulations 2019, Appendix 5 to this Guide.

As for the prohibition on investments in Crimea, the exception is drafted in these terms:[2] 10.07

Provided that a person notifies HM Treasury no later than five working days before the day on which an act is carried out, no prohibition relating to investments in Crimea are contravened by a person meeting an obligation under a contract that was concluded before 20 December 2014.

2. Licences

As a corollary of exceptions, the central licensing provision of the 2018 Act is section 15(2)(b), which provides that persons may take any actions which would otherwise breach the prohibitions in the regulations, if they do so under authority of a licence granted by an appropriate Minister. Licensing grounds for sanctions may include: 10.08

a. payments to satisfy the essential needs and/or payments necessary for basic expenses of natural or legal persons, entities or bodies, such as food, rent, and energy;
b. payment for insurance;
c. payment of reasonable professional fees and the reimbursement of reasonable and necessary incurred expenses associated with the provision of legal services;
d. payment of fees or service charges for routine holding or maintenance of frozen funds or economic resources;
e. payments required in extraordinary situations or for extraordinary expenses;
f. payments required by a court order;
g. payment due under contracts, agreements or obligations that were concluded or arose before the date on which the natural or legal person, entity or body referred to in the asset freeze was sanctioned;
h. payment necessary to ensure human safety, environmental protection or evacuations, or for the verification and destruction of chemical weapons;
i. payment intended to be used for official purposes of a diplomatic mission, consular post or international organization;
j. export of goods or transfer of technology for humanitarian purposes; or
k. brokering, technical assistance, and other services provided for humanitarian purposes.

Further, in relation to the practical details of such licenses, section 15(3) deals with the contents, scope, and duration of licences issued by an appropriate Minister. A licence must specify the acts it authorizes. It may be general or granted to a category of persons or to a particular person. It may be subject to conditions. It may be of indefinite duration or be finite and therefore subject to an expiry date. A general licence may authorize multiple parties to undertake specific activities, for example 10.09

[2] Ibid.

certain types of transactions relating to humanitarian aid. A licence may be varied or revoked, and any such changes will be communicated to any affected designated person or their authorized representative. There is flexibility here for Executive discretion.

10.10 Working through the Russian example, the licensing provisions are set out at sanction regulations 64 to 68 inclusive.[3] Notably, in respect of the prohibitions on dealing with transferable securities and money market instruments (emphasis added):[4]

> There are *no* grounds under which a licence can be granted in relation to these prohibitions. There is an exception for acts done for the purposes of national security or the prevention of serious crime.

3. Immigration Exceptions

10.11 As for immigration sanctions, section 15 of the 2018 Act also provides a power to make exceptions to a travel ban either for an individual or for a group of individuals.[5] This provides the flexibility to disapply the effects of a travel ban on a case-by-case basis, for example to allow an individual to travel to attend an international conference convened by an intergovernmental organization. This can be done either in the regulation itself or by a direction of the appropriate Minister at a later date. Section 15(6) clarifies that exceptions to the prohibitions and requirements in any regulations to be made may be made to support activity carried out for the purposes of national security or the prevention or detection of serious crime.

C. PROTECTION FOR COMPLIANCE

10.12 What happens if a person refuses to continue dealing with someone who is the target of sanctions, in breach of contract? Section 44 of the 2018 Act ensures that such a person, who may have been liable to civil proceedings as a result of compliance with sanctions regulations contained within the Act, is not liable if they reasonably believe that they were acting in compliance with regulations in place at the time. Section 44 aims to protect people from any adverse results generated by compliance (for example, a breach of a contract to supply goods that are prohibited from export by sanctions).

10.13 As for the burden and standard of proof in any criminal proceedings brought for breach of provisions in specific sanctions regimes, the Russian example, at its regulation 56(2)[6] is instructive:

[3] The Russia (Sanctions) (EU Exit) Regulations 2019, Appendix 4 to this Guide.

[4] Guidance for the financial and investment restrictions in Russia, Appendix 5 to this Guide.

[5] The provision in the sanctions against Russia is found at its Regulation 69, Appendix 4 to this Guide.

[6] Appendix 4 to this Guide. The formulation of burden and standard is the same as for self-defence in English criminal law. Once the defence cross a basic 'evidential' threshold, the burden is on the prosecution to disprove it beyond reasonable doubt, or in the modern parlance, so that the jury (or tribunal of fact) is sure.

If evidence is adduced which is sufficient to raise an issue with respect to the defence, the court must assume that the defence is satisfied unless the prosecution proves beyond reasonable doubt that it is not.

D. GUIDANCE

This section of the Guide draws heavily from 'Post EU Exit Guide to Financial Sanctions (Jan 2019)' issued by HM Treasury. 10.14

1. Crediting Frozen Accounts

It is important to note that as for crediting frozen accounts, the effect of asset freezing legislation and guidance is to permit without a licence: 10.15

- a relevant firm to credit a frozen account with interest or other earnings due on the frozen account, so long as those funds are themselves frozen immediately.
- a person to transfer funds to a relevant firm for crediting a frozen account where the transfer is in order to discharge obligations that were concluded or arose before the date the person became sanctioned. This is an important restriction on the scope of the effect of sanctions, and a clear attempt to ensure proportionality. It may lead to arbitrary outcomes, e.g. who is to say 'on the ground' at which point in 2014 obligations in Crimea may have assisted the Russian annexation? As a matter of law and commercial necessity, there must be a bright-line threshold date.
- a relevant firm, to reiterate, without the need for a licence, to credit a frozen account with payments from a third party, provided that the incoming funds are also frozen and, that it informs OFSI of the transaction without delay. This is a pragmatic attempt to balance proportionality with allowing OFSI to maintain oversight.

2. Protection for Non-designated Independent Persons

As for protection for an independent person holding legal or equitable interest in frozen funds or economic resources, the legislation creates an exception to allow independent persons to transfer their legal or equitable interests in frozen funds or economic resources to another person, where immediately before the transfer all the provisions in 1–4 below are present: 10.16

1. That independent person is not a designated person;
2. That independent person holds the interest in the funds or economic resources;
3. That independent person does not hold the interest jointly with a designated person; and

4. That independent person is not owned or controlled, directly or indirectly by a designated person (see Chapter 3 of this Guide for the meaning of 'owned or controlled').

3. Ring-fencing

10.17 By way of context, under 'Ring-fencing', in the wake of the financial crisis, as from 1 January 2019, each large UK bank must separate core retail banking from the rest of its business, to comply with the Financial Services (Banking Reform) Act 2013. UK targeted financial sanctions regimes contain an exception permitting banks subject to the ring-fencing legislation to transfer funds from account A in a non-ring-fenced body, to account B in a ring-fenced body (as defined in the legislation) where accounts A and B are held or controlled (directly or indirectly) by a designated person. The 2018 Act does nothing to undermine the ring-fencing provisions.

4. OFSI Licensing Review and Non-retrospectivity

10.18 By way of licensing overview, it is important to note that OFSI can only issue licences where there are specific and relevant licensing grounds enabling them to do so, and where the conditions in those grounds have been met. The available grounds can be found in the legislation underpinning each particular financial sanctions regime.[7]

10.19 Notably, licences cannot be issued retrospectively by OFSI. A licence is a written permission from OFSI allowing a future act that would otherwise breach prohibitions imposed by UK targeted financial sanctions. A licence does not compel any party, including the financial institutions involved in the payment route, to take any action. Rather, its purpose is to confirm that the proposed transaction or activity is lawful under financial sanctions regulations.

5. Licensing Grounds: UK Regimes

10.20 The following extract (Table 6.A) is reproduced verbatim from 'Post EU Exit Guide to Financial Sanctions (Jan 2019)' issued by HM Treasury.

6. Licensing Grounds: Other Domestic Regimes

10.21 In order to understand the context of the 2018 Act, it is important to note that the UK's other domestic targeted financial sanctions regimes do not have specific

[7] https://www.gov.uk/government/collections/financial-sanctions-regime-specific-consolidated-lists-and-releases.

Table 6.A OFSI's approach to licensing grounds

Basic needs	• The legislation confirms that the ground is present to enable the basic needs of a designated person, or (in the case of an individual) any financially dependent family of such a person to be met.
	• Expenditure to meet basic needs of an individual should be considered to be expenses which are necessary to ensure that designated persons or financially dependent family members are not imperilled.
	• In respect of a person other than an individual e.g. an entity, the legislation confirms that basic needs *includes*:
	  • payment of insurance premiums
	  • payment of reasonable fees for the provision of property management services
	  • payment of remuneration, allowances or pensions of employees
	  • payment of tax
	  • rent or mortgage payments
	  • utility charges
	• The list of basic needs detailed above is not exhaustive but is indicative of the type of basic needs intended to be caught. Therefore, expenditure to meet the basic needs of an entity should be expenses strictly necessary to ensure the continued existence of the designated entity.
	• Basic needs licences do not necessarily enable a designated person to continue the lifestyle or business activities they had before they were designated.

Fees for the provision of legal services	• Both legal fees and disbursements must be reasonable. It is for the applicant to demonstrate to OFSI that the legal fees and disbursements are reasonable. In support of the applicant application, the applicant should:
	  • provide an estimate of the likely fees;
	  • provide a breakdown of how the fees will be charged; and
	  • identify any disbursements, such as payments for counsel and expert witnesses.
	• OFSI considers that the Supreme Court Cost Guides or the sums that could be expected to be recouped if costs were awarded, provide a useful starting point for assessing the reasonableness of legal fees and disbursements.
	• If the applicant are seeking fees of a level in excess of those, the applicant need to demonstrate why those increased fees are reasonable in the given case.
	• Fees and disbursements must relate specifically to the provision of legal advice, involvement in litigation or in dispute resolution.

Routine maintenance of frozen funds and economic resources	• The fees or service charges must be reasonable and result in the routine holding or maintenance of funds or economic resources frozen. • The re-design, refurbishment or redevelopment in order to improve the value of a frozen economic resource is generally not covered, although each application will be considered on a case by case basis.
Extraordinary expenses	• This involves an expense which will be extraordinary in nature, and therefore not recurring or easily anticipated. • It cannot be used where other licensing grounds are more suitable or as a way or avoiding the clear limitations of those other grounds.
Pre-existing judicial decisions etc.	• This enables the use of frozen funds or economic resources that are the subject of a judicial decision or lien which was established before the date of designation and enforceable in the UK. The use of the funds or economic resources must be to implement or satisfy in whole or in part the pre-existing judicial decision or lien and cannot be for the direct or indirect benefit of a designated person.

(*Continued*)

Table 6.A Continued

Humanitarian assistance activity etc.	• This enables payments to facilitate: • any humanitarian activity; or • where applicable, any activity whose purposes are consistent with the objectives of UN Security Council Resolutions (which will be set out in the applicable SAMLA regulations). • Humanitarian assistance includes the work of international and non-governmental organisations carrying out relief activities for the benefit of the applicable civilian population, which may include the delivery of humanitarian aid or peace-building programmes. • A licence may still be required even if this activity is using government funds.
Diplomatic missions	• This enables anything to be done in order that the proper functions of a diplomatic mission or consular post or an international organisation enjoying immunities in accordance with international law, may be carried out.
Extraordinary situations	• This applies to non-UN designated persons and enables anything to be done to deal with an extraordinary situation. This will enable a situation which is extraordinary in nature but does not necessarily involve an expense. • This may, for example, allow for funds to be released to support disaster relief or provide aid in extraordinary situations. It cannot be used where other grounds are more suitable or as a way of avoiding the clear limitations of other grounds.
Prior obligations	• The obligation must have arisen prior to the date of designation and cannot relate to trade provisions (specified in the regulations). In addition, it cannot result in funds or economic resources being made available (directly or indirectly) to the designated person.

licensing grounds. By contrast, they contain a general power to issue licences. OFSI will exercise these powers according to the provisions of the particular domestic regime in question, with an eye to the stated policy objectives of each regime.

10.22 The other domestic regimes are found in the following legislation:

- Terrorist Asset-Freezing etc. Act 2010 (TAFA 2010)
- Anti-Terrorism Crime and Security Act 2001 (ATCSA 2001)
- Counter-Terrorism Act 2008 (CTA 2008)

7. General Licences

10.23 A General Licence, created by OFSI, as the name suggests, permits multiple legal or natural persons to undertake certain financial activity which would otherwise be prohibited by sanctions legislation.

10.24 OFSI publishes active General Licences and maintains accompanying guidance on its website. OFSI does not accept applications for General Licences. Rather, they are drafted and issued by OFSI under such conditions as HM Treasury deems appropriate from time to time. Guidance states that they 'will usually be considered in relation to unforeseeable circumstances where HM Treasury has decided that issuing a general licence will best support the Government's policy priorities'.

By way of example, a General Licence could be used to respond to a humanitarian crisis in a conflict zone, where it may be necessary to undertake otherwise prohibited financial activity to facilitate the provision of providing food and medical aid via local entities. 10.25

HM Treasury can vary, suspend, or revoke General Licences at any time. OFSI aims to discuss proposed changes to General Licences with relevant stakeholders before considering such action. In the example of a humanitarian crisis the consultation aim may be of secondary importance and fall away. 10.26

Once a General Licence has been created, a condition of the licence may be that to rely on it the applicant will need to register with OFSI and receive confirmation that the applicant registration has been received before proceeding with transactions or activity in line with the terms of the licence. It is important to note that it remains the responsibility of anyone relying on a general licence to ensure the activities they undertake fall within the conditions detailed within it. 10.27

If such a condition is present, to register, an applicant must provide OFSI with the following information: 10.28

- The name of the applicant company or individual, including contact details;
- The General Licence the applicant intends to use;
- The specific transactions the applicant intends to conduct, in line with permissions of the relevant General Licence;
- The proposed payment route(s), in full including account numbers and sort codes;
- Which designated persons are expected to be engaged; and
- Estimate of the value (in GBP) of the proposed transaction.

If any of these details change, an applicant must update the applicant registration details with OFSI before continuing to use a General Licence. This duty to update allows OFSI to monitor the perimeter of targeted financial sanctions. 10.29

Breaching a General Licence is also a serious criminal offence. Pre-Brexit, offences relating to UK financial sanctions carry a maximum of seven years' imprisonment on indictment (applying to all of the UK) and, on summary conviction, to a maximum of six months' imprisonment in England, Wales, and Northern Ireland, and twelve months in Scotland. 10.30

Each General Licence may include reporting requirements and or requirements to keep records of transactions undertaken by registered users. 10.31

Requirements will be stated in each General Licence and may vary between licences. 10.32

- Reporting conditions are where those making use of the General Licence must report all activity under the licence to OFSI within a set number of days, as directed by the licence;
- Record Keeping requirements are where those making use of the licence must maintain records of the activity under the General Licence for a set period of time, as directed by the Licence. OFSI may request to review records.

10.33 Finally, General Licences can be found on the website GOV.UK: https://www.gov.uk/government/publications/counter-financing-of-terrorism-general-licenses.

8. Applying for a Licence

10.34 The applicant must provide evidence to support an application and demonstrate that all criteria of the relevant licensing ground (where applicable) have been met. Incomplete applications will not be considered and will be returned to the applicant for re-submission.

10.35 OFSI will endeavour to assist applicants who contact them to understand the licensing process as well as our evidentiary requirements. However, they cannot provide legal advice and applicants should consider taking independent legal advice before applying, especially for complicated matters.

10.36 OFSI expects that legal and professional advisers will have fully considered the relevant law and formed a view about an application before approaching OFSI for guidance or submitting an application.

10.37 OFSI does not charge for licences.

9. Submitting an Application

10.38 Applicants should use the form available on GOV.UK to apply for a licence from OFSI.[8]

10.39 Applicants will generally be required to provide:

- the licensing ground(s) being relied upon in the application including supporting arguments;
- full information on the parties involved in the proposed transaction, e.g. the
- designated person(s);
- any financial institution(s) involved (e.g. remitter, correspondent, beneficiary);
- ultimate beneficiary of the transaction;
- the complete payment route including account details;
- the amount (or estimated amount) of the proposed transaction.

10.40 The applicant should always refer to the up-to-date version of the legislation for the relevant sanction regime. Links to these can be found on the relevant financial sanctions regime pages.[9]

[8] https://www.gov.uk/guidance/licences-that-allow-activity-prohibited-by-financial-sanctions.

[9] https://www.gov.uk/government/collections/financial-sanctions-regime-specific-consolidated-lists-and-releases.

10. Counter-terrorism Regimes

If the applicant is seeking a licence under either the Terrorism and Terrorist Financing or the ISIL (Da'esh) and Al-Qaida organizations regime, the applicant should email OFSI (ofsi@hmtreasury.gov.uk) setting out the full details of the proposed transaction. 10.41

OFSI's licensing policy for the counter-terrorism regime can be found on GOV.UK. 10.42

11

ENFORCEMENT

A. Enforcement under the 2018 Act 11.01
1. The Mechanism for Imposing Fines 11.01
2. Overview of 2018 Amendments 11.03
3. Detailed Guidance from OFSI 11.08
B. International Assessment 11.14

A. ENFORCEMENT UNDER THE 2018 ACT

1. The Mechanism for Imposing Fines

11.01 By way of context, OFSI issues monetary penalties for sanctions breaches, under section 146 of the Policing and Crime Act 2017. This basic mechanism is preserved by the 2018 Act.

11.02 One recent example[1] saw OFSI issue a GBP 10,000 penalty against a UK company who had engaged in a relatively low-level transaction of just GBP 204 with a designated person. OFSI stated its reasoning thus:

> Travelex had direct, in-person, contact with a designated person (DP) in the UK... despite having access to their passport , , , [they] allowed the individual to utilise funds that should have been frozen. No matter the value of the transaction, the breach directly contravened the policy intention of the asset freeze.

2. Overview of 2018 Amendments

11.03 Turning to the 2018 Act, section 17 provides for the enforcement of sanctions. Subsection (3) allows sanctions regimes to set out the powers and duties of any person who is to enforce the regulations.

11.04 By subsections (4) and (5), sanctions regulations produced under the powers in the 2018 Act can create new criminal offences and set sentences of up to ten years imprisonment following conviction on indictment. Subsection (6) enables

[1] https://assets.publishing.service.gov.uk/government/uploads/system/uploads/attachment_data/file/804021/Travelex_monetary_penalty.pdf.

regulations to apply, with or without modification, provisions of the Customs and Excise Management Act 1979 for the purposes of enforcement. Subsection (8) enables the regulations to specify that investigatory powers in Chapter 1 of Part 2 of the Serious Organised Crime and Police Act 2005 can be used to investigate breaches of sanctions.

As for enforcement outside the context of criminal courts, subsection (9) enables 11.05
regulations to specify whether the civil monetary penalty regime in Part 8 of Policing and Crime Act 2017[2] applies where prohibitions are breached. That Act created powers to impose monetary penalties for financial sanctions offences and brings financial sanctions offences into the scope of Deferred Prosecution Agreements (DPAs under the Crime and Courts Act 2013) and Serious Crime Prevention Orders (SCPOs under the Serious Crime Act 2007).

DPAs are court-approved agreements between an organization (a legal person 11.06
such as a corporate body or unincorporated association, but not a natural person) and a prosecutor who is considering prosecuting the organization for an offence. They only apply to persons in England and Wales.

Finally, consequential amendments made in Schedule 3 of the 2018 Act preserve 11.07
these powers for breaches of financial sanctions and bring other breaches of sanctions offences within the scope of DPAs, discussed above, and the Serious Crime Prevention Orders Provision under this subsection will clearly identify which sanctions are financial sanctions that, when breached, may attract a civil monetary penalty. HM Government has indicated that it does not intend to impose civil monetary penalties in respect of breaches of trade sanctions.

3. Detailed Guidance from OFSI

Post-Brexit, OFSI retains responsibility for monitoring compliance with financial 11.08
sanctions and for assessing suspected breaches. It also has the power to impose monetary penalties for breaches of financial sanctions and has issued statutory guidance[3] on the exercise of these powers. OFSI guidance helpfully sets out, in its own words:

- an explanation of the powers given to the Treasury in the 2017 Act
- a summary of our compliance and enforcement approach
- an overview of how we will assess whether to apply a monetary penalty, and what we will take into account
- an overview of the process that will decide the level of penalty
- an explanation of how we will impose a penalty, including timescales at each stage and your rights of review and appeal

---

[2] By way of recent example, see again ibid.

[3] https://assets.publishing.service.gov.uk/government/uploads/system/uploads/attachment_data/file/708990/Monetary_Penalties_Guidance_web.pdf.

11.09 As for context for broader enforcement of these fines, OFSI has the power to impose monetary penalties[4] for breaches of financial sanctions under powers in the Policing and Crime Act 2017. The value of a monetary penalty may range from 50 per cent of the total breach up to £1m—whichever is the greater value.

11.10 Further, OFSI may refer cases to law enforcement agencies for investigation and potential criminal prosecution.

11.11 To mark the seriousness with which HM Government approaches breach of sanctions, the level of penalties for breaches have already been expanded and, for custodial sentences, increased by the Policing and Crime Act 2017. The pre-Brexit context is that offences relating to UK financial sanctions carried a maximum of seven years' imprisonment on indictment (applying to all of the UK) and, on summary conviction, a maximum of six months' imprisonment in England, Wales, and Northern Ireland, and twelve months in Scotland. Custodial sentences for ATCSA 2001 and CTA 2008 have been similarly increased.

11.12 As mentioned in section A.2 of this Chapter, breaches of financial sanctions legislation are included on the list of offences for which a DPA can be made.

11.13 Breaches of financial sanctions are included on the list of offences for which a SCPO may be imposed.

B. INTERNATIONAL ASSESSMENT

11.14 The UK underwent a fourth round Mutual Evaluation Report (MER) by the Financial Action Task Force (FATF)[5] in 2018. The assessment was that[6] 'Overall, the UK has a strong system to implement targeted financial sanctions (TFS) without delay under the relevant UNSCRs.'

11.15 The MER found that 'The creation of OFSI in March 2016 reflects the importance that the UK attaches to financial sanctions.' On the more critical side, the report found minor shortcomings in relation to enforcement actions taken with respect to sanctions breaches, delays in communicating designations, and inconsistent appreciation and application sanctions compliance across financial institutions.

11.16 As for Designation, the MER found that:[7]

> The UK has a leading role in international sanctions policy and generating listings at the UN. The UK is on the UN Security Council and CFT is one of its priorities for the UNSCR 1267 Sanctions Committee. Between 2010 and the on-site visit, the UK has co-sponsored more than 41 designation proposals to the 1267 Committee and has made 8 designation proposals concerning UK nationals.

---

[4] See further guidance on the broader context at these helpful FAQs https://www.gov.uk/government/publications/financial-sanctions-faqs.

[5] Financial Action Task Force, Mutual Evaluation Report, United Kingdom (2018) http://www.fatf-gafi.org/media/fatf/documents/reports/mer4/MER-United-Kingdom-2018.pdf.

[6] Ibid para. 96.

[7] Ibid para. 243.

12

INFORMATION AND REPORTING OBLIGATIONS

A.	Overview of Existing Obligations	12.01
B.	Section 16: Information	12.04
C.	Guidance on Reporting Obligations	12.09

A. OVERVIEW OF EXISTING OBLIGATIONS

The 2018 Act broadens the scope of reporting obligations. Since 2017, the combined effect of statute[1] and regulations[2] require relevant businesses and professionals (e.g. financial institutions, lawyers, and accountants) to report to the Office of Financial Sanctions Implementation (OFSI) whenever they know or suspect that a customer or counter-party is an asset-freeze target or has breached a financial sanction. Failure to do so is a criminal offence.[3] 12.01

There is a distinction to be drawn here between the duties imposed by the criminal law[4] on every natural and legal person (not to breach sanctions), and the enhanced duties to report suspected breaches. Since 2017 these obligations were imposed on prescribed institutions and business entities, within scope of the AML regime.[5] 12.02

The 2018 Act allows for the latter, i.e. sanctions reporting obligations, to be imposed on any individual or firm, not merely those within scope of the MLRs.[6] 12.03

---

[1] Proceeds of Crime Act 2002 (POCA 2002).

[2] The Money Laundering, Terrorist Financing and Transfer of Funds (Information on the Payer) Regulations 2017.

[3] See the offences under Part 7 POCA 2002.

[4] In each sanction regime, see Part 9 of the Russia (Sanctions) (EU Exit) Regulations 2019, UK Statutory Instruments 2019 No. 855 (the 'Russia sanctions').

[5] See Chapter 5 of OFSI Guidance, at Appendix 8 to this Guide.

[6] Ibid.

B. SECTION 16: INFORMATION

12.04 New powers under section 16 of the 2018 Act enable HM Government to monitor compliance with the regulations[7] and obtain evidence if it believes that the regulations have been contravened or circumvented. In relation to targeted financial sanctions, the powers may be used to require people to report cases where they become aware or have reasonable grounds to suspect they are dealing with a designated person or a designated person has committed an offence. HM Government's stated intention is that the regulations under section 1 will set out what information these persons must report. Part 8 of the Russia sanctions provides a detailed example.

12.05 This provision therefore enables the UK to replicate the wide scope of the existing reporting requirement under directly applicable EU law,[8] which falls away post-Brexit. Regulation 70 of the Russia sanctions places reporting obligations on 'relevant firms',[9] so continuing a narrower focus than all natural and legal persons.

12.06 In relation to targeted financial sanctions, for example, new regimes under the 2018 Act give the government powers to request information from a designated person on the funds or economic resources they hold, own, or control or that someone else does on their behalf, and how those funds are disposed of; an example is seen at Russia sanctions regulation 72. HM Government may request information on expenditure by or on behalf of the designated person.

12.07 New regimes created under section 1 of the 2018 Act can also require registers or records to be maintained,[10] and allow the government to request from any person in or resident in the UK any information that the government may reasonably require to assess compliance with licences. Russia sanctions regulation 77 provides for officials to be allowed to enter the premises of a licensed person in order to make such an assessment.

12.08 The regulations under section 16 also allow HM Government to disclose information received on the basis of these provisions. This includes disclosure to police officers, office holders of the Crown in the UK Government or devolved administrations, regulatory bodies in the UK, and international partners. For example, the Russia sanctions regulation 78 extends the list to include British Overseas Territories, British Dependent Territories, and domestic Legal Aid authorities.

C. GUIDANCE ON REPORTING OBLIGATIONS

12.09 OFSI issued guidance in January 2020, which is reproduced at Appendix 8 to this Guide. The key distinction in the official guidance is between the obligations under

[7] i.e. new regimes promulgated under section 1 of the 2018 Act.
[8] See Chapter 5 of OFSI Guidance, at Appendix 8 to this Guide.
[9] Defined at Russia sanctions, regulation 71.
[10] See section 16(1)(a)(ii) of the 2018 Act.

EU regimes (see paragraphs 5.1 through to 5.1.3) and domestic regimes (see paragraph 5.2) EU obligations persist throughout the transition period.[11] Most sanctions regimes laid under the 2018 Act will not fully come into force until 1 January 2021, as per the terms of each regime. The Guidance from OFSI helpfully sets out domestic reporting obligations arising from anti-terrorism legislation. The orders themselves are available online.[12]

Further Guidance is available as to the precise steps to take in reporting a breach to OFSI (see paragraph 5.3). A fundamental distinction is maintained between the duties to file Suspicious Activity Reports (SARs) under POCA 2002 to the National Crime Agency, and the obligations to report suspected sanctions breaches to OFSI (see paragraph 5.7) . Filing the former does not remove the need for the latter. 12.10

[11] The Withdrawal Agreement states that the transition period ends on 31 December 2020. EU law will continue to be the mechanism for the UK to implement UN and EU sanctions during this period.

[12] https://www.gov.uk/government/publications/financial-sanctions-uk-freezing-orders.

13

ANTI-MONEY LAUNDERING

A. Anti-money Laundering Powers in the UK Post-Brexit 13.01
1. Overview of the Amendments Made by the 2018 Act 13.01
2. Pre-Brexit AML Regime under EU Law 13.05
3. The Impact of the 2018 Act on AML in the UK 13.12
4. The Core AML Power: Section 49 13.15
5. AML Topics on Which Further Regulations May Issue 13.18

B. Anti-money Laundering in British Overseas Territories 13.40
1. The Statutory Scheme 13.40
2. Commentary 13.44

C. AML Update 2020: The Implementation of '5MLD' 13.48
1. Extension of Scope of Regulations: Tax Advisers, Letting Agents, and Art Dealers 13.51
2. Further Requirements for Policies, Controls, and Procedures (Regulation 19) 13.55
3. Extended Training Requirements (Regulation 24) 13.58
4. Supervisors Approving Individuals (Regulation 26) 13.59
5. Customer Due Diligence (Regulation 27 and Regulation 28) 13.62
6. Change to Dealing with Discrepancies on Registers (Under Regulation 30A) 13.66
7. Changes to Enhanced Due Diligence (Chapter 2, 2017 MLRs) 13.73
8. Trust Registration 13.81
9. E-money Thresholds for CDD 13.82
10. Duty to Respond to Information Requests: Accounts and Safe-deposit Boxes 13.83
11. Crypto Registration with FCA 13.84

A. ANTI-MONEY LAUNDERING POWERS IN THE UK POST-BREXIT

1. Overview of the Amendments Made by the 2018 Act

13.01 Just as the UK had grown to depend on the EU in the field of sanctions, so in Anti-Money Laundering ('AML', which will be taken to include countering the finance of terrorism for the purposes of this Chapter of the Guide) the UK became reliant on the direct effect of EU Directives.[1]

The 2018 Act, Part 2 Schedule 2, provides the powers for the HM Government to continue to make provision in relation to AML post-Brexit, specifically to introduce further secondary legislation from time to time in the following wide ranging topics: the detection, investigation, and prevention of money laundering or terrorist financing, and the implementation of Financial Action Taskforce (FATF) standards.[2] 13.02

For the avoidance of doubt, practitioners will note that the 4th and 5th Money Laundering Directives continue to have effect in UK law post-Brexit (through the MLRs which transpose them) by virtue of sections 2(1) and 7(1) of the EU (Withdrawal) Act 2018.[3] The mechanism within the 2018 Act is that any future amendments to the AML regime will need to be made by HM Government via domestic secondary legislation (under the 2018 Act, as the EU route is no longer available). 13.03

A further AML focus of the 2018 Act is on registers of beneficial ownership in British Overseas Territories (BOTs). This high-profile amendment to the Act, section 51, required HM Government to make provision for public registers of beneficial ownership of companies in all BOTs by the end of 2020. The deadline has moved, see section B. of this Chapter below. The list of BOTs excludes the Isle of Man, Jersey, and Guernsey but includes significant offshore jurisdictions such as the British Virgin Islands and Cayman Islands. Section 51 is dealt with at the end of this Chapter. 13.04

2. Pre-Brexit AML Regime under EU Law

Pre-Brexit, the core of the UK AML regime derived from the EU's Fourth Money Laundering Directive (4MLD) which encompassed recommendations made by the global AML body, the Financial Action Task Force (FATF), physically based at the OECD in Paris. FATF is an inter-governmental global standard-setting body for AML policy that promotes the implementation of legal, regulatory, and operational measures for combating money laundering[4] and terrorist financing. 13.05

FATF produces Recommendations aiming to set out a comprehensive and consistent framework[5] adopted by its members in order to combat money laundering 13.06

[1] The basis of which was the seminal section 2(1) European Communities Act 1972, 'All such rights, powers, liabilities, obligations and restrictions from time to time created or arising by or under the Treaties, and all such remedies and procedures from time to time provided for by or under the Treaties, as in accordance with the Treaties are without further enactment to be given legal effect or used in the United Kingdom shall be recognised and available in law, and be enforced ... etc.'

[2] The FATF Recommendations are the global standard, see http://www.fatf-gafi.org/publications/fatfrecommendations/documents/fatf-recommendations.html.

[3] Section 2(1) EU(W)A 2018: 'EU-derived domestic legislation, as it has effect in domestic law immediately before exit day, continues to have effect in domestic law on and after exit day.'

[4] http://www.fatf-gafi.org/about/.

[5] http://www.fatf-gafi.org/media/fatf/documents/recommendations/pdfs/FATF%20Recommendations%202012.pdf.

and terrorist financing. FATF's thirty-seven full members are periodically subjected to a Mutual Evaluation that comprises a peer to peer review. The Mutual Evaluation is undertaken by representatives from fellow member states who assess the extent to which the member has implemented the FATF Recommendations. The Mutual Evaluations give FATF insight into emerging risks on an international scale and highlight areas of weakness enabling the Recommendations to frequently be updated and remain a credible deterrent. The recent FATF evaluation of the UK is discussed in Chapter 1 of this Guide.

13.07 By way of brief historical context, AML legislation in the UK has been largely reactive to the evolution in the interpretation of international standards and is subject to frequent change. Looking at the recent past, the EU's Third Money Laundering Directive (3MLD) came into force December 2005 and was transposed into UK law in the Money Laundering Regulations 2007.[6] The EU implemented 4MLD in June 2017 having given Member States two years to adopt the requirements at a national level and reflect the changes made to the 3MLD regime; this included a greater emphasis on undertaking a risk-based approach to fulfilling AML requirements (targeting resources where the perceived risk is highest) which is classically underpinned by a written risk assessment, periodically updated as part of an on-going monitoring regime. Further changes include a stricter approach to the application of customer due diligence in relation to domestic Politically Exposed Persons (PEPs) and a refined concept of simplified due diligence. The changes made in 4MLD reflected the updated FATF recommendations of 2012.

13.08 In June 2017, the UK transposed 4MLD into national law under powers conferred by section 2(2) of the European Communities Act 1972, by enacting the Money Laundering, Terrorist financing and Transfer of Funds (Information on the Payer) Regulations Act 2017 (Money Laundering Regulations 2017) which replaced the Money Laundering Regulations 2007.

13.09 The Fifth Money Laundering Directive (5MLD) came into force in July 2018 and Member States have until January 2020 to implement the revised measures. 5MLD has a greater focus on the prevention of terrorist financing. This was due to political pressure, the recent context being increased terrorist activity in Europe. Its effects on UK legislation are considered in detail at the end of this Chapter.

13.10 Commentators have noted that 5MLD has a focus on virtual currencies in the financial markets[7] and FATF is moving to give detailed guidance on the supervision of virtual assets.[8] Further context is the *Mossack Fonseca* disclosures, the so-called 'Panama Papers',[9] and also the so-called 'Paradise Papers' leaks.[10]

---

[6] http://www.legislation.gov.uk/uksi/2007/2157/contents/made.

[7] http://blog.macfarlanes.com/post/102expn/fifth-money-laundering-directive.

[8] http://www.fatf-gafi.org/publications/fatfgeneral/documents/supervisor-forum-2020.html.

[9] https://www.theguardian.com/world/2017/feb/10/panama-papers-mossack-fonseca-offices-raided-over-odebrecht-bribery-scandal.

[10] https://www.theguardian.com/news/2017/nov/05/what-are-the-paradise-papers-and-what-do-they-tell-us.

Key amendments in 5MLD include a requirement for greater transparency of beneficial ownership of corporate entities and trusts, expansion of scope of the MLRs to include virtual currency exchanges and virtual currency wallet providers, as well as prescribed Enhanced Due Diligence for business transactions involving pre-defined high-risk countries,[11] as set out by the European Commission. All of these aspects are considered at the end of this Chapter. 13.11

3. The Impact of the 2018 Act on AML in the UK

For the avoidance of doubt, MLRs in place on 31 January 2020 remain in force post-Brexit. This is because they are EU derived legislation which is retained by section 2(1) of the EU (Withdrawal) Act 2018. They remain as domestic 'regulations', i.e. with the status of binding secondary legislation, due to the effect of section 7 of the EU(W)A 2018.[12] 13.12

However, the 2018 Act is a key piece of Brexit legislation as it enables the UK to overhaul its domestic AML and sanctions regime—the power to impose its own AML and sanctions regulations independently of the EU law. 13.13

HM Government has stated '[t]he desire to implement 5MLD standards compliments the UK's approach to continue to be agile in legislating against emerging AML risk', per the Government White Paper[13] on the then Bill, which outlined the intention to create new legislation post-Brexit, to enable amendments to be made to the Money Laundering Regulations 2017. Without this, the UK would simply not be able to address emerging risk, or implement updated FATF recommendations as they are issued, e.g. recent guidance on the risk-based approach to be taken in respect of Virtual Assets.[14] The UK pre-Brexit utilized provisions within the European Communities Act 1972 to transpose EU Directives relating to AML into UK law. The European Union (Withdrawal) Act 2018 repealed the European Communities Act 1972 and froze the AML and terrorist financing regulatory regime as at 31 January 2020. 13.14

4. The Core AML Power: Section 49

The core power is in section 49[15] of the 2018 Act, which enables an appropriate Minister (Secretary of State or HM Treasury) to make regulations in respect 13.15

[11] http://www.allenovery.com/news/en-gb/articles/Pages/Tighter-AML-controls-imposed-by-Europe%E2%80%99s-Fifth-Anti-money-Laundering-Directive.aspx.

[12] Section 7 EU(W)A 2018: ' (1) Anything which— (a) was, immediately before exit day, primary legislation of a particular kind, subordinate legislation of a particular kind or another enactment of a particular kind, and (b) continues to be domestic law on and after exit day by virtue of section 2, continues to be domestic law as an enactment of the same kind.'

[13] https://assets.publishing.service.gov.uk/government/uploads/system/uploads/attachment_data/file/609986/Public_consultation_on_the_UK_s_future_legal_framework_for_imposing_and_implementing_sanctions__Print_pdf_version_.pdf.

[14] http://www.fatf-gafi.org/publications/fatfrecommendations/documents/guidance-rba-virtual-assets.html.

[15] And Schedule 2 to the 2018 Act, given force by section 49(2).

of money laundering, terrorist financing, and to implement relevant measures as required by FATF. This empowers an appropriate Minister to make, amend, and repeal secondary legislation relating to AML and terrorist financing once the UK leaves the EU. This power further ensures that the UK can continue to comply with the international standards set by FATF, and address emerging risks relating to money laundering and terrorist financing. In the absence of the 2018 Act the UK would soon have fallen behind, proliferation finance[16] and virtual assets being areas of recent development.

13.16 Recent FATF meetings have focused on further guidance for the Risk Based Approach (RBA) to be applied in the Securities Sector, as well as further work on the RBA to be adopted by lawyers, accountants, and TCSP providers. Other trends are the regulation of virtual assets/crypto currencies.

13.17 As per section 49(3) of the Act, for these purposes money laundering and terrorist financing are defined by reference to existing UK statutory definitions set out respectively in the Proceeds of Crime Act 2002; the Terrorism Act 2000; the Anti-terrorism, Crime and Security Act 2001; the Terrorist Asset-Freezing etc. Act 2010; and the ISIL (Da'esh) and Al-Qaida (Asset-Freezing) Regulations 2011.

5. AML Topics on Which Further Regulations May Issue

13.18 As noted, there was no immediate substantive change to the detail of existing MLRs as a result of Brexit. The fundamental difference is that the UK has reassumed control of its AML regime. The UK's approach to implementing targeted financial sanctions against Russia has already diverged, in subtle ways,[17] from the EU regime. Practitioners will be keen to analyse any nod in the Schedule to future priorities for change in AML regulation.

13.19 As discussed above, section 49 of the 2018 Act is couched in general terms as to allowing HM Government to amend rules enabling or facilitating the detection of, or facilitating the prevention of, money laundering (ML) and terrorist financing (TF), or implementing international standards, such as FATF. The voluminous Money Laundering Regulations (MLRs) 2017[18] are very much more detailed and nuanced, as is the FATF guidance and recommendations.[19]

13.20 To this end, Schedule 2 of the 2018 Act specifies topics which are intended by Parliament to be within the scope of section 49, for the avoidance of doubt and potential litigation. There is a caveat[20] that the schedule is 'Without prejudice to the generality of section 49' so that any omission from the list in it would not be an automatic bar to HM Government legislating.

---

[16] https://www.aima.org/article/countering-the-financing-of-terrorism-and-sanctions-post-brexit.html.

[17] See Appendix 5, p. 247 of this Guide.

[18] The Money Laundering, Terrorist Financing and Transfer of Funds (Information on the Payer) Regulations 2017 found at http://www.legislation.gov.uk/uksi/2017/692/pdfs/uksi_20170692_en.pdf

[19] http://www.fatf-gafi.org/publications/?hf=10&b=0&s=desc(fatf_releasedate).

[20] Paragraph 1, Schedule 2 of the 2018 Act.

Practitioners will note that the remaining Schedule 2 paragraphs (i.e. paras 2–17 set out at Appendix 1 to this Guide) cover the broad topics addressed in the Money Laundering Regulations 2017, which transposed 4MLD (and the enforcement provisions of the associated FTR) into UK law.[21] 13.21

i) Potential Expansion of the Population Subject to AML Regulation

There is a very wide discretion for the UK to expand its supervised population for AML purposes to include, by paragraph 24, any 'relevant business' which means business of a kind which entails risks relating to money laundering, terrorist financing or other threats to the integrity of the financial system. 13.22

This new definition is much broader than the existing scope of UK MLRs.[22] At present its Regulation 8 lists categories of persons to whom AML regulations apply. The 2018 Act introduces the prospect of defining the scope of AML supervision by type of work done, rather than by profession/service offered. This latter approach is closer to that adopted elsewhere, e.g. the Cayman Islands. In Cayman, a person is within scope of AML supervision not because (s)he or it falls within a category of persons (per se) but whether or not (s)he or it is conducting 'relevant financial business'.[23] 13.23

The final limb for potential inclusion in future AML supervision, for businesses which entail 'other threats to the integrity of the financial system' seems to be overreach on its face. If the risk is 'other than' those relating to money laundering or terrorist financing (e.g. it is a prudential, or a risk of fraud or corruption) then it calls for 'other' regulation, not AML supervision. The 2018 Act is, in this respect, couched in the widest terms to allow the UK government to introduce AML regulations in respect of a very broad range of its domestic population. 13.24

ii) Risk Assessments

Schedule 2 to the 2018 Act at paragraph 2(1)[24] allows future section 49 regulations to require the relevant Departments of HM Government, persons carrying on relevant business and supervisory authorities to undertake a risk assessment in these familiar terms: 'to identify and assess risks relating to money laundering, terrorist financing or other threats to the integrity of the international financial system'. There is an element of 'belt and braces' here, as the MLRs 2017 subsist,[25] in so far as the existing supervised population is concerned, but see the 13.25

[21] MLRs in place on 29 March 2019 remain in force because they are EU-derived legislation which is retained by section 2(1) of the EU (Withdrawal) Act 2018. They remain as domestic 'regulations', i.e. with the status of binding secondary legislation, because of section 7 of the EU(W)Act 2018.

[22] http://www.legislation.gov.uk/uksi/2017/692/pdfs/uksi_20170692_en.pdf.

[23] Section 2, Cayman Islands Proceeds of Crime Law, see original scheme at https://www.cima.ky/upimages/commonfiles/1499349646ProceedsofCrimeLaw2017Revision.PDF.

[24] All paragraph numbers in the remainder of this section of the Guide refer to Schedule 2 of the 2018 Act.

[25] Regs 16,17, and 18 of the 2017 MLRs deal with the point at present.

above passage for potential broadening of scope to all those undertaking relevant business.

13.26 Moreover, the government will be able to, paragraph 2(2), 'make provision about factors to be taken into account in the assessment of such risks'. This may go far beyond the high-level approach of National Risk Assessments and reports/guidelines set out in current MLR 17(2) in respect of supervisory authorities. Granted, the current MLRs at regulation 18(2)(b) already list relatively standard and general risk factors (customers, geography, products/services/ transactions, and delivery channels). There is the potential here for a much more prescriptive approach to be imposed by government on supervisory authorities, and persons within the scope of the MLRs as to which additional factors they must take into account.

iii) Policies and Procedures and Introduction of Prescribed Measures

13.27 Paragraph 3 states that section 49 of the 2018 Act may be used by HM Government to pass regulations requiring the same population as above to have appropriate policies, procedures, and controls in place in relation to the size and nature of the business, enforcing a risk-based approach as outlined in 4MLD. Again, practitioners may see little new here; all of this is currently and will still be required as a result of the 2017 MLRs (which all survive Brexit), and the use of 'require' is not to be taken as meaning 'require for the first time', except to the extent that the scope of those being regulated for AML is broadened.

13.28 By contrast, paragraph 4 is more novel and wide-ranging, HM Government may now issue further regulations to the existing supervised population: 'Require relevant persons to take prescribed measures in relation to their customers in prescribed circumstances'.

13.29 This is not the natural corollary of Regulation 21 2017 MLRs (which is focused on internal controls). It can be assumed that the new paragraph seeks to ensure HM Government could make amendments to Part 3 of current MLRs, as to customer due diligence (including simplified and enhanced levels). There is scope in the future for the UK to take a different approach to the detail of AML regulation than the EU. Doubtless the UK will always seek to comply with FATF recommendations, guidance, and Mutual Evaluation reports. As mentioned, there have been two recent examples[26] of nuanced UK divergence from previous EU implementation of sanctions, so the prospect is more than theoretical.

iv) Information Sharing and Registers

13.30 On information sharing, paragraph 5 of Schedule 2 to the 2018 Act allows HM Government to bring in new regulations on information sharing, currently contained within Part 8 of the 2017 MLRs.

[26] See Appendix 5 to this Guide, p. 247.

5MLD can be seen underpinning paragraph 6, with a power for HM Government to require beneficial ownership registers for prescribed entities, trust, or other arrangements. No geographical restriction is imposed here. This is further explored in sections 50 and 51 of the 2018 Act in respect of British Overseas Territories, discussed in more detail at the end of this Chapter. 13.31

v) Supervisory Functions

Paragraphs 7 to 14 confirm that new regulations made under section 49 could confer supervisory functions on prescribed bodies and gives a non-exhaustive list of powers or duties that could be conferred on such supervisory authorities (at present HMRC and the FCA, which includes the Office for Professional Body AML Supervision (OPBAS). 13.32

vi) Criminal Offences and Other Penalties

By paragraph 15 there is a power for HM Government to make provisions 'creating criminal offences for the purposes of the enforcement of the requirements imposed by or under' regulations made by section 49. Although the safeguards as to Ministerial reporting in relation to criminal offences are not repeated in the Schedule, they stand. 13.33

As for mode of trial, paragraph 18 provides for any future regulations made under section 49 to contain provision for criminal offences to be punishable on both summary conviction (magistrates or equivalent) and indictment (trial by jury). The maximum sentences that can be imposed by regulations made under paragraph 15 are identical to those currently provided for in the Money Laundering Regulations 2017, which may include imprisonment for up to three months (on summary conviction before a magistrates' court or equivalent) or up to two years (on conviction on indictment at a Crown Court). 13.34

There is a separate penalty regime established under Part 7 of the Proceeds of Crime Act 2002 for criminal offences relating to money laundering. This regime provides for longer prison sentences not exceeding five or fourteen years (depending on the offence). 13.35

vii) Geographical Scope

As for extra-territoriality, paragraph 22 confirms that regulations made under section 49 may impose requirements in relation to conduct outside the UK by a UK natural or legal person. This is a continuation of the policy position under the Money Laundering Regulations 2017 and captures—for example—instances where a person in an overseas branch of a UK firm commits an offence under regulations made for the purpose of preventing money laundering. 13.36

viii) Future-proofing and Definitions

Paragraph 23(1) confirms that regulations made under section 49 may, subject to any modifications that the appropriate Minister considers appropriate, make provision corresponding or similar to the Money Laundering Regulations 2017 (as these 13.37

had effect immediately prior to the UK's withdrawal from the EU). This provides flexibility to ensure that section 49 can be used to make future regulations similar to any provisions of the Money Laundering Regulations 2017 that are amended prior to the UK's withdrawal from the EU. Paragraph 23(1)(b) confirms that regulations made by section 49 can be used to amend or revoke the Money Laundering Regulations 2017.

13.38 Finally, paragraph 24 defines certain terms used in section 49 and Schedule 2. In particular, it confirms that the definitions of 'money laundering' and 'terrorist financing' have the meaning currently used in the Money Laundering Regulations 2017.

13.39 There is consistency for now, with Schedule 2 importing the potential for divergence from the EU in the future. The 2018 Act could be used by HM Government to extend the existing suite of AML supervision to a broader population and/or to amend any of the current AML regulations, in any or all respects. This goes beyond what was necessary to deal with the compliance consequences to the UK of Brexit.

B. ANTI-MONEY LAUNDERING IN BRITISH OVERSEAS TERRITORIES

1. The Statutory Scheme

13.40 As per the Fifth Money Laundering Directive (5MLD[27]) the UK must publish a register of beneficial owners of overseas entities. Under section 51 of the 2018 Act an obligation will extend to BOTs (listed below) but not the Crown Dependencies of Jersey, Guernsey, and the Isle of Man.

13.41 Section 51 of the 2018 Act envisages that the governments of BOTs will establish a publicly available beneficial ownership register of companies that are registered in its jurisdiction.

13.42 A subsequently amended deadline of 31 December 2020[28] appeared under section 51(2): 'The Secretary of State must, no later than 31 December 2020, prepare a draft Order in Council requiring the government of any British Overseas Territory that has not introduced a publicly accessible register of the beneficial ownership of companies within its jurisdiction to do so. The 2018 Act allows the UK Government a degree of flexibility in determining whether a particular BOT has complied. This, by section 51(7):

> a 'publicly accessible register of the beneficial ownership of companies' means a register which, in the opinion of the Secretary of State, provides information broadly equivalent to that available in accordance with the provisions of Part 21A of the Companies Act 2006.

---

[27] https://eur-lex.europa.eu/legal-content/EN/TXT/PDF/?uri=CELEX:32018L0843&from=EN.

[28] 2023 is the new deadline.

The BOTs are, as defined in Schedule 6 of the British Nationality Act 1981: 13.43

Anguilla
Bermuda[29]
British Antarctic Territory
British Virgin Islands
British Indian Ocean Territory
Cayman Islands.[30]
Falkland Islands
Gibraltar
Montserrat
Pitcairn Islands
Saint Helena, Ascension and Tristan da Cunha
Saint Helena
Ascension Island
Tristan da Cunha
South Georgia and the South Sandwich Islands
Turks and Caicos Islands

2. Commentary

After the passage of the 2018 Act, HM Government indicated that it will issue an Order in Council instructing BOTs to establish fully operational public registers of beneficial ownership by 2023, if they have not done so by the end of 2020.[31] 13.44

Placing a requirement on BOTs to introduce such a register raises fundamental questions about the role of the UK Parliament in legislating for jurisdictions which are not represented at Westminster. The Cayman Islands Government has taken this point of principle in its public response. Further, the Cayman Islands Government has described the action by the UK Parliament as 'a potential constitutional overreach', the rationale being that the 2018 Act clearly touches on financial services, an area of policy that is devolved to the territory. The Cayman Islands Government announced that it would therefore mount a legal challenge to such an Order, if it were ever made. 13.45

[29] Bermuda's Fourth Round Mutual Evaluation Report (MER) was published in January 2020, https://www.cfatf-gafic.org/home/cfatf-news/616-fourth-round-mutual-evaluation-report-of-bermuda-2.

[30] Its Fourth Round MER is here: https://www.cfatf-gafic.org/documents/4th-round-meval-reports/11255-fourth-round-mutual-evaluation-report-for-cayman-islands/file.

[31] https://www.caymancompass.com/2018/12/23/fco-beneficial-ownership-register-to-be-made-public-by-2023/.

13.46 On the other hand, the Cayman Islands have indicated a high-level political commitment[32] to complying with the Caribbean Financial Action Task Force (CFATF) recommendations (as part of its response to the CFATF Mutual Evaluation).[33] The net effect may be that Cayman will want to maintain the same standards as the UK.

13.47 Debate has focused on vexed question of whether the system adopted in the British Virgin Islands[34] and elsewhere, i.e. a verified but non-public register of beneficial ownership, available to law enforcement and competent authorities at short notice, is in fact more useful in the global efforts to stem money laundering than a public register, unverified and containing errors. The cost, economic consequences, necessity or otherwise, and timescale for implementation have not been assessed. In this respect, the 2018 Act provides a stimulus for ongoing political debate, but no clear remedy.

C. AML UPDATE 2020: THE IMPLEMENTATION OF '5MLD'

13.48 This part of the Guide sets out the January 2020 changes to the UK regime implementing '5MLD', the Fifth Money Laundering Directive. This reform represents the last time the UK will be driven by an EU Directive in AML; from this point the 2018 Act will be used instead. As has been noted throughout this guide, there is the clear potential for divergence between the UK and EU.[35]

13.49 By way of background, 5MLD was adopted by the European Parliament in April 2018. Four driving factors have been identified by commentators:[36]

1. Terrorist attacks in Europe during the preceding five years;
2. The 'Panama Papers' leak was said to put the spot-light on offshore jurisdictions masking beneficial ownership;
3. Adoption of crypto-currencies;
4. EU's reiteration of desire to implement FATF standards.

13.50 The latest reforms are made via amendments[37] to the Anti-Money Laundering (AML) regulations (the Money Laundering, Terrorist Financing and Transfer of Funds (Information on the Payer) Regulations 2017 (as amended)). Each significant amendment will be considered in turn.

---

[32] http://www.mondaq.com/caymanislands/x/844486/Money+Laundering/Cayman+Readies+For+AntiMoney+Laundering+Update.

[33] Ongoing at the time of publication of this Guide, see https://www.cfatf-gafic.org/home/cfatf-news/608-outcomes-of-the-cfatf-l-november-2019-plenary-meeting?highlight=WyJjYXltYW4iLCJjYXltYW4ncyIsImlzbGFuZHMiLCJpc2xhbmQiLCJpc2xhbmQncyIsImNheW1hbiBpc2xhbmRzIl0=.

[34] http://www.bvi.gov.vg/media-centre/beneficial-secure-search-system-goes-live.

[35] See the statements of the UK Chancellor on 'divergence' in the weeks before Brexit https://www.bbc.com/news/uk-politics-51161808.

[36] https://risk.lexisnexis.co.uk/insights-resources/infographic/5th-money-laundering-directive.

[37] Made by the Money Laundering and Terrorist Financing (Amendment) Regulations 2019, found here: http://www.legislation.gov.uk/uksi/2019/1511/pdfs/uksi_20191511_en.pdf.

1. Extension of Scope of Regulations: Tax Advisers, Letting Agents, and Art Dealers

As for the scope of application of the MLRs, as to whom is included, the definition of a 'tax adviser' has been expanded[38] to include providing material aid, or assistance or advice on tax affairs of other persons including where provided through a third party. This is an expansion of the skeletal core definition: 'a firm or sole practitioner who by way of business provides advice about the tax affairs of other persons, when providing such services'. Legal practices and other mixed disciplinary entities will need to exercise caution. If they are providing services which now fall under the revised definition, they must comply with all the requirements of the regulations. 13.51

Further, the scope of AML regulation is expanded from estate agents to include high-value letting agents, as defined.[39] 13.52

Crypto-asset exchange providers are considered below at section C.11 of this Chapter. 13.53

Finally, the extension of AML regulation now includes high value 'art market participants'.[40] The fuller definition here of a 'work of art' is set in the context of the definitions provided in the 1994 VAT Act, beyond the scope of this Guide. 13.54

2. Further Requirements for Policies, Controls, and Procedures (Regulation 19)

As for those who find themselves within scope, further requirements are expressly made in respect of mandatory policies, controls, and procedures. These must now provide for identification and scrutiny of transactions that are *either* complex or unusually large. Previously, only transactions that were *both* had to be identified and scrutinized: see now regulation 19(4)(a). Further, it is now expressly required that such systems and controls must now ensure the assessment and mitigation of the risks associated with new products and new business practices (including new delivery mechanisms) is taken into account, per regulation 19(4)(c). In the case of group parent undertakings, these must include policies on the sharing of information about customers, customer accounts, and transactions between subsidiaries of a parent group: see regulation 20(b). 13.55

By way of example, the recent guidance[41] to UK lawyers is that: 13.56

> Whether a transaction is 'complex' or 'unusually large' should be judged both in relation to the normal activity of the practice and the normal activity of the client. When new technology is adopted, appropriate measures must be taken in order to assess and mitigate any money laundering or terrorist financing risks this adoption may cause. This requirement has now been extended

[38] By the amending regulation 4(2).

[39] See the amending regulation 4(3) and (4): high-value is of a monthly rent exceeding 10,000 euros.

[40] By the amending regulation 4(6), again with the threshold of 10,000 euros.

[41] Reiterated in Legal Sector Affinity Group Guidance, January 2020.

to require that this same process be followed when new products or business practices are introduced. This may be included in your Practice-Wide Risk Assessment.

13.57 Further, per the same Legal Sector Affinity Group Guidance, 'New products or business practices (for example entry into new areas of legal practice or changes to the structure or operational model of the practice) must be assessed in terms of AML risk and incorporated into your practice-wide risk assessment and PCPs [policies, controls and procedures]'.

3. Extended Training Requirements (Regulation 24)

13.58 Under the amended regulations, the existing training requirements on staff under regulation 24 are extended from 'relevant employees' to include any agents a practice uses for the purpose of its business. The test for whether an agent or employee needs training is if their work is relevant to the AML compliance of the practice, or they are involved in the identification, mitigation, prevention, or detection of money laundering or terrorist financing risk within the business. The training requirement will not include all staff in a practice, nor every agent engaged by it, e.g. window cleaners, caterers, or IT maintenance. A risk-based approach is required. There is an element of proportionality in 'appropriate' measures, see regulation 24(1)(a).

4. Supervisors Approving Individuals (Regulation 26)

13.59 Statutory and professional body supervisors[42] have a gate-keeper role to sectors such as law and accountancy.

13.60 Regulation 26 now includes a more explicit statement that supervisory authorities must be provided with sufficient information to determine whether a sole practitioner, or a Beneficial Owner, Officer, or Manager (so-called BOOMs) of a firm has been convicted of a relevant offence.

13.61 In practice, this may mean there is an obligation on supervisory bodies to obtain, and regulated firms to provide, a criminal record check (e.g. Disclosure and Barring Service[43]) of relevant BOOMs.

5. Customer Due Diligence (Regulation 27 and Regulation 28)

13.62 For those in scope, in respect of existing clients, Part 3 Customer (or Client) Due Diligence (CDD) must be renewed[44] when a regulated entity has any legal duty in the course of the calendar year to contact a client under the International Tax Compliance Regulations 2015[45] or to review information where it is: relevant to

[42] The latter are themselves supervised for AML by OPBAS, see https://www.fca.org.uk/opbas.
[43] https://www.gov.uk/government/organisations/disclosure-and-barring-service.
[44] See amending regulation 5(1)(c).
[45] S.I. 2015/878, amended by S.I. 2017/598.

their client risk assessment (or where appropriate practice-wide/matter risk assessment); or where it concerns beneficial ownership information of the customer, including information which helps the regulated person understand the ownership or control structure of any entity that is the beneficial owner of the client.

Further, amendments to original regulation 28 require regulated persons to update their records relating to the beneficial ownership of corporate clients. Such persons also need to understand the ownership and control structure of their corporate customers, and record any difficulties encountered in identifying beneficial ownership. As for original regulation 28(3), in addition to previous requirements in relation to undertaking due diligence on a non-natural person (e.g. trusts), the regulated entity must now[46] also take reasonable measures to understand the ownership and control structure of that person.[47] 13.63

Looking at the original regulation 28(8), there is now an additional requirement that will apply in a narrowly defined set of circumstances. Where a client is a body corporate and the practice has exhausted all possible means of identifying their beneficial owners but has not succeeded or is not satisfied that an individual is the beneficial owner, the regulated entity must[48] take reasonable measures to identify and verify the identity of the senior person responsible for managing the body corporate, and record in writing all actions and difficulties encountered in doing so. 13.64

Further clarity is provided[49] in that an electronic identification process using electronic identification services means and trust services[50] may be regarded as reliable, where they are secure from fraud and misuse and capable of providing appropriate assurance customers are who they say they are. The amending regulations add to the previous guidance, in practical recognition of the increased use of electronic identity verification (EIV) and expressly adding a further option to conduct EIV with a trust service. The only electronic identification and trust services (eIDAS) EU[51]-approved scheme currently available in the UK is GOV.UK Verify.[52] Post-Brexit the UK may approve other schemes. 13.65

6. Change to Dealing with Discrepancies on Registers (Under Regulation 30A)

By way of background, under 4MLD, EU member states were required to establish or a central register of beneficial owner information on registered corporate or other legal entities identifying persons of significant control. There is a requirement that 13.66

[46] By amending regulation 5(2).
[47] See amending regulation 5(2).
[48] By the amending regulation 5(2)(b).
[49] See the amending regulation 5(2)(c).
[50] as defined in EU Regulation 2014/910/EU.
[51] EU 910/2014, the EU Regulation on electronic identification and trust services for electronic transactions.
[52] Though this is in itself an offering which contains five alternative portals to verification of identity, see https://www.gov.uk/government/publications/introducing-govuk-verify/introducing-govuk-verify.

this information must be publicly accessible. As a result, HM Government brought in a Persons of Significant Control Register in 2016, allowing information to be reported from that date. Debate continues as to the merits of unverified public registers, versus private verified registers available to law enforcement online at short notice.

13.67 By regulation 30A, there is a new requirement for regulated persons to report to Companies House discrepancies between the information the firm holds on their customers compared with the information held in the Companies House Register. Companies House has issued helpful guidance[53] as to what constitutes a reportable discrepancy, and precisely how to report it.

13.68 The effect of the original regulation was that before establishing a business relationship with a company (registered or unregistered as defined in the Unregistered Companies Regulations 2009(1)), a limited liability partnership, or a Scottish partnership, a regulated entity must obtain proof of registration or an excerpt from the relevant register.

13.69 Regulation 30A(3) brings in a significant change in the regulations, in that persons will have a responsibility to report discrepancies between information collected (as above) from the relevant Register, and information collated while undertaking duties and responsibilities under the regulations (e.g. due diligence or ongoing monitoring).

13.70 Entities finding such discrepancies whilst fulfilling their AML duties must report them, but there is not a positive requirement for practices to actively seek out such discrepancies.

13.71 Neither does this responsibility to report apply where the information is subject to legal professional privilege (LPP).

13.72 Any discrepancy should be reported to Companies House (via a new online reporting tool available on the Companies House website) as soon as reasonably possible.

7. Changes to Enhanced Due Diligence (Chapter 2, 2017 MLRs)

13.73 There are three significant changes to enhanced due diligence (EDD) requirements under existing regulation 33. The first two (i.e. so-called 'red flag' transactions and high risk third countries) expand the situations in which EDD must be applied. The final reform has the effect adding additional factors to be considered in assessing risk, and therefore whether EDD should apply at all.

13.74 First, looking at 'red flag' transactions, changes to existing EDD requirements mean that a regulated person must apply EDD in any of the following circumstances (N.B. previously it was only necessary if all the listed elements were met):

- where the transaction is complex;
- where the transaction is unusually large; or

[53] https://www.gov.uk/guidance/report-a-discrepancy-about-a-beneficial-owner-on-the-psc-register-by-an-obliged-entity.

- where there is an unusual pattern of transactions, or the transaction or transactions have no apparent economic or legal purpose.

As mentioned above, whether or not a transaction is 'complex' or 'unusually large' should be judged in relation to the normal activity of the practice and the normal activity of the client. 13.75

Second, when assessing whether a situation is high risk, and thus whether EDD should be applied, the new factors to be considered include: 13.76

- whether the person is a beneficiary of a life insurance policy;
- whether the person is seeking residence/citizen rights in exchange for investments in that EEA state;
- whether the firm operates without face to face meeting and without electronic identity systems to mitigate this; or
- whether the person is involved in the trade of oil, arms, precious metals, tobacco products, cultural artefacts, ivory and other items related to protected species, and other items of archaeological, historical, cultural, and religious significance, or of rare scientific value.

Arguably,[54] whether the person is a beneficiary of a life insurance policy is only likely to be indicative of higher AML risk where the retainer bears direct relevance to the policy.

As for high risk jurisdictions, EDD and ongoing monitoring are now required when either the client or counterparty to a transaction is 'established in' a high-risk third country[55] as per original regulation 33(1)(b). 13.77

As at 10 January 2020, those high-risk countries are: Afghanistan, Lao PDR, Yemen, Tunisia, Bosnia and Herzegovina, Syria, Ethiopia, Pakistan, Guyana, Uganda, Sri Lanka, Iran, Iraq, Vanuatu, Trinidad and Tobago, and North Korea (DPRK). 13.78

A client or counterparty is to be treated as 'established in' a country, where any of the following apply: it was incorporated in the country; it has a principal place of business in the country; (if a financial institution or credit institution) its principal regulatory authority is based in the country; or (if a natural person) being resident in, but not merely because they were born in the country. 13.79

The new regulation 33(3A) stipulates that where EDD is to be applied due to a party to the transaction being 'established in' a high risk third country, it must include obtaining: additional information on the client and on the client's beneficial owner; additional information on the intended nature of the business relationship; obtaining information on the source of funds and source of wealth of the client and of the client's beneficial owner; obtaining information on the 13.80

[54] As the Legal Sector Affinity Group maintain in their 2020 Guidance.

[55] A 'high-risk third country' is one which has been identified by the European Commission in delegated acts adopted under Article 9.2 of the fourth money laundering directive as a high-risk third country.

reasons for the transactions; obtaining the approval of senior management of the practice for establishing or continuing the business relationship; and conducting enhanced monitoring of the business relationship by increasing the number and timing of controls applied and selecting patterns of transactions that need further examination.

8. Trust Registration

13.81 While there had been indication via a consultation paper[56] that there may be changes to the trust registration regime, these have not been included in this legislation. The UK's Legal Sector Affinity Group[57] anticipates HM Government may seek to implement changes at another time.

9. E-money Thresholds for CDD

13.82 Amendments to original regulation 38 regarding electronic money mean that firms can only forego customer due diligence measures in situations where:

- the maximum amount which can be stored electronically is €150 (previously €250);
- the payment instrument used in connection with the electronic money (the relevant payment instrument) is:
  - not reloadable, or
  - is subject to a maximum limit on monthly payment transactions of €150, which can only be used in the UK (NB the threshold was previously €250);
- the relevant payment instrument is used exclusively to purchase goods or services anonymous electronic money cannot be used to fund the relevant payment instrument.

10. Duty to Respond to Information Requests: Accounts and Safe-deposit Boxes

13.83 As of 10 September 2020, new Part 5A imposes duties on credit institutions and the providers of safe custody services to respond to requests for information, via a central automated mechanism. A law enforcement authority or the Gambling Commission may request details related to accounts and safe-deposit boxes including, but not limited to, name, date of birth, and address of the holders or beneficial owners.

[56] https://assets.publishing.service.gov.uk/government/uploads/system/uploads/attachment_data/file/860491/5MLD_Consultation_Response.pdf.

[57] Ibid.

11. Crypto Registration with FCA

As for 'crypto-asset exchange providers', these are brought within scope of the MLRs by the amending regulation 4(1)(b)(j).[58] Businesses carrying out certain crypto-asset activities will need to comply with the MLRs in relation to those activities from 10 January 2020, and to register with the Financial Conduct Authority during 2020.[59] 13.84

The implementation of 5MLD in January 2020 marked the last occasion on which UK AML reforms were driven by an EU Directive, whether there will be future divergence in interpretation of FATF standards is moot. 13.85

[58] Custodian wallet providers come into scope per 4(1)(b)(k); they are entities that provide services to safeguard and administer virtual assets on behalf of customers.

[59] Per FCA website https://www.fca.org.uk/firms/financial-crime/cryptoassets-aml-ctf-regime.

APPENDIX 1

Sanctions and Anti-Money Laundering Act 2018

2018 CHAPTER 13

An Act to make provision enabling sanctions to be imposed where appropriate for the purposes of compliance with United Nations obligations or other international obligations or for the purposes of furthering the prevention of terrorism or for the purposes of national security or international peace and security or for the purposes of furthering foreign policy objectives; to make provision for the purposes of the detection, investigation and prevention of money laundering and terrorist financing and for the purposes of implementing Standards published by the Financial Action Task Force relating to combating threats to the integrity of the international financial system; and for connected purposes. [23rd May 2018]

BE IT ENACTED by the Queen's most Excellent Majesty, by and with the advice and consent of the Lords Spiritual and Temporal, and Commons, in this present Parliament assembled, and by the authority of the same, as follows:—

PART 1
SANCTIONS REGULATIONS

CHAPTER 1
POWER TO MAKE SANCTIONS REGULATIONS

Power to make sanctions regulations

1 Power to make sanctions regulations

(1) An appropriate Minister may make sanctions regulations where that Minister considers that it is appropriate to make the regulations—
(a) for the purposes of compliance with a UN obligation,
(b) for the purposes of compliance with any other international obligation, or
(c) for a purpose within subsection (2).

(2) A purpose is within this subsection if the appropriate Minister making the regulations considers that carrying out that purpose would—
   (a) further the prevention of terrorism, in the United Kingdom or elsewhere,
   (b) be in the interests of national security,
   (c) be in the interests of international peace and security,
   (d) further a foreign policy objective of the government of the United Kingdom,
   (e) promote the resolution of armed conflicts or the protection of civilians in conflict zones,
   (f) provide accountability for or be a deterrent to gross violations of human rights, or otherwise promote—
      (i) compliance with international human rights law, or
      (ii) respect for human rights,
   (g) promote compliance with international humanitarian law,
   (h) contribute to multilateral efforts to prevent the spread and use of weapons and materials of mass destruction, or
   (i) promote respect for democracy, the rule of law and good governance.

(3) Regulations under this section must state the purpose (or purposes) of the regulations, and any purpose stated must be—
   (a) compliance with a UN obligation, or other international obligation, specified in the regulations, or
   (b) a particular purpose that is within subsection (2).

(4) Section 2 contains additional requirements in relation to regulations stating a purpose within subsection (2) above.

(5) In this section 'sanctions regulations' means regulations which do one or more of the following—
   (a) impose financial sanctions (see section 3);
   (b) impose immigration sanctions (see section 4);
   (c) impose trade sanctions (see section 5 and Schedule 1);
   (d) impose aircraft sanctions (see section 6);
   (e) impose shipping sanctions (see section 7);
   (f) impose sanctions within section 8 (other sanctions for purposes of UN obligations);
   (g) make supplemental provision in connection with any provision of the regulations or other regulations made under this section.

(6) In this section 'supplemental provision' includes any provision authorised by any other provision of this Act to be made by regulations under this section (see in particular sections 9 to 17, 19 to 21 and 54).

(7) In this Act any reference to a gross violation of human rights is to conduct which—
   (a) constitutes, or
   (b) is connected with,

   the commission of a gross human rights abuse or violation; and whether conduct constitutes or is connected with the commission of such an abuse or violation is to be determined in accordance with section 241A of the Proceeds of Crime Act 2002.

(8) In this Act—

   'UN obligation' means an obligation that the United Kingdom has by virtue of a UN Security Council Resolution;

   'UN Security Council Resolution' means a resolution adopted by the Security Council of the United Nations;

   'international obligation' means an obligation of the United Kingdom created or arising by or under any international agreement.

(9) For the purposes of any provision of this Act which refers to an 'appropriate Minister', the following are appropriate Ministers—
(a) the Secretary of State;
(b) the Treasury.
(10) None of paragraphs (a) to (i) of subsection (2) is to be taken to limit the meaning of any other of those paragraphs.

2 Additional requirements for regulations for a purpose within section 1(2)

(1) This section applies to regulations under section 1 any of whose purposes (as stated under section 1(3)) is a discretionary purpose.
In this section 'discretionary purpose' means a purpose which is not compliance with a UN obligation or other international obligation but is within section 1(2).
(2) An appropriate Minister may not decide that it is appropriate to make regulations to which this section applies unless, in respect of each discretionary purpose stated in the regulations, that Minister—
(a) has considered whether there are good reasons to pursue that purpose and has determined that there are, and
(b) has considered whether the imposition of sanctions is a reasonable course of action for that purpose and has determined that it is.
(3) In subsection (2)(b) 'sanctions' means prohibitions and requirements of the kinds which are imposed by the regulations for the purpose in question (or both for that purpose and for another purpose of the regulations).
(4) In relation to any regulations to which this section applies, the appropriate Minister making the regulations ('the Minister') must at the required time lay before Parliament a report which explains in respect of each discretionary purpose stated under section 1(3) in the regulations—
(a) why the Minister considers that carrying out that purpose would meet one or more of the conditions in paragraphs (a) to (i) of section 1(2),
(b) why the Minister considers that there are good reasons to pursue that purpose, and
(c) why the Minister considers that the imposition of sanctions (within the meaning given by subsection (3)) is a reasonable course of action for that purpose.
(5) Nothing in subsection (4) requires the report to contain anything the disclosure of which may, in the opinion of the Minister, damage national security or international relations.
(6) In subsection (4) 'the required time' means—
(a) in the case of regulations contained in a statutory instrument which is laid before Parliament after being made, the same time as the instrument is laid before Parliament;
(b) in the case of regulations contained in a statutory instrument a draft of which is laid before Parliament, the same time as the draft is laid.

Types of sanction

3 Financial sanctions

(1) For the purposes of section 1(5)(a) regulations 'impose financial sanctions' if they impose prohibitions or requirements for one or more of the following purposes—
(a) freezing funds or economic resources owned, held or controlled by designated persons (see section 9);
(b) preventing financial services from being provided to, or for the benefit of—
(i) designated persons,
(ii) persons connected with a prescribed country, or
(iii) a prescribed description of persons connected with a prescribed country;

(c) preventing financial services from being procured from, or for the benefit of—
   (i) designated persons,
   (ii) persons connected with a prescribed country, or
   (iii) a prescribed description of persons connected with a prescribed country;

(d) preventing funds or economic resources from being made available to, or for the benefit of—
   (i) designated persons,
   (ii) persons connected with a prescribed country, or
   (iii) a prescribed description of persons connected with a prescribed country;

(e) preventing funds or economic resources from being received from—
   (i) designated persons,
   (ii) persons connected with a prescribed country, or
   (iii) a prescribed description of persons connected with a prescribed country;

(f) preventing financial services from being provided, where the services relate to financial products, or financial products of a prescribed description, issued by designated persons;

(g) preventing persons from owning, controlling or having a prescribed interest in persons (other than individuals) which are—
   (i) designated persons,
   (ii) connected with a prescribed country, or
   (iii) of a prescribed description and connected with a prescribed country.

(2) For the purposes of section 1(5)(a) regulations also 'impose financial sanctions' if they impose prohibitions or requirements for the purpose of preventing persons from entering into, or continuing to be a party to, arrangements for commercial purposes, or for prescribed commercial purposes, with—
   (a) designated persons,
   (b) persons connected with a prescribed country, or
   (c) a prescribed description of persons connected with a prescribed country.

(3) In subsection (1) any reference to funds, economic resources or financial services being made available, received, procured or provided is to their being made available, received, procured or provided (as the case may be) directly or indirectly.

(4) In subsection (2) 'arrangements' includes any agreement, understanding, scheme, transaction or series of transactions (whether or not legally enforceable).

(5) Sections 60 and 61 contain definitions for the purposes of this Act of— 'economic resources',
'financial products',
'financial services',
'freeze', and
'funds'.

(6) Section 62 makes provision about the meaning of —
   (a) funds or economic resources being 'owned, held or controlled' or 'made available' (see subsection (4) of that section),
   (b) a person 'owning' or 'controlling' another person (see subsection (5) of that section), and
   (c) a person being 'connected with' a country (see subsection (6) of that section).

4 Immigration sanctions

(1) For the purposes of section 1(5)(b) regulations 'impose immigration sanctions' if they provide for designated persons (see section 9) to be excluded persons for the purposes of section 8B of the Immigration Act 1971.

(2) As to the effect of such provision, see section 8B of the Immigration Act 1971 (as amended by paragraph 1 of Schedule 3 to this Act).

5 Trade sanctions

(1) For the purposes of section 1(5)(c) regulations 'impose trade sanctions' if they impose prohibitions or requirements for one or more of the purposes mentioned in Part 1 of Schedule 1.
(2) Part 2 of that Schedule makes further provision in connection with regulations which impose trade sanctions.

6 Aircraft sanctions

(1) For the purposes of section 1(5)(d) regulations 'impose aircraft sanctions' if they impose prohibitions or requirements for one or more of the following purposes—
  (a) detaining disqualified aircraft (see subsection (6)) within the United Kingdom, or controlling the movement of disqualified aircraft within the United Kingdom and the airspace over the United Kingdom;
  (b) ensuring that disqualified aircraft—
    (i) do not overfly the United Kingdom, or
    (ii) leave the airspace over the United Kingdom;
  (c) preventing persons from owning, chartering or operating aircraft registered in a prescribed country;
  (d) preventing aircraft from being registered in a prescribed country;
  (e) preventing the registration of—
    (i) aircraft in which a designated person (see section 9) holds a prescribed interest (or designated persons, taken together, hold a prescribed interest), or
    (ii) aircraft chartered by demise to designated persons.
(2) For the purposes of section 1(5)(d) regulations also 'impose aircraft sanctions' if they authorise directions within subsection (3), (4) or (5).
(3) Directions are within this subsection if they are given for a purpose mentioned in subsection (1)(a) or (b) and either—
  (a) they are given by the Secretary of State to—
    (i) the CAA,
    (ii) a person who holds a licence under Chapter 1 of Part 1 of the Transport Act 2000 (air traffic services), or
    (iii) an airport operator, or
  (b) they are given to the operator or pilot in command of a disqualified aircraft by—
    (i) the Secretary of State, or
    (ii) a person mentioned in paragraph (a)(i), (ii) or (iii).
(4) Directions are within this subsection if they are given by the Secretary of State to the CAA for the purpose of terminating the registration of any aircraft mentioned in subsection (1)(e).
(5) Directions are within this subsection if they are given by the Secretary of State to the operator or pilot in command of a British-controlled aircraft for the purpose of preventing the aircraft from—
  (a) overflying a prescribed country, or
  (b) landing in a prescribed country.
(6) In this section 'disqualified aircraft' means aircraft—
  (a) owned, chartered or operated by—
    (i) designated persons,

(ii) persons connected with a prescribed country, or
(iii) a prescribed description of persons connected with a prescribed country,
(b) registered in a prescribed country, or
(c) originating from a prescribed country.

(7) Provision authorising directions by virtue of subsection (2) may include provision—
(a) as to the effect of any such directions so far as they are inconsistent with requirements or permissions under any other enactment;
(b) requiring a person not to disclose any such directions if the Secretary of State notifies the person to that effect.

(8) For the purposes of this section any reference to the United Kingdom includes a reference to the territorial sea.

(9) In this section 'aircraft'—
(a) subject to paragraph (b), includes—
(i) unmanned aircraft, and
(ii) aircraft capable of spaceflight activities;
(b) does not include the naval, military or air-force aircraft of any country.

(10) In this section—
'airport' means the aggregate of the land, buildings and works comprised in an aerodrome within the meaning of the Civil Aviation Act 1982 (see section 105(1) of that Act);
'airport operator', in relation to an airport, means the person by whom the airport is managed;
'British-controlled aircraft' has the same meaning as in section 92 of the Civil Aviation Act 1982;
'the CAA' means the Civil Aviation Authority;
'enactment' includes an enactment mentioned in any of paragraphs (a) to (d) of section 54(6);
'operator', in relation to an aircraft, means the person having the management of the aircraft, and cognate expressions are to be construed accordingly;
'pilot in command', in relation to an aircraft, means the pilot designated by the operator as being in command and charged with the safe conduct of its flight, without being under the direction of any other pilot in the aircraft;
'registration' means registration in the register of aircraft kept by the CAA.

7 Shipping sanctions

(1) For the purposes of section 1(5)(e) regulations 'impose shipping sanctions' if they impose prohibitions or requirements for one or more of the following purposes—
(a) detaining within the United Kingdom, or controlling the movement within the United Kingdom of—
(i) disqualified ships (see subsection (8)), or
(ii) specified ships (see section 14);
(b) ensuring that disqualified ships or specified ships—
(i) do not enter the United Kingdom, or
(ii) leave the United Kingdom;
(c) preventing persons from owning, controlling, chartering or operating—
(i) ships registered in a prescribed country,
(ii) ships flying the flag of a prescribed country, or
(iii) specified ships;
(d) preventing ships from—
(i) being registered in a prescribed country, or
(ii) flying the flag of a prescribed country;

(e) preventing the registration of—
  (i) ships in which a designated person (see section 9) holds a prescribed interest (or designated persons, taken together, hold a prescribed interest),
  (ii) ships in which persons connected with a prescribed country hold a prescribed interest, or
  (iii) specified ships.

(2) For the purposes of section 1(5)(e) regulations also 'impose shipping sanctions' if they authorise directions within subsection (3), (4) or (5).

(3) Directions are within this subsection if they are given for a purpose mentioned in subsection (1)(a) or (b) and either—
(a) they are given to a harbour authority by the Secretary of State, or
(b) they are given to the master or pilot of a disqualified ship or a specified ship by—
  (i) the Secretary of State, or
  (ii) a harbour authority.

(4) Directions are within this subsection if they are given by the Secretary of State to the Registrar for the purpose of terminating the registration of any ship mentioned in subsection (1)(e).

(5) Directions are within this subsection if they are given by the Secretary of State to the master or pilot of a British ship (see subsections (12) and (13)) for the purpose of preventing the ship from travelling to—
(a) the sea or other waters within the seaward limits of the territorial sea adjacent to a prescribed country, or a particular place in that sea or those waters, or
(b) harbours in a prescribed country.

(6) For the purposes of section 1(5)(e) regulations also 'impose shipping sanctions' if, for the purpose of the implementation of so much of a UN Security Council Resolution as provides for the taking of measures in relation to ships designated for purposes of that resolution, they make provision—
(a) relating to such ships and corresponding to provision that may be made by virtue of subsection (1)(a), (b), (c) or (e),
(b) authorising directions corresponding to directions within subsection (3) to be given in relation to, or to the master or pilot of, such a ship, or
(c) authorising directions corresponding to directions within subsection (4) to be given in relation to such a ship.

(7) Provision made by virtue of subsection (6) may describe the ships to which it relates by reference to the instrument in which the ships are designated, including by reference to that instrument as varied or supplemented from time to time.

(8) In this section 'disqualified ships' means ships—
(a) owned, controlled, chartered, operated or crewed by—
  (i) designated persons,
  (ii) persons connected with a prescribed country, or
  (iii) a prescribed description of persons connected with a prescribed country,
(b) registered in a prescribed country,
(c) flying the flag of a prescribed country, or
(d) originating from a prescribed country.

(9) Provision authorising directions by virtue of this section may include provision as to the effect of any such directions so far as they are inconsistent with requirements under any other enactment.

(10) Provision made by virtue of this section may include provision as to the meaning of any reference in the provision to a ship being 'crewed' by persons.

(11) In subsection (1) any reference to the United Kingdom includes a reference to the territorial sea.

(12) In this section 'British ship' means a ship which—

(a) is registered under Part 2 of the Merchant Shipping Act 1995,

(b) is a Government ship within the meaning of that Act,

(c) is registered under the law of a relevant British possession,

(d) is not registered under the law of a country outside the United Kingdom but is wholly owned by persons each of whom has a United Kingdom connection, or

(e) is registered under an Order in Council under section 1 of the Hovercraft Act 1968.

(13) For the purposes of subsection (12)(d), a person has a 'United Kingdom connection' if the person is—

(a) a British citizen, a British overseas territories citizen or a British Overseas citizen,

(b) an individual who is habitually resident in the United Kingdom, or

(c) a body corporate which is established under the law of a part of the United Kingdom and has its principal place of business in the United Kingdom.

(14) In this section—

'enactment' includes an enactment mentioned in any of paragraphs (a) to (d) of section 54(6);

'harbour authority' has the same meaning as in the Merchant Shipping Act 1995 (see section 313(1) of that Act);

'master' includes every person (except a pilot) having command or charge of a ship and, in relation to a fishing vessel, means the skipper;

'pilot', in relation to a ship, means any person not belonging to the ship who has the conduct of the ship;

'the Registrar' means the Registrar General of Shipping and Seamen or, where functions of that person are being discharged by another person, that other person;

'registration' means registration in the register of British ships maintained by the Registrar;

'relevant British possession' means—

(a) any of the Channel Islands,

(b) the Isle of Man, or

(c) any British overseas territory;

'ship' includes every description of vessel (including a hovercraft) used in navigation, except the naval, military or air-force ships of any country.

8 Other sanctions for purposes of UN obligations

(1) For the purposes of section 1(5)(f), regulations impose sanctions within this section if they impose prohibitions or requirements, not otherwise authorised by this Part, which the appropriate Minister making the regulations considers that it is appropriate to impose for the purposes of compliance with a UN obligation.

(2) The reference in subsection (1) to prohibitions or requirements includes prohibitions or requirements imposed on or otherwise relating to designated persons (see section 9).

Designation of persons

9 'Designated persons'

(1) Subsection (2) applies for the purposes of sections 3 and 4, Schedule 1 and sections 6 to 8.

(2) In each of those provisions, 'designated persons' means—
(a) persons designated under any power contained in the regulations that authorises an appropriate Minister to designate persons for the purposes of the regulations or of any provisions of the regulations, or
(b) persons who are designated persons under any provision included in the regulations by virtue of section 13 (persons named by or under UN Security Council Resolutions).

(3) In subsection (2) 'the regulations' means the regulations mentioned in section 3, 4, 5(1), 6, 7 or 8 (as the case may be).

(4) As regards designation of persons by virtue of subsection (2)(a), see sections 10 to 12.

(5) In this Act 'person' includes (in addition to an individual and a body of persons corporate or unincorporate) any organisation and any association or combination of persons.

10 Designation powers: general

(1) In this Act a 'designation power', in relation to regulations under section 1, means a power (contained in the regulations by virtue of section 9(2)(a)) for an appropriate Minister to designate persons for the purposes of the regulations or of any provisions of the regulations.

(2) Regulations under section 1 which contain a designation power may make provision about the way in which the power must or may be exercised, including provision authorising the appropriate Minister to whom the power is granted—
(a) to designate a person by name;
(b) to provide that persons of a description specified by that Minister are designated persons;
(c) to designate different persons for the purposes of different provisions of the regulations.

(3) Regulations under section 1 which contain a designation power must provide that where an appropriate Minister—
(a) has made a designation under the power, or
(b) has varied or revoked a designation made under the power (see section 22),

that Minister must without delay take such steps as are reasonably practicable to inform the designated person of the designation, variation or revocation.

(4) The regulations may include provision, additional to that required by subsection (3), as to steps to be taken as regards notification or publicity where a designation has been made under the designation power or a designation made under the power has been varied or revoked.

(5) The regulations need not require a person to be notified of an intention to designate the person.

(6) Sections 11 and 12 contain provision about criteria for designation under a designation power.

11 Designation of a person by name under a designation power

(1) This section applies to regulations under section 1 which authorise an appropriate Minister ('the Minister') to designate persons by name.

(2) The regulations must contain provision which prohibits the Minister from designating a person by name except where the Minister—
(a) has reasonable grounds to suspect that that person is an involved person (see subsection (3)), and
(b) considers that the designation of that person is appropriate, having regard to—
(i) the purpose of the regulations as stated under section 1(3), and
(ii) the likely significant effects of the designation on that person (as they appear to the Minister to be on the basis of the information that the Minister has).

(3) The regulations must provide that 'an involved person' means a person who—
(a) is or has been involved in an activity specified in the regulations,
(b) is owned or controlled directly or indirectly by a person who is or has been so involved,
(c) is acting on behalf of or at the direction of a person who is or has been so involved, or
(d) is a member of, or associated with, a person who is or has been so involved.

(4) An activity may not be specified in the regulations by virtue of subsection (3) unless the Minister considers that specifying the activity is appropriate having regard to the purpose of the regulations as stated under section 1(3).

(5) The regulations may, in the case of any activity specified in the regulations, make provision as to the meaning for the purposes of the regulations of a person's being involved in that activity.

(6) The regulations may make provision, for the purposes of the regulations, as to the meaning of a person's—
(a) being 'owned or controlled directly or indirectly by' another person, and
(b) being 'associated with' another person.

(7) The regulations must, in relation to any case where the Minister designates a person by name, require the information given under the provision made under section 10(3) to include a statement of reasons.

(8) In subsection (7) a 'statement of reasons' means a brief statement of the matters that the Minister knows, or has reasonable grounds to suspect, in relation to that person which have led the Minister to make the designation.

(9) The regulations may authorise matters to be excluded from that statement where the Minister considers that they should be excluded—
(a) in the interests of national security or international relations,
(b) for reasons connected with the prevention or detection of serious crime in the United Kingdom or elsewhere, or
(c) in the interests of justice,

(but the regulations may not authorise the Minister to provide no statement of reasons).

12 Designation of persons by description under a designation power

(1) This section applies to regulations under section 1 which grant a power for an appropriate Minister ('the Minister') to provide that persons of a specified description are designated persons.

(2) The regulations must contain provision which prohibits the exercise of that power except where conditions A to C are met.

(3) Condition A is that the description of persons specified is such that a reasonable person would know whether that person fell within it.

(4) Condition B is that, at the time the description is specified, it is not practicable for the Minister to identify and designate by name all the persons falling within that description at that time.

(5) Condition C is that the Minister—
(a) has reasonable grounds to suspect—
(i) in a case where the specified description is members of a particular organisation, that that organisation is an involved person, or
(ii) in the case of any other specified description, that any person falling within that description would necessarily be an involved person, and
(b) considers that the designation of persons of the specified description is appropriate, having regard to—
(i) the purpose of the regulations as stated under section 1(3), and

(ii) the likely significant effects of the designation (as they appear to the Minister to be on the basis of the information that the Minister has) on persons of that description.

(6) Subsections (3) to (6) of section 11 apply to regulations which contain provision mentioned in subsection (2) above.

(7) The regulations must, in relation to any case where the Minister provides that persons of a specified description are designated persons, require the information given under the provision made under section 10(3) to include a statement of reasons.

(8) In subsection (7) a 'statement of reasons' means a brief statement of the matters that the Minister knows, or has reasonable grounds to suspect, in relation to persons of the specified description which have led the Minister to make the provision designating persons of that description.

(9) The regulations may authorise matters to be excluded from that statement where the Minister considers that they should be excluded—

(a) in the interests of national security or international relations,

(b) for reasons connected with the prevention or detection of serious crime in the United Kingdom or elsewhere, or

(c) in the interests of justice,

(but the regulations may not authorise the Minister to provide no statement of reasons).

(10) In this section 'organisation' includes any body, association or combination of persons.

13 Persons named by or under UN Security Council Resolutions

(1) This section applies where—

(a) the purpose, or a purpose, of a provision of regulations under section 1 is compliance with an obligation to take particular measures in relation to UN—named persons that the United Kingdom has by virtue of a UN Security Council Resolution ('the Resolution'), and

(b) for that provision of the regulations to achieve its purpose as regards that obligation, the relevant UN-named persons need to be designated persons for the purposes of that provision.

(2) The regulations must provide for those persons to be designated persons for the purposes of that provision.

(3) Provision under subsection (2) may be expressed in any way and may in particular refer to the Resolution, or any other instrument, as varied or supplemented from time to time.

(4) In this section—

a 'UN-named person' means a person for the time being named (by the Security Council or a subsidiary organ of the Security Council) for the purposes of the Resolution so far as it provides for the taking of the measures in question, and

'the relevant UN-named persons' means each such person.

Specified ships

14 'Specified ships'

(1) In each of section 7 and Schedule 1 'specified ships' means ships (within the meaning of that provision) specified under any power contained in the regulations that authorises an appropriate Minister to specify ships for the purposes of the regulations or of any provisions of the regulations.

In this subsection 'the regulations' means the regulations mentioned in section 7 or section 5(1) (as the case may be).

(2) Subsections (3) to (8) apply to regulations under section 1 which authorise an appropriate Minister ('the Minister') to specify ships.

(3) The regulations may make provision about the way in which the power must or may be exercised, including provision authorising the Minister to specify ships by their International Maritime Organisation number.

(4) The regulations may make provision as to the steps to be taken as regards notification and publicity where the power is exercised.

(5) The regulations need not require a person to be notified of an intention to specify a ship.

(6) The regulations must contain provision which prohibits the Minister from specifying a ship except where the Minister—

(a) has reasonable grounds to suspect that the ship is, has been, or is likely to be, involved in an activity specified in the regulations, and

(b) considers that it is appropriate for that ship to be specified, having regard to the purpose of the regulations as stated under section 1(3).

(7) An activity may not be specified in the regulations by virtue of subsection (6)(a) unless the Minister considers that specifying the activity is appropriate having regard to the purpose of the regulations as stated under section 1(3).

(8) The regulations may, in the case of any activity specified in the regulations, make provision as to the meaning for the purposes of the regulations of a ship's being involved in that activity.

Contents of sanctions regulations: further provision

15 Exceptions and licences

(1) In this section 'regulations' means regulations under section 1.

(2) Regulations may—

(a) create exceptions to any prohibition or requirement imposed by the regulations;

(b) provide for a prohibition imposed by the regulations not to apply to anything done under the authority of a licence issued by an appropriate Minister specified in the regulations;

(c) provide for a requirement imposed by the regulations to be subject to such exceptions as an appropriate Minister specified in the regulations may direct.

(3) Regulations may, as respects any licences or directions provided for under subsection (2)(b) or (c)—

(a) provide that a licence or direction may be general or issued to a category of persons or a particular person;

(b) provide that a licence or direction must specify what is authorised by the licence or excepted by the direction;

(c) make provision as to what may, or may not, be authorised by a licence or excepted by a direction;

(d) provide that a licence or direction may contain conditions;

(e) provide that a licence or direction may not be issued unless criteria specified by the regulations are met;

(f) make provision as to the duration of licences or directions, which may enable them to be of indefinite duration or a defined duration;

(g) make provision enabling licences or directions to be varied, revoked or suspended;

(h) make provision as to notifications or publicity to be given in connection with licences or directions.

(4) Where regulations provide for designated persons to be excluded persons for the purposes of section 8B of the Immigration Act 1971, the regulations may—
   (a) create exceptions from subsections (1) to (3) of that section in relation to any person who under the regulations is an excluded person (a 'relevant person');
   (b) authorise an appropriate Minister specified in the regulations to direct that, in relation to any relevant person specified, or of a description specified, in the direction, subsections (1) to (3) of that section have effect subject to exceptions specified in the direction.
(5) Regulations may, as respects any directions provided for under subsection (4)(b), make any provision mentioned (in relation to directions) in subsection (3)(d) to (h).
(6) The exceptions that may be created under subsection (2)(a) include exceptions in relation to acts done for the purposes of—
   (a) national security;
   (b) the prevention or detection of serious crime in the United Kingdom or elsewhere.
   In this subsection 'act' includes an omission.
(7) Nothing in subsection (6) is to be taken to limit subsection (2).

16 Information

(1) Regulations under section 1 may make provision—
   (a) requiring persons of a prescribed description—
      (i) to inform an appropriate authority of prescribed matters;
      (ii) to create and retain registers or records;
   (b) authorising an appropriate authority to require persons of a prescribed description to provide information, or produce documents, of a prescribed description;
   (c) conferring powers to inspect and copy prescribed documents or information;
   (d) conferring powers of entry in relation to powers conferred by virtue of paragraph (b) or (c), and about the exercise of any such powers of entry;
   (e) authorising or restricting the disclosure of information, including provision—
      (i) about the purposes for which information held in connection with anything done under or by virtue of the regulations may be used;
      (ii) about the persons to whom any such information may be disclosed.
(2) Without prejudice to anything in subsection (1), regulations under section 1 may include provision authorising or requiring prescribed information about a person designated by or under the regulations to be notified to prescribed persons or to be publicised.
(3) In subsection (1) 'appropriate authority' means—
   (a) an appropriate Minister, or
   (b) such other person as may be prescribed.

17 Enforcement

(1) In this section 'regulations' means regulations under section 1.
(2) Regulations may make provision—
   (a) for the enforcement of any prohibitions or requirements imposed by regulations;
   (b) for the enforcement of any prohibitions or requirements imposed under regulations, including, in particular, prohibitions or requirements imposed by—
      (i) conditions of a licence or direction issued by virtue of section 15, or
      (ii) directions given by virtue of sections 6 and 7;
   (c) for preventing any prohibitions or requirements mentioned in paragraph (a) or (b) from being circumvented.

(3) The provision that may be made by virtue of subsection (2) includes provision as to the powers and duties of any person who is to enforce the regulations.

(4) Regulations—

(a) may create criminal offences for the purposes of the enforcement of prohibitions or requirements mentioned in subsection (2)(a) or (b) or for the purposes of preventing such prohibitions or requirements from being circumvented, and

(b) may include provision dealing with matters relating to any offences created for such purposes by regulations (including provision that creates defences).

(5) Regulations may not provide for an offence under regulations to be punishable with imprisonment for a period exceeding—

(a) in the case of conviction on indictment, 10 years;

(b) in the case of summary conviction—

(i) in relation to England and Wales, 12 months or, in relation to offences committed before section 154(1) of the Criminal Justice Act 2003 comes into force, 6 months;

(ii) in relation to Scotland, 12 months;

(iii) in relation to Northern Ireland, 6 months.

(6) Regulations may include provision applying, for the purpose of the enforcement of any relevant prohibition or requirement, any provision of the Customs and Excise Management Act 1979 specified in the regulations, with or without modifications.

(7) In subsection (6) a 'relevant prohibition or requirement' means—

(a) a prohibition or requirement imposed by regulations for a purpose mentioned in—

(i) section 3(1)(b) to (g) or (2), or

(ii) Part 1 of Schedule 1, or

(b) a prohibition or requirement imposed by a condition of a licence or direction issued by virtue of section 15 in relation to a prohibition or requirement mentioned in paragraph (a).

(8) Regulations may provide that a particular offence which is—

(a) created by virtue of this section, and

(b) specified by the regulations,

is an offence to which Chapter 1 of Part 2 of the Serious Organised Crime and Police Act 2005 (investigatory powers) applies.

(9) Regulations may provide that a particular provision of the regulations which—

(a) contains a prohibition or requirement imposed for a purpose mentioned in section 3(1) or (2), and

(b) is specified by the regulations,

is to be regarded as not being financial sanctions legislation for the purposes of Part 8 of the Policing and Crime Act 2017 (financial sanctions: monetary penalties).

18 Report in respect of offences in regulations

(1) In this section 'relevant regulations' means regulations under section 1 which create any offence for the purposes of—

(a) the enforcement of any prohibitions or requirements imposed by or under regulations under section 1, or

(b) preventing any such prohibitions or requirements from being circumvented.

(2) The appropriate Minister making any relevant regulations ('the Minister') must at the required time lay before Parliament a report which—

(a) specifies the offences created by the regulations, indicating the prohibitions or requirements to which those offences relate,

(b) states that the Minister considers that there are good reasons for those prohibitions or requirements to be enforceable by criminal proceedings and explains why the Minister is of that opinion, and

(c) in the case of any of those offences which are punishable with imprisonment—

(i) states the maximum terms of imprisonment that apply to those offences,

(ii) states that the Minister considers that there are good reasons for those maximum terms, and

(iii) explains why the Minister is of that opinion.

(3) Subsection (4) applies where an offence created by the regulations relates to a particular prohibition or requirement and the Minister considers that a good reason—

(a) for that prohibition or requirement to be enforceable by criminal proceedings, or

(b) for a particular maximum term of imprisonment to apply to that offence,

is consistency with another enactment relating to the enforcement of a similar prohibition or requirement.

(4) The report must identify that other enactment.

(5) In subsection (3) 'another enactment' means any provision of or made under an Act, other than a provision of the regulations to which the report relates.

(6) In subsection (2) 'the required time' means—

(a) in the case of regulations contained in a statutory instrument which is laid before Parliament after being made, the same time as the instrument is laid before Parliament;

(b) in the case of regulations contained in a statutory instrument a draft of which is laid before Parliament, the same time as the draft is laid.

(7) This section applies to regulations which amend other regulations under section 1 so as to create an offence as it applies to regulations which otherwise create an offence.

19 Enforcement: goods etc on ships

(1) The provision that may be made by virtue of section 17(2) (enforcement of prohibitions or requirements) includes provision as to the powers and duties of prescribed persons in relation to—

(a) British ships in foreign waters or international waters,

(b) ships without nationality in international waters, and

(c) foreign ships in international waters.

(2) Regulations may make provision by virtue of this section only for the purpose of enforcing relevant prohibitions or requirements.

(3) A prohibition or requirement is a 'relevant prohibition or requirement' for the purposes of this section if it is—

(a) a prohibition or requirement specified by the regulations which is imposed by regulations for a purpose mentioned in any of paragraphs 2 to 7, 15(a), (b) or (c) or 16(a) of Schedule 1, or

(b) a prohibition or requirement imposed by a condition of a licence or direction issued by virtue of section 15 in relation to a prohibition or requirement mentioned in paragraph (a).

(4) The powers that may be conferred by virtue of this section include powers to—

(a) stop a ship;

(b) board a ship;

(c) require any person found on a ship boarded by virtue of this section to provide information or produce documents;

(d) inspect and copy such documents or information;

(e) stop any person found on such a ship and search that person for—
   (i) prohibited goods, or
   (ii) any thing that might be used to cause physical injury or damage to property or to endanger the safety of any ship;
(f) search a ship boarded by virtue of this section, or any thing found on such a ship (including cargo), for prohibited goods;
(g) seize goods found on a ship, in any thing found on a ship, or on any person found on a ship (but see subsection (8));
(h) for the purpose of exercising a power mentioned in paragraph (e), (f) or (g), require a ship to be taken to, and remain in, a port or anchorage in the United Kingdom or any other country willing to receive it.

(5) Regulations that confer a power mentioned in subsection (4)(a) to (f) or (h) must provide that a person may not exercise the power in relation to a ship unless the person has reasonable grounds to suspect that the ship is carrying prohibited goods (and the regulations need not require the person to have reasonable grounds to suspect that an offence is being or has been committed).

(6) Regulations that confer a power mentioned in subsection (4)(e)(i) or (f) must provide that the power may be exercised only to the extent reasonably required for the purpose of discovering prohibited goods.

(7) Regulations that confer a power mentioned in subsection (4)(e)(ii) on a person ('the officer') may permit the search of a person only where the officer has reasonable grounds to believe that that person might use a thing in a way mentioned in subsection (4)(e)(ii).

(8) Regulations that confer a power mentioned in subsection (4)(g) on a person—
(a) must provide for the power to be exercisable on a ship only where that person is lawfully on the ship (whether in exercise of powers conferred by virtue of this section or otherwise), and
(b) may permit the seizure only of—
   (i) goods which that person has reasonable grounds to suspect are prohibited goods, or
   (ii) things within subsection (4)(e)(ii).

(9) Regulations that confer a power on a person by virtue of this section may authorise that person to use reasonable force, if necessary, in the exercise of the power.

(10) Regulations that confer a power by virtue of this section must provide that—
(a) the power may be exercised in relation to a British ship in foreign waters only with the authority of the Secretary of State, and
(b) in relation to foreign waters other than the sea and other waters within the seaward limits of the territorial sea adjacent to any relevant British possession, the Secretary of State may give authority only if the State in whose waters the power would be exercised consents to the exercise of the power.

(11) Regulations that confer a power by virtue of this section must provide that—
(a) the power may be exercised in relation to a foreign ship only with the authority of the Secretary of State, and
(b) the Secretary of State may give authority only if—
   (i) the home state has requested the assistance of the United Kingdom for the purpose of enforcing relevant prohibitions or requirements,
   (ii) the home state has authorised the United Kingdom to act for that purpose, or
   (iii) the United Nations Convention on the Law of the Sea 1982 (Cmnd 8941) or a UN Security Council Resolution otherwise permits the exercise of the powers in relation to the ship.

(12) The reference in subsection (11) to the United Nations Convention on the Law of the Sea includes a reference to any modifications of that Convention agreed after the passing of this Act that have entered into force in relation to the United Kingdom.

(13) In this section—

'arrangements' includes any agreement, understanding, scheme, transaction or series of transactions (whether or not legally enforceable);

'British ship' means a ship falling within paragraph (a), (c), (d) or (e) of section 7(12);

'foreign ship' means a ship which—

(a) is registered in a State other than the United Kingdom, or

(b) is not so registered but is entitled to fly the flag of a State other than the United Kingdom;

'foreign waters' means the sea and other waters within the seaward limits of the territorial sea adjacent to any relevant British possession or State other than the United Kingdom;

'goods' includes technology within the meaning of Schedule 1 (see paragraph 37 of that Schedule);

'home state', in relation to a foreign ship, means—

(a) the State in which the ship is registered, or

(b) the State whose flag the ship is otherwise entitled to fly;

'international waters' means waters beyond the territorial sea of the United Kingdom or of any other State or relevant British possession;

'prohibited goods' means goods which have been, or are being, dealt with in contravention of a relevant prohibition or requirement (see subsection (3));

'regulations' means regulations under section 1;

'relevant British possession' has the same meaning as in section 7 (see subsection (14) of that section);

'ship' has the same meaning as in section 7 (see subsection (14) of that section);

'ship without nationality' means a ship which—

(a) is not registered in, or otherwise entitled to fly the flag of, any State or relevant British possession, or

(b) sails under the flags of two or more States or relevant British possessions, or under the flags of a State and relevant British possession, using them according to convenience.

(14) In the definition of 'prohibited goods' in subsection (13), the reference to goods dealt with in contravention of a relevant prohibition or requirement includes a reference to a case where—

(a) arrangements relating to goods have been entered into that have not been fully implemented, and

(b) if those arrangements were to be fully implemented, the goods would be dealt with in contravention of that prohibition or requirement.

20 Goods etc on ships: non-UK conduct

(1) Regulations may make provision conferring on prescribed persons powers exercisable—

(a) in relation to—

(i) British ships in foreign waters or international waters,

(ii) ships without nationality in international waters, and

(iii) foreign ships in international waters,

(b) for the purpose of—

(i) investigating the suspected carriage of relevant goods on such ships, or

(ii) preventing the continued carriage on such ships of goods suspected to be relevant goods.

(2) The powers that may be conferred by virtue of this section include powers to—
  (a) stop a ship;
  (b) board a ship;
  (c) require any person found on a ship boarded by virtue of this section to provide information or produce documents;
  (d) inspect and copy such documents or information;
  (e) stop any person found on such a ship and search that person for—
    (i) relevant goods, or
    (ii) any thing that might be used to cause physical injury or damage to property or to endanger the safety of any ship;
  (f) search a ship boarded by virtue of this section, or any thing found on such a ship (including cargo), for relevant goods;
  (g) seize goods found on a ship, in any thing found on a ship, or on any person found on a ship (but see subsection (6));
  (h) for the purpose of exercising a power mentioned in paragraph (e), (f) or (g), require a ship to be taken to, and remain in, a port or anchorage in the United Kingdom or any other country willing to receive it.

(3) Regulations that confer a power mentioned in subsection (2)(a) to (f) or (h) must provide that a person may not exercise the power in relation to a ship unless the person has reasonable grounds to suspect that the ship is carrying relevant goods.

(4) Regulations that confer a power mentioned in subsection (2)(e)(i) or (f) must provide that the power may be exercised only to the extent reasonably required for the purpose of discovering relevant goods.

(5) Regulations that confer a power mentioned in subsection (2)(e)(ii) on a person ('the officer') may permit the search of a person only where the officer has reasonable grounds to believe that that person might use a thing in a way mentioned in subsection (2)(e)(ii).

(6) Regulations that confer a power mentioned in subsection (2)(g) on a person—
  (a) must provide for the power to be exercisable on a ship only where that person is lawfully on the ship (whether in exercise of powers conferred by virtue of this section or otherwise), and
  (b) may permit the seizure only of—
    (i) goods which that person has reasonable grounds to suspect are relevant goods, or
    (ii) things within subsection (2)(e)(ii).

(7) Regulations that confer a power on a person by virtue of this section may authorise that person to use reasonable force, if necessary, in the exercise of the power.

(8) Regulations that confer a power by virtue of this section must provide that—
  (a) the power may be exercised in relation to a British ship in foreign waters only with the authority of the Secretary of State, and
  (b) in relation to foreign waters other than the sea and other waters within the seaward limits of the territorial sea adjacent to any relevant British possession, the Secretary of State may give authority only if the State in whose waters the power would be exercised consents to the exercise of the power.

(9) Regulations that confer a power by virtue of this section must provide that—
  (a) the power may be exercised in relation to a foreign ship only with the authority of the Secretary of State, and
  (b) the Secretary of State may give authority only if—
    (i) the home state has requested the assistance of the United Kingdom for a purpose mentioned in subsection (1)(b),

(ii) the home state has authorised the United Kingdom to act for such a purpose, or
(iii) the United Nations Convention on the Law of the Sea 1982 (Cmnd 8941) or a UN Security Council Resolution otherwise permits the exercise of the powers in relation to the ship.

(10) The reference in subsection (9) to the United Nations Convention on the Law of the Sea includes a reference to any modifications of that Convention agreed after the passing of this Act that have entered into force in relation to the United Kingdom.

(11) In this section—
'regulations' means regulations under section 1;
'relevant goods' means goods in relation to which relevant non-UK conduct is occurring or has occurred;
'relevant non-UK conduct' means conduct outside the United Kingdom by a person other than a United Kingdom person that would constitute a contravention of a relevant prohibition or requirement if the conduct had been—
(a) in the United Kingdom, or
(b) by a United Kingdom person;
'relevant prohibition or requirement' has the same meaning as in section 19 (see subsection (3) of that section);
'United Kingdom person' has the same meaning as in section 21 (see subsection (2) of that section).

(12) In the definition of 'relevant non-UK conduct' in subsection (11), the reference to conduct that would constitute a contravention of a relevant prohibition or requirement if the conduct had been in the United Kingdom or by a United Kingdom person includes a reference to a case where—
(a) arrangements relating to goods have been entered into that have not been fully implemented, and
(b) if those arrangements were to be fully implemented (and if the conduct had been in the United Kingdom or by a United Kingdom person) the goods would be dealt with in contravention of that prohibition or requirement.

(13) In this section, the following expressions have the same meaning as in section 19—
'arrangements',
'British ship', 'foreign ship', 'foreign waters', 'goods',
'home state', 'international waters',
'relevant British possession', 'ship', and
'ship without nationality'.

21 Extra-territorial application

(1) Prohibitions or requirements may be imposed by or under regulations under section 1 in relation to—
(a) conduct in the United Kingdom or in the territorial sea by any person;
(b) conduct elsewhere, but only if the conduct is by a United Kingdom person.

(2) In subsection (1) 'United Kingdom person' means—
(a) a United Kingdom national, or
(b) a body incorporated or constituted under the law of any part of the United Kingdom.

(3) For this purpose a United Kingdom national is an individual who is—
(a) a British citizen, a British overseas territories citizen, a British National (Overseas) or a British Overseas citizen,

(b) a person who under the British Nationality Act 1981 is a British subject, or
(c) a British protected person within the meaning of that Act.

(4) Her Majesty may by Order in Council provide for this section to have effect as if the list of persons in subsection (2) included a body incorporated or constituted under the law of any of the following named in the Order—
(a) any of the Channel Islands;
(b) the Isle of Man;
(c) any of the British overseas territories.

(5) In this section 'conduct' includes acts and omissions.

(6) Nothing in this section limits the provision that may be made in regulations under section 1 by virtue of section 19 or 20.

CHAPTER 2
REVIEW BY APPROPRIATE MINISTER, AND OTHER REVIEWS

Revocation, variation and review of designations

22 Power to vary or revoke designation made under regulations

(1) In this section and section 23—
'a relevant designation' means a designation made under a designation power contained in regulations under section 1;
'the Minister', in relation to a relevant designation, means the appropriate Minister who made that designation.

(2) A relevant designation may at any time be varied or revoked by the Minister.

(3) If at any time the Minister considers that the required conditions are not met in respect of a relevant designation, the Minister must revoke the designation.

(4) In subsection (3) 'the required conditions' means—
(a) if the designation is of a named person, the conditions of the provision included in the regulations under section 11(2) (reading that provision, so far as made under section 11(2)(b), as if references to the designation were references to leaving the designation in place),
(b) if the designation is of persons of a specified description, the conditions of the provision included in the regulations under section 12(2) (reading that provision, so far as made under section 12(5)(b), as if references to the designation were references to leaving the designation in place).

23 Right to request variation or revocation of designation

(1) At any time while a relevant designation has effect, the designated person may—
(a) request the Minister to vary the designation, or
(b) request the Minister to revoke the designation.

(2) But where a request under this section has been made in respect of a designation, no further request may be made under this section in respect of that designation unless the grounds on which the further request is made are or include that there is a significant matter which has not previously been considered by the Minister.

(3) On a request under this section the Minister must decide whether to vary or revoke the designation or to take no action with respect to it (but see section 22(3)).

(4) In this section —

'the designated person' means the person named by the designation or, where the designation is of persons of a specified description, any person of that description;

'the Minister' has the meaning given by section 22(1); 'relevant designation' has the meaning given by section 22(1).

24 Periodic review of certain designations

(1) This section applies where—

(a) regulations under section 1 which contain a designation power are in force, and

(b) any qualifying designations have been made by an appropriate Minister under the power.

(2) That appropriate Minister must in each review period—

(a) consider each qualifying designation which has effect, and

(b) decide in the case of each such designation whether to vary or revoke the designation or to take no action with respect to it (but see section 22(3)).

(3) In this section a 'qualifying designation' means a designation which designates a named person, or persons of a specified description, for the purposes of any provision of the regulations that—

(a) imposes a prohibition or requirement for a purpose mentioned in section 3(1) (a), (b)(i) or (d)(i) (asset-freezing etc), or

(b) provides for designated persons to be excluded persons for the purposes of section 8B of the Immigration Act 1971.

(4) For the purposes of this section each of the following is a 'review period'—

(a) the period of 3 years beginning with the date when the regulations are made, and

(b) each period of 3 years that begins with the date of completion of a review under this section of qualifying designations under the regulations.

25 Right of UN-named person to request review

(1) This section applies where—

(a) the purpose, or a purpose, of a provision of regulations under section 1 is compliance with an obligation to take particular measures that the United Kingdom has by virtue of a UN Security Council Resolution ('the Resolution'),

(b) a person is a designated person for the purposes of that provision, and

(c) the person is such a designated person under provision included in the regulations by virtue of section 13 (persons named by or under UN Security Council Resolutions).

(2) The person may request the Secretary of State to use the Secretary of State's best endeavours to secure that the person's name is removed from the relevant UN list.

(3) But where a person has made a request under this section in respect of a designation, that person may make no further request under this section in respect of that designation unless the grounds on which the further request is made are or include that there is a significant matter which has not previously been considered by the Secretary of State.

(4) On a request under this section the Secretary of State must decide whether or not to comply with the request.

(5) For the purposes of this section a person's name is 'removed from the relevant UN list' if the person ceases to be named (by the Security Council or a subsidiary organ of the Security Council) for the purposes of the Resolution so far as it provides for the taking of the measures in question.

Revocation and review in relation to ships

26 Power to revoke specification of ship made under regulations

(1) In this section and section 27—

'a ship specification' means a specification of a ship made under a power contained in regulations under section 1 by virtue of section 14;

'the Minister', in relation to a ship specification, means the appropriate Minister who made that specification.

(2) A ship specification may at any time be revoked by the Minister.

(3) If at any time the Minister considers that the required conditions are not met in respect of a ship specification, the Minister must revoke the specification.

(4) In subsection (3) 'the required conditions' means the conditions of the provision included in the regulations under section 14(6).

27 Right to request revocation of specification of ship

(1) At any time while a ship specification has effect, any person affected by it may request the Minister to revoke the specification.

(2) But where a person has made a request under this section in respect of a specification, no further request may be made under this section by that person or any other person in respect of that specification unless the grounds on which the further request is made are or include that there is a significant matter which has not previously been considered by the Minister.

(3) On a request under this section the Minister must decide whether to revoke the specification or to take no action with respect to it (but see section 26(3)).

(4) In this section—

'the Minister', and 'ship specification',

have the meaning given by section 26(1).

28 Periodic review where ships are specified

(1) This section applies where—

(a) regulations under section 1 are in force which by virtue of section 14 contain a power to specify a ship, and

(b) any specifications have been made by an appropriate Minister under that power.

(2) That appropriate Minister must in each review period—

(a) consider each specification of a ship which has effect under the regulations, and

(b) decide in the case of each such specification whether to revoke it or to take no action with respect to it (but see section 26(3)).

(3) For the purposes of this section each of the following is a 'review period'—

(a) the period of 3 years beginning with the date when the regulations are made, and

(b) each period of 3 years that begins with the date of completion of a review under this section of specifications made under the regulations.

29 UN-designated ship: right to request review

(1) This section applies where a provision of regulations under section 1 is made by virtue of section 7(6) or paragraph 15 of Schedule 1 in relation to ships designated by the Security Council or a subsidiary organ of the Security Council for any purposes of a UN Security Council Resolution ('the Resolution').

(2) Any person affected by that provision may request the Secretary of State to use the Secretary of State's best endeavours to secure that a ship so designated ceases to be designated for any purposes of the Resolution.

(3) But where a person has made a request under this section in respect of the designation of a ship, no further request may be made under this section by that person or any other person in respect of that designation unless the grounds on which the further request is made are or include that there is a significant matter which has not previously been considered by the Secretary of State.

(4) On a request under this section the Secretary of State must decide whether or not to comply with the request.

Review of regulations

30 Review by appropriate Minister of regulations under section 1

(1) Subsection (2) applies where any regulations under section 1 are in force.

(2) The appropriate Minister who made the regulations must in each relevant period review whether the regulations are still appropriate for the purpose stated in them under section 1(3).

(3) If a purpose so stated in any regulations under section 1 is a purpose other than compliance with a UN obligation or other international obligation, any review of those regulations under this section must also include a consideration of—

(a) whether carrying out that purpose would meet any one or more of the conditions in paragraphs (a) to (i) of section 1(2),

(b) whether there are good reasons to pursue that purpose, and

(c) whether the imposition of sanctions is a reasonable course of action for that purpose.

(4) In subsection (3)(c) 'sanctions' means prohibitions and requirements of the kinds which are imposed by the regulations for the purpose in question (or both for that purpose and for another purpose of the regulations).

(5) An appropriate Minister who has carried out a review under this section must lay before Parliament a report containing—

(a) the conclusions of the review,

(b) the reasons for those conclusions, and

(c) a statement of any action that that Minister has taken or proposes to take in consequence of the review.

(6) Nothing in subsection (5) requires the report to contain anything the disclosure of which may, in the opinion of that Minister, damage national security or international relations.

(7) For the purposes of this section each of the following is a 'relevant period' in relation to regulations under section 1—

(a) the period of one year beginning with the date when the regulations are made;

(b) each period of one year that begins with the date when a report under this section containing the conclusions of a review of the regulations is laid before Parliament.

31 Independent review of regulations with counter-terrorism purpose

(1) The Secretary of State must appoint a person to review the operation of such asset—freeze provisions of relevant regulations made by the Secretary of State as the Secretary of State may from time to time refer to that person.

(2) The Treasury must appoint a person to review the operation of such asset-freeze provisions of relevant regulations made by the Treasury as the Treasury may from time to time refer to that person.

(3) The persons appointed under subsections (1) and (2) may be the same person.

(4) In each calendar year, by 31 January—

(a) the person appointed under subsection (1) must notify the Secretary of State of what (if any) reviews under that subsection that person intends to carry out in that year, and

(b) the person appointed under subsection (2) must notify the Treasury of what (if any) reviews under that subsection that person intends to carry out in that year.

(5) Reviews of which notice is given under subsection (4) in a particular year—

(a) may not relate to any provisions that have not been referred before the giving of the notice, and

(b) must be completed during that year or as soon as reasonably practicable after the end of it.

(6) The person who conducts a review under this section must as soon as reasonably practicable after completing the review send a report on its outcome to—

(a) the Secretary of State, if the review is under subsection (1), or

(b) the Treasury, if the review is under subsection (2).

(7) On receiving a report under this section the Secretary of State or (as the case may be) the Treasury must lay a copy of it before Parliament.

(8) The Secretary of State may pay the expenses of a person who conducts a review under subsection (1) and also such allowances as the Secretary of State may determine.

(9) The Treasury may pay the expenses of a person who conducts a review under subsection (2) and also such allowances as the Treasury may determine.

(10) For the purposes of this section, regulations are 'relevant regulations' if—

(a) they are regulations under section 1, and

(b) they state under section 1(3) at least one purpose which—

(i) is not compliance with a UN obligation or other international obligation, and

(ii) relates to counter-terrorism.

(11) A purpose 'relates to counter-terrorism' if the report under section 2 in respect of the regulations indicated that, in the opinion of the appropriate Minister making them, the carrying out of that purpose would further the prevention of terrorism in the United Kingdom or elsewhere.

(12) For the purposes of this section a provision of relevant regulations is an 'asset-freeze provision' if and to the extent that it—

(a) imposes a prohibition or requirement for a purpose mentioned in section 3(1) (a), (b) or (d), or

(b) makes provision in connection with such a prohibition or requirement.

(13) If a provision is referred under this section which contains a designation power, any review under this section of the operation of that provision may not include a review of any decisions to designate under that power.

32 Periodic reports on exercise of power to make regulations under section 1

(1) The Secretary of State must as soon as reasonably practicable after the end of each reporting period lay before Parliament a report which—

(a) specifies the regulations under section 1, if any, that were made in that reporting period,

(b) identifies which, if any, of those regulations—

(i) stated a relevant human rights purpose, or

(ii) amended or revoked regulations stating such a purpose,

(c) specifies any recommendations which in that reporting period were made by a Parliamentary Committee in connection with a relevant independent review, and

(d) includes a copy of any response to those recommendations which was made by the government to that Committee in that reporting period.

(2) Nothing in subsection (1)(d) requires a report under this section to contain anything the disclosure of which may, in the opinion of the Secretary of State, damage national security or international relations.

(3) For the purposes of this section the following are reporting periods—

(a) the period of 12 months beginning with the day on which this Act is passed ('the first reporting period'), and

(b) each period of 12 months that ends with an anniversary of the date when the first reporting period ends.

(4) For the purposes of this section—

(a) regulations 'state' a purpose if the purpose is stated under section 1(3) in the regulations;

(b) a purpose is a 'relevant human rights purpose' if, in the opinion of the Secretary of State, carrying out that purpose would provide accountability for or be a deterrent to gross violations of human rights.

(5) In this section—

'the government' means the government of the United Kingdom;

'gross violation of human rights' has the meaning given by section 1(7);

a 'Parliamentary Committee' means a committee of the House of Commons or a committee of the House of Lords or a joint committee of both Houses;

a 'relevant independent review', in relation to a Parliamentary Committee, means a consideration by that Committee of whether the power to make regulations under section 1 should be exercised in connection with a gross violation of human rights.

Procedure for requests to, and reviews by, appropriate Minister

33 Procedure for requests to, and reviews by, appropriate Minister

(1) An appropriate Minister may by regulations make provision about the procedure to be followed in connection with a request under section 23, 25, 27 or 29 or a review under section 24, 28 or 30.

(2) Regulations made under this section in relation to a request under section 23, 25, 27 or 29 must require—

(a) the decision on any such request to be made as soon as reasonably practicable after the receipt by the appropriate Minister dealing with the request of the information needed for making the decision, and

(b) the person who made the request to be informed of the decision and the reasons for it as soon as reasonably practicable after the decision is made.

(3) The regulations may authorise matters to be excluded from the reasons given for the decision where the appropriate Minister who made the decision considers that those matters should be excluded—

(a) in the interests of national security or international relations,

(b) for reasons connected with the prevention or detection of serious crime in the United Kingdom or elsewhere, or

(c) in the interests of justice,

(but the regulations may not authorise that Minister to provide no reasons).

CHAPTER 3
TEMPORARY POWERS IN RELATION TO EU SANCTIONS LISTS

34 Temporary powers in relation to EU sanctions lists

(1) This section applies where—
 (a) a provision of retained EU sanctions law relates to persons named in any Annex, instrument or other document, or
 (b) a provision of an instrument made by the Council of the European Union (however expressed) requires or recommends that persons named, or of a description specified, in that instrument or any other document must not

or should not be admitted to the United Kingdom (see section 8B of the Immigration Act 1971).

(2) An Annex, instrument or other document mentioned in subsection (1)(a) or (b) is an 'EU sanctions list' for the purposes of this section.

(3) An appropriate Minister may, in respect of any EU sanctions list—
 (a) direct that a person's name is to be treated as added to the list with effect from a date specified in the direction, or
 (b) direct that a person's name is to be treated as removed from the list with effect from a date specified in the direction.

(4) The giving of a direction under paragraph (a) or (b) of subsection (3) does not prevent the giving of any subsequent direction under either of those paragraphs in respect of the same person.

(5) The power to give a direction under this section is not exercisable after two years beginning with the day on which this section comes into force.

(6) In this section 'a provision of retained EU sanctions law' means a provision of retained EU law which corresponds to any provision that by virtue of any of sections 3 and 5 to 7 could be made by regulations under section 1 in relation to designated persons.

(7) Section 35 makes further provision about directions under this section.

35 Directions under section 34: further provision

(1) An appropriate Minister may not under section 34 direct that a person's name is to be treated as added to an EU sanctions list except where that Minister—
 (a) has reasonable grounds to suspect that the person is an involved person (see subsections (2) and (3) below), and
 (b) considers that it is appropriate to give the direction, having regard to—
  (i) the purpose of the EU provision which relates to persons in that list (see subsections (4) and (5) below), and
  (ii) the likely significant effects of the direction on the person to whom it relates (as they appear to that Minister to be on the basis of the information that the Minister has).

(2) In subsection (1)(a) 'an involved person' means a person who—
 (a) is or has been involved in an activity which is specified, by regulations made by an appropriate Minister, in relation to the list in question,
 (b) is owned or controlled directly or indirectly by a person who is or has been so involved,
 (c) is acting on behalf of or at the direction of a person who is or has been so involved, or
 (d) is a member of, or associated with, a person who is or has been so involved.

(3) An activity may not be specified by regulations under subsection (2)(a) unless the appropriate Minister making the regulations considers that specifying the activity is appropriate having regard to the purpose of the EU provision which relates to persons in the list in question.

(4) In subsections (1) and (3) any reference to the 'purpose' of any EU provision is to such purpose, or purposes, as may be prescribed in relation to that provision by regulations made by an appropriate Minister.

(5) Any purpose prescribed under subsection (4) must be a purpose that it is reasonable to assume was the purpose (or one of the purposes) of the provision in question.

(6) Regulations under subsection (2)(a) which specify an activity may also make provision as to the meaning, for the purposes of subsection (2) as it applies in relation to the list in question, of a person's—

(a) being involved in the specified activity;

(b) being 'owned or controlled directly or indirectly by' another person;

(c) being 'associated with' another person.

(7) Regulations made by an appropriate Minister may make provision as to the steps to be taken as regards notification and publicity where a direction is given under section 34.

(8) Regulations made under subsection (7) must, in relation to any case where a direction under section 34 has been given, require the appropriate Minister who gave the direction ('the Minister') to take without delay such steps as are reasonably practicable—

(a) to inform the person to whom it relates that the direction has been given, and

(b) where the direction is under section 34(3)(a), to include with that information a brief statement of the matters that the Minister knows, or has reasonable grounds to suspect, in relation to that person which have led the Minister to give the direction.

(9) The regulations may authorise the statement required by virtue of subsection (8)(b) to exclude matters where the Minister considers that they should be excluded—

(a) in the interests of national security or international relations,

(b) for reasons connected with the prevention or detection of serious crime in the United Kingdom or elsewhere, or

(c) in the interests of justice,

(but the regulations may not authorise the Minister to provide no such statement).

(10) The regulations need not require a person to be notified of an intention to make a direction under section 34.

(11) In this section—

'EU sanctions list' has the same meaning as in section 34; 'EU provision' means—

(a) a provision of retained EU sanctions law (within the meaning of section 34), or

(b) a provision of an instrument made by the Council of the European Union.

36 Rights of person on EU sanctions list

(1) A person whose name is included, or treated as included, in an EU sanctions list may make a request for a direction under section 34(3)(b) that the person's name be treated as removed from the list.

This is subject to section 37 (UN-named persons).

(2) Any request under this section must be made—

(a) if the person is treated as included in the list by virtue of a direction under section 34(3)(a), to the appropriate Minister who gave that direction;

(b) in any other case, to an appropriate Minister.

(3) Where a request under this section has been made for a direction in respect of a person and a list, no further request may be made under this section in respect of that person and that list unless the grounds on which the further request is made are or include that there is a significant matter which has not previously been considered.

(4) On a request under this section the appropriate Minister to whom the request is made must decide whether or not to comply with the request.

(5) An appropriate Minister may by regulations make provision about the procedure to be followed in connection with a request under this section or section 37.

(6) Regulations made under subsection (5) in relation to a request under this section or section 37 must require—

(a) the decision on any such request to be made as soon as reasonably practicable after the receipt by the appropriate Minister dealing with the request of the information needed for making the decision, and

(b) the person who made the request to be informed of the decision and the reasons for it as soon as reasonably practicable after the decision is made.

(7) The regulations may authorise matters to be excluded from the reasons given for the decision where the appropriate Minister who made the decision considers that those matters should be excluded—

(a) in the interests of national security or international relations,

(b) for reasons connected with the prevention or detection of serious crime in the United Kingdom or elsewhere, or

(c) in the interests of justice,

(but the regulations may not authorise that Minister to provide no reasons).

(8) In this section 'EU sanctions list' has the same meaning as in section 34.

37 Rights of UN-named person on EU sanctions list

(1) This section applies where—

(a) a person whose name is included or treated as included in an EU sanctions list is a person in relation to whom, by virtue of a UN Security Council Resolution ('the Resolution'), the United Kingdom has an obligation to take particular measures, and

(b) that obligation is met by—

(i) provision mentioned in section 34(1)(a) which relates to that EU sanctions list, or

(ii) the application to the person, by virtue of that EU sanctions list, of any provision of section 8B of the Immigration Act 1971.

(2) The person—

(a) may not make a request under section 36 in respect of the EU sanctions list concerned, but

(b) may at any relevant time make a request under this section for the Secretary of State to use the Secretary of State's best endeavours to secure that the person's name is removed from the relevant UN list.

(3) Where a person has made a request under this section by virtue of being on an EU sanctions list, the person may make no further request under this section by virtue of being on that list unless the grounds on which the further request is made are or include that there is a significant matter which has not previously been considered by the Secretary of State.

(4) On a request under this section the Secretary of State must decide whether or not to comply with the request.

(5) For the purposes of this section a person's name is 'removed from the relevant UN list' if the person ceases to be named (by the Security Council or a subsidiary organ of the Security Council) for the purposes of the Resolution so far as it provides for the taking of the measures in question.

(6) In subsection (2) a 'relevant time' means a time when no provision of regulations under section 1 has been made the purpose (or a purpose) of which is compliance with the United Kingdom's obligation to take the measures in question.

(7) For the purposes of subsection (3) a person is 'on' an EU sanctions list if the person's name is included or treated as included in that list.
(8) In this section 'EU sanctions list' has the same meaning as in section 34.

CHAPTER 4
COURT REVIEWS

38 Court review of decisions

(1) This section applies to—
  (a) any decision under section 23(3) or 24(2) (decision, following a request to or review by an appropriate Minister, on whether a designation of a person made under a designation power should be varied or revoked);
  (b) any decision under section 27(3) or 28(2) (decision, following a request to or review by an appropriate Minister, on whether a ship specification should be revoked);
  (c) any decision under section 25(4), 29(4), 36(4) or 37(4) not to comply with a request;
  (d) any other decision of an appropriate Minister in connection with functions of that Minister under this Part or regulations under this Part, other than—
    (i) a decision to make or vary, or not to revoke or vary, a designation under a designation power where the designated person has a right to make a request under section 23 or would have but for section 23(2),
    (ii) a decision to make a ship specification, or not to revoke a ship specification, where a person has a right to make a request in respect of that specification under section 27 or would have but for section 27(2), or
    (iii) a decision to give a direction under section 34(3)(a) where the person has a right to make a request under section 36 or would have but for section 36(3) or 37.
(2) The appropriate person may apply to the High Court or, in Scotland, the Court of Session, for the decision to be set aside.
(3) 'The appropriate person' means—
  (a) in relation to a decision within subsection (1)(a), the person named by the designation or, where the designation is of persons of a specified description, any person of that description;
  (b) in relation to a decision within subsection (1)(b) or (d), any person affected by the decision;
  (c) in relation to a decision within subsection (1)(c), the person who made the request.
(4) In determining whether the decision should be set aside, the court must apply the principles applicable on an application for judicial review.
(5) If the court decides that a decision should be set aside it may make any such order, or give any such relief, as could in the absence of this section be made or given in proceedings for judicial review of the decision; but this is subject to section 39(1) to (4).
(6) In this section and section 39 'a ship specification' means a specification of a ship made under a power contained in regulations under section 1 by virtue of section 14.

39 Court reviews: further provision

(1) Subsection (2) applies to the court in any of the following proceedings—
  (a) any proceedings on an application under section 38 in respect of a decision mentioned in section 38(1)(a), (b) or (c) ('a relevant application');
  (b) any proceedings on a claim arising from any matter to which a relevant application relates;

(c) if—
(i) a designation made under a designation power contained in regulations under section 1 is revoked without an application under section 38 being made,
(ii) a ship specification (within the meaning of section 38) is revoked without such an application being made, or
(iii) a corrective direction is given under section 34(3)(b) without such an application being made,

any proceedings on a relevant claim.

(2) If the court would, in the absence of this subsection, have power to award damages, the court may not award damages unless—
(a) the reason (or one of the reasons) that the court would have that power is that it is satisfied that the tort of negligence was committed, or, in Scotland, that there has been negligence, or
(b) the court is satisfied that the decision concerned was made in bad faith.

(3) In subsection (1)(c)—
a 'corrective direction' means a direction given in respect of a person and a list following the giving of a direction under section 34(3)(a) in respect of that person and list;
a 'relevant claim' means a claim made by (as the case may be)—
(a) a person designated by the designation,
(b) a person affected by the ship specification, or
(c) the person in respect of whom the direction under section 34(3)(a) was given,

which arises from any matter relating to the designation, ship specification or direction.

(4) In subsection (2) 'the decision concerned' means—
(a) in relation to proceedings within subsection (1)(a) or (b) where the relevant application was in respect of a decision mentioned in section 38(1)(a), the decision in respect of which the relevant application was made or the designation to which that decision related;
(b) in relation to any other proceedings within subsection (1)(a) or (b), the decision in respect of which the relevant application was made;
(c) in relation to proceedings within subsection (1)(c), the designation or ship specification or the decision to give the direction under section 34(3)(a).

(5) A decision mentioned in sub-paragraph (i), (ii) or (iii) of section 38(1)(d) may not be questioned by way of proceedings for judicial review (and nor may a decision to which section 38 applies).

40 Rules of court

(1) Sections 66 to 68 of the Counter-Terrorism Act 2008 (supplementary provisions relating to rules of court and special advocates) apply in relation to proceedings—
(a) on an application under section 38 (court review of decisions), or
(b) on a claim arising from any matter to which such an application relates,

as they apply in relation to financial restrictions proceedings within the meaning of section 65 of that Act, but with the following modification.

(2) That modification is that any reference in those sections to the Treasury is to be read, in relation to proceedings on an application under section 38 of this Act in respect of a decision of the Secretary of State or a claim arising from any matter to which such an application relates, as a reference to the Secretary of State.

(3) The first time after the passing of this Act that rules of court are made in exercise of the powers conferred by subsection (1) in relation to proceedings in England and Wales—
(a) on an application under section 38, or

(b) on a claim arising from any matter to which such an application relates,

those rules (together with any related rules of court) may be made by the Lord Chancellor instead of by the person who would otherwise make them.

(4) The first time after the passing of this Act that rules of court are made in exercise of the powers conferred by subsection (1) in relation to proceedings in Northern Ireland—

(a) on an application under section 38, or

(b) on a claim arising from any matter to which such an application relates,

those rules (together with any related rules of court) may be made by the Lord Chancellor instead of by the person who would otherwise make them.

(5) Before making rules of court under this section, the Lord Chancellor must consult—

(a) in relation to rules applicable to proceedings in England and Wales, the Lord Chief Justice of England and Wales;

(b) in relation to rules applicable to proceedings in Northern Ireland, the Lord Chief Justice of Northern Ireland.

(6) The Lord Chancellor is not required to undertake any other consultation before making the rules.

(7) The requirements of subsection (5)(a) and (b) may be satisfied by consultation that took place wholly or partly before the passing of this Act.

(8) Rules of court made by the Lord Chancellor under this section—

(a) must be laid before Parliament, and

(b) if not approved by a resolution of each House before the end of 28 days beginning with the day on which they were made, cease to have effect at the end of that period.

(9) In calculating a period of 28 days for the purposes of subsection (8), no account is to be taken of any time during which Parliament is dissolved or prorogued or during which both Houses are adjourned for more than 4 days.

(10) If rules cease to have effect in accordance with subsection (8)(b)—

(a) that does not affect anything done under the rules, and

(b) subsection (3) or (as the case may be) (4) applies as if the rules had not been made.

(11) The following provisions do not apply to rules of court made by the Lord Chancellor under this section—

(a) section 3(6) of the Civil Procedure Act 1997 (Parliamentary procedure for civil procedure rules);

(b) section 56(1), (2) and (4) of the Judicature (Northern Ireland) Act 1978 (statutory rules procedure).

(12) Section 4(1) of the Statutory Instruments Act 1946 (statutory instruments which are required to be laid before Parliament) applies to any such rules applicable to proceedings in Northern Ireland as it applies to a statutory instrument which is required to be laid before Parliament after being made.

(13) Until section 85 of the Courts Act 2003 (process for making civil procedure rules) comes into force, in subsection (11)(a) above 'section 3(6)' is to be read as 'section 3(2)'.

(14) In this section—

'related rules of court' means rules of court that—

(a) are contained in the same instrument as the rules mentioned in subsection (3) or (as the case may be) (4), and

(b) relate specifically to the same kind of proceedings as those rules,

'rules of court' means rules for regulating the practice and procedure to be followed in the High Court or the Court of Appeal.

CHAPTER 5

MISCELLANEOUS

41 Procedure for dealing with goods etc seized from ships

(1) The Secretary of State may by regulations make provision about the procedure to be followed in connection with goods seized under a power conferred by regulations under section 1 by virtue of section 19 or 20.

(2) Regulations under this section relating to goods seized on suspicion of being prohibited goods or relevant goods may include provision—

(a) requiring prescribed persons to be notified of the seizure of the goods;

(b) requiring the Secretary of State to determine whether the seized goods were, at the time of their seizure, prohibited goods (where the goods were seized under a power conferred by virtue of section 19) or relevant goods (where the goods were seized under a power conferred by virtue of section 20);

(c) enabling the making of a claim by prescribed persons in relation to the seized goods;

(d) about the determination by a prescribed court of any such claim;

(e) about the publicity to be given to any such determination by a court;

(f) for and about the return of seized goods to prescribed persons before or after any such determination of a claim by a court;

(g) about the treatment of seized goods not so returned (including, in prescribed circumstances, their destruction or sale);

(h) for and about the payment of compensation by the Secretary of State following a determination by a court that the goods were not, at the time of their seizure, prohibited goods (where the goods were seized under a power conferred by virtue of section 19) or relevant goods (where the goods were seized under a power conferred by virtue of section 20).

(3) In this section—

'goods' has the same meaning as in sections 19 and 20 (see subsections (13) of those sections);

'prohibited goods' has the same meaning as in section 19 (see subsection (13) of that section);

'relevant goods' has the same meaning as in section 20 (see subsection (11) of that section).

42 Suspension of prohibitions and requirements

(1) An appropriate Minister may make regulations ('suspending regulations') providing that—

(a) while the suspending regulations have effect, or

(b) for a specified period,

a specified prohibition or requirement of regulations under section 1 is not to have effect.

(2) In this section 'specified' means specified in the suspending regulations.

(3) A period specified under subsection (1)(b) may be expressed in any way, including, for example, being expressed in a way such that—

(a) the period begins, or ends, when a specified condition is met, or

(b) the period begins when a specified condition is met and lasts for so long as the suspending regulations or a specified provision of those regulations has effect.

43 Guidance about regulations under section 1

(1) Where regulations are made under section 1, the appropriate Minister who made the regulations must issue guidance about any prohibitions and requirements imposed by the regulations.

(2) The guidance may include guidance about—
(a) best practice for complying with the prohibitions and requirements;
(b) the enforcement of the prohibitions and requirements;
(c) circumstances where the prohibitions and requirements do not apply.

44 Protection for acts done for purposes of compliance

(1) This section applies to an act done in the reasonable belief that the act is in compliance with—
(a) regulations under section 1, or
(b) directions given by virtue of section 6 or 7.
(2) A person is not liable to any civil proceedings to which that person would, in the absence of this section, have been liable in respect of the act.
(3) In this section 'act' includes an omission.

45 Revocation and amendment of regulations under section 1

(1) Section 1 includes a power, by further regulations under that section ('new regulations')—
(a) to revoke any regulations under that section, or
(b) to amend any regulations under that section where the condition in subsection (2) below is met.
(2) The condition referred to in subsection (1)(b) is that the appropriate Minister making the new regulations—
(a) considers that the regulations being amended will, as amended, be sanctions regulations within the meaning given by section 1(5) that are appropriate for the purpose stated in them under section 1(3), and
(b) if any purpose stated in the regulations being amended is a purpose other than compliance with a UN obligation or other international obligation, considers in respect of each such purpose—
(i) that carrying out that purpose would meet one or more of the conditions in paragraphs (a) to (i) of section 1(2),
(ii) that there are good reasons to pursue that purpose, and
(iii) that the imposition of sanctions is a reasonable course of action for that purpose.
(3) In subsection (2)(b)(iii) 'sanctions' means prohibitions and requirements of the kinds imposed by the amended regulations for the purpose in question (or both for that purpose and for another purpose of those regulations).
In this subsection 'the amended regulations' means the regulations being amended as those regulations will be when amended.
(4) Except as permitted by subsection (5), the purpose stated under section 1(3) in any regulations under section 1 may not be amended (but this does not prevent regulations under that section from being revoked and replaced by regulations with a purpose that is to any extent different from that of the revoked regulations).
(5) Where the purpose stated under section 1(3) in any regulations under section 1 is or includes compliance with a specified UN obligation or other international obligation, regulations made by virtue of this section may amend that purpose so as to—
(a) add a reference to a UN obligation, or other international obligation, to which the United Kingdom is for the time being subject,
(b) substitute such a reference for another reference to a UN obligation or other international obligation, or

(c) remove a reference to a UN obligation, or other international obligation, to which the United Kingdom is no longer subject.

(6) The requirements of section 1(1) and (3), section 2 and section 30 do not apply in relation to regulations made by virtue of this section.

(7) In relation to section 1, this section has effect in place of section 14 of the Interpretation Act 1978 (implied power to revoke and amend).

46 Report where regulations for a purpose within section 1(2) are amended

(1) This section applies where—

(a) by virtue of section 45 regulations under section 1 are amended by further regulations under section 1 ('new regulations'), and

(b) the regulations being amended state under section 1(3) a purpose other than compliance with a UN obligation or other international obligation.

(2) The appropriate Minister making the new regulations must at the required time lay before Parliament a report which explains why that Minister is of the opinion mentioned in section 45(2)(b).

(3) Nothing in subsection (2) requires the report to contain anything the disclosure of which may in the opinion of that Minister damage national security or international relations.

(4) In subsection (2) 'the required time' means—

(a) where the new regulations are contained in a statutory instrument which is laid before Parliament after being made, the same time as the instrument is laid before Parliament;

(b) where a draft of a statutory instrument containing the new regulations is laid before Parliament, the same time as the draft is laid.

47 Power to amend Part 1 so as to authorise additional sanctions

(1) An appropriate Minister may by regulations amend this Part so as to authorise regulations under section 1 to impose prohibitions or requirements of kinds—

(a) which are not for the time being authorised by Chapter 1 (ignoring section 8), but

(b) which are kinds of prohibition or requirement that the United Kingdom—

(i) has any UN obligation or other international obligation to impose, or

(ii) has at any time had any UN obligation or other international obligation to impose.

(2) Without prejudice to the generality of subsection (1) or section 54(2), regulations under this section—

(a) may amend the definition of 'sanctions regulations' in section 1(5), and

(b) where they make any such amendment, may amend this Part in connection with that amendment.

(3) For the avoidance of doubt, regulations under this section may not add to or amend the purposes mentioned in section 1(1) or amend section 1(2).

48 Power to make provision relating to certain appeals

(1) In this section an 'immigration designation' means a designation of a person (whether by name or by description) which—

(a) is made under a designation power contained in regulations under section 1, and

(b) designates the person for the purposes of any provision of the regulations that provides for designated persons to be excluded persons for the purposes of section 8B of the Immigration Act 1971.

(2) In this section an 'immigration claim' means any representation made by a person to an appropriate Minister which—
(a) is made in connection with an immigration designation of that person, and
(b) is within subsection (3).
(3) A representation is within this subsection if it is a representation by a person—
(a) that removal from the United Kingdom of that person would—
(i) breach the United Kingdom's obligations under the Human Rights Convention ('human rights obligations'), or
(ii) breach the United Kingdom's obligations under the Refugee Convention ('Refugee Convention obligations'),
(b) that requiring that person to leave the United Kingdom would breach human rights obligations or breach Refugee Convention obligations, or
(c) that refusal of entry of that person into the United Kingdom would breach human rights obligations or breach Refugee Convention obligations.
(4) The Secretary of State may by regulations make provision—
(a) about the effect of an immigration claim, or a prescribed description of immigration claim, for the purposes of prescribed provisions of the Immigration Acts;
(b) for a decision of a prescribed description made by an appropriate Minister under this Part, or such a decision so far as relating to prescribed matters, to be treated as a decision from which a person may appeal under section 82(1) of the Nationality, Immigration and Asylum Act 2002 ('the 2002 Act');
(c) modifying Part 5 of the 2002 Act in relation to an appeal relating to such a decision;
(d) preventing the court in proceedings on an application under section 38 above from considering prescribed issues where—
(i) an immigration claim has been made and the circumstances are such as may be prescribed, or
(ii) a representation within subsection (3) is made in the proceedings and the circumstances are such as may be prescribed;
(e) in relation to any case where under regulations under section 1 above a person is an excluded person for the purposes of section 8B of the Immigration Act 1971, disapplying any of subsections (1), (2) and (3) of that section until the end of a prescribed period or until the occurrence of a prescribed event.
(5) In this section 'the Human Rights Convention' and 'the Refugee Convention' have the same meaning as in section 8B of the Immigration Act 1971.

PART 2
ANTI-MONEY LAUNDERING

49 Money laundering and terrorist financing etc

(1) An appropriate Minister may by regulations make provision for one or more of the following purposes—
(a) enabling or facilitating the detection or investigation of money laundering, or preventing money laundering;
(b) enabling or facilitating the detection or investigation of terrorist financing, or preventing terrorist financing;

(c) the implementation of Standards published by the Financial Action Task Force from time to time relating to combating threats to the integrity of the international financial system.

(2) Schedule 2 makes further provision about regulations under this section.

(3) In this Part—

'money laundering' has the meaning given by section 340(11) of the Proceeds of Crime Act 2002;

'terrorist financing' means an act which constitutes an offence under—

(a) section 15 (fund-raising), 16 (use and possession), 17 (funding arrangements), 18 (money laundering) or 63 (terrorist finance: jurisdiction) of the Terrorism Act 2000,

(b) paragraph 7(2) or (3) of Schedule 3 (freezing orders: offences) to the Anti-terrorism, Crime and Security Act 2001,

(c) regulation 10 (contravention and circumvention of prohibitions) of the ISIL (Da'esh) and Al-Qaida (Asset-Freezing) Regulations 2011 (S.I. 2011/2742), or

(d) section 11 (freezing of funds and economic resources), 12 (making funds or financial services available to designated person), 13 (making funds or financial services available for benefit of designated person), 14 (making economic resources available to designated person), 15 (making economic resources available for benefit of designated person) or 18 (circumventing prohibitions etc) of the Terrorist Asset-Freezing etc Act 2010.

50 Reports on progress towards register of beneficial owners of overseas entities

(1) The Secretary of State must, after the end of each reporting period, publish a report explaining the progress that has been made during that period towards putting in place a register of beneficial owners of overseas entities.

(2) For the purposes of this section, the following are reporting periods—

(a) the period of 12 months beginning with the day on which this Act is passed;

(b) the period of 12 months beginning with the day after the end of the period mentioned in paragraph (a);

(c) the period of 12 months beginning with the day after the end of the period mentioned in paragraph (b).

(3) The first and second reports under this section must include—

(a) a statement setting out the steps that are to be taken in the next reporting period towards putting the register in place, and

(b) an assessment of when the register will be put in place.

(4) The third report under this section must include a statement setting out what further steps, if any, are to be taken towards putting the register in place.

(5) Where a report is published under this section the Secretary of State must lay a copy of it before Parliament.

(6) For the purposes of this section 'a register of beneficial owners of overseas entities' means a public register—

(a) which contains information about overseas entities and persons with significant control over them, and

(b) which in the opinion of the Secretary of State will assist in the prevention of money laundering.

51 Public registers of beneficial ownership of companies registered in British Overseas Territories

(1) For the purposes of the detection, investigation or prevention of money laundering, the Secretary of State must provide all reasonable assistance to the governments of the British

Overseas Territories to enable each of those governments to establish a publicly accessible register of the beneficial ownership of companies registered in each government's jurisdiction.

(2) The Secretary of State must, no later than 31 December 2020, prepare a draft Order in Council requiring the government of any British Overseas Territory that has not introduced a publicly accessible register of the beneficial ownership of companies within its jurisdiction to do so.

(3) The draft Order in Council under subsection (2) must set out the form that the register must take.

(4) If an Order in Council contains requirements of a kind mentioned in subsection (2)—
 (a) it must be laid before Parliament after being made, and
 (b) if not approved by a resolution of each House of Parliament before the end of 28 days beginning with the day on which it is made, it ceases to have effect at the end of that period (but without that affecting the power to make a new Order under this section).

(5) In calculating a period of 28 days for the purposes of subsection (4), no account is to be taken of any time during which Parliament is dissolved or prorogued or during which both Houses are adjourned for more than four days.

(6) For the purposes of this section, 'British Overseas Territories' means a territory listed in Schedule 6 of the British Nationality Act 1981.

(7) For the purposes of this section, 'a publicly accessible register of the beneficial ownership of companies' means a register which, in the opinion of the Secretary of State, provides information broadly equivalent to that available in accordance with the provisions of Part 21A of the Companies Act 2006.

PART 3
GENERAL

Supplementary

52 Crown application

(1) Regulations under section 1 or 49 may make provision binding the Crown.

(2) The regulations may not provide for the Crown to be criminally liable.

(3) Nothing in this Act affects Her Majesty in Her private capacity (within the meaning of the Crown Proceedings Act 1947).

53 Saving for prerogative powers

(1) Nothing in this Act affects any power to exclude a person from the United Kingdom by virtue of the prerogative of the Crown.

(2) Nothing in this Act affects any power exercisable in relation to ships by virtue of the prerogative of the Crown.

54 Regulations: general

(1) Regulations under this Act may—
 (a) make different provision for different purposes;
 (b) confer functions on a prescribed person;
 (c) confer jurisdiction on any court or tribunal.

(2) Regulations under this Act may make supplemental, incidental, consequential, transitional or saving provision, including—
(a) in the case of regulations under section 1 or 49, provision amending, repealing or revoking enactments (whenever passed or made), and
(b) in the case of regulations under section 1 which repeal or revoke an enactment, provision for persons designated by or under that enactment to be treated as persons designated under the regulations.
(3) Regulations under section 1 may amend the definition of 'terrorist financing' in section 49(3) so as to remove any reference to a provision of regulations that is revoked by regulations under section 1.
(4) Regulations under section 1 may amend the definition of 'terrorist financing' in section 49(3) so as to add a reference to a provision of regulations under section 1 that contains an offence, but only if—
(a) each purpose of the regulations containing the offence, as stated under section 1(3), is compliance with a UN obligation or other international obligation, or
(b) paragraph (a) does not apply but the report under section 2 in respect of the regulations containing the offence indicates that, in the opinion of the appropriate Minister making those regulations, the carrying out of a purpose stated in those regulations under section 1(3) would further the prevention of terrorism in the United Kingdom or elsewhere.
(5) Any power under this Act to make regulations is exercisable by statutory instrument.
(6) In this section 'enactment' includes—
(a) an enactment contained in any Order in Council, order, rules, regulations or other instrument made under an Act,
(b) an enactment contained in, or in an instrument made under, an Act of the Scottish Parliament,
(c) an enactment contained in, or in an instrument made under, a Measure or Act of the National Assembly for Wales,
(d) an enactment contained in, or in an instrument made under, Northern Ireland legislation, and
(e) any retained direct EU legislation.
(7) In subsection (2)(b) the reference to persons 'designated' by or under a repealed or revoked enactment includes, where the enactment is retained direct EU legislation, persons listed in or under that enactment.
(8) This section does not apply to regulations under—
(a) section 56 (regulations under section 1: transitory provision), or
(b) section 64 (commencement).

55 Parliamentary procedure for regulations

(1) Subsection (3) applies to a statutory instrument which—
(a) contains non-UN regulations under section 1 (see subsection (7)),
(b) does not contain any UN regulations under that section, and
(c) is not a statutory instrument mentioned in subsection (5)(a) to (d).
(2) Subsection (3) also applies to a statutory instrument which contains only regulations under section 49 which make new provision about high-risk countries (see subsection (9)).
(3) A statutory instrument to which this subsection applies—
(a) must be laid before Parliament after being made, and

(b) if not approved by a resolution of each House of Parliament before the end of 28 days beginning with the day on which it is made, ceases to have effect at the end of that period (but without that affecting anything done under the regulations or the power to make new regulations).

(4) In calculating a period of 28 days for the purposes of subsection (3), no account is to be taken of any time during which Parliament is dissolved or prorogued or during which both Houses are adjourned for more than 4 days.

(5) A statutory instrument containing (whether alone or with other provision)—

(a) regulations under section 1 that repeal, revoke or amend any provision of primary legislation,

(b) regulations under section 47,

(c) regulations under section 48, or

(d) regulations under section 49,

may not be made unless a draft of the instrument has been laid before, and approved by a resolution of, each House of Parliament.

This subsection does not apply to a statutory instrument to which subsection (3) applies by virtue of subsection (2).

(6) A statutory instrument containing regulations under this Act which is not—

(a) a statutory instrument to which subsection (3) applies,

(b) a statutory instrument mentioned in subsection (5)(a) to (d),

(c) a statutory instrument containing only regulations under section 56, or

(d) a statutory instrument containing only regulations under section 64,

is subject to annulment in pursuance of a resolution of either House of Parliament.

(7) In subsection (1) 'UN regulations' means regulations under section 1 that—

(a) are regulations the stated purpose of which, or one of the stated purposes of which, is compliance with a UN obligation, or

(b) amend regulations under section 1 the stated purpose of which, or one of the stated purposes of which, is compliance with a UN obligation,

and 'non-UN regulations' means any regulations under section 1 which are not UN regulations.

(8) For the purposes of subsection (7), a purpose is a 'stated purpose' of regulations under section 1 if it is stated under section 1(3) in the regulations.

(9) For the purposes of subsection (2), regulations under section 49 'make new provision about high-risk countries' if they add or remove an entry in a list of countries in relation to which enhanced customer due diligence measures are required to be taken by virtue of—

(a) the Money Laundering Regulations 2017 (S.I. 2017/692), or

(b) regulations under section 49.

(10) In this section 'primary legislation' means—

(a) an Act of Parliament,

(b) an Act of the Scottish Parliament,

(c) a Measure or Act of the National Assembly for Wales, or

(d) Northern Ireland legislation.

56 Regulations under section 1: transitory provision

(1) If the appropriate Minister making a statutory instrument containing (whether alone or with other provision) any regulations under section 1 considers it is appropriate to do so in consequence of, or otherwise in connection with, the withdrawal of the United Kingdom from the

EU, the instrument may provide that it comes into force, or that any provision of regulations contained in the instrument comes into force, on such day as that Minister may by regulations under this section appoint.

(2) Any power of an appropriate Minister to appoint a day under this section includes—
(a) a power to appoint different days for different purposes, and
(b) a power to appoint a time on a day if that Minister considers it appropriate to do so (including a time that has effect by reference to the coming into force of any other enactment).

(3) Any power under this section to make regulations is exercisable by statutory instrument.

(4) Subsection (5) applies in the case of a statutory instrument—
(a) which contains provision by virtue of subsection (1) of this section, and
(b) to which section 55(3) applies by virtue of subsection (1) of that section.

(5) Where this subsection applies—
(a) the reference in section 55(3)(b) to the day on which the statutory instrument is made is to be read as a reference to the first day on which any provision of the regulations contained in the instrument comes into force for any purpose in accordance with regulations under this section, and
(b) any reference in section 55(3) or (4) to 28 days is to be read as a reference to 60 days.

(6) In this section 'enactment' includes an enactment mentioned in any of paragraphs (a) to (d) of section 54(6).

57 Duties to lay certain reports before Parliament: further provision

(1) In this section 'a reporting provision' means section 2(4), 18(2) or 46(2) or paragraph 21(2) of Schedule 2 (duties to lay before Parliament certain reports relating to regulations).

(2) Where more than one reporting provision applies in relation to particular regulations under section 1, the reports to which those provisions relate may be contained in a single document.

(3) If a reporting provision is not complied with, the appropriate Minister who should have complied with that provision must publish a written statement explaining why that Minister failed to comply with it.

(4) Subsection (5) applies where a reporting provision applies and—
(a) a statutory instrument containing the regulations concerned, or
(b) a draft of such an instrument,
is laid before the House of Commons and House of Lords on different days.

(5) Where this subsection applies, the reporting provision in question is to be read as requiring the laying of a copy of the report to which that provision relates—
(a) before the House of Commons at the time the instrument or draft mentioned in subsection (4) is laid before the House of Commons, and
(b) before the House of Lords at the time that instrument or draft is laid before the House of Lords.

58 Retained EU rights

(1) If and to the extent that anything in the European Union (Withdrawal) Act 2018 would, in the absence of this section, prevent any power within subsection (2) from being exercised so as to modify anything which is retained EU law by virtue of section 4 of that Act (saving for certain rights etc), it does not prevent that power from being so exercised.

(2) The following powers fall within this subsection—
   (a) any power conferred by this Act, or by regulations under this Act, on a Minister of the Crown within the meaning of the Ministers of the Crown Act 1975 (however that power is expressed);
   (b) any power conferred by regulations under Schedule 2 on a supervisory authority.

(3) In this section 'modify' has the same meaning as in the European Union (Withdrawal) Act 2018.

59 Consequential amendments and repeals

(1) Part 1 of the Terrorist Asset-Freezing etc Act 2010 is repealed, except for—
   (a) paragraphs 1 to 5 of Schedule 1 to that Act (amendments of rules of court), and
   (b) section 45(1) of that Act so far as it introduces that Schedule.

(2) Neither paragraphs 1 to 5 of Schedule 1 to that Act, nor the exception of those paragraphs from the repeal made by subsection (1), affects any power to amend or revoke any provision of—
   (a) the Rules of the Court of Judicature (Northern Ireland) 1980 (S.R. 1980/346), or
   (b) the Civil Procedure Rules 1998 (S.I. 1998/3132)).

(3) Subsection (1) does not affect the power in section 54 of the Terrorist Asset-Freezing etc Act 2010 to make provision by Order in Council extending to any of the Channel Islands, the Isle of Man or any British overseas territory.

(4) Part 1 of Schedule 3 contains amendments consequential on Parts 1 and 2 of this Act.

(5) Part 2 of Schedule 3 contains repeals and other provision consequential on subsection (1).

Definitions

60 Meaning of 'funds', 'economic resources' and 'freeze'

(1) In this Act 'funds' means financial assets and benefits of every kind, including (but not limited to)—
   (a) cash, cheques, claims on money, drafts, money orders and other payment instruments;
   (b) deposits, balances on accounts, debts and debt obligations;
   (c) publicly and privately traded securities and debt instruments, including stocks and shares, certificates representing securities, bonds, notes, warrants, debentures and derivative products;
   (d) interest, dividends and other income on or value accruing from or generated by assets;
   (e) credit, rights of set-off, guarantees, performance bonds and other financial commitments;
   (f) letters of credit, bills of lading and bills of sale;
   (g) documents providing evidence of an interest in funds or financial resources;
   (h) any other instrument of export financing.

(2) In this Act 'economic resources' means assets of every kind, whether tangible or intangible, movable or immovable, which are not funds but can be used to obtain funds, goods or services.

(3) In this Act references to 'freezing' funds are to preventing funds from being dealt with; and for the purposes of this subsection funds are 'dealt with' if—
   (a) they are used, altered, moved, or transferred or access is allowed to them,
   (b) they are dealt with in any other way that would result in any change in volume, amount, location, ownership, possession, character or destination, or
   (c) any other change is made that would enable their use, including portfolio management.

(4) In this Act references to 'freezing' economic resources are to preventing economic resources from being dealt with; and for the purposes of this subsection economic resources are 'dealt with' if—
   (a) they are exchanged for funds, goods or services, or
   (b) they are used in exchange for funds, goods or services (whether by being pledged as security or otherwise).

61 Meaning of 'financial services' and 'financial products'

(1) In this Act 'financial services' means any service of a financial nature, including (but not limited to)—
   (a) insurance-related services consisting of—
      (i) direct life assurance;
      (ii) direct insurance other than life assurance;
      (iii) reinsurance and retrocession;
      (iv) insurance intermediation, such as brokerage and agency;
      (v) services auxiliary to insurance, such as consultancy, actuarial, risk assessment and claim settlement services;
   (b) banking and other financial services consisting of—
      (i) accepting deposits and other repayable funds;
      (ii) lending (including consumer credit, mortgage credit, factoring and financing of commercial transactions);
      (iii) financial leasing;
      (iv) payment and money transmission services (including credit, charge and debit cards, travellers' cheques and bankers' drafts);
      (v) providing guarantees or commitments;
      (vi) financial trading (as defined in subsection (2));
      (vii) participating in issues of any kind of securities (including underwriting and placement as an agent, whether publicly or privately) and providing services related to such issues;
      (viii) money brokering;
      (ix) asset management, such as cash or portfolio management, all forms of collective investment management, pension fund management, custodial, depository and trust services;
      (x) settlement and clearing services for financial assets (including securities, derivative products and other negotiable instruments);
      (xi) providing or transferring financial information, and financial data processing or related software (but only by suppliers of other financial services);
      (xii) providing advisory and other auxiliary financial services in respect of any activity listed in sub-paragraphs (i) to (xi) (including credit reference and analysis, investment and portfolio research and advice, advice on acquisitions and on corporate restructuring and strategy).

(2) In subsection (1)(b)(vi), 'financial trading' means trading for own account or for account of customers, whether on an investment exchange, in an over-the—counter market or otherwise, in financial products.

(3) In this Act 'financial products' means—
   (a) money market instruments (including cheques, bills and certificates of deposit);
   (b) foreign exchange;

(c) derivative products (including futures and options);
(d) exchange rate and interest rate instruments (including products such as swaps and forward rate agreements);
(e) transferable securities;
(f) other negotiable instruments and financial assets (including bullion).

62 Interpretation

(1) In this Act—

'appropriate Minister' is to be read in accordance with section 1(9); 'country' includes any territory, region or other place;

'designation power' has the meaning given by section 10(1); 'economic resources' has the meaning given by section 60(2); 'financial products' has the meaning given by section 61(3); 'financial services' has the meaning given by section 61(1);

'freeze', in relation to funds or economic resources, has the meaning given by section 60(3) and (4);

'funds' has the meaning given by section 60(1);

'international obligation' has the meaning given by section 1(8); 'person' has the meaning given by section 9(5);

'prescribed', in any provision relating to regulations, means prescribed by the regulations;

'retained direct EU legislation' has the same meaning as in the European Union (Withdrawal) Act 2018;

'retained EU law' has the same meaning as in that Act;

'the Security Council' means the Security Council of the United Nations; 'the territorial sea' (without more) means the territorial sea adjacent to the
United Kingdom;

'terrorism' has the same meaning as in the Terrorism Act 2000 (see section 1(1) to (4) of that Act);

'UN obligation' has the meaning given by section 1(8);

'UN Security Council Resolution' has the meaning given by section 1(8).

(2) Any reference in this Act to a person named 'for the purposes of' a UN Security Council Resolution so far as it provides for the taking of particular measures includes any person who, by virtue of—
(a) being named for any purposes by the Security Council or a subsidiary organ of the Security Council, and
(b) the terms of the resolution,

is a person in relation to whom the resolution provides for the measures to be taken.

(3) Any reference in this Act to ships designated 'for purposes of' a UN Security Council Resolution which provides for the taking of measures in relation to ships includes any ship which, by virtue of—
(a) being designated for any purposes by the Security Council or a subsidiary organ of the Security Council, and
(b) the terms of the resolution,

is a ship in relation to which the resolution provides for the measures to be taken.

(4) Regulations under section 1 may make provision as to the meaning of any reference in the regulations to funds, economic resources or technology (or a particular description of funds, economic resources or technology) being—
(a) owned by a person,

(b) held by a person,
(c) controlled by a person, or
(d) made available to or for the benefit of a person.

(5) Regulations under section 1 may make provision as to the meaning of any reference in the regulations to a person 'owning' or 'controlling' another person.

(6) Regulations under section 1 may make provision as to the connection that is required between—
(a) a person, or a person of a prescribed description, and
(b) a country,
in order for the person to be regarded as 'connected with' that country for the purposes of any provision of the regulations.

Final provisions

63 Extent

(1) Subject to the following provisions of this section, this Act extends to England and Wales, Scotland and Northern Ireland.

(2) Any amendment or repeal made by Schedule 3 of any provision of—
(a) the Senior Courts Act 1981,
(b) the Crime and Courts Act 2013, or
(c) the Charities Act 2011,
does not extend to Scotland or Northern Ireland.

(3) Her Majesty may by Order in Council provide for any of the provisions of Part 1, section 51 and this Part, or any regulations under Part 1 (whether made before or after the making of the Order in Council), to extend with or without modifications to—
(a) any of the Channel Islands;
(b) the Isle of Man;
(c) any of the British overseas territories.

(4) The power conferred by subsection (3), so far as relating to regulations, includes power to provide for the regulations as amended from time to time to extend as mentioned in that subsection.

(5) Her Majesty may by Order in Council provide for the repeal in section 59(1) (repeal of provisions of the Terrorist Asset-Freezing etc Act 2010) to extend to—
(a) any of the Channel Islands;
(b) the Isle of Man;
(c) any of the British overseas territories.

(6) The power under section 36 of the Immigration Act 1971 may be exercised so as to extend to any of the Channel Islands or the Isle of Man any amendment made by this Act of any part of that Act (with or without modifications).

(7) The power under section 272(6) of the Investigatory Powers Act 2016 may be exercised so as to extend to the Isle of Man or any of the British overseas territories any amendment made by this Act of any part of that Act (with or without modifications).

64 Commencement

(1) The following provisions come into force on the day on which this Act is passed—
(a) section 32;
(b) section 50;
(c) sections 52 to 56;
(d) sections 60 to 63;

(e) this section;

(f) section 65.

(2) The remaining provisions of this Act come into force on such day as the Secretary of State may by regulations appoint.

(3) Different days may be appointed for different purposes.

(4) The Secretary of State may by regulations make transitional or saving provision in connection with the coming into force of any provision of this Act.

(5) Any power under this section to make regulations is exercisable by statutory instrument.

65 Short title

This Act may be cited as the Sanctions and Anti-Money Laundering Act 2018.

SCHEDULES

SCHEDULE 1

Section 5

TRADE SANCTIONS

PART 1

TRADE SANCTIONS

1 The purposes referred to in section 5(1) are the purposes set out in paragraphs 2 to 16.

2 Preventing the export of goods of a prescribed description—

(a) to, or for the benefit of—

(i) designated persons (see section 9),

(ii) persons connected with a prescribed country, or

(iii) a prescribed description of persons connected with a prescribed country, or

(b) to, for the benefit of, or for use in, a prescribed country.

3 Preventing the import of all goods, or of goods of a prescribed description—

(a) which are consigned from a prescribed country,

(b) which originate in a prescribed country,

(c) which are consigned from or imported, manufactured, produced or owned by—

(i) designated persons,

(ii) persons connected with a prescribed country, or

(iii) a prescribed description of persons connected with a prescribed country,

(d) for the benefit of—

(i) designated persons,

(ii) persons connected with a prescribed country, or

(iii) a prescribed description of persons connected with a prescribed country, or

(e) for the benefit of a prescribed country.

4 Preventing the movement outside the United Kingdom of goods of a prescribed description—

(a) to, or for the benefit of—

(i) designated persons,

(ii) persons connected with a prescribed country, or

(iii) a prescribed description of persons connected with a prescribed country,

(b) to, or for the benefit of, a prescribed country,
(c) from a prescribed country,
(d) which originate in a prescribed country, or
(e) in specified ships (see section 14).

5 Preventing a transfer of technology of a prescribed description—
(a) to, or for the benefit of—
(i) designated persons,
(ii) persons connected with a prescribed country, or
(iii) a prescribed description of persons connected with a prescribed country,
(b) to a place (see paragraph 36) in a prescribed country,
(c) to, or for the benefit of, persons outside the United Kingdom, where the transfer is from a designated person, a person connected with a prescribed country or a place in a prescribed country,
(d) to a place outside the United Kingdom, where the transfer is from a designated person, a person connected with a prescribed country or a place in a prescribed country,
(e) to persons (other than designated persons) in the United Kingdom, where the person effecting, or responsible for, the transfer has reason to believe that the technology may be used in a prescribed country, or
(f) to a place in the United Kingdom, where the person effecting, or responsible for, the transfer has reason to believe that the technology may be used in a prescribed country.

6 Preventing goods or technology of a prescribed description from being made available—
(a) to, or for the benefit of—
(i) designated persons,
(ii) persons connected with a prescribed country, or
(iii) a prescribed description of persons connected with a prescribed country,
(b) for the benefit of, or for use in, a prescribed country, or
(c) for use in connection with specified ships.

7 Preventing the acquisition of goods or technology of a prescribed description—
(a) from, or for the benefit of—
(i) designated persons,
(ii) persons connected with a prescribed country,
(iii) a prescribed description of persons connected with a prescribed country, or
(iv) persons on board specified ships, or
(b) in, or which originate in, a prescribed country.

8 Preventing land, or land of a prescribed description, from being made available to, or for the benefit of—
(a) designated persons,
(b) persons connected with a prescribed country, or
(c) a prescribed description of persons connected with a prescribed country.

9 Preventing the acquisition of land, or land of a prescribed description—
(a) from, or for the benefit of—
(i) designated persons,
(ii) persons connected with a prescribed country, or
(iii) a prescribed description of persons connected with a prescribed country, or
(b) in a prescribed country.

10 Preventing—
(a) activities of a prescribed description relating (directly or indirectly) to military activities from being carried on for the benefit of—

(i) designated persons,
(ii) persons connected with a prescribed country, or
(iii) a prescribed description of persons connected with a prescribed country, or

(b) activities of a prescribed description from being carried on, where the activities relate (directly or indirectly) to military activities carried on, or proposed to be carried on, in a prescribed country.

11 Preventing all services, or services of a prescribed description, from being provided—

(a) to, or for the benefit of—
(i) designated persons,
(ii) persons connected with a prescribed country, or
(iii) a prescribed description of persons connected with a prescribed country, or

(b) in the United Kingdom by a prescribed description of persons connected with a prescribed country.

12 Preventing all services, or services of a prescribed description, from being procured—

(a) from, or for the benefit of—
(i) designated persons,
(ii) persons connected with a prescribed country, or
(iii) a prescribed description of persons connected with a prescribed country, or

(b) for provision in a prescribed country.

13 Preventing services, or services of a prescribed description, from being provided or procured, where the services relate to

(a) the export of goods of a prescribed description to, or for the benefit of, persons as mentioned in paragraph 2(a),
(b) the export of goods of a prescribed description to, for the benefit of, or for use in, a prescribed country,
(c) the import of goods, or goods of a prescribed description, which are consigned from, or originate in, a prescribed country,
(d) the import of goods, or goods of a prescribed description, which are consigned from or imported, manufactured, produced or owned by persons as mentioned in paragraph 3(c),
(e) the import of goods, or goods of a prescribed description, for the benefit of persons as mentioned in paragraph 3(d),
(f) the import of goods, or goods of a prescribed description, for the benefit of a prescribed country,
(g) the movement of goods of a prescribed description to, or for the benefit of, persons as mentioned in paragraph 4(a),
(h) the movement of goods of a prescribed description to, or for the benefit of, a prescribed country,
(i) the movement of goods of a prescribed description from a prescribed country, or which originate in a prescribed country,
(j) the movement of goods of a prescribed description in specified ships,
(k) the transfer of technology of a prescribed description to, or for the benefit of, persons as mentioned in sub-paragraph (a), (c) or (e) of paragraph 5,
(l) the transfer of technology of a prescribed description to a place as mentioned in sub-paragraph (b), (d) or (f) of paragraph 5,
(m) the making available of goods or technology of a prescribed description to, or for the benefit of, persons as mentioned in paragraph 6(a),
(n) the making available of goods or technology of a prescribed description for the benefit of, or for use in, a prescribed country,

(o) the making available of goods or technology of a prescribed description for use in connection with specified ships,
(p) the acquisition of goods or technology of a prescribed description from, or for the benefit of, persons as mentioned in paragraph 7(a),
(q) the acquisition of goods or technology of a prescribed description in, or which originate in, a prescribed country,
(r) the making available of land, or land of a prescribed description, to, or for the benefit of, persons as mentioned in paragraph 8,
(s) the acquisition of land, or land of a prescribed description, from, or for the benefit of, persons as mentioned in paragraph 9(a),
(t) the acquisition of land, or land of a prescribed description, in a prescribed country,
(u) the carrying on of activities of a prescribed description as mentioned in sub-paragraph (a) of paragraph 10 for the benefit of persons as mentioned in that sub-paragraph,
(v) the carrying on of activities of a prescribed description as mentioned in paragraph 10(b), or
(w) the provision or procurement of other services, or services of a prescribed description, which relate to a matter mentioned in any of sub-paragraphs (a) to (v).

14 Preventing services, or services of a prescribed description, from being provided or procured, where the services relate to—
(a) the provision of other services, or services of a prescribed description, to, or for the benefit of, persons as mentioned in paragraph 11(a),
(b) the provision of other services, or services of a prescribed description, in the United Kingdom by a prescribed description of persons connected with a prescribed country,
(c) the procurement of other services, or services of a prescribed description, from, or for the benefit of, persons as mentioned in paragraph 12(a),
(d) the procurement of other services, or services of a prescribed description, for provision in a prescribed country,
(e) projects, industries, sectors or infrastructure of a prescribed description in a prescribed country,
(f) activities of a prescribed description carried on, or proposed to be carried on, in a prescribed country,
(g) trade with a prescribed country,
(h) aircraft registered in a prescribed country,
(i) ships registered in a prescribed country,
(j) specified ships, or
(k) the provision or procurement of other services, or services of a prescribed description, which relate to a matter mentioned in any of sub-paragraphs (e) to (j).

15 So far as a UN Security Council Resolution provides for the taking of measures in relation to ships designated for purposes of that resolution, and so far as the purposes set out in this paragraph are relevant to that resolution, preventing—
(a) the movement outside the United Kingdom of goods of a prescribed description in such ships,
(b) goods or technology of a prescribed description from being made available for use in connection with such ships,
(c) the acquisition of goods or technology of a prescribed description from persons on board such ships, or
(d) the provision or procurement of services which relate to such ships.

16 Preventing—
(a) the export, import, movement, making available or acquisition of objects of cultural interest, or objects of cultural interest of a prescribed description, which have been removed from a prescribed country, or
(b) services of a prescribed description from being provided or procured, where the services relate to objects of cultural interest, or objects of cultural interest of a prescribed description, which have been removed from a prescribed country.

PART 2
FURTHER PROVISION

Further provision

17 Regulations which include provision for a purpose mentioned in Part 1 may describe goods wholly or partly by reference to—
(a) the uses to which the goods, or any information recorded on or derived from them, may be put,
(b) the types of users of the goods, or of any such information,
(c) the industries, sectors, infrastructure or projects to which the goods, or any such information, may relate, or
(d) the place where the goods originate.

18 Regulations which include provision for a purpose mentioned in paragraph 2 or 3 may describe goods wholly or partly by reference to their being of an amount, quantity or value in excess of a prescribed amount, quantity or value.

19 Regulations which include provision for a purpose mentioned in Part 1 may describe technology wholly or partly by reference to—
(a) the uses to which the technology may be put,
(b) the industries, sectors, infrastructure or projects to which the technology may relate, or
(c) any activities carried on, or proposed to be carried on, to which the technology may relate.

20 Regulations which include provision for a purpose mentioned in Part 1 may describe services wholly or partly by reference to—
(a) the uses to which the services may be put,
(b) the industries, sectors, infrastructure or projects to which the services may relate,
(c) any goods, technology or land to which the services may relate,
(d) any activities carried on, or proposed to be carried on, to which the services may relate (including the export, import, movement, transfer, making available, acquisition, development, manufacture, production, maintenance or use of goods, technology or land), or
(e) any other services to which the services in question may relate.

21 Regulations which include provision for a purpose mentioned in Part 1 may include provision having the effect that references to specified provisions of orders made under the Export Control Act 2002 are to operate as references to specified provisions of such orders as amended from time to time.

22 Regulations which include provision for a purpose mentioned in Part 1 may include provision having the effect that references to a specified Annex of Council Regulation (EC) No 428/2009 of 5 May 2009 (setting up a Community regime for the control of exports, transfer, brokering and transit of dual-use items) are to operate as references to that Annex as amended from time to time.

23 Regulations which include provision for a purpose mentioned in Part 1 may include provision having the effect that references to a technical list of goods or technology (including a list by reference to which any UN obligation operates) are to operate as references to that list as revised or re-issued from time to time.

24 Regulations which include provision for a purpose mentioned in paragraph 2 may include provision in relation to the removal from the United Kingdom of vehicles, ships and aircraft (as an export of goods), whether or not they are moving under their own power or carrying goods or passengers.

25 Regulations which include provision for a purpose mentioned in paragraph 3 may include provision in relation to the taking into the United Kingdom of vehicles, ships and aircraft (as an import of goods), whether or not they are moving under their own power or carrying goods or passengers.

26 (1) This paragraph applies where regulations include provision for a purpose mentioned in paragraph 15 in relation to ships designated by the Security Council or a subsidiary organ of the Security Council for purposes of a UN Security Council Resolution.

(2) The provision may describe the ships by reference to the instrument in which the ships are designated, including by reference to that instrument as varied or supplemented from time to time.

Enforcement

27 (1) This paragraph applies in relation to any provision of CEMA which specifies a maximum period of imprisonment with which an offence is punishable on conviction on indictment.

(2) Regulations under this paragraph may modify any such provision in the case of an offence committed in connection with a prohibition or requirement—

(a) imposed for a purpose mentioned in Part 1, and

(b) specified in the regulations.

(3) The modification may not have the effect that such an offence is punishable with imprisonment for a period exceeding 10 years.

28 (1) For the purpose of the enforcement of any relevant prohibition or requirement, regulations under this paragraph may modify any provision of CEMA which—

(a) determines whether any thing is liable to forfeiture under CEMA by virtue of a contravention of the prohibition or requirement,

(b) provides for the treatment of any thing which is so liable by virtue of such a contravention, or

(c) confers any power exercisable in relation to a ship, aircraft or vehicle.

(2) In sub-paragraph (1) a 'relevant prohibition or requirement' means a prohibition or requirement—

(a) imposed for a purpose mentioned in Part 1, and

(b) specified in the regulations under this paragraph.

Restriction

29 Regulations may not contain prohibitions for a purpose mentioned in Part 1 which have the effect of prohibiting any of the following activities—

(a) the communication of information in the ordinary course of scientific research,

(b) the making of information generally available to the public, or

(c) the communication of information that is generally available to the public, unless the interference by the regulations in the freedom to carry on the activity in question is necessary (and no more than is necessary).

30 The question whether any such interference is necessary is to be determined by the appropriate Minister making the regulations—
(a) by reference to the circumstances prevailing at the time the regulations are made, and
(b) having considered the purpose of the regulations as stated under section 1(3) and the need to respect the freedom to carry on that activity.

Interpretation

31 In this Schedule, any reference to goods, technology, land or services being moved, made available, acquired, provided or procured is to their being moved, made available, acquired, provided or procured (as the case may be) directly or indirectly.

32 For the purposes of this Schedule—
(a) 'export' means export from the United Kingdom,
(b) goods removed to the Isle of Man from the United Kingdom are not to be regarded as exported, and
(c) goods transported out of the United Kingdom by aircraft or ship as stores within the meaning of CEMA (see section 1(1) and (4) of that Act) are to be regarded as exported.

33 For the purposes of this Schedule—
(a) 'import' means import into the United Kingdom, but
(b) goods removed to the United Kingdom from the Isle of Man are not to be regarded as imported.

Sub-paragraph (a) does not apply for the purposes of paragraph 34.

34 Paragraph 33(b) does not apply to goods imported into the Isle of Man in contravention of any prohibition or requirement and which are of a description the import of which into the United Kingdom is subject to a corresponding prohibition or requirement imposed by regulations for a purpose mentioned in paragraph 3.

35 For the purposes of this Schedule—
(a) goods, technology or land are 'acquired' by a person if the person buys, leases, hires, borrows or accepts as a gift the goods, technology or land (as the case may be), and 'acquisition' is to be construed accordingly, and
(b) a reference to goods which 'originate' in a country includes a reference to goods which are manufactured or produced in that country.

36 In paragraph 5 'place' includes—
(a) any vehicle, ship or aircraft,
(b) any installation (including a floating installation or one resting on the seabed or its subsoil or on other land covered with water or its subsoil), or
(c) any tent or movable structure.

37 In this Schedule—
'aircraft' includes unmanned aircraft and aircraft capable of spaceflight activities;
'CEMA' means the Customs and Excise Management Act 1979; 'objects of cultural interest' includes objects of historical or scientific
interest;
'regulations' means regulations under section 1;
'ship' includes every description of vessel (including a hovercraft) used in navigation;
'specified ship' has the meaning given by section 14;

'technology' means information (including information comprised in software) that is capable of use in connection with—

(a) the development, production or use of any goods or software, or

(b) the development of, or the carrying out of, an industrial or commercial activity or an activity of any other kind whatsoever;

'transfer', in relation to any technology, means a transfer by any means (or combination of means), including oral communication and the transfer of goods on which the technology is recorded or from which it can be derived, other than the export of such goods.

38 Nothing in section 3 prevents any reference to services in this Schedule from including financial services.

SCHEDULE 2

Section 49

MONEY LAUNDERING AND TERRORIST FINANCING ETC

Regulations under section 49

1 Without prejudice to the generality of section 49, regulations under that section may do any thing mentioned in paragraphs 2 to 17.

2 (1) Require—

(a) the Secretary of State or the Treasury, or both of them acting jointly,

(b) supervisory authorities (within the meaning given by paragraph 24), and

(c) such persons carrying on relevant business (within the meaning given by that paragraph) as are prescribed for the purposes of this paragraph,

to identify and assess risks relating to money laundering, terrorist financing or other threats to the integrity of the international financial system.

(2) Make provision about factors to be taken into account in the assessment of such risks.

3 Require any person carrying on relevant business who is of a description prescribed for the purposes of this paragraph ('a relevant person') to have policies, controls and procedures which—

(a) are policies, controls and procedures for mitigating and managing risks relating to money laundering, terrorist financing or other threats to the integrity of the international financial system,

(b) are of prescribed kinds, and

(c) are appropriate having regard to the size and nature of the business that the person carries on.

4 Require relevant persons to take prescribed measures in relation to their customers in prescribed circumstances.

5 Make provision for and in connection with—

(a) the provision of information by prescribed persons, and

(b) the disclosure of information, including provision about—

(i) the purposes for which information held in connection with anything done under the regulations may be used, and

(ii) the persons to whom any such information may be disclosed.

6 Make provision for and in connection with the creation, production and retention of—

(a) registers, and

(b) records,

including registers of people with significant control and registers and records relating to the beneficial ownership of prescribed entities, trusts or other arrangements.

7 (1) Confer supervisory functions on the Financial Conduct Authority, the Commissioners for Her Majesty's Revenue and Customs and such other bodies as may be prescribed ('supervisory authorities') in relation to relevant persons, including powers or duties to—
(a) collect information,
(b) give directions,
(c) issue guidance,
(d) approve individuals in their capacity as relevant persons or as owner of, or in positions of control over or responsibility in, relevant persons that are not individuals, and
(e) cooperate with other supervisory authorities or other prescribed persons.
(2) Make provision about the exercise of functions conferred on supervisory authorities under sub-paragraph (1).

8 (1) Confer supervisory functions on a prescribed body (an 'oversight body') in relation to bodies prescribed as, or seeking to be prescribed as, supervisory authorities, including powers or duties to—
(a) collect information,
(b) give directions,
(c) issue guidance, and
(d) give recommendations as to whether bodies should be, or should cease to be, prescribed as supervisory authorities.
(2) Make provision about the exercise of functions conferred on an oversight body under sub-paragraph (1).

9 Make provision for and in connection with the registration of relevant persons by supervisory authorities, including—
(a) provision which prohibits a person from carrying on a business of a prescribed description unless registered, and
(b) provision about the suspension or cancellation of a person's registration.

10 Make provision enabling supervisory authorities to enter into arrangements with other bodies for the purposes of the enforcement of the regulations.

11 (1) Confer investigatory powers on—
(a) supervisory authorities, and
(b) prescribed enforcement partners within the meaning given by paragraph 24.
(2) Make provision about the exercise of investigatory powers.
(3) Make provision enabling investigatory powers to be exercised by a supervisory authority in relation to persons supervised by another supervisory authority.
(4) In this paragraph 'investigatory powers' includes powers of entry, search, inspection, seizure of documents or information and retention of documents or information.

12 (1) Authorise supervisory authorities to impose charges on persons supervised by them in respect of expenses incurred for the purposes of the regulations.
(2) Make provision in connection with any charges for which provision is made under sub-paragraph (1), including provision for charges to meet expenses incurred by enforcement partners for the purposes of the regulations.
(3) Where provision is made by virtue of paragraph 11(3), authorise supervisory authorities to impose charges on other supervisory authorities in respect of expenses incurred in relation to the exercise of powers in accordance with such provision.

(4) Authorise an oversight body to impose charges on supervisory authorities or persons seeking to be prescribed as supervisory authorities in respect of the exercise by the oversight body of functions conferred on it by the regulations.

(5) Make provision in connection with any charges for which provision is made under sub-paragraph (3) or (4).

13 (1) Authorise the Financial Conduct Authority and the Commissioners for Her Majesty's Revenue and Customs to impose civil monetary penalties in relation to the contravention of prescribed requirements.

(2) Authorise supervisory authorities to impose civil penalties (other than monetary penalties) in relation to the contravention of prescribed requirements, including—

(a) the publication of statements of censure,

(b) the suspension or revocation of, or restrictions on, any permission or authorisation granted by a supervisory authority,

(c) the suspension or cancellation of, or restrictions on, a person's registration as mentioned in paragraph 9, and

(d) restrictions on the holding of management responsibilities.

(3) Authorise an oversight body to—

(a) impose civil monetary penalties, and

(b) publish statements of censure,

in relation to the contravention of prescribed requirements by supervisory authorities.

(4) Make provision in connection with any civil penalties for which provision is made under sub-paragraph (1), (2) or (3), including provision for publishing details of persons who have incurred penalties.

14 Make provision for and in connection with the grant of injunctions (or, in Scotland, interdicts) and other orders by prescribed courts in relation to the contravention of prescribed requirements.

15 Make provision—

(a) creating criminal offences for the purposes of the enforcement of requirements imposed by or under regulations under section 49, and

(b) dealing with matters relating to any offences created for such purposes by regulations under section 49,

but see paragraphs 18 and 19.

16 Make provision for and in connection with reviews of, and appeals against, decisions of—

(a) prescribed supervisory authorities, and

(b) an oversight body.

17 Make provision exempting prescribed persons from prescribed requirements, generally or in prescribed circumstances.

Criminal offences: restrictions and relationship with civil penalties

18 Regulations under section 49 may not provide for an offence created by such regulations to be punishable with imprisonment for a period exceeding—

(a) in the case of conviction on indictment, 2 years;

(b) in the case of summary conviction, 3 months.

19 Regulations under section 49 may provide for the creation of a criminal offence only if the regulations also provide for either or both of the following in relation to the offence—

(a) a mental element necessary for its commission;

(b) a defence to it (for example, a defence grounded on a person's knowledge or belief, or a defence that a person took all reasonable steps and exercised all due diligence).

20 Regulations under section 49 which confer a power to impose a civil monetary penalty must provide that a person is not liable to such a penalty in respect of acts or omissions for which the person has been convicted of a criminal offence created by such regulations.

Criminal offences: report in respect of offences in regulations

21 (1) In this paragraph 'relevant regulations' means regulations under section 49 which create any offence for the purposes of the enforcement of any requirements imposed by or under regulations under section 49.

(2) The appropriate Minister making any relevant regulations ('the Minister') must at the required time lay before Parliament a report which—

(a) specifies the offences created by the regulations, indicating the requirements to which those offences relate,

(b) states that the Minister considers that there are good reasons for those requirements to be enforceable by criminal proceedings and explains why the Minister is of that opinion, and

(c) in the case of any of those offences which are punishable with imprisonment—

(i) states the maximum terms of imprisonment that apply to those offences,

(ii) states that the Minister considers that there are good reasons for those maximum terms, and

(iii) explains why the Minister is of that opinion.

(3) Sub-paragraph (4) applies where an offence created by the regulations relates to particular requirements and the Minister considers that a good reason—

(a) for those requirements to be enforceable by criminal proceedings, or

(b) for a particular maximum term of imprisonment to apply to that offence,

is consistency with another enactment relating to the enforcement of similar requirements.

(4) The report must identify that other enactment.

(5) In sub-paragraph (3) 'another enactment' means any provision of or made under an Act, other than a provision of the regulations to which the report relates.

(6) In sub-paragraph (2) 'the required time' means the same time as the draft of the statutory instrument containing the regulations is laid before Parliament.

(7) This paragraph applies to regulations which amend other regulations under section 49 so as to create an offence as it applies to regulations which otherwise create an offence.

Extra-territorial application

22 (1) Regulations under section 49 may impose requirements in relation to conduct outside the United Kingdom by a United Kingdom person.

(2) In sub-paragraph (1) 'United Kingdom person' means—

(a) a United Kingdom national,

(b) a body incorporated or constituted under the law of any part of the United Kingdom, or

(c) a body within paragraph (3) or (4) of regulation 9 of the Money Laundering Regulations 2017 (bodies to be regarded for the purposes of those Regulations as carrying on business in the United Kingdom)', as that regulation has effect immediately before it is saved by section 2 of the European Union (Withdrawal) Act 2018.

(3) For this purpose a United Kingdom national is an individual who is—
(a) a British citizen, a British overseas territories citizen, a British National (Overseas) or a British Overseas citizen,
(b) a person who under the British Nationality Act 1981 is a British subject, or
(c) a British protected person within the meaning of that Act.
(4) In this paragraph 'conduct' includes acts and omissions.

Money Laundering Regulations 2017

23 (1) Without prejudice to anything in section 49, paragraphs 1 to 22 or section 54(2), regulations under section 49 may—
(a) subject to any modifications the appropriate Minister making those regulations considers appropriate, make provision corresponding or similar to any provision of retained money laundering Regulations as those Regulations have effect immediately after being saved by section 2 or 3 of the European Union (Withdrawal) Act 2018;
(b) amend or revoke any retained money laundering Regulations.
(2) In sub-paragraph (1) 'retained money laundering Regulations' means—
(a) the Money Laundering Regulations 2017;
(b) Regulation (EU) 2015/847 of the European Parliament and of the Council of 20 May 2015 on information accompanying transfers of funds;
(c) any provision made under Directive (EU) 2015/849 of the European Parliament and of the Council of 20 May 2015 on the prevention of the use of the financial system for the purposes of money laundering or terrorist financing by virtue of Article 290 or 291(2) of the Treaty on the Functioning of the European Union.
(3) In paragraph 15 (offences), any reference to regulations under section 49 includes the Money Laundering Regulations 2017.
(4) In paragraph 21 (report in respect of offences)—
(a) the reference in sub-paragraph (1) to requirements imposed by or under regulations under section 49 includes requirements imposed by or under the Money Laundering Regulations 2017, and
(b) the reference in sub-paragraph (7) to other regulations under section 49 includes the Money Laundering Regulations 2017.

Interpretation

24 In this Schedule—
'enforcement partners' means bodies with which supervisory authorities enter into arrangements for the purposes of the enforcement of regulations under section 49;
'money laundering' has the meaning given by section 49;
'Money Laundering Regulations 2017' means the Money Laundering, Terrorist Financing and Transfer of Funds (Information on the Payer) Regulations 2017 (S.I. 2017/692);
'oversight body' means a body on which functions are conferred under paragraph 8(1);
'relevant business' means business of a kind which entails risks relating to money laundering, terrorist financing or other threats to the integrity of the financial system;
'relevant person' means a person on whom requirements are imposed under paragraph 3;
'requirements' includes prohibitions;

'supervisory authority' means the Financial Conduct Authority, the Commissioners for Her Majesty's Revenue and Customs or any other body on which functions are conferred under paragraph 7(1);
'terrorist financing' has the meaning given by section 49.

SCHEDULE 3

Section 59(4) and (5)

CONSEQUENTIAL AMENDMENTS

PART 1
AMENDMENTS CONSEQUENTIAL ON PARTS 1 AND 2

Immigration Act 1971 (c. 77)

1 (1) Section 8B of the Immigration Act 1971 (persons excluded from the United Kingdom under international obligations) is amended as follows.
(2) In the heading for 'international obligations' substitute 'certain instruments'.
(3) For subsection (4) substitute—

'(4) "Excluded person" means—
(a) a person named by or under, or of a description specified in, an instrument falling within subsection (5), or
(b) a person who under regulations under section 1 of the Sanctions and Anti-Money Laundering Act 2018 is an excluded person for the purposes of this section (see section 4 of that Act).'

(4) In subsection (5A)(b), for the words from the beginning to 'that subsection' substitute 'the person is within subsection (4)(a) and not within subsection (4)(b)
and has been exempted from the application of subsection (1), (2) or (3), as the case may be,'.
(5) After subsection (5A) insert—

"(5B) In relation to any person within subsection (4)(b), subsections (1) to (3) are subject to any exception created under, or direction given by virtue of, section 15(4) of the Sanctions and Anti-Money Laundering Act 2018 (power to create exceptions etc)."

Senior Courts Act 1981 (c. 54)

2 In paragraph 2 of Schedule 1 to the Senior Courts Act 1981 (business allocated to the Queen's Bench Division), after sub-paragraph (be) insert—

'(bf) all proceedings—
(i) on an application under section 38 of the Sanctions and Anti-Money Laundering Act 2018 (court review of decisions), or
(ii) on a claim arising from any matter to which such an application relates;'."

Regulation of Investigatory Powers Act 2000 (c. 23)

3 (1) Section 18 of the Regulation of Investigatory Powers Act 2000 (exceptions to matters excluded from legal proceedings) is amended as follows.
(2) In subsection (1), after paragraph (de) insert—

'(df) any proceedings—
(i) on an application under section 38 of the Sanctions and Anti-Money Laundering Act 2018 (court review of decisions), or
(ii) on a claim arising from any matter to which such an application relates,
or any proceedings arising out of such proceedings;'.

(3) In subsection (2), after paragraph (zd) insert—

'(ze) in the case of proceedings falling within paragraph (df), to—
(i) a person, other than the Secretary of State or the Treasury (as the case may be), who is or was a party to the proceedings, or
(ii) any person who for the purposes of the proceedings (but otherwise than by virtue of appointment as a special advocate) represents a person falling within sub—paragraph (i);'.

Serious Organised Crime and Police Act 2005 (c. 15)

4 In section 61(1) of the Serious Organised Crime and Police Act 2005 (offences to which investigatory powers etc apply), after paragraph (i) insert—
'(j) any offence under regulations under section 1 of the Sanctions and Anti-Money Laundering Act 2018 (sanctions regulations) which is specified by those regulations by virtue of section 17(8) of that Act.'

Serious Crime Act 2007 (c. 27)

5 (1) Schedule 1 to the Serious Crime Act 2007 (offences in relation to which a serious crime prevention order may be made) is amended as follows.
(2) In paragraph 13B after sub-paragraph (5) insert—

"(5A) An offence under regulations made under section 1 of the Sanctions and Anti-Money Laundering Act 2018."

(3) In paragraph 16MA after sub-paragraph (5) insert—

"(5A) An offence under regulations made under section 1 of the Sanctions and Anti-Money Laundering Act 2018."

(4) In paragraph 29A after sub-paragraph (5) insert—

"(5A) An offence under regulations made under section 1 of the Sanctions and Anti-Money Laundering Act 2018."

(5) In the italic headings before each of paragraphs 13B, 16MA and 29A, omit 'Financial'.

Crime and Courts Act 2013 (c. 22)

6 (1) Part 2 of Schedule 17 to the Crime and Courts Act 2013 (offences in relation to which a deferred prosecution agreement may be entered into) is amended as follows.
(2) In paragraph 26A, after sub-paragraph (5) insert—

"(5A) An offence under regulations made under section 1 of the Sanctions and Anti-Money Laundering Act 2018 (sanctions regulations)."

(3) After paragraph 27 insert—

"27A An offence under regulations made under section 49 of the Sanctions and Anti-Money Laundering Act 2018 (money laundering and terrorist financing etc)."

Investigatory Powers Act 2016 (c. 25)

7 In Schedule 3 to the Investigatory Powers Act 2016 (exceptions to section 56), after paragraph 9 insert—

"*Sanctions proceedings*

9A (1) Section 56(1) does not apply in relation to any proceedings—

(a) on an application under section 38 of the Sanctions and Anti-Money Laundering Act 2018 (court review of decisions), or

(b) on a claim arising from any matter to which such an application relates,

or any proceedings arising out of such proceedings.

(2) But sub-paragraph (1) does not permit the disclosure of anything to—

(a) any person, other than the Secretary of State or the Treasury (as the case may be), who is or was a party to the proceedings, or

(b) any person who—

(i) represents such a person for the purposes of the proceedings, and

(ii) does so otherwise than by virtue of appointment as a special advocate."

Policing and Crime Act 2017 (c. 3)

8 (1) Part 8 of the Policing and Crime Act 2017 (financial sanctions) is amended as follows.

(2) In section 143(4) (meaning of 'financial sanctions legislation') after paragraph (e) insert—

"(f) a provision of regulations made under section 1 of the Sanctions and Anti-Money Laundering Act 2018 that contains a prohibition or requirement imposed for a purpose mentioned in section 3(1) or (2) of that Act."

(3) After section 143(4) insert—

"(4A) But "financial sanctions legislation" does not include any provision of regulations made under section 1 of the Sanctions and Anti-Money Laundering Act 2018 which is specified in the regulations as a provision to be regarded as not being financial sanctions legislation for the purposes of this Part."

(4) Omit sections 152 to 156 (avoidance of delay: temporary regulations).

PART 2
REPEALS ETC CONSEQUENTIAL ON REPEALS IN TERRORIST ASSET-FREEZING ETC ACT 2010

Repeals and revocations

9 The following provisions are repealed or revoked—

Title	*Extent of repeal or revocation*
Senior Courts Act 1981	In Schedule 1, paragraph 2(bc).
Regulation of Investigatory Powers Act 2000	In section 18, subsection (1)(dc) and, in subsection (2)(zb), the words "or (dc)".
Counter-Terrorism Act 2008	Section 28(2)(d).
Charities Act 2011	In section 178(1), in Case J, paragraph (a).

Title	*Extent of repeal or revocation*
Electronic Money Regulations 2011 (S.I. 2011/99)	In regulation 13(8)(d), the words "the Terrorist Asset-Freezing etc Act 2010,".
Legal Aid, Sentencing and Punishment of Offenders 2012	In Schedule 5, paragraph 71.
Financial Services Act 2012	In Schedule 18, paragraph 132.
Counter-Terrorism and Security Act 2015	Section 45(2). Section 46(1)(b). Section 49(4)(c).
Investigatory Powers Act 2016	In Schedule 3, paragraph 11. In Schedule 10, paragraph 25.
Payment Services Regulations 2017 (S.I. 2017/752)	Regulation 14(5)(e).
Sanctions and Anti-Money Laundering Act 2018	In section 49(3), in the definition of "terrorist financing", paragraph (d).

Consequential amendment

10 In Schedule 3 to the Investigatory Powers Act 2016 (exceptions to section 56), in paragraph 12, for 'neither paragraph 10 nor paragraph 11 permits' substitute 'paragraph 10 does not permit'.

APPENDIX 2

Statutory Instruments 2018 No. 1269
Exiting The European Union Sanctions
The Sanctions Review Procedure (EU Exit) Regulations 2018

Made - - - - 27th November 2018
Laid before Parliament - - - - - - - - 30th November 2018
Coming into force - - 7th January 2019
The Secretary of State, in exercise of the powers conferred by sections 33 and 54(2) of the Sanctions and Anti-Money Laundering Act 2018([1]), makes the following Regulations:

Citation and commencement

1. These Regulations may be cited as the Sanctions Review Procedure (EU Exit) Regulations 2018 and come into force on 7th January 2019.

Interpretation

2. In these Regulations— 'address'—
   (a) in relation to an individual, means the address where that individual usually resides;
   (b) in relation to a company incorporated in the United Kingdom, means the address of the registered office that a company is required to have under section 86 of the Companies Act 2006([2]);
   (c) in relation to any other company, means the address of its principal place of business in its country of incorporation or, if applicable, its registered office;
   (d) in relation to an unincorporated body, organisation, association, or combination of persons, means the address of their main place of business or activity;

   'Minister' means the appropriate Minister dealing with a request under any of the sections mentioned in regulation 3([3]);

   'requester' means the person who makes a request under any of the sections mentioned in regulation 3;

---

[1] 2018 c. 13. Section 33 provides that Regulations may be made by an 'appropriate Minister' which is defined in section 1(9) as the Secretary of State or the Treasury.

[2] 2006 c 46.

[3] Sections 22 and 26 of the Act provide that the appropriate Minister is the Minister who made the designation or specification that is the subject of the request. Sections 25 and 29 provide that the appropriate Minister is the Secretary of State.

a reference without more to a numbered section is a reference to the section of the Sanctions and Anti-Money Laundering Act 2018 bearing that number.

Requests to which these Regulations apply

3. These Regulations apply to a request under any of the following sections—
(a) section 23 (right to request variation or revocation of designation);
(b) section 25 (right of UN-named person to request review);
(c) section 27 (right to request revocation of specification of ship);
(d) section 29 (UN-designated ship: right to request review).

Content of request

4.—(1) A request must be made in writing in English.
(2) A request must include the requester's—
(a) name;
(b) address;
(c) correspondence address, if different; and
(d) proof of identity, if the requester is an individual.
(3) Where a person is acting on behalf of the requester, that person must provide confirmation of authority to act on behalf of the requester.
(4) A request must specify whether it is for—
(a) a variation under section 23;
(b) revocation under section 23;
(c) review under section 25;
(d) revocation under section 27;
(e) review under section 29.
(5) A request must explain—
(a) where the request is for a variation under section 23, why the designation should be varied and what variation is requested;
(b) where the request is for revocation under section 23, why the designation should be revoked;
(c) where the request is for review under section 25, why the requester's name should be removed from the relevant UN list;
(d) where the request is for revocation under section 27, how the requester is affected by the ship specification and why the specification should be revoked;
(e) where the request is for review under section 29, how the requester is affected by the designation and why the designation should cease.
(6) A request must include relevant evidence of the explanation provided under paragraph (5), where such evidence is available to the requester.
(7) Where a request includes any evidence which is not in English, the request must include a translation of that evidence into English, and the translation must—
(a) include a signed declaration by the translator that the translation is an accurate translation of the evidence;
(b) include the date of the translation and the full name and contact details of the translator.
(8) Where the request is a further request under any of the sections mentioned in regulation 3, the further request must explain what the significant matter giving rise to the further request is, and why it is significant.

Submission of request

5.—(1) A request must be made electronically to sanctions.reassessment@fco.gov.uk.

(2) But where it is not reasonably practicable for the requester to make a request electronically, a request may be submitted in hard copy to Sanctions Unit, Foreign and Commonwealth Office, King Charles Street, London SW1A 2AH.

Further information

6.—(1) The Minister may ask the requester for further information about the request.

(2) The requester must provide any such further information, where such information is available to the requester, as soon as reasonably practicable.

Decision on request

7. The Minister must make the decision on the request as soon as reasonably practicable after receiving the information needed for making the decision.

Notification of decision

8.—(1) The Minister must inform the requester in writing of the decision on the request and the reasons for it, as soon as reasonably practicable after the decision is made.

(2) Where the decision is in relation to a request under section 27 (right to request revocation of specification of ship) or section 29 (UN-designated ship: right to request review), the Minister may also inform any person affected by the ship specification or designation of the decision and the reasons for it.

(3) Matters may be excluded from the reasons given where the Minister considers that they should be excluded—

(a) in the interests of national security or international relations;

(b) for reasons connected with the prevention or detection of serious crime in the United Kingdom or elsewhere; or

(c) in the interests of justice.

Publicity

9.—(1) The Minister may take steps to publicise the decision on a request, and the reasons for it.

(2) Matters may be excluded from the published reasons where the Minister considers that they should be excluded—

(a) in the interests of national security or international relations;

(b) for reasons connected with the prevention or detection of serious crime in the United Kingdom or elsewhere; or

(c) in the interests of justice.

Signed by the authority of the Secretary of State

Alan Duncan
Minister of State
27th November 2018 Foreign and Commonwealth Office

EXPLANATORY NOTE

(This note is not part of the Regulations)

Chapter 2 of Part 1 of the Sanctions and Anti-Money Laundering Act 2018 (c.13) ('the Act') enables certain persons to request a review, variation or revocation of a designation or ship specification that has been made under the Act. The request is to be dealt with by the appropriate Minister, i.e. the Minister who made the decision or, in the case of UN listings, the Secretary of State. These Regulations make provision for the procedure applicable to such requests.

Regulations 4 and 5 make provision about the information that must be contained in a request and the manner in which requests must be made and.

Regulation 6 enables the Minister to seek further information in relation to the request.

Regulation 7 makes provision about decisions on a request, in particular that a decision must be made as soon as reasonably practicable after the appropriate Minister has received the information necessary to make a decision.

Regulations 8 and 9 make provision about notification and publication of decisions and reasons. They allow matters to be excluded from the reasons given for a decision on specified grounds, namely in the interests of national security or international relations, for the prevention or detection of serious crime, or in the interests of justice.

A full impact assessment has not been produced for this instrument as no impact on the private or voluntary sectors is foreseen.

APPENDIX 3

STATUTORY INSTRUMENTS

2018 No. 1213 (C. 85)

SANCTIONS

The Sanctions and Anti-Money Laundering Act 2018 (Commencement. 1) Regulations 2018

Made - - - - 21st November 2018

The Secretary of State, in exercise of the power conferred by section 64(2) of the Sanctions and Anti-Money Laundering 2018([1]), makes the following Regulations:

Citation

1. These Regulations may be cited as the Sanctions and Anti-Money Laundering Act 2018 (Commencement No. 1) Regulations 2018.

Commencement

2. The following provisions of the Sanctions and Anti-Money Laundering Act 2018 come into force on the day after the day on which these Regulations are made—
   (a) sections 1 to 31;
   (b) sections 33 to 48;
   (c) sections 57 and 58;
   (d) section 59(4) so far as it relates to the provisions coming into force in accordance with paragraph (f) of this regulation;
   (e) Schedule 1;
   (f) paragraphs 1 to 7, and sub-paragraphs (1) to (3) of paragraph 8, of Schedule 3.

Alan Duncan

Minister of State

21st November 2018 Foreign and Commonwealth Office

---

[1] 2018 c.13.

EXPLANATORY NOTE

(This note is not part of the Regulations)

These Regulations bring into force certain provisions of the Sanctions and Anti-Money Laundering Act 2018 ('the Act') relating to sanctions. Certain provisions of the Act came into force on Royal Assent by virtue of section 64(1) of the Act. The remaining provisions of the Act, including the repeal of certain existing legislation relating to sanctions, and certain provisions relating to anti-money laundering under Part 2 of the Act, are intended to be brought into force at a later date.

APPENDIX 4

STATUTORY INSTRUMENTS

2019 No. 855

EXITING THE EUROPEAN UNION SANCTIONS

The Russia (Sanctions) (EU Exit) Regulations 2019

Approved by both Houses of Parliament
Made - - - - 10th April 2019
Laid before Parliament 11th April 2019
Coming into force in accordance with regulation 1(2) and (3)

The Secretary of State([1]), in exercise of the powers conferred by sections 1(1)(c) and (3)(b), 3(1)(a), (b)(ii) and (iii), (c)(ii) and (iii), (d), (e)(iii), (g)(iii), (2)(b) and (c), 4, 5, 7(2) and (5), 9(2)(a), 10(2)(a) and (c), (3) and (4), 11(2) to (9), 15(2)(a) and (b), (3), (4)(b), (5) and (6), 16, 17(2) to (9), 19, 20, 21(1), 54(1) and (2)(a), 62(4) to (6) of, and paragraphs 2(a)(iii) and (b), 3(a) and (b), 4(a) (iii), (b) and (c), 5(a)(ii) and (iii) and (b), 6(a)(ii) and (iii) and (b), 7(a)(iii) and (b), 9, 10(b), 11(a)
(ii) and (iii), 13(a), (b), (c), (g), (h), (i), (k), (l), (m), (n), (p), (q), (t), (v) and (w), 14(a), (e), (f) and (k), 17, 19 to 23 and 27 of Schedule 1 to, the Sanctions and Anti-Money Laundering Act 2018([2]), and having decided, upon consideration of the matters set out in section 2(2) of that Act, that it is appropriate to do so, makes the following Regulations:

PART 1
GENERAL

Citation and commencement

1.—(1) These Regulations may be cited as the Russia (Sanctions) (EU Exit) Regulations 2019.

(2) Subject to paragraph (3), these Regulations come into force on exit day.

(3) The following provisions of these Regulations come into force on the day after the day on which the Regulations are made—

---

[1] The power to make regulations under Part 1 of the Sanctions and Anti-Money Laundering Act 2018 is conferred on an 'appropriate Minister'. Section 1(9)(a) of the Act defines an 'appropriate Minister' as including the Secretary of State.

[2] 2018 c.13.

(a) this regulation;
(b) regulation 2 (interpretation);
(c) regulation 4 (purposes);
(d) Part 2;
(e) Schedule 1 (rules for interpretation of regulations 7(2) and 16(7)).

Interpretation

2. In these Regulations—
'the Act' means the Sanctions and Anti-Money Laundering Act 2018;
'arrangement' includes any agreement, understanding, scheme, transaction or series of transactions, whether or not legally enforceable (but see paragraph 12 of Schedule 1 for the meaning of that term in that Schedule);
'CEMA' means the Customs and Excise Management Act 1979([3]);
'the Commissioners' means the Commissioners for Her Majesty's Revenue and Customs;
'conduct' includes acts and omissions;
'Crimea' means the Autonomous Republic of Crimea and the city of Sevastopol;
'document' includes information recorded in any form and, in relation to information recorded otherwise than in legible form, references to its production include producing a copy of the information in legible form;
'the EU Russia Regulations' means the following, as they have effect in EU law—
(a) Council Regulation (EU) No 269/2014 of 17 March 2014 (concerning restrictive measures in respect of actions undermining or threatening the territorial integrity, sovereignty and independence of Ukraine)([4]),
(b) Council Regulation (EU) No 692/2014 of 23 June 2014 (concerning restrictive measures in response to the illegal annexation of Crimea and Sevastopol)([5]), and
(c) Council Regulation (EU) No 833/2014 of 31 July 2014 (concerning restrictive measures in view of Russia's actions destabilising the situation in Ukraine)([6]);
'trade licence' means a licence under regulation 65; 'Treasury licence' means a licence under regulation 64(1); the 'Ukraine Financial Sanctions Regulations' means—
(a) The Ukraine (European Union Financial Sanctions) (No.2) Regulations 2014([7]), and
(b) The Ukraine (European Union Financial Sanctions) (No.3) Regulations 2014([8]); 'United Kingdom person' has the same meaning as in section 21 of the Act;
'working day' means any day other than—
(a) Saturday or Sunday,
(b) Christmas Day or Good Friday, or
(c) a day which is a bank holiday under the Banking and Financial Dealings Act 1971 in any part of the United Kingdom.

---

[3] 1979 c.2. Amendments have been made to this Act and are cited, where relevant, in respect of the applicable regulations.
[4] OJ L 78, 17.3.2014, p. 6–15.
[5] OJ L 183 24.6.2014, p. 9.
[6] OJ L 229, 31.7.2014, p. 1–11.
[7] S.I. 2014/693, as modified by the Wales Act 2014 (c.29), section 4(4)(a) and amended by S.I. 2017/560, S.I. 2017/754 and S.I. 2018/682 and as prospectively amended by S.I. 2018/1149.
[8] S.I. 2014/2054, as amended by S.I. 2014/2445, S.I. 2014/3230, S.I. 2017/560, S.I. 2017/754, 2018/682 and as prospectively amended by S.I. 2018/1149.

Application of prohibitions and requirements outside the United Kingdom

3.—(1) A United Kingdom person may contravene a relevant prohibition by conduct wholly or partly outside the United Kingdom.

(2) Any person may contravene a relevant prohibition by conduct in the territorial sea.

(3) In this regulation a 'relevant prohibition' means any prohibition imposed—

(a) by regulation 9(2) (confidential information),

(b) by Part 3 (Finance),

(c) by Part 5 (Trade),

(d) under Part 6 (Ships), or

(e) by a condition of a Treasury licence or a trade licence.

(4) A United Kingdom person may comply, or fail to comply, with a relevant requirement by conduct wholly or partly outside the United Kingdom.

(5) Any person may comply, or fail to comply, with a relevant requirement by conduct in the territorial sea.

(6) In this regulation a 'relevant requirement' means any requirement imposed—

(a) by or under Part 8 (Information and records), or by reason of a request made under a power conferred by that Part, or

(b) by a condition of a Treasury licence or a trade licence.

(7) Nothing in this regulation is to be taken to prevent a relevant prohibition or a relevant requirement from applying to conduct (by any person) in the United Kingdom.

Purposes

4. The regulations contained in this instrument that are made under section 1 of the Act are for the purposes of encouraging Russia to cease actions destabilising Ukraine or undermining or threatening the territorial integrity, sovereignty or independence of Ukraine.

PART 2
DESIGNATION OF PERSONS

Power to designate persons

5.—(1) The Secretary of State may designate persons by name for the purposes of any of the following—

(a) regulations 11 to 15 (asset-freeze etc.);

(b) regulation 20 (immigration).

(2) The Secretary of State may designate different persons for the purposes of different provisions mentioned in paragraph (1).

Designation criteria

6.—(1) The Secretary of State may not designate a person under regulation 5 unless the Secretary of State—

(a) has reasonable grounds to suspect that that person is an involved person, and

(b) considers that the designation of that person is appropriate, having regard to—

(i) the purposes stated in regulation 4, and
(ii) the likely significant effects of the designation on that person (as they appear to the Secretary of State to be on the basis of the information that the Secretary of State has).

(2) In this regulation an 'involved person' means a person who—
(a) is or has been involved in destabilising Ukraine or undermining or threatening the territorial integrity, sovereignty or independence of Ukraine,
(b) is owned or controlled directly or indirectly (within the meaning of regulation 7) by a person who is or has been so involved,
(c) is acting on behalf of or at the direction of a person who is or has been so involved, or
(d) is a member of, or associated with, a person who is or has been so involved.

(3) For the purposes of this regulation a person is 'involved in destabilising Ukraine or undermining or threatening the territorial integrity, sovereignty or independence of Ukraine' if—
(a) the person is responsible for, engaging in, providing support for, or promoting any policy or action which destabilises Ukraine or undermines or threatens the territorial integrity, sovereignty or independence of Ukraine;
(b) the person provides financial services, or makes available funds, economic resources, goods or technology that could contribute to destabilising Ukraine or undermining or threatening the territorial integrity, sovereignty or independence of Ukraine;
(c) the person provides financial services, or makes available funds, economic resources, goods or technology, to—
(i) a person who is responsible for a policy or action which falls within paragraph (a), or
(ii) a person who provides financial services, or makes available funds, economic resources, goods or technology, as mentioned in sub-paragraph (b);
(d) the person obstructs the work of international organisations in Ukraine;
(e) the person conducts business with a separatist group in the Donbas region;
(f) the person is a relevant person trading or operating in Crimea; or
(g) the person assists with the contravention of a relevant provision.

(4) In paragraph (3)(f), a person ('P') "is a 'relevant person' if—
(a) P is not an individual;
(b) the ownership or control of P has been transferred contrary to the law of Ukraine.

(5) In paragraph (2)(d), being 'associated with' a person includes obtaining a financial benefit or other material benefit from that person.

(6) In this regulation 'relevant provision' means—
(a) any provision of Part 3 or Part 5;
(b) any provision of the law of a country other than the United Kingdom made for purposes corresponding to a purpose of any provision of Part 3 or Part 5.

(7) Nothing in any sub-paragraph of paragraph (3) is to be taken to limit the meaning of any of the other sub-paragraphs of that paragraph.

Meaning of 'owned or controlled directly or indirectly'

7.—(1) A person who is not an individual ('C') is 'owned or controlled directly or indirectly' by another person ('P') if either of the following two conditions is met (or both are met).

(2) The first condition is that P—
(a) holds directly or indirectly more than 50% of the shares in C,

(b) holds directly or indirectly more than 50% of the voting rights in C, or
(c) holds the right directly or indirectly to appoint or remove a majority of the board of directors of C.

(3) Schedule 1 contains provision applying for the purpose of interpreting paragraph (2).

(4) The second condition is that it is reasonable, having regard to all the circumstances, to expect that P would (if P chose to) be able, in most cases or in significant respects, by whatever means and whether directly or indirectly, to achieve the result that affairs of C are conducted in accordance with P's wishes.

Notification and publicity where designation power used

8.—(1) Paragraph (2) applies where the Secretary of State—
(a) has made a designation under regulation 5, or
(b) has by virtue of section 22 of the Act varied or revoked a designation made under that regulation.

(2) The Secretary of State—
(a) must without delay take such steps as are reasonably practicable to inform the designated person of the designation, variation or revocation, and
(b) must take steps to publicise the designation, variation or revocation.

(3) The information given under paragraph (2)(a) where a designation is made must include a statement of reasons.

(4) In this regulation a 'statement of reasons', in relation to a designation, means a brief statement of the matters that the Secretary of State knows, or has reasonable grounds to suspect, in relation to the designated person which have led the Secretary of State to make the designation.

(5) Matters that would otherwise be required by paragraph (4) to be included in a statement of reasons may be excluded from it where the Secretary of State considers that they should be excluded—
(a) in the interests of national security or international relations,
(b) for reasons connected with the prevention or detection of serious crime in the United Kingdom or elsewhere, or
(c) in the interests of justice.

(6) The steps taken under paragraph (2)(b) must—
(a) unless one or more of the restricted publicity conditions is met, be steps to publicise generally—
(i) the designation, variation or revocation, and
(ii) in the case of a designation, the statement of reasons;
(b) if one or more of those conditions is met, be steps to inform only such persons as the Secretary of State considers appropriate of the designation, variation or revocation and (in the case of a designation) of the contents of the statement of reasons.

(7) The 'restricted publicity conditions' are as follows—
(a) the designation is of a person believed by the Secretary of State to be an individual under the age of 18;
(b) the Secretary of State considers that disclosure of the designation, variation or revocation should be restricted—
(i) in the interests of national security or international relations,

(ii) for reasons connected with the prevention or detection of serious crime in the United Kingdom or elsewhere, or
(iii) in the interests of justice.

(8) Paragraph (9) applies if—
(a) when a designation is made one or more of the restricted publicity conditions is met, but
(b) at any time when the designation has effect, it becomes the case that none of the restricted publicity conditions is met.

(9) The Secretary of State must—
(a) take such steps as are reasonably practicable to inform the designated person that none of the restricted publicity conditions is now met, and
(b) take steps to publicise generally the designation and the statement of reasons relating to it.

Confidential information in certain cases where designation power used

9.—(1) Where the Secretary of State in accordance with regulation 8(6)(b) informs only certain persons of a designation, variation or revocation and (in the case of a designation) of the contents of the statement of reasons, the Secretary of State may specify that any of that information is to be treated as confidential.

(2) A person ('P') who—
(a) is provided with information that is to be treated as confidential in accordance with paragraph (1), or
(b) otherwise obtains such information, must not, subject to paragraph (3), disclose it if P knows, or has reasonable cause to suspect, that the information is to be treated as confidential.

(3) The prohibition in paragraph (2) does not apply to any disclosure made by P with lawful authority.

(4) For this purpose information is disclosed with lawful authority only if and to the extent that—
(a) the disclosure is by, or is authorised by, the Secretary of State,
(b) the disclosure is by or with the consent of the person who is or was the subject of the designation,
(c) the disclosure is necessary to give effect to a requirement imposed under or by virtue of these Regulations or any other enactment, or
(d) the disclosure is required, under rules of court, tribunal rules or a court or tribunal order, for the purposes of legal proceedings of any description.

(5) This regulation does not prevent the disclosure of information that is already, or has previously been, available to the public from other sources.

(6) A person who contravenes the prohibition in paragraph (2) commits an offence.

(7) The High Court (in Scotland, the Court of Session) may, on the application of—
(a) the person who is the subject of the information, or
(b) the Secretary of State,

grant an injunction (in Scotland, an interdict) to prevent a breach of the prohibition in paragraph (2).

(8) In paragraph (4)(c), 'enactment' has the meaning given by section 54(6) of the Act.

PART 3
FINANCE

CHAPTER 1
Finance restrictions in relation to designated persons

Meaning of 'designated person'

10. In this Chapter a 'designated person' means a person who is designated under regulation 5 for the purposes of regulations 11 to 15.

Asset-freeze in relation to designated persons

11.—(1) A person ('P') must not deal with funds or economic resources owned, held or controlled by a designated person if P knows, or has reasonable cause to suspect, that P is dealing with such funds or economic resources.

(2) Paragraph (1) is subject to Part 7 (Exceptions and licences).

(3) A person who contravenes the prohibition in paragraph (1) commits an offence.

(4) For the purposes of paragraph (1) a person 'deals with' funds if the person—

(a) uses, alters, moves, transfers or allows access to the funds,

(b) deals with the funds in any other way that would result in any change in volume, amount, location, ownership, possession, character or destination, or

(c) makes any other change, including portfolio management, that would enable use of the funds.

(5) For the purposes of paragraph (1) a person 'deals with' economic resources if the person—

(a) exchanges the economic resources for funds, goods or services, or

(b) uses the economic resources in exchange for funds, goods or services (whether by pledging them as security or otherwise).

(6) The reference in paragraph (1) to funds or economic resources that are 'owned, held or controlled' by a person includes, in particular, a reference to—

(a) funds or economic resources in which the person has any legal or equitable interest, regardless of whether the interest is held jointly with any other person and regardless of whether any other person holds an interest in the funds or economic resources;

(b) any tangible property (other than real property), or bearer security, that is comprised in funds or economic resources and is in the possession of the person.

(7) For the purposes of paragraph (1) funds or economic resources are to be treated as owned, held or controlled by a designated person if they are owned, held or controlled by a person who is owned or controlled directly or indirectly (within the meaning of regulation 7) by the designated person.

(8) For the avoidance of doubt, the reference in paragraph (1) to a designated person includes P if P is a designated person.

Making funds available to designated person

12.—(1) A person ('P') must not make funds available directly or indirectly to a designated person if P knows, or has reasonable cause to suspect, that P is making the funds so available.

(2) Paragraph (1) is subject to Part 7 (Exceptions and licences).
(3) A person who contravenes the prohibition in paragraph (1) commits an offence.
(4) The reference in paragraph (1) to making funds available indirectly to a designated person includes, in particular, a reference to making them available to a person who is owned or controlled directly or indirectly (within the meaning of regulation 7) by the designated person.

Making funds available for benefit of designated person

13.—(1) A person ('P') must not make funds available to any person for the benefit of a designated person if P knows, or has reasonable cause to suspect, that P is making the funds so available.
(2) Paragraph (1) is subject to Part 7 (Exceptions and licences).
(3) A person who contravenes the prohibition in paragraph (1) commits an offence.
(4) For the purposes of this regulation—
(a) funds are made available for the benefit of a designated person only if that person thereby obtains, or is able to obtain, a significant financial benefit, and
(b) 'financial benefit' includes the discharge (or partial discharge) of a financial obligation for which the designated person is wholly or partly responsible.

Making economic resources available to designated person

14.—(1) A person ('P') must not make economic resources available directly or indirectly to a designated person if P knows, or has reasonable cause to suspect—
(a) that P is making the economic resources so available, and
(b) that the designated person would be likely to exchange the economic resources for, or use them in exchange for, funds, goods or services.
(2) Paragraph (1) is subject to Part 7 (Exceptions and licences).
(3) A person who contravenes the prohibition in paragraph (1) commits an offence.
(4) The reference in paragraph (1) to making economic resources available indirectly to a designated person includes, in particular, a reference to making them available to a person who is owned or controlled directly or indirectly (within the meaning of regulation 7) by the designated person.

Making economic resources available for benefit of designated person

15.—(1) A person ('P') must not make economic resources available to any person for the benefit of a designated person if P knows, or has reasonable cause to suspect, that P is making the economic resources so available.
(2) Paragraph (1) is subject to Part 7 (Exceptions and licences).
(3) A person who contravenes the prohibition in paragraph (1) commits an offence.
(4) For the purposes of paragraph (1)—
(a) economic resources are made available for the benefit of a designated person only if that person thereby obtains, or is able to obtain, a significant financial benefit, and
(b) 'financial benefit' includes the discharge (or partial discharge) of a financial obligation for which the designated person is wholly or partly responsible.

CHAPTER 2

Other financial and investment restrictions

Dealing with transferable securities or money-market instruments

16.—(1) A person ('P') must not, directly or indirectly, deal with a transferable security or money-market instrument falling within paragraph (2) if P knows, or has reasonable cause to suspect, that P is dealing with such a transferable security or money-market instrument.

(2) A transferable security or money-market instrument falls within this paragraph if it has a maturity exceeding 30 days and is issued after 1 August 2014 by—

(a) a person mentioned in any of paragraphs 1 to 5 of Schedule 2;

(b) a person, other than an individual, which is—

(i) incorporated or constituted under the law of a non-UK country, and

(ii) owned by a person within sub-paragraph (a); or

(c) a person, other than an individual, acting on behalf or at the direction of a person within sub-paragraph (a) or sub-paragraph (b).

(3) A person ('P') must not, directly or indirectly, deal with a transferable security or money-market instrument falling within paragraph (4) if P knows, or has reasonable cause to suspect, that P is dealing with such a transferable security or money-market instrument.

(4) A transferable security or money-market instrument falls within this paragraph if it has a maturity exceeding 30 days and is issued after 12 September 2014 by—

(a) a person mentioned in any of paragraphs 6 to 11 of Schedule 2;

(b) a person, other than an individual, which is—

(i) incorporated or constituted under the law of a non-UK country, and

(ii) owned by a person within sub-paragraph (a); or

(c) a person, other than an individual, acting on behalf or at the direction of a person within sub-paragraph (a) or sub-paragraph (b).

(5) Paragraphs (1) and (3) are subject to regulation 63 (exception for acts done for purposes of national security or prevention of serious crime).

(6) A person who contravenes a prohibition in paragraph (1) or (3) commits an offence.

(7) For the purposes of this regulation, and regulations 17 (loans and credit arrangements) and 59 (exceptions relating to loans and credit arrangements), a person ('C') is 'owned' by another person ('P') if P—

(a) holds directly or indirectly more than 50% of the shares in C, or

(b) holds directly or indirectly more than 50% of the voting rights in C.

(8) Schedule 1 applies for the purpose of interpreting paragraph (7).

(9) For the purposes of this regulation, a reference to 'dealing with' a transferable security or money-market instrument includes a reference to purchasing or selling the security or instrument, providing investment services relating to the security or instrument or assisting in the issuance of the security or instrument.

(10) In this regulation—

'investment services' means—

(a) the reception and transmission of orders in relation to one or more financial instruments,

(b) the execution of orders on behalf of clients,
(c) dealing on own account,
(d) portfolio management,
(e) the provision of investment advice,
(f) the underwriting of financial instruments or placing of financial instruments on a firm commitment basis,
(g) the placing of financial instruments without a firm commitment basis, or
(h) any service in relation to the admission to trading on a regulated market or trading on a multilateral trading facility;

'money-market instrument' means an instrument of a kind normally dealt in on the money market, such as treasury bills, certificates of deposit and commercial papers, excluding instruments of payment;

'non-UK country' means a country that is not the United Kingdom;

'transferable security' means a security, negotiable on the capital market, of any of the following kinds, but excluding instruments of payment—

(a) shares in companies and other securities equivalent to shares in companies, partnerships or other entities, and depositary receipts in respect of shares;
(b) bonds or other forms of securitised debt, including depositary receipts in respect of such securities;
(c) any other securities giving the right to purchase or sell any security of a kind mentioned in paragraph (a) or (b).

Loans and credit arrangements

17.—(1) A person ('P') must not directly or indirectly grant a relevant loan if P knows, or has reasonable cause to suspect, that P is granting a relevant loan.

(2) A person must not directly or indirectly enter into any arrangement to grant a relevant loan if the person knows, or has reasonable cause to suspect, that the arrangement relates to a relevant loan.

(3) Paragraphs (1) and (2) are subject to regulations 59 and 63 (exceptions).

(4) A person who contravenes a prohibition in paragraph (1) or (2) commits an offence.

(5) In this regulation—

'non-UK country' means a country that is not the United Kingdom; 'relevant loan' means a loan or credit—

(a) with a maturity exceeding 30 days,
(b) made or granted to a relevant person, and
(c) which is first made or granted at any time after exit day;

'relevant person' means—

(a) a person falling within Schedule 2;
(b) a person, other than an individual, which is—
    (i) incorporated or constituted under the law of a non-UK country, and
    (ii) owned (within the meaning of regulation 16(7)) by a person within sub-paragraph (a); or
(c) a person, other than an individual, acting on behalf or at the direction of a person within sub-paragraph (a) or sub-paragraph (b).

Investments in relation to Crimea

18.—(1) A person ('P') must not carry on an activity mentioned in paragraph (2) if P knows, or has reasonable cause to suspect, that P is carrying on such an activity.

(2) The activities in this paragraph are—

(a) directly or indirectly acquiring or extending a participation, or acquiring any ownership interest, in land located in Crimea;

(b) directly or indirectly acquiring or extending a participation, or acquiring any ownership interest in or control over, a relevant entity;

(c) directly or indirectly granting any loan or credit, entering into any arrangement to grant any loan or credit, or otherwise providing funds, including for example equity capital—

(i) to a relevant entity, or

(ii) for the documented purpose of financing any such entity;

(d) directly or indirectly establishing any joint venture—

(i) in Crimea, or

(ii) with a relevant entity;

(e) providing investment services directly related to an activity referred to in sub-paragraphs (a) to (d) above.

(3) Paragraph (1) is subject to Part 7 (Exceptions and licences).

(4) A person who contravenes a prohibition in paragraph (1) commits an offence.

(5) In this regulation—

'investment services' has the same meaning as it has in regulation 16;

'relevant entity' means a person, other than an individual, which has a place of business located in Crimea.

CHAPTER 3
Further provision

Circumventing etc. prohibitions

19.—(1) A person must not intentionally participate in activities knowing that the object or effect of them is (whether directly or indirectly)—

(a) to circumvent any of the prohibitions in regulations 11 to 18, or

(b) to enable or facilitate the contravention of any such prohibition.

(2) A person who contravenes the prohibition in paragraph (1) commits an offence.

PART 4
IMMIGRATION

Immigration

20. A person who is designated under regulation 5 for the purposes of this regulation is an excluded person for the purposes of section 8B of the Immigration Act 1971([9]).

[9] 1971 c. 77, as amended by the Immigration and Asylum Act 1999 (c.33), s.8 and the Immigration Act 2016 (c.19), s.76.

PART 5
TRADE

CHAPTER 1

Interpretation

Interpretation of this Part

21.—(1) In this Part—

'brokering service' means any service to secure, or otherwise in relation to, an arrangement, including (but not limited to)—

(a) the selection or introduction of persons as parties or potential parties to the arrangement,

(b) the negotiation of the arrangement,

(c) the facilitation of anything that enables the arrangement to be entered into, and

(d) the provision of any assistance that in any way promotes or facilitates the arrangement;

'dual-use goods' means—

(a) any thing for the time being specified in Annex I of the Dual-Use Regulation, other than any thing which is dual-use technology, and

(b) any tangible storage medium on which dual-use technology is recorded or from which it can be derived;

'the Dual-Use Regulation' means Council Regulation (EC) No 428/2009 of 5 May 2009 setting up a Community regime for the control of exports, transfer, brokering and transit of dual-use items;

'dual-use technology' means any thing for the time being specified in Annex I of the Dual-Use Regulation which is described as software or technology;

'energy-related goods' means any thing falling within Part 2 of Schedule 3; 'infrastructure-related goods' means any thing falling within Part 3 of Schedule 3; 'military goods' means—

(a) any thing for the time being specified in Schedule 2 to the Export Control Order 2008([10]), other than any thing which is military technology, and

(b) any tangible storage medium on which military technology is recorded or from which it can be derived;

'military technology' means any thing for the time being specified in Schedule 2 to the Export Control Order 2008 which is described as software or technology;

'technical assistance', in relation to goods or technology, means—

(a) technical support relating to the repair, development, production, assembly, testing, use or maintenance of the goods or technology, or

(b) any other technical service relating to the goods or technology;

'technology' has the meaning given in paragraph 37 of Schedule 1 to the Act; 'transfer' has the meaning given in paragraph 37 of Schedule 1 to the Act.

(2) For the purposes of this Part, a person is to be regarded as 'connected with' Russia if the person is—

(a) an individual who is, or an association or combination of individuals who are, ordinarily resident in Russia,

[10] S.I. 2008/3231. Schedule 2 was substituted by S.I. 2017/85 and subsequently amended by S.I 2017/697 and S.I. 2018/165. There are other instruments which amend other parts of the Order.

(b) an individual who is, or an association or combination of individuals who are, located in Russia,
(c) a person, other than an individual, which is incorporated or constituted under the law of Russia, or
(d) a person, other than an individual, which is domiciled in Russia.

(3) For the purposes of this Part, a person is to be regarded as 'connected with' Crimea if the person is—
(a) an individual who is, or an association or combination of individuals who are, ordinarily resident in Crimea,
(b) an individual who is, or an association or combination of individuals who are, located in Crimea, or
(c) a person, other than an individual, which has its registered office, central administration or principal place of business located in Crimea.

(4) Paragraphs 32 to 36 of Schedule 1 to the Act (trade sanctions) apply for the purpose of interpreting expressions in this Part.

(5) In this Part, any reference to the United Kingdom includes a reference to the territorial sea.

CHAPTER 2

Military goods, military technology and related activities

Export of military goods

22.—(1) The export of military goods to, or for use in, Russia is prohibited.

(2) Paragraph (1) is subject to Part 7 (Exceptions and licences).

Import of arms and related materiel

23.—(1) The import of arms and related materiel which are consigned from Russia is prohibited.

(2) The import of arms and related materiel which originate in Russia is prohibited.

(3) Paragraphs (1) and (2) are subject to Part 7 (Exceptions and licences).

(4) In this regulation 'arms and related materiel' means—
(a) military goods, and
(b) any thing which falls within chapter 93 of the Goods Classification Table, other than military goods.

(5) For the purposes of the definition of 'arms and related materiel', whether a thing 'falls within chapter 93 of the Goods Classification Table' is to be interpreted in accordance with paragraph 1 of Schedule 3.

Supply and delivery of military goods

24.—(1) A person must not—
(a) directly or indirectly supply or deliver military goods from a third country to a place in Russia;
(b) directly or indirectly supply or deliver military goods from a place in Russia to a third country.

(2) Paragraph (1) is subject to Part 7 (Exceptions and licences).

(3) A person who contravenes a prohibition in paragraph (1) commits an offence, but—
(a) it is a defence for a person charged with the offence of contravening paragraph (1)(a) to show that the person did not know and had no reasonable cause to suspect that the goods were destined (or ultimately destined) for Russia;

(b) it is a defence for a person charged with the offence of contravening paragraph (1)(b) to show that the person did not know and had no reasonable cause to suspect that the supply or delivery was from a place in Russia, whether directly or indirectly.

(4) In this regulation 'third country' means a country that is not the United Kingdom, the Isle of Man or Russia.

Making available or acquiring military goods and military technology

25.—(1) A person must not—

(a) directly or indirectly make military goods or military technology available to a person connected with Russia;

(b) directly or indirectly make military goods or military technology available for use in Russia;

(c) directly or indirectly acquire military goods or military technology from a person connected with Russia;

(d) directly or indirectly acquire military goods or military technology which originate in Russia;

(e) directly or indirectly acquire military goods or military technology located in Russia.

(2) Paragraph (1) is subject to Part 7 (Exceptions and licences).

(3) A person who contravenes a prohibition in paragraph (1) commits an offence, but—

(a) it is a defence for a person charged with an offence of contravening paragraph (1)(a) or (c) ('P') to show that P did not know and had no reasonable cause to suspect that the person was connected with Russia;

(b) it is a defence for a person charged with the offence of contravening paragraph (1)(b) to show that the person did not know and had no reasonable cause to suspect that the goods or technology were for use in Russia;

(c) it is a defence for a person charged with the offence of contravening paragraph (1)(d) to show that the person did not know and had no reasonable cause to suspect that the goods or technology originated in Russia;

(d) it is a defence for a person charged with the offence of contravening paragraph (1)(e) to show that the person did not know and had no reasonable cause to suspect that the goods or technology were located in Russia.

Transfer of military technology

26.—(1) A person must not—

(a) transfer military technology to a place in Russia;

(b) transfer military technology to a person connected with Russia;

(c) transfer military technology to persons outside the United Kingdom or to a place outside the United Kingdom, where the transfer is from a place in Russia.

(2) Paragraph (1) is subject to Part 7 (Exceptions and licences).

(3) A person who contravenes a prohibition in paragraph (1) commits an offence, but—

(a) it is a defence for a person charged with the offence of contravening paragraph (1)(a) to show that the person did not know and had no reasonable cause to suspect that the transfer was to a place in Russia;

(b) it is a defence for a person charged with the offence of contravening paragraph (1)(b) ('P') to show that P did not know and had no reasonable cause to suspect that the person was connected with Russia;

(c) it is a defence for a person charged with the offence of contravening paragraph (1)(c) to show that the person did not know and had no reasonable cause to suspect that the transfer was from a place in Russia.

Technical assistance relating to military goods and military technology

27.—(1) A person must not directly or indirectly provide technical assistance relating to military goods or military technology—

(a) to a person connected with Russia, or

(b) for use in Russia.

(2) Paragraph (1) is subject to Part 7 (Exceptions and licences).

(3) A person who contravenes a prohibition in paragraph (1) commits an offence, but—

(a) it is a defence for a person charged with an offence of contravening paragraph (1)(a) ('P') to show that P did not know and had no reasonable cause to suspect that the person was connected with Russia;

(b) it is a defence for a person charged with an offence of contravening paragraph (1)(b) to show that the person did not know and had no reasonable cause to suspect that the goods or technology were for use in Russia.

Financial services and funds relating to military goods and military technology

28.—(1) A person must not directly or indirectly provide, to a person connected with Russia, financial services in pursuance of or in connection with an arrangement whose object or effect is—

(a) the export of military goods,

(b) the direct or indirect supply or delivery of military goods,

(c) directly or indirectly making military goods or military technology available to a person,

(d) the transfer of military technology, or

(e) the direct or indirect provision of technical assistance relating to military goods or military technology.

(2) A person must not directly or indirectly make funds available to a person connected with Russia in pursuance of or in connection with an arrangement mentioned in paragraph (1).

(3) A person must not directly or indirectly provide financial services or funds in pursuance of or in connection with an arrangement whose object or effect is—

(a) the export of military goods to, or for use in, Russia;

(b) the direct or indirect supply or delivery of military goods to a place in Russia;

(c) directly or indirectly making military goods or military technology available—

(i) to a person connected with Russia, or

(ii) for use in Russia;

(d) the transfer of military technology—

(i) to a person connected with Russia, or

(ii) to a place in Russia; or

(e) the direct or indirect provision of technical assistance relating to military goods or military technology—

(i) to a person connected with Russia, or

(ii) for use in Russia.

(4) A person must not directly or indirectly procure financial services from a person connected with Russia in pursuance of or in connection with an arrangement mentioned in paragraph (1).

(5) A person must not directly or indirectly procure financial services in pursuance of or in connection with an arrangement mentioned in paragraph (3).

(6) Paragraphs (1) to (5) are subject to Part 7 (Exceptions and licences).

(7) A person who contravenes a prohibition in any of paragraphs (1) to (5) commits an offence,

but—

(a) it is a defence for a person charged with an offence of contravening paragraph (1), (2) or (4) ('P') to show that P did not know and had no reasonable cause to suspect that the person was connected with Russia;

(b) it is a defence for a person charged with the offence of contravening paragraph (3) to show that the person did not know and had no reasonable cause to suspect that the financial services or funds (as the case may be) were provided in pursuance of or in connection with an arrangement mentioned in that paragraph;

(c) it is a defence for a person charged with the offence of contravening paragraph (5) to show that the person did not know and had no reasonable cause to suspect that the financial services were procured in pursuance of or in connection with an arrangement mentioned in paragraph (3).

Brokering services: non-UK activity relating to military goods and military technology

29.—(1) A person must not directly or indirectly provide brokering services in relation to an arrangement ('arrangement A') whose object or effect is—

(a) the direct or indirect supply or delivery of military goods from a third country to a place in Russia;

(b) directly or indirectly making military goods available in a third country for direct or indirect supply or delivery—
  (i) to a person connected with Russia, or
  (ii) to a place in Russia;

(c) directly or indirectly making military technology available in a third country for transfer—
  (i) to a person connected with Russia, or
  (ii) to a place in Russia;

(d) the transfer of military technology from a place in a third country—
  (i) to a person connected with Russia, or
  (ii) to a place in Russia;

(e) the direct or indirect provision, in a non-UK country, of technical assistance relating to military goods or military technology—
  (i) to a person connected with Russia, or
  (ii) for use in Russia;

(f) the direct or indirect provision, in a non-UK country, of financial services—
  (i) to a person connected with Russia, where arrangement A, or any other arrangement in connection with which arrangement A is entered into, is an arrangement mentioned in regulation 28(1), or

(ii) where arrangement A, or any other arrangement in connection with which arrangement A is entered into, is an arrangement mentioned in regulation 28(3);

(g) directly or indirectly making funds available, in a non-UK country, to a person connected with Russia, where arrangement A, or any other arrangement in connection with which arrangement A is entered into, is an arrangement mentioned in regulation 28(1); or

(h) the direct or indirect provision of funds from a non-UK country, where arrangement A, or any other arrangement in connection with which arrangement A is entered into, is an arrangement mentioned in regulation 28(3).

(2) Paragraph (1) is subject to Part 7 (Exceptions and licences).

(3) A person who contravenes a prohibition in paragraph (1) commits an offence, but it is a defence for a person charged with that offence to show that the person did not know and had no reasonable cause to suspect that the brokering services were provided in relation to an arrangement mentioned in that paragraph.

(4) In this regulation—

'non-UK country' means a country that is not the United Kingdom; 'third country' means—

(a) for the purposes of paragraph (1)(a) and (b), a country that is not the United Kingdom, the Isle of Man or Russia,

(b) for the purposes of any other provision of paragraph (1), a country that is not the United Kingdom or Russia.

Enabling or facilitating military activities

30.—(1) A person must not directly or indirectly provide—

(a) technical assistance,

(b) armed personnel,

(c) financial services or funds, or

(d) brokering services in relation to an arrangement whose object or effect is to provide, in a non-UK country, anything mentioned in sub-paragraphs (a) to (c),

where such provision enables or facilitates the conduct of military activities carried on or proposed to be carried on by the Russian military or any other military end-user who is a person connected with Russia.

(2) Paragraph (1) is subject to Part 7 (Exceptions and licences).

(3) A person who contravenes the prohibition in paragraph (1) commits an offence, but it is a defence for a person charged with that offence to show that the person did not know and had no reasonable cause to suspect that the provision as mentioned in paragraph (1) would enable or facilitate the conduct of military activities carried on or proposed to be carried on by the Russian military or any other military end-user who is a person connected with Russia.

(4) In this regulation—

'non-UK country' means a country that is not the United Kingdom;

'technical assistance' means the provision of technical support or any other technical service.

(5) Nothing in this regulation is to be taken to limit the meaning of any of the prohibitions contained in this Part.

CHAPTER 3

Dual-use goods, dual-use technology and related activities

Interpretation of this Chapter

31. For the purposes of this Chapter—
   (a) goods are 'for military use' if they are—
      (i) for use by the Russian military or any other military end-user, or
      (ii) for any military use;
   (b) technology is 'for military use' if it—
      (i) relates to military activities carried on or proposed to be carried on by the Russian military or any other military end-user, or
      (ii) is for any military use.

Export of dual-use goods

32.—(1) The export to Russia of dual-use goods for military use is prohibited.
   (2) The export of dual-use goods for military use in Russia is prohibited.
   (3) The export of dual-use goods to or for use by a person mentioned in Schedule 4 is prohibited.
   (4) Paragraphs (1) and (2) are subject to Part 7 (Exceptions and licences).

Supply and delivery of dual-use goods

33.—(1) A person must not—
      (a) directly or indirectly supply or deliver dual-use goods for military use from a third country to a place in Russia;
      (b) directly or indirectly supply or deliver dual-use goods from a third country to or for use by a person mentioned in Schedule 4.
   (2) Paragraph (1) is subject to Part 7 (Exceptions and licences).
   (3) A person who contravenes a prohibition in paragraph (1) commits an offence, but—
      (a) it is a defence for a person charged with the offence of contravening paragraph (1)(a) to show that the person did not know and had no reasonable cause to suspect that—
         (i) the goods were destined (or ultimately destined) for Russia, or
         (ii) the goods were for military use;
      (b) it is a defence for a person charged with the offence of contravening paragraph (1)(b) ('P') to show that P did not know and had no reasonable cause to suspect that the person to whom, or for whose use, the goods were supplied or delivered was a person mentioned in Schedule 4.
   (4) In this regulation 'third country' means a country that is not the United Kingdom, the Isle of Man or Russia.

Making dual-use goods and dual-use technology available

34.—(1) A person must not—
      (a) directly or indirectly make available, to a person connected with Russia, dual-use goods for military use or dual-use technology for military use;
      (b) directly or indirectly make available dual-use goods for military use in Russia or dual-use technology for military use in Russia;

(c) directly or indirectly make dual-use goods available to or for use by a person mentioned in Schedule 4.

(2) Paragraph (1) is subject to Part 7 (Exceptions and licences).

(3) A person who contravenes a prohibition in paragraph (1) commits an offence, but—

(a) it is a defence for a person charged with an offence of contravening paragraph (1)(a) ('P') to show that P did not know and had no reasonable cause to suspect that—

(i) the person was connected with Russia, or

(ii) the goods or technology were for military use;

(b) it is a defence for a person charged with an offence of contravening paragraph (1)(b) to show that the person did not know and had no reasonable cause to suspect that the goods or technology were for military use in Russia;

(c) it is a defence for a person charged with an offence of contravening paragraph (1)(c) ('P') to show that P did not know and had no reasonable cause to suspect that the person to whom or for whose benefit the goods were made available was a person mentioned in Schedule 4.

Transfer of dual-use technology

35.—(1) A person must not—

(a) transfer dual-use technology for military use to a place in Russia;

(b) transfer dual-use technology for military use to a person connected with Russia;

(c) transfer dual-use technology to a person mentioned in Schedule 4.

(2) Paragraph (1) is subject to Part 7 (Exceptions and licences).

(3) A person who contravenes a prohibition in paragraph (1) commits an offence, but—

(a) it is a defence for a person charged with the offence of contravening paragraph (1)(a) to show that the person did not know and had no reasonable cause to suspect that—

(i) the transfer was to a place in Russia, or

(ii) the technology was for military use;

(b) it is a defence for a person charged with the offence of contravening paragraph (1)(b) ('P') to show that P did not know and had no reasonable cause to suspect that—

(i) the person was connected with Russia, or

(ii) the technology was for military use;

(c) it is a defence for a person charged with an offence of contravening paragraph (1)(c) ('P') to show that P did not know and had no reasonable cause to suspect that the person to whom the technology was transferred was a person mentioned in Schedule 4.

Technical assistance relating to dual-use goods and dual-use technology

36.—(1) A person must not directly or indirectly—

(a) provide technical assistance relating to dual-use goods for military use or dual-use technology for military use to a person connected with Russia;

(b) provide technical assistance relating to dual-use goods for military use in Russia or dual-use technology for military use in Russia;

(c) provide technical assistance relating to dual-use goods or dual-use technology to a person mentioned in Schedule 4;

(d) provide technical assistance relating to dual-use goods or dual-use technology for use by a person mentioned in Schedule 4.

(2) Paragraph (1) is subject to Part 7 (Exceptions and licences).

(3) A person who contravenes a prohibition in paragraph (1) commits an offence, but—

(a) it is a defence for a person charged with the offence of contravening paragraph (1)(a) ('P') to show that P did not know and had no reasonable cause to suspect that—

(i) the person was connected with Russia, or

(ii) the goods or technology were for military use;

(b) it is a defence for a person charged with the offence of contravening paragraph (1)(b) to show that the person did not know and had no reasonable cause to suspect that the goods or technology were for military use in Russia;

(c) it is a defence for a person charged with the offence of contravening paragraph (1)(c) ('P') to show that P did not know and had no reasonable cause to suspect that the person was a person mentioned in Schedule 4;

(d) it is a defence for a person charged with the offence of contravening paragraph (1)(d) to show that the person did not know and had no reasonable cause to suspect that the goods or technology were for use by a person mentioned in Schedule 4.

Financial services and funds relating to dual-use goods and dual-use technology

37.—(1) A person must not directly or indirectly provide, to a person connected with Russia, financial services in pursuance of or in connection with an arrangement whose object or effect is—

(a) the export of dual-use goods for military use,

(b) the direct or indirect supply or delivery of dual-use goods for military use,

(c) directly or indirectly making dual-use goods for military use or dual-use technology for military use available to a person,

(d) the transfer of dual-use technology for military use, or

(e) the direct or indirect provision of technical assistance relating to dual-use goods for military use or dual-use technology for military use.

(2) A person must not directly or indirectly make funds available to a person connected with Russia in pursuance of or in connection with an arrangement mentioned in paragraph (1).

(3) A person must not directly or indirectly provide, to a person mentioned in Schedule 4, financial services or funds in pursuance of or in connection with an arrangement whose object or effect is—

(a) the export of dual-use goods,

(b) the direct or indirect supply or delivery of dual-use goods,

(c) directly or indirectly making dual-use goods or technology available to a person,

(d) the transfer of dual-use technology, or

(e) the direct or indirect provision of technical assistance relating to dual-use goods or dual-use technology.

(4) A person must not directly or indirectly provide financial services or funds in pursuance of or in connection with an arrangement whose object or effect is—

(a) the export to Russia of dual-use goods for military use;

(b) the export of dual-use goods for military use in Russia;

(c) the export of dual-use goods to or for use by a person mentioned in Schedule 4;

(d) the direct or indirect supply or delivery of dual-use goods for military use to a place in Russia;

(e) the direct or indirect supply or delivery of dual-use goods to or for use by a person mentioned in Schedule 4;
(f) directly or indirectly making available, to a person connected with Russia, dual-use goods for military use or dual-use technology for military use;
(g) directly or indirectly making available dual-use goods for military use in Russia or dual-use technology for military use in Russia;
(h) directly or indirectly making dual-use goods or dual-use technology available to or for use by a person mentioned in Schedule 4.
(i) the transfer of dual-use technology for military use—
(i) to a person connected with Russia, or
(ii) to a place in Russia;
(j) the transfer of dual-use technology to a person mentioned in Schedule 4;
(k) the direct or indirect provision of technical assistance relating to dual-use goods for military use or dual-use technology for military use to a person connected with Russia;
(l) the direct or indirect provision of technical assistance relating to dual-use goods for military use in Russia or dual-use technology for military use in Russia;
(m) the direct or indirect provision of technical assistance relating to dual-use goods or dual-use technology to a person mentioned in Schedule 4;
(n) the direct or indirect provision of technical assistance relating to dual-use goods or dual-use technology for use by a person mentioned in Schedule 4.

(5) Paragraphs (1) to (4) are subject to Part 7 (Exceptions and licences).
(6) A person who contravenes a prohibition in any of paragraphs (1) to (4) commits an offence,

but—
(a) it is a defence for a person charged with an offence of contravening a prohibition in paragraph (1) or (2) ('P') to show that P did not know and had no reasonable cause to suspect that the person was connected with Russia;
(b) it is a defence for a person charged with an offence of contravening a prohibition in paragraph (3) ('P') to show that P did not know and had no reasonable cause to suspect that the person was a person mentioned in Schedule 4;
(c) it is a defence for a person charged with an offence of contravening a prohibition in paragraph (4) to show that the person did not know and had no reasonable cause to suspect that the financial services or funds (as the case may be) were provided in pursuance of or in connection with an arrangement mentioned in that paragraph.

Brokering services: non-UK activity relating to dual-use goods and dual-use technology

38.—(1) A person ('P') must not directly or indirectly provide brokering services in relation to an arrangement ('arrangement A') whose object or effect is—
(a) the direct or indirect supply or delivery of dual-use goods for military use from a third country to a place in Russia;
(b) the direct or indirect supply or delivery of dual-use goods to or for use by a person mentioned in Schedule 4;

(c) directly or indirectly making dual-use goods for military use available in a third country for direct or indirect supply or delivery—
(i) to a person connected with Russia, or
(ii) to a place in Russia;
(d) directly or indirectly making dual-use technology for military use available in a third country for transfer—
(i) to a person connected with Russia, or
(ii) to a place in Russia;
(e) directly or indirectly making dual-use goods or dual-use technology available to or for use by a person mentioned in Schedule 4.
(f) the transfer of dual-use technology for military use from a place in a third country—
(i) to a person connected with Russia, or
(ii) to a place in Russia;
(g) the transfer of dual-use technology from a place in a third country to a person mentioned in Schedule 4;
(h) the direct or indirect provision, in a non-UK country, of technical assistance relating to dual-use goods for military use or dual-use technology for military use—
(i) to a person connected with Russia, or
(ii) for use in Russia;
(i) the direct or indirect provision, in a non-UK country, of technical assistance relating to dual-use goods or dual-use technology to a person mentioned in Schedule 4.
(j) the direct or indirect provision, in a non-UK country, of financial services—
(i) to a person connected with Russia, where arrangement A, or any other arrangement in connection with which arrangement A is entered into, is an arrangement mentioned in regulation 37(1), or
(ii) where arrangement A, or any other arrangement in connection with which arrangement A is entered into, is an arrangement mentioned in regulation 37(3);
(k) directly or indirectly making funds available, in a non-UK country, to a person connected with Russia, where arrangement A, or any other arrangement in connection with which arrangement A is entered into, is an arrangement mentioned in regulation 37(1); or
(l) the direct or indirect provision of funds from a non-UK country, where arrangement A, or any other arrangement in connection with which arrangement A is entered into, is an arrangement mentioned in regulation 37(3).

(2) Paragraph (1) is subject to Part 7 (Exceptions and licences).

(3) A person who contravenes a prohibition in paragraph (1) commits an offence, but it is a defence for a person charged with that offence to show that the person did not know and had no reasonable cause to suspect that the brokering services were provided in relation to an arrangement mentioned in that paragraph.

(4) In this regulation—

'non-UK country' means a country that is not the United Kingdom; 'third country' means—
(a) for the purposes of paragraph (1)(a) and (c), a country that is not the United Kingdom, the Isle of Man or Russia,
(b) for the purposes of any other provision of paragraph (1), a country that is not the United Kingdom or Russia.

CHAPTER 4

Energy-related goods and related activities

Interpretation of this Chapter

39. For the purposes of this Chapter 'Russia' includes Russia's exclusive economic zone and continental shelf (which terms are to be interpreted in accordance with the United Nations Convention on the Law of the Sea)([11]).

Export of energy-related goods

40.—(1) The export of energy-related goods for use in Russia is prohibited.

(2) Paragraph (1) is subject to Part 7 (Exceptions and licences).

Supply and delivery of energy-related goods

41.—(1) A person must not directly or indirectly supply or deliver energy-related goods for use in Russia from a third country to a place in Russia.

(2) Paragraph (1) is subject to Part 7 (Exceptions and licences).

(3) A person who contravenes the prohibition in paragraph (1) commits an offence, but it is a defence for a person charged with that offence to show that the person did not know and had no reasonable cause to suspect that—

(a) the goods were destined (or ultimately destined) for Russia, or

(b) the goods were for use in Russia.

(4) In this regulation 'third country' means a country that is not the United Kingdom, the Isle of Man or Russia.

Making energy-related goods available

42.—(1) A person must not directly or indirectly make energy-related goods available for use in Russia.

(2) Paragraph (1) is subject to Part 7 (Exceptions and licences).

(3) A person who contravenes a prohibition in paragraph (1) commits an offence, but it is a defence for a person charged with that offence to show that the person did not know and had no reasonable cause to suspect that the goods were for use in Russia.

Technical assistance relating to energy-related goods

43.—(1) A person must not directly or indirectly—

(a) provide technical assistance relating to energy-related goods for use in Russia; or

(b) provide, to a person connected with Russia, technical assistance relating to energy-related goods.

(2) Paragraph (1) is subject to Part 7 (Exceptions and licences).

(3) A person who contravenes a prohibition in paragraph (1) commits an offence, but—

(a) it is a defence for a person charged with the offence in paragraph (1)(a) to show that the person did not know and had no reasonable cause to suspect that the goods were for use in Russia;

---

[11] Command 8941.

(b) it is a defence for a person charged with the offence in paragraph (1)(b) ('P') to show that P did not know and had no reasonable cause to suspect that the person was connected with Russia.

Financial services and funds relating to energy-related goods and energy-related technology

44.—(1) A person must not directly or indirectly provide, to a person connected with Russia, financial services in pursuance of or in connection with an arrangement whose object or effect is—

(a) the export of energy-related goods,

(b) the direct or indirect supply or delivery of energy-related goods,

(c) directly or indirectly making energy-related goods available to a person, or

(d) the direct or indirect provision of technical assistance relating to energy-related goods.

(2) A person must not directly or indirectly make funds available to a person connected with Russia in pursuance of or in connection with an arrangement mentioned in paragraph (1).

(3) A person must not directly or indirectly provide financial services or funds in pursuance of or in connection with an arrangement whose object or effect is—

(a) the export to Russia of energy-related goods for use in Russia;

(b) the direct or indirect supply or delivery of energy-related goods for use in Russia;

(c) directly or indirectly making energy-related goods available for use in Russia;

(d) the direct or indirect provision of technical assistance relating to energy-related goods to a person connected with Russia;

(e) the direct or indirect provision of technical assistance relating to energy-related goods for use in Russia;

(4) Paragraphs (1) to (3) are subject to Part 7 (Exceptions and licences).

(5) A person who contravenes a prohibition in any of paragraphs (1) to (3) commits an offence,

but—

(a) it is a defence for a person charged with an offence of contravening a prohibition in paragraph (1) or (2) ('P') to show that P did not know and had no reasonable cause to suspect that the person was connected with Russia;

(b) it is a defence for a person charged with an offence of contravening a prohibition in paragraph (3) to show that the person did not know and had no reasonable cause to suspect that the financial services or funds (as the case may be) were provided in pursuance of or in connection with an arrangement mentioned that paragraph.

Brokering services: non-UK activity relating to energy-related goods and energy-related technology

45.—(1) A person ('P') must not directly or indirectly provide brokering services in relation to an arrangement ('arrangement A') whose object or effect is—

(a) the direct or indirect supply or delivery of energy-related goods for use in Russia from a third country to a place in Russia;

(b) directly or indirectly making energy-related goods available for use in Russia;

(c) the direct or indirect provision, in a non-UK country, of technical assistance relating to energy-related goods—

(i) to a person connected with Russia, or

(ii) for use in Russia;

(d) the direct or indirect provision, in a non-UK country, of financial services—
  (i) to a person connected with Russia, where arrangement A, or any other arrangement in connection with which arrangement A is entered into, is an arrangement mentioned in regulation 44(1), or
  (ii) where arrangement A, or any other arrangement in connection with which arrangement A is entered into, is an arrangement mentioned in regulation 44(3);
(e) directly or indirectly making funds available, in a non-UK country, to a person connected with Russia, where arrangement A, or any other arrangement in connection with which arrangement A is entered into, is an arrangement mentioned in regulation 44(1); or
(f) the direct or indirect provision of funds from a non-UK country, where arrangement A, or any other arrangement in connection with which arrangement A is entered into, is an arrangement mentioned in regulation 44(3).

(2) Paragraph (1) is subject to Part 7 (Exceptions and licences).

(3) A person who contravenes a prohibition in paragraph (1) commits an offence, but it is a defence for a person charged with that offence to show that the person did not know and had no reasonable cause to suspect that the brokering services were provided in relation to an arrangement mentioned in that paragraph.

(4) In this regulation—

'non-UK country' means a country that is not the United Kingdom;

'third country' means a country that is not the United Kingdom, the Isle of Man or Russia.

Prohibition on providing other energy-related services

46.—(1) A person must not provide, directly or indirectly, relevant energy services.

(2) Paragraph (1) is subject to Part 7 (Exceptions and licences).

(3) A person who contravenes the prohibition in paragraph (1) commits an offence, but it is a defence for a person charged with that offence to show that the person did not know and had no reasonable cause to suspect that the person was providing relevant energy services.

(4) In this regulation—

'relevant energy services' means specified services necessary for a relevant oil exploration or production project;

'relevant oil exploration or production project' means a project in Russia within any of the following descriptions—
(a) oil exploration and production in waters deeper than 150 metres;
(b) oil exploration and production in the offshore area north of the Arctic Circle; or
(c) a project that has the potential to produce oil from resources located in shale formations by way of hydraulic fracturing, excluding exploration and production through shale formations to locate or extract oil from non-shale reservoirs;

'specified services' means any of the following—
(a) drilling;
(b) well testing;
(c) logging and completion services;
(d) supply of specialised floating vessels.

CHAPTER 5

Exports and imports, and related activities, in relation to Crimea

Imports from Crimea

47.—(1) The import of goods which originate in Crimea is prohibited.

(2) Paragraph (1) is subject to Part 7 (Exceptions and licences).

Export of infrastructure-related goods to Crimea

48.—(1) The export of infrastructure-related goods to, or for use in, Crimea, is prohibited.

(2) Paragraph (1) is subject to Part 7 (Exceptions and licences).

Supply and delivery of infrastructure-related goods

49.—(1) A person must not directly or indirectly supply or deliver infrastructure-related goods from a third country to a place in Crimea.

(2) Paragraph (1) is subject to Part 7 (Exceptions and licences).

(3) A person who contravenes the prohibition in paragraph (1) commits an offence, but it is a defence for a person charged with that offence to show that the person did not know and had no reasonable cause to suspect that the goods were destined (or ultimately destined) for Crimea.

(4) In this regulation, 'third country' means a country that is not the United Kingdom, the Isle of Man or Crimea.

Making infrastructure-related goods available

50.—(1) A person must not—

(a) directly or indirectly make infrastructure-related goods available to a person connected with Crimea;

(b) directly or indirectly make infrastructure-related goods available for use in Crimea.

(2) Paragraph (1) is subject to Part 7 (Exceptions and licences).

(3) A person who contravenes a prohibition in paragraph (1) commits an offence, but—

(a) it is a defence for a person charged with the offence of contravening paragraph (1)(a) ('P') to show that P did not know and had no reasonable cause to suspect that the person was connected with Crimea;

(b) it is a defence for a person charged with the offence of contravening paragraph (1)(b) to show that the person did not know and had no reasonable cause to suspect that the goods were for use in Crimea.

Technical assistance relating to infrastructure-related goods

51.—(1) A person must not directly or indirectly provide technical assistance relating to infrastructure-related goods—

(a) to a person connected with Crimea, or

(b) for use in Crimea.

(2) Paragraph (1) is subject to Part 7 (Exceptions and licences).

(3) A person who contravenes a prohibition in paragraph (1) commits an offence, but—

(a) it is a defence for a person charged with the offence of contravening paragraph (1)(a) ('P') to show that P did not know and had no reasonable cause to suspect that the person was connected with Crimea;

(b) it is a defence for a person charged with the offence of contravening paragraph (1)(b) to show that the person did not know and had no reasonable cause to suspect that the goods were for use in Crimea.

Financial services and funds relating to infrastructure-related goods etc.

52.—(1) A person must not directly or indirectly provide, to a person connected with Crimea, financial services in pursuance of or in connection with an arrangement whose object or effect is—

(a) the export of infrastructure-related goods,

(b) the direct or indirect supply or delivery of infrastructure-related goods,

(c) directly or indirectly making infrastructure-related goods available to a person, or

(d) the direct or indirect provision of technical assistance relating to infrastructure-related goods.

(2) A person must not directly or indirectly make funds available to a person connected with Crimea in pursuance of or in connection with an arrangement mentioned in paragraph (1).

(3) A person must not directly or indirectly provide financial services or funds in pursuance of or in connection with an arrangement whose object or effect is—

(a) the import of goods which originate in Crimea;

(b) the export of infrastructure-related goods to, or for use in, Crimea,

(c) the direct or indirect supply or delivery of infrastructure-related goods to a place in Crimea,

(d) directly or indirectly making infrastructure-related goods available—

(i) to a person connected with Crimea, or

(ii) for use in Crimea,

(e) the direct or indirect provision of technical assistance relating to infrastructure-related goods—

(i) to a person connected with Crimea, or

(ii) for use in Crimea.

(4) Paragraphs (1) to (3) are subject to Part 7 (Exceptions and licences).

(5) A person who contravenes a prohibition in any of paragraphs (1) to (3) commits an offence,

but—

(a) it is a defence for a person charged with an offence of contravening paragraph (1) or (2) ('P') to show that P did not know and had no reasonable cause to suspect that the person was connected with Crimea;

(b) it is a defence for a person charged with an offence of contravening a prohibition in paragraph (3) to show that the person did not know and had no reasonable cause to suspect that the financial services or funds (as the case may be) were provided in pursuance of or in connection with an arrangement mentioned in that paragraph.

Brokering services: non-UK activity relating to infrastructure-related goods and goods from Crimea

53.—(1) A person must not directly or indirectly provide brokering services in relation to an arrangement ('arrangement A') whose object or effect is—

(a) the import of goods which originate in Crimea;

(b) the direct or indirect supply or delivery of infrastructure-related goods from a third country to a place in Crimea,

(c) directly or indirectly making infrastructure-related goods available in a third country for direct or indirect supply or delivery—
(i) to a person connected with Crimea, or
(ii) to a place in Crimea,
(d) the direct or indirect provision, in a non-UK country, of technical assistance relating to infrastructure-related goods—
(i) to a person connected with Crimea, or
(ii) for use in Crimea,
(e) the direct or indirect provision, in a non-UK country, of financial services—
(i) to a person connected with Crimea, where arrangement A, or any other arrangement in connection with which arrangement A is entered into, is an arrangement mentioned in regulation 52(1), or
(ii) where arrangement A, or any other arrangement in connection with which arrangement A is entered into, is an arrangement mentioned in regulation 52(3) in relation to infrastructure-related goods,
(f) directly or indirectly making funds available, in a non-UK country, to a person connected with Crimea, where arrangement A, or any other arrangement in connection with which arrangement A is entered into, is an arrangement mentioned in regulation 52(1), or
(g) the direct or indirect provision of funds from a non-UK country, where arrangement A, or any other arrangement in connection with which arrangement A is entered into, is an arrangement mentioned in regulation 52(3) in relation to infrastructure-related goods.

(2) Paragraph (1) is subject to Part 7 (Exceptions and licences).

(3) A person who contravenes a prohibition in paragraph (1) commits an offence, but it is a defence for a person charged with that offence to show that the person did not know and had no reasonable cause to suspect that the brokering services were provided in relation to an arrangement mentioned in that paragraph.

(4) In this regulation—

'non-UK country' means a country that is not the United Kingdom;

'third country' means a country that is not the United Kingdom, the Isle of Man or Crimea.

CHAPTER 6

Other services relating to Crimea

Prohibition on providing certain services relating to Crimea

54.—(1) A person must not provide—
(a) services relating to a relevant infrastructure sector in Crimea; or
(b) services relating to tourism in Crimea.

(2) Paragraph (1) is subject to Part 7 (Exceptions and licences).

(3) A person who contravenes the prohibition in paragraph (1) commits an offence, but—
(a) it is a defence for a person charged with the offence in paragraph (1)(a) ('P') to show that P did not know and had no reasonable cause to suspect that P was providing services relating to a relevant infrastructure sector in Crimea;
(b) it is a defence for a person charged with the offence in paragraph (1)(b) ('P') to show that P did not know and had no reasonable cause to suspect that P was providing services relating to tourism in Crimea.

(4) In this regulation—
'services relating to a relevant infrastructure sector in Crimea' means technical assistance, brokering, construction or engineering services directly relating to infrastructure in Crimea in any of the following sectors—

(a) transport;
(b) telecommunications;
(c) energy;
(d) the prospection, exploration and production of oil, gas and mineral resources; 'technical assistance' means the provision of technical support or any other technical service.

CHAPTER 7
Further provision

Circumventing etc. prohibitions

55.—(1) A person must not intentionally participate in activities knowing that the object or effect of them is, whether directly or indirectly—

(a) to circumvent any of the prohibitions in Chapters 2 to 6 of this Part, or
(b) to enable or facilitate the contravention of any such prohibition.

(2) A person who contravenes a prohibition in paragraph (1) commits an offence.

Defences

56.—(1) Paragraph (2) applies where a person relies on a defence under any of Chapters 2 to 6 of this Part.

(2) If evidence is adduced which is sufficient to raise an issue with respect to the defence, the court must assume that the defence is satisfied unless the prosecution proves beyond reasonable doubt that it is not.

PART 6
SHIPS

Movement of ships

57.—(1) The Secretary of State may give a Crimean ports direction to a master or pilot of a British ship which is a cruise ship.

(2) In this regulation, a 'Crimean ports direction' is a direction prohibiting a ship from entering a port or any ports located in Crimea.

(3) It is an offence for a person to whom a direction under this regulation is given to fail to comply with the direction.

(4) A Crimean ports direction—

(a) may be given to any master or pilot of a British ship which is a cruise ship, or to masters and pilots of British ships which are cruise ships generally;
(b) may be of indefinite duration or a defined duration.

(5) The Secretary of State may vary, revoke or suspend a Crimean ports direction at any time.

(6) In this regulation, 'cruise ship' means a ship providing cruise services.

(7) Any expression used in this Part and in section 7 of the Act (shipping sanctions) has the same meaning in this Part as it has in that section.

PART 7
EXCEPTIONS AND LICENCES

Asset-freeze etc.: exceptions from prohibitions

58.—(1) The prohibition in regulation 11 (asset-freeze in relation to designated persons) is not contravened by an independent person ('P') transferring to another person a legal or equitable interest in funds or economic resources where, immediately before the transfer, the interest—

(a) is held by P, and

(b) is not held jointly with the designated person.

(2) In paragraph (1) 'independent person' means a person who—

(a) is not the designated person, and

(b) is not owned or controlled directly or indirectly (within the meaning of regulation 7) by the designated person.

(3) The prohibitions in regulations 11 to 13 (asset-freeze in relation to, and making funds available to or for the benefit of, designated persons) are not contravened by a relevant institution crediting a frozen account with interest or other earnings due on the account.

(4) The prohibitions in regulations 12 and 13 (making funds available to, or for the benefit of, designated persons) are not contravened by a relevant institution crediting a frozen account where it receives funds transferred to that institution for crediting to that account.

(5) The prohibitions in regulations 12 and 13 are not contravened by the transfer of funds to a relevant institution for crediting to an account held or controlled (directly or indirectly) by a designated person, where those funds are transferred in discharge (or partial discharge) of an obligation which arose before the date on which the person became a designated person.

(6) The prohibitions in regulations 11 to 13 are not contravened in relation to a designated person ('P') by a transfer of funds from account A to account B, where—

(a) account A is with a relevant institution which carries on an excluded activity within the meaning of section 142D of the Financial Services and Markets Act 2000([12]),

(b) account B is with a ring-fenced body within the meaning of section 142A of the Financial Services and Markets Act 2000([13]), and

(c) accounts A and B are held or controlled (directly or indirectly) by P.

(7) In this regulation—

'designated person' has the same meaning as it has in Chapter 1 Part 3 (Finance);

'frozen account' means an account with a relevant institution which is held or controlled (directly or indirectly) by a designated person;

'relevant institution' means a person that has permission under Part 4A of the Financial Services and Markets Act 2000([14]) (permission to carry on regulated activity).

---

[12] 2000 c.8. Section 142D was inserted by section 4(1) of the Financial Services (Banking Reform) Act 2013 (c.33).

[13] Section 142A was inserted by section 4(1) of the Financial Services (Banking Reform) Act 2013 (c.33).

[14] Part 4A was inserted by the Financial Services Act 2012 (c.21), section 11(2) and amended by S.I. 2018/135.

(8) The definition of 'relevant institution' in paragraph (7) is to be read with section 22 of the Financial Services and Markets Act 2000([15]), any relevant order under that section([16]) and Schedule 2 to that Act([17]).

Exceptions relating to loans and credit arrangements

59.—(1) The prohibitions in regulation 17 (loans and credit arrangements) are not contravened by the grant of—

(a) a relevant loan that has a specific and documented objective of making funds available for non-restricted trade;

(b) a relevant loan that has a specific and documented objective of making emergency funds available to meet applicable solvency or liquidity criteria for a relevant subsidiary;

(c) a relevant loan consisting of a drawdown or disbursement made under an arrangement entered into before 15th September 2014, where the conditions in paragraph (2) are met.

(2) The conditions referred to in paragraph (1)(c) are that—

(a) all the terms and conditions of such drawdowns or disbursements—

(i) were agreed before 15th September 2014;

(ii) have not been modified on or after that date; and

(b) a contractual maturity date has been fixed for the repayment in full of all funds made available and for the cancellation of all the rights and obligations under the arrangement.

(3) In this regulation—

'non-restricted trade' means any trade that is not prohibited under Part 5; 'relevant loan' has the meaning given to it in regulation 17;

'relevant subsidiary' means a person, other than an individual, which is—

(a) incorporated or constituted under the law of any part of the United Kingdom, and

(b) owned (within the meaning of regulation 16(7)) by a person mentioned in paragraphs 1 to 5 of Schedule 2.

Exceptions relating to investments in relation to Crimea

60.—(1) The prohibitions in regulation 18 (investments in relation to Crimea) are not contravened by any act done by a person ('P') in satisfaction of an obligation of P arising under a contract concluded before 20 December 2014, or an ancillary contract necessary for the satisfaction of such a contract, provided that P has notified the Treasury no later than the day five working days before the day on which the act is carried out.

(2) The prohibitions in regulation 18 are not contravened by activities carried on by a person with entities outside Crimea where the related investment is not destined for an entity in Crimea.

---

[15] Section 22 was amended by; the Financial Guidance and Claims Act 2018 (c.10), Part 2, s.27(4); the Financial Services Act 2012, section 7(1); and S.I. 2018/135.

[16] S.I. 2001/544, as amended by S.I. 2017/500.

[17] Schedule 2 was amended by; the Dormant Bank and Building Society Accounts Act 2008 (c.31), section 15, Schedule 2, para. 1; the Regulation of Financial Services (Land Transactions) Act 2003 (c.24), section 1; the Financial Services Act 2012, section 7(2) to (5) and section 8; S.I. 2013/1881; and it is prospectively amended by S.I. 2018/135.

Trade: exception for emergencies in certain cases

61.—(1) The prohibitions in regulations 40 to 45 (prohibitions relating to energy-related goods etc.) and regulations 48 to 54 (prohibitions relating to infrastructure in Crimea etc.) are not contravened by a person ('P') where the P provides justification to the Secretary of State within the relevant period that the act is an act dealing with an emergency.

(2) In this regulation—

'an act dealing with an emergency' means an act assisting with the urgent prevention or mitigation of an event likely to have a serious and significant impact on human health or safety, infrastructure or the environment;

'relevant period', in relation to an act, means the period of 5 working days beginning with the day on which the act is done.

Exception relating to trade restrictions in relation to Crimea

62.—(1) A prohibition in regulation 47 (imports from Crimea) or regulation 52(3)(a) (financial services and funds in relation to imports from Crimea) is not contravened by any action in relation to goods which—

(a) originate in Crimea, and

(b) are the subject of a certificate of origin.

(2) In this regulation a 'certificate of origin' means a document issued by the Government of Ukraine or a person acting on behalf of the Government of Ukraine confirming that the goods originate in Ukraine.

Exception for acts done for purposes of national security or prevention of serious crime

63.—(1) Where an act would, in the absence of this paragraph, be prohibited by regulation 9(2) (confidentiality) or any prohibition in Part 3 (Finance) or 5 (Trade), or under or by virtue of Part 6 (Ships) that prohibition does not apply to the act if the act is one which a responsible officer has determined would be in the interests of—

(a) national security, or

(b) the prevention or detection of serious crime in the United Kingdom or elsewhere.

(2) Where, in the absence of this paragraph, a thing would be required to be done under or by virtue of a provision of Part 8 (Information and records) or Part 10 (Maritime enforcement), that requirement does not apply if a responsible officer has determined that not doing the thing in question would be in the interests of—

(a) national security, or

(b) the prevention or detection of serious crime in the United Kingdom or elsewhere.

(3) In this regulation 'responsible officer' means a person in the service of the Crown or holding office under the Crown, acting in the course of that person's duty.

Treasury licences

64.—(1) The prohibitions in regulations 11 to 15 (asset-freeze etc.) and 18 (investments in relation to Crimea) do not apply to anything done under the authority of a licence issued by the Treasury under this paragraph.

(2) The Treasury may issue a licence which authorises acts by a particular person only—

(a) in the case of acts which would otherwise be prohibited by regulations 11 to 15, where the Treasury consider that it is appropriate to issue the licence for a purpose set out in Part 1 of Schedule 5, and
(b) in the case of acts which would otherwise be prohibited by regulation 18, where the Treasury consider that it is appropriate to issue the licence for a purpose set out in Part 2 of Schedule 5.

Trade licences

65. The prohibitions in Chapters 2 to 6 of Part 5 (Trade) do not apply to anything done under the authority of a licence issued by the Secretary of State under this regulation.

Licences: general provisions

66.—(1) This regulation applies in relation to Treasury licences and trade licences.
(2) A licence must specify the acts authorised by it.
(3) A licence may be general or may authorise acts by a particular person or persons of a particular description.
(4) A licence may —
(a) contain conditions;
(b) be of indefinite duration or a defined duration.
(5) A person who issues a licence may vary, revoke or suspend it at any time.
(6) A person who issues, varies, revokes or suspends a licence which authorises acts by a particular person must give written notice to that person of the issue, variation, revocation or suspension of the licence.
(7) A person who issues, varies, revokes or suspends a general licence or a licence which authorises acts by persons of a particular description must take such steps as that person considers appropriate to publicise the issue, variation, revocation or suspension of the licence.

Finance: licensing offences

67.—(1) A person ('P') commits an offence if P knowingly or recklessly—
(a) provides information that is false in a material respect, or
(b) provides or produces a document that is not what it purports to be, for the purpose of obtaining a Treasury licence (whether for P or anyone else).
(2) A person who purports to act under the authority of a Treasury licence but who fails to comply with any condition of the licence commits an offence.

Trade: licensing offences

68.—(1) A person ('P') commits an offence if P knowingly or recklessly—
(a) provides information that is false in a material respect, or
(b) provides or produces a document that is not what it purports to be, for the purpose of obtaining a trade licence (whether for P or anyone else).
(2) A person who purports to act under the authority of a trade licence but who fails to comply with any condition of the licence commits an offence.
(3) A licence in respect of which an offence under paragraph (1) has been committed is to be treated as void from the time at which it was issued.

Section 8B(1) to (3) of Immigration Act 1971: directions

69.—(1) The Secretary of State may direct that, in relation to any person within regulation 20 whose name is specified, or who is of a specified description, section 8B(1) and (2) of the Immigration Act 1971, or section 8B(3) of that Act, have effect subject to specified exceptions.

(2) A direction under this regulation—

(a) may contain conditions.

(b) must be of a defined duration (and that duration may be expressed in any way, including, for example, being expressed in a way such that the direction ceases to have effect on, or within a specified period after, the occurrence of a specified event).

(3) The Secretary of State may vary, revoke or suspend a direction under this regulation at any time.

(4) On the issue, variation, revocation or suspension of a direction under this regulation, the Secretary of State may take such steps as the Secretary of State considers appropriate to publicise the issue, variation, revocation or suspension of the direction.

(5) In this regulation 'specified' means specified in a direction under this regulation.

PART 8
INFORMATION AND RECORDS

Finance: reporting obligations

70.—(1) A relevant firm must inform the Treasury as soon as practicable if—

(a) it knows, or has reasonable cause to suspect, that a person—

(i) is a designated person, or

(ii) has committed an offence under any provision of Part 3 (Finance) or regulation 67 (finance: licensing offences), and

(b) the information or other matter on which the knowledge or cause for suspicion is based came to it in the course of carrying on its business.

(2) Where a relevant firm informs the Treasury under paragraph (1), it must state—

(a) the information or other matter on which the knowledge or suspicion is based, and

(b) any information it holds about the person by which the person can be identified.

(3) Paragraph (4) applies if—

(a) a relevant firm informs the Treasury under paragraph (1) that it knows, or has reasonable cause to suspect, that a person is a designated person, and

(b) that person is a customer of the relevant firm.

(4) The relevant firm must also state the nature and amount or quantity of any funds or economic resources held by it for the customer at the time when it first had the knowledge or suspicion.

(5) A relevant institution must inform the Treasury without delay if that institution—

(a) credits a frozen account in accordance with regulation 58(4) (finance: exceptions from prohibitions), or

(b) transfers funds from a frozen account in accordance with regulation 58(6).

(6) A person who fails to comply with a requirement in paragraph (1), (2) or (4) commits an offence.

(7) In this regulation—
'designated person' has the same meaning as it has in Chapter 1 of Part 3 (Finance); 'frozen account' has the same meaning as it has in regulation 58;
'relevant firm' is to be read in accordance with regulation 71; 'relevant institution' has the same meaning as it has in regulation 58.

'Relevant firm'

71.—(1) The following are relevant firms for the purposes of regulation 70—
(a) a person that has permission under Part 4A of the Financial Services and Markets Act 2000 (permission to carry on regulated activity);
(b) an undertaking that by way of business—
(i) operates a currency exchange office,
(ii) transmits money (or any representation of monetary value) by any means, or
(iii) cashes cheques that are made payable to customers;
(c) a firm or sole practitioner that is—
(i) a statutory auditor within the meaning of Part 42 of the Companies Act 2006 (statutory auditors)([18]), or
(ii) a local auditor within the meaning of section 4(1) of the Local Audit and Accountability Act 2014 (general requirements for audit)([19]);
(d) a firm or sole practitioner that provides to other persons, by way of business—
(i) accountancy services,
(ii) legal or notarial services,
(iii) advice about tax affairs, or
(iv) trust or company services within the meaning of paragraph (2);
(e) a firm or sole practitioner that carries out, or whose employees carry out, estate agency work;
(f) the holder of a casino operating licence within the meaning given by section 65(2)(a) of the Gambling Act 2005 (nature of a licence)([20]);
(g) a person engaged in the business of making, supplying, selling (including selling by auction) or exchanging—
(i) articles made from gold, silver, platinum or palladium, or
(ii) precious stones or pearls.

(2) In paragraph (1) 'trust or company services' means any of the following services—
(a) forming companies or other legal persons;
(b) acting, or arranging for another person to act—
(i) as a director or secretary of a company,
(ii) as a partner of a partnership, or
(iii) in a similar capacity in relation to other legal persons;
(c) providing a registered office, business address, correspondence or administrative address or other related services for a company, partnership or any other legal person or arrangement;

[18] 2006 c.46. Section 1210 was amended by; S.I. 2017/516; S.I. 2017/1164; S.I. 2013/3115; S.I. 2012/1809; S.I. 2008/1950; S.I. 2008/567; and S.I. 2008/565.
[19] 2014 c.2.
[20] 2005 c.19.

(d) acting, or arranging for another person to act, as—
   (i) a trustee of an express trust or similar legal arrangement, or
   (ii) a nominee shareholder for a person.

(3) In paragraph (1)—

'estate agency work' is to be read in accordance with section 1 of the Estate Agents Act 1979([21]), but as if references in that section to disposing of or acquiring an interest in land included (despite anything in section 2 of that Act) references to disposing of or acquiring an estate or interest in land outside the United Kingdom where that estate or interest is capable of being owned or held as a separate interest;

'firm' means any entity that, whether or not a legal person, is not an individual, and includes a body corporate and a partnership or other unincorporated body.

(4) Paragraph (1)(a) and (b) is to be read with section 22 of the Financial Services and Markets Act 2000, any relevant order under that section and Schedule 2 to that Act.

(5) For the purposes of regulation 70(1), information or another matter comes to a relevant firm 'in the course of carrying on its business' if the information or other matter comes to the firm—
   (a) in the case of a relevant firm within paragraph(1)(a), in the course of carrying on an activity in respect of which the permission mentioned in that provision is required;
   (b) in the case of a relevant firm within paragraph (1)(c)(i), in the course of carrying out statutory audit work within the meaning of section 1210 of the Companies Act 2006 (meaning of statutory auditor)([22]);
   (c) in the case of a relevant firm within paragraph (1)(c)(ii), in the course of carrying out an audit required by the Local Audit and Accountability Act 2014;
   (d) in the case of a relevant firm within paragraph (1)(f), in the course of carrying on an activity in respect of which the licence mentioned in that provision is required;
   (e) in the case of a relevant firm within any other provision of paragraph (1), in the course of carrying on an activity mentioned in that provision.

Finance: powers to request information

72.—(1) The Treasury may request a designated person to provide information about—
   (a) funds or economic resources owned, held or controlled by or on behalf of the designated person, or
   (b) any disposal of such funds or economic resources.

(2) The Treasury may request a designated person to provide such information as the Treasury may reasonably require about expenditure—
   (a) by the designated person, or
   (b) for the benefit of the designated person.

(3) For the purposes of paragraph (2), expenditure for the benefit of a designated person includes expenditure on the discharge (or partial discharge) of a financial obligation for which the designated person is wholly or partly responsible.

---

[21] 1979 c.38, amended by paragraph 40 of Schedule 1 to the Law Reform (Miscellaneous Provisions) (Scotland) Act 1985 (c.73); paragraph 42 of Schedule 2 to the Planning (Consequential Provisions) Act 1990 (c.11); paragraph 28 of Schedule 2 to the Planning (Consequential Provisions) (Scotland) Act 1997 (c.11); section 70 of the Enterprise and Regulatory Reform Act 2013 (c.24); S.I. 2001/1283; S.I. 2000/121; and S.I. 1991/2684.

[22] Section 1210 has been amended by S.I. 2017/516, S.I. 2017/1164, S.I. 2008/565 and S.I. 2008/1950.

(4) The power in paragraph (1) or (2) is exercisable only where the Treasury believe that it is necessary for the purpose of monitoring compliance with or detecting evasion of any provision of Part 3 (Finance).

(5) The Treasury may request a person acting under a Treasury licence to provide information about—

(a) funds or economic resources dealt with under the licence,

(b) funds, economic resources or financial services made available under the licence, or

(c) any matter to which a licence relates, where that licence authorises an act that would otherwise be prohibited under regulation 18 (investments in Crimea).

(6) The Treasury may request a person to provide information within paragraph (7) if the Treasury believe that the person may be able to provide the information.

(7) Information within this paragraph is such information as the Treasury may reasonably require for the purpose of—

(a) establishing for the purposes of any provision of Chapter 1 of Part 3 (Finance)—

(i) the nature and amount or quantity of any funds or economic resources owned, held or controlled by or on behalf of a designated person,

(ii) the nature and amount or quantity of any funds, financial services or economic resources made available directly or indirectly to, or for the benefit of, a designated person, or

(iii) the nature of any financial transactions entered into by a designated person;

(b) monitoring compliance with or detecting evasion of—

(i) any provision of Part 3,

(ii) regulation 70 (finance: reporting obligations), or

(iii) any condition of a Treasury licence;

(c) detecting or obtaining evidence of the commission of an offence under Part 3 or regulation 67 (finance: licensing offences) or 70 (finance: reporting obligations).

(8) The Treasury may specify the way in which, and the period within which, information is to be provided.

(9) If no such period is specified, the information which has been requested must be provided within a reasonable time.

(10) A request may include a continuing obligation to keep the Treasury informed as circumstances change, or on such regular basis as the Treasury may specify.

(11) Information requested under this regulation may relate to any period of time during which a person is, or was, a designated person.

(12) Information requested by virtue of paragraph (1)(b), (2) or (7)(a)(iii) may relate to any period before a person became a designated person (as well as, or instead of, any subsequent period).

(13) Expressions used in this regulation have the same meaning as they have in Part 3.

Finance: production of documents

73.—(1) A request under regulation 72 may include a request to produce specified documents or documents of a specified description.

(2) Where the Treasury request that documents be produced, the Treasury may—

(a) take copies of or extracts from any document so produced,

(b) request any person producing a document to give an explanation of it, and

(c) where that person is a body corporate, partnership or unincorporated body other than a partnership, request any person who is—

(i) in the case of a partnership, a present or past partner or employee of the partnership, or
(ii) in any other case, a present or past officer or employee of the body concerned,
to give such an explanation.

(3) Where the Treasury request a designated person or a person acting under a Treasury licence to produce documents, that person must—
(a) take reasonable steps to obtain the documents (if they are not already in the person's possession or control);
(b) keep the documents under the person's possession or control (except for the purpose of providing them to the Treasury or as the Treasury may otherwise permit).

(4) In this regulation 'designated person' has the same meaning as it has in Chapter 1 of Part 3 (Finance).

Finance: information offences

74.—(1) A person commits an offence, if that person—
(a) without reasonable excuse, refuses or fails within the time and in the manner specified (or, if no time has been specified, within a reasonable time) to comply with any request under regulation 72 (finance: powers to request information);
(b) knowingly or recklessly gives any information, or produces any document, which is false in a material particular in response to such a request;
(c) with intent to evade any provision of regulation 72 or 73 (finance: production of documents), destroys, mutilates, defaces, conceals or removes any document;
(d) otherwise intentionally obstructs the Treasury in the exercise of their powers under regulation 72 or 73.

(2) Where a person is convicted of an offence under this regulation, the court may make an order requiring that person, within such period as may be specified in the order, to comply with the request.

Trade: application of information powers in CEMA

75.—(1) Section 77A of CEMA([23]) applies in relation to a person carrying on a relevant activity as it applies in relation to a person concerned in the importation or exportation of goods but as if—
(a) in subsection (1), the reference to a person concerned in the importation or exportation of goods for which for that purpose an entry is required by regulation 5 of the Customs Controls on Importation of Goods Regulations 1991([24]) or an entry or specification is required by or under CEMA were to a person carrying on a relevant activity;
(b) any other reference to importation or exportation were to a relevant activity;
(c) any reference to goods were to the goods, technology, services or funds to which the relevant activity relates.

(2) For the purposes of paragraph (1), a 'relevant activity' means an activity—
(a) which would, unless done under the authority of a trade licence, constitute a contravention of any prohibition in Chapters 2 to 6 of Part 5 (Trade), except any prohibition on imports or exports, or

[23] Section 77A was inserted by the Finance Act 1987 (c.16), section 10 and amended by S.I. 1992/3095.

[24] S.I. 1991/2724 as amended by S.I. 1992/3095, S.I. 1993/3014 and S.I. 2011/1043 and is prospectively revoked by S.I. 2018/1247.

(b) which would constitute a contravention of the prohibition in regulation 55(1) (circumventing etc. prohibitions).

General trade licences: records

76.—(1) This regulation applies in relation to a person ('P') who does any act authorised by a general licence issued under regulation 65 (trade licences) ('the licence').

(2) P must keep a register or record containing such details as may be necessary to allow the following information to be identified in relation to each act done under the authority of the licence—

(a) a description of the act;

(b) a description of any goods, technology, services or funds to which the act relates;

(c) the date of the act or the dates between which the act took place;

(d) the quantity of any goods or funds to which the act relates;

(e) P's name and address;

(f) the name and address of any consignee of goods to which the act relates or any recipient of technology, services or funds to which the act relates;

(g) in so far as it is known to P, the name and address of the end-user of the goods, technology, services or funds to which the act relates;

(h) if different from P, the name and address of the supplier of any goods to which the act relates;

(i) any further information required by the licence.

(3) The register or record relating to an act must be kept until the end of the calendar year in which the register or record is created and for a further period of 4 years from the end of that calendar year.

(4) P must notify the Secretary of State in writing of P's name and the address at which the register or record may be inspected, and must make a further such notification if those details change.

(5) A notification under paragraph (4) must be given no later than 30 days after—

(a) P first does any act authorised by the licence, or

(b) there is any change to the details previously notified.

(6) A person who fails to comply with a requirement in paragraph (2), (3) or (4) commits an offence.

General trade licences: inspection of records

77.—(1) A person authorised by the Secretary of State or the Commissioners (an 'official') may at any reasonable hour enter premises notified under regulation 76(4) for the purposes of monitoring compliance with or detecting evasion of regulation 76(2) or (3).

(2) An official may require any person on the premises to produce any register or record required to be kept under regulation 76, or any document included in such a register or record, that is in the person's possession or control.

(3) An official may inspect and copy any such register, record or document.

(4) An official must, if requested to do so, produce documentary evidence that he or she is authorised to exercise a power conferred by this regulation.

(5) A person commits an offence if, without reasonable excuse, the person—

(a) intentionally obstructs an official in the performance of any of the official's functions under this regulation, or

(b) fails to produce a register, record or document when reasonably required to do so by an official under this regulation.

Disclosure of information

78.—(1) The Secretary of State, the Treasury or the Commissioners may, in accordance with this regulation, disclose—

(a) any information obtained under or by virtue of Part 7 (Exceptions and licences), this Part or Part 10 (Maritime enforcement), or

(b) any information held in connection with—

(i) anything done under or by virtue of Part 2 (Designation of persons), Part 3 (Finance), Part 5 (Trade), Part 6 (Ships), or

(ii) any exception or licence under Part 7 or anything done in accordance with such an exception or under the authority of such a licence.

(2) Information referred to in paragraph (1) may be disclosed for, or in connection with, any of the following purposes—

(a) any purpose stated in regulation 4;

(b) the exercise of functions under these Regulations;

(c) facilitating, monitoring or ensuring compliance with these Regulations;

(d) taking any action with a view to instituting, or otherwise for the purposes of, any proceedings in the United Kingdom—

(i) for an offence under any provision of these Regulations,

(ii) for an offence under CEMA in connection with any prohibition in Part 5 on imports or exports, or

(iii) in relation to a monetary penalty under section 146 of the Policing and Crime Act 2017 (breach of financial sanctions legislation);

(e) taking any action with a view to instituting, or otherwise for the purposes of, any proceedings in any of the Channel Islands, the Isle of Man, or any British overseas territory, for an offence—

(i) under a provision in any such jurisdiction that is similar to a provision of these Regulations, or

(ii) in connection with a prohibition in any such jurisdiction that is similar to a prohibition referred to in sub-paragraph (d)(ii);

(f) compliance with an international obligation([25]);

(g) facilitating the exercise by an authority outside the United Kingdom or by an international organisation of functions which correspond to functions under these Regulations.

(3) Information referred to in paragraph (1) may be disclosed to the following persons—

(a) a police officer;

(b) any person holding or acting in any office under or in the service of—

(i) the Crown in right of the Government of the United Kingdom,

(ii) the Crown in right of the Scottish Government, the Northern Ireland Executive or the Welsh Government,

(iii) the States of Jersey, Guernsey or Alderney or the Chief Pleas of Sark,

(iv) the Government of the Isle of Man, or

(v) the Government of any British overseas territory;

(c) any law officer of the Crown for Jersey, Guernsey or the Isle of Man;

[25] Section 1(8) of the Act defines an 'international obligation' as an obligation of the United Kingdom created or arising by or under any international agreement.

(d) the Scottish Legal Aid Board;
(e) the Financial Conduct Authority, the Prudential Regulation Authority, the Bank of England, the Jersey Financial Services Commission, the Guernsey Financial Services Commission or the Isle of Man Financial Services Authority;
(f) any other regulatory body (whether or not in the United Kingdom);
(g) any organ of the United Nations;
(h) the Council of the European Union, the European Commission or the European External Action Service;
(i) the Government of any country;
(j) any other person where the Secretary of State, the Treasury or the Commissioners (as the case may be) consider that it is appropriate to disclose the information.

(4) Information referred to in paragraph (1) may be disclosed to any person with the consent of a person who, in their own right, is entitled to the information.

(5) In paragraph (4) 'in their own right' means not merely in the capacity as a servant or agent of another person.

(6) In paragraph (1)(b)—
(a) the reference to information includes information obtained at a time when any provision of these Regulations is not in force, and
(b) the reference to a licence under Part 7 includes—
(i) a licence or authorisation which has effect or is treated as if it were a licence which had been issued under that Part, and
(ii) a licence which is deemed to have been issued under that Part.

Part 7: supplementary

79.—(1) A disclosure of information under regulation 78 does not breach any restriction on such disclosure imposed by statute or otherwise.

(2) But nothing in that regulation authorises a disclosure that—
(a) contravenes the data protection legislation, or
(b) is prohibited by any of Parts 1 to 7 or Chapter 1 of Part 9 of the Investigatory Powers Act 2016([26]).

(3) Nothing in this Part is to be read as requiring a person who has acted or is acting as counsel or solicitor for any person to disclose any privileged information in their possession in that capacity.

(4) Regulation 78 does not limit the circumstances in which information may be disclosed apart from that regulation.

(5) Nothing in this Part limits any conditions which may be contained in a Treasury licence or a trade licence.

(6) In this regulation—
'the data protection legislation' has the same meaning as in the Data Protection Act 2018 (see section 3 of that Act)([27]);

---

[26] 2016 c.25. Parts 2 and 5 have been amended by the Policing and Crime Act 2017 (c.3), Schedule 9(3), para 74 and Part 7 has been amended by the Data Protection Act 2018 (c. 12), Schedule 19(1), para 202. Chapter 1 of Part 9 has been amended by regulation 6 of the Investigatory Powers Act 2016 (Commencement No. 3 and Transitory, Transitional and Savings Provisions) Regulations 2017 (S.I. 2017/859).

[27] 2018 c.12. There are amendments to this Act that are not relevant to these Regulations.

'privileged information' means information with respect to which a claim to legal professional privilege (in Scotland, to confidentiality of communications) could be maintained in legal proceedings.

PART 9
ENFORCEMENT

Penalties for offences

80.—(1) A person who commits an offence under any provision of Part 3 (Finance), regulation 67 (finance: licensing offences) or Part 6 (Ships) is liable—
(a) on summary conviction in England and Wales, to imprisonment for a term not exceeding 12 months or a fine (or both);
(b) on summary conviction in Scotland, to imprisonment for a term not exceeding 12 months or a fine not exceeding the statutory maximum (or both);
(c) on summary conviction in Northern Ireland, to imprisonment for a term not exceeding 6 months or a fine not exceeding the statutory maximum (or both);
(d) on conviction on indictment, to imprisonment for a term not exceeding 7 years or a fine (or both).

(2) A person who commits an offence under any provision of Part 5 (Trade) is liable—
(a) on summary conviction in England and Wales, to imprisonment for a term not exceeding 12 months or a fine (or both);
(b) on summary conviction in Scotland, to imprisonment for a term not exceeding 12 months or a fine not exceeding the statutory maximum (or both);
(c) on summary conviction in Northern Ireland, to imprisonment for a term not exceeding 6 months or a fine not exceeding the statutory maximum (or both);
(d) on conviction on indictment, to imprisonment for a term not exceeding 10 years or a fine (or both).

(3) A person who commits an offence under regulation 9(6) (confidentiality), 68 (trade: licensing offences), 76(6) (general trade licences: records) or 77(5) (general trade licences: inspection of records) is liable—
(a) on summary conviction in England and Wales, to imprisonment for a term not exceeding 12 months or a fine (or both);
(b) on summary conviction in Scotland, to imprisonment for a term not exceeding 12 months or a fine not exceeding the statutory maximum (or both);
(c) on summary conviction in Northern Ireland, to imprisonment for a term not exceeding 6 months or a fine not exceeding the statutory maximum (or both);
(d) on conviction on indictment, to imprisonment for a term not exceeding 2 years or a fine (or both).

(4) A person who commits an offence under regulation 70(6) or 74 (information offences in connection with Part 3) is liable—
(a) on summary conviction in England and Wales, to imprisonment for a term not exceeding 6 months or a fine (or both);
(b) on summary conviction in Scotland, to imprisonment for a term not exceeding 6 months or a fine not exceeding level 5 on the standard scale (or both);
(c) on summary conviction in Northern Ireland, to imprisonment for a term not exceeding 6 months or a fine not exceeding level 5 on the standard scale (or both).

(5) In relation to an offence committed before section 154(1) of the Criminal Justice Act 2003([28]) comes into force the reference in each of paragraphs (1)(a), (2)(a) and (3)(a) to 12 months is to be read as a reference to 6 months.

Liability of officers of bodies corporate etc.

81.—(1) Where an offence under these Regulations, committed by a body corporate—

(a) is committed with the consent or connivance of any director, manager, secretary or other similar officer of the body corporate, or any person who was purporting to act in any such capacity, or

(b) is attributable to any neglect on the part of any such person,

that person as well as the body corporate is guilty of the offence and is liable to be proceeded against and punished accordingly.

(2) In paragraph (1) 'director', in relation to a body corporate whose affairs are managed by its members, means a member of the body corporate.

(3) Paragraph (1) also applies in relation to a body that is not a body corporate, with the substitution for the reference to a director of the body of a reference—

(a) in the case of a partnership, to a partner;

(b) in the case of an unincorporated body other than a partnership—

(i) where the body's affairs are managed by its members, to a member of the body;

(ii) in any other case, to a member of the governing body.

(4) Section 171(4) of CEMA (which is a provision similar to this regulation) does not apply to any offence under these Regulations to which that provision would, in the absence of this paragraph, apply.

Jurisdiction to try offences

82.—(1) Where an offence under regulation 9(6) (confidentiality), Part 3 (Finance), regulation 67 (finance: licensing offences) or regulation 70(6) or 74 (information offences in connection with Part 3) is committed in the United Kingdom—

(a) proceedings for the offence may be taken at any place in the United Kingdom, and

(b) the offence may for all incidental purposes be treated as having been committed at any such place.

(2) Where an offence under these Regulations is committed outside the United Kingdom—

(a) proceedings for the offence may be taken at any place in the United Kingdom, and

(b) the offence may for all incidental purposes be treated as having been committed at any such place.

(3) In the application of paragraph (2) to Scotland, any such proceedings against a person may be taken—

(a) in any sheriff court district in which the person is apprehended or is in custody, or

(b) in such sheriff court district as the Lord Advocate may determine.

(4) In paragraph (3) 'sheriff court district' is to be read in accordance with the Criminal Procedure (Scotland) Act 1995 (see section 307(1) of that Act)([29]).

[28] 2003 c.44. Amendments have been made to section 154(1), but none are relevant to these Regulations.

[29] 1995 c.46.

Procedure for offences by unincorporated bodies

83.—(1) Paragraphs (2) and (3) apply if it is alleged that an offence under these Regulations has been committed by an unincorporated body (as opposed to by a member of the body).

(2) Proceedings in England and Wales or Northern Ireland for such an offence must be brought against the body in its own name.

(3) For the purposes of proceedings, for such an offence brought against an unincorporated body—

(a) rules of court relating to the service of documents have effect as if the body were a body corporate;

(b) the following provisions apply as they apply in relation to a body corporate

(i) section 33 of the Criminal Justice Act 1925([30]) and Schedule 3 to the Magistrates' Courts Act 1980([31]);

(ii) section 18 of the Criminal Justice Act (Northern Ireland) 1945([32]) and Article 166 of, and Schedule 4 to, the Magistrates' Courts (Northern Ireland) Order 1981([33]).

(4) A fine imposed on an unincorporated body on its conviction of an offence under these Regulations is to be paid out of the funds of the body.

Time limit for proceedings for summary offences

84.—(1) Proceedings for an offence under these Regulations which is triable only summarily may be brought within the period of 12 months beginning with the date on which evidence sufficient in the opinion of the prosecutor to justify the proceedings comes to the prosecutor's knowledge.

(2) But such proceedings may not be brought by virtue of paragraph (1) more than 3 years after the commission of the offence.

(3) A certificate signed by the prosecutor as to the date on which the evidence in question came to the prosecutor's knowledge is conclusive evidence of the date on which it did so; and a certificate to that effect and purporting to be so signed is to be treated as being so signed unless the contrary is proved.

(4) In relation to proceedings in Scotland—

(a) section 136(3) of the Criminal Procedure (Scotland) Act 1995 (date of commencement of summary proceedings)([34]) applies for the purposes of this regulation as it applies for the purposes of that section, and

(b) references in this regulation to the prosecutor are to be treated as references to the Lord Advocate.

Trade enforcement: application of CEMA

85.—(1) Where the Commissioners investigate or propose to investigate any matter with a view to determining—

(a) whether there are grounds for believing that a relevant offence has been committed, or

---

[30] 1925 c.8, as amended by Statute Law (Repeals) Act 2004 (c.14), section 1(1) and (3) and Schedule 1(17)(11), para. 1. Other amendments have been made to section 33 that are not relevant to these Regulations.

[31] 1980 c.43. Amendments have been made to Schedule 3 that are not relevant to these Regulations.

[32] 1945 c.15 (N.I.).

[33] S.I. 1981/1675 (N.I. 26).

[34] There have been no amendments to section 136(3).

(b) whether a person should be prosecuted for such an offence,

the matter is to be treated as an assigned matter.

(2) In paragraph (1) 'assigned matter' has the meaning given by section 1(1) of CEMA([35]).

(3) In this regulation a 'relevant offence' means an offence under—

(a) Part 5 (Trade),

(b) regulation 68 (trade: licensing offences),

(c) regulation 76(6) (general trade licences: records), or

(d) regulation 77(5) (general trade licences: inspection of records).

(4) Section 138 of CEMA([36]) (arrest of persons) applies to a person who has committed, or whom there are reasonable grounds to suspect of having committed, a relevant offence as it applies to a person who has committed, or whom there are reasonable grounds to suspect of having committed, an offence for which the person is liable to be arrested under the customs and excise Acts, but as if—

(a) any reference to an offence under, or for which a person is liable to be arrested under, the customs and excise Acts were to a relevant offence;

(b) in subsection (2), the reference to any person so liable were to a person who has committed, or whom there are reasonable grounds to suspect of having committed, a relevant offence.

(5) The provisions of CEMA mentioned in paragraph (6) apply in relation to proceedings for a relevant offence as they apply in relation to proceedings for an offence under the customs and excise Acts, but as if—

(a) any reference to the customs and excise Acts were to any of the provisions mentioned in paragraph (3)(a) to (d);

(b) in section 145(6), the reference to an offence for which a person is liable to be arrested under the customs and excise Acts were to a relevant offence;

(c) in section 151, the reference to any penalty imposed under the customs and excise Acts were to any penalty imposed under these Regulations in relation to a relevant offence;

(d) in section 154(2)—

(i) the reference to proceedings relating to customs or excise were to proceedings under any of the provisions mentioned in paragraph (3)(a) to (d), and

(ii) the reference to the place from which any goods have been brought included a reference to the place to which goods have been exported, supplied or delivered or the place to or from which technology has been transferred.

(6) The provisions of CEMA are sections 145, 146, 147, 148(1), 150, 151, 152, 154 and 155([37]) (legal proceedings).

---

[35] The definition of 'assigned matter' in section 1(1) of CEMA was amended by the Commissioners for Revenue and Customs Act 2005 (c.11), Schedule 4, paragraph 22(a), the Scotland Act 2012 (c. 11), section 24(7), the Wales Act 2014 (c.29), section 7(1).

[36] Section 138 of CEMA was amended by; the Police and Criminal Evidence Act 1984 (c. 60), section 114(1), Schedule 6, paragraph 37, and Part 1 of Schedule 7;, the Finance Act 1988 (c. 39), section 11; the Serious and Organised Crime Act 2005 (c. 15), Part 4 of Schedule 7, paragraph 54,; S.I 1989/1341; and S.I. 2007/288.

[37] Section 145 of CEMA was amended by the Police and Criminal Evidence Act 1984, section 114(1), the Commissioners for Revenue and Customs Act 2005, Schedule 4, paragraph 23(a), and S.I. 2014/834. Section 147 was amended by the Criminal Justice Act 1982 (c. 48), Schedule 14, paragraph 42, the Finance Act 1989, section 16(2), and the Criminal Justice Act 2003, Part 2 of Schedule 3, paragraph 50. Section 152

Trade offences in CEMA: modification of penalty

86.—(1) Paragraph (2) applies where a person is guilty of an offence under section 50(2) of CEMA in connection with a prohibition mentioned in regulations 23 or 47(1) (imports).

(2) Where this paragraph applies, the reference to 7 years in section 50(4)(b) of CEMA([38]) is to be read as a reference to 10 years.

(3) Paragraph (4) applies where a person is guilty of an offence under section 68(2) of CEMA in connection with a prohibition mentioned in regulations 22(1), 32, 40(1) or 48 (exports).

(4) Where this paragraph applies, the reference to 7 years in section 68(3)(b) of CEMA([39]) is to be read as a reference to 10 years.

(5) Paragraph (6) applies where a person is guilty of an offence under section 170(2) of CEMA in connection with a prohibition mentioned in regulation 22(1), 23, 32, 40(1), 47(1) or 48 (exports and imports).

(6) Where this paragraph applies, the reference to 7 years in section 170(3)(b) of CEMA([40]) is to be read as a reference to 10 years.

Application of Chapter 1 of Part 2 of Serious Organised Crime and Police Act 2005

87. Chapter 1 of Part 2 of the Serious Organised Crime and Police Act 2005 (investigatory powers)([41]) applies to any offence under Part 3 (Finance) or regulation 67 (finance: licensing offences).

Monetary penalties

88. Each provision in Part 5 (Trade) which contains a prohibition imposed for a purpose mentioned in section 3(1) or (2) of the Act is to be regarded as not being financial sanctions legislation for the purposes of Part 8 of the Policing and Crime Act 2017([42]).

PART 10
MARITIME ENFORCEMENT

Exercise of maritime enforcement powers

89.—(1) A maritime enforcement officer may, for a purpose mentioned in paragraph (2) or (3), exercise any of the maritime enforcement powers in relation to—

(a) a British ship in foreign waters or international waters,

(b) a ship without nationality in international waters, or

(c) a foreign ship in international waters,

and a ship within sub-paragraph (a), (b) or (c) is referred to in this Part as 'a relevant ship'.

---

was amended by the Commissioners for Revenue and Customs Act 2005, Schedule 4, paragraph 26, and Schedule 5. Section 155 was amended by the Commissioners for Revenue and Customs Act 2005, Schedule, 4, paragraph 27, and Schedule 5.

[38] The words '7 years' were inserted in section 50(4)(b) of CEMA by the Finance Act 1988, section 12.

[39] The words '7 years' were inserted in section 68(3)(b) of CEMA by the Finance Act 1988, section 12.

[40] The words '7 years' were inserted in section 170(3)(b) of CEMA by the Finance Act 1988, section 12.

[41] 2005 c.15, as amended by Schedule 3, para. 4 of the Act.

[42] 2017 c.3; see section 143(4)(f) and (4A).

(2) The maritime enforcement powers may be exercised for the purpose of enforcing any of the following—

(a) a prohibition in any of regulations 22 to 26 (trade sanctions relating to military goods and military technology);

(b) a prohibition in any of regulations 32 to 35 (trade sanctions relating to dual-use goods and dual-use technology);

(c) a prohibition in any of regulations 40 to 42 (trade sanctions relating to energy-related goods);

(d) a prohibition in any of regulation 47 to 50 (exports and imports etc. in relation to Crimea);

(e) a prohibition imposed by a condition of a trade licence in relation to a prohibition mentioned in sub-paragraph (a) to (d).

(3) The maritime enforcement powers may also be exercised in relation to a relevant ship for the purpose of—

(a) investigating the suspected carriage of relevant goods on the ship, or

(b) preventing the continued carriage on the ship of goods suspected to be relevant goods.

(4) In this Part, 'the maritime enforcement powers' are the powers conferred by regulations 91 and 92.

(5) This regulation is subject to regulation 93 (restrictions on exercise of maritime enforcement powers).

Maritime enforcement officers

90.—(1) The following persons are 'maritime enforcement officers' for the purposes of this Part—

(a) a commissioned officer of any of Her Majesty's ships;

(b) a member of the Ministry of Defence Police (within the meaning of section 1 of the Ministry of Defence Police Act 1987([43]));

(c) a constable—

(i) who is a member of a police force in England and Wales,

(ii) within the meaning of section 99 of the Police and Fire Reform (Scotland) Act 2012([44]), or

(iii) who is a member of the Police Service of Northern Ireland or the Police Service of Northern Ireland Reserve;

(d) a special constable—

(i) appointed under section 27 of the Police Act 1996([45]),

(ii) appointed under section 9 of the Police and Fire Reform (Scotland) Act 2012, or

(iii) in Northern Ireland, appointed by virtue of provision incorporating section 79 of the Harbours, Docks, and Piers Clauses Act 1847([46]);

[43] 1987 c.4. Section 1 was amended by; paragraph 41 of Schedule 7 to the Police Act 1996 (c.16); paragraph 16 of Schedule 4 to the Police (Northern Ireland) Act 1998 (c.32); section 78(2) of the Police (Northern Ireland) Act 2000 (c.32); section 79(3) of the Police Reform Act 2002 (c.30); and by S.I. 2013/602.

[44] 2012 asp.8 (Scottish Act).

[45] 1996 c.16. Section 27 was amended by paragraphs 22 and 26 of Schedule 16(1) to the Police Reform and Social Responsibility Act 2011 (c.13).

[46] 1847 c.27. Section 79 was amended by S.I. 2006/2167.

(e) a constable who is a member of the British Transport Police Force;

(f) a port constable, within the meaning of section 7 of the Marine Navigation Act 2013([47]), or a person appointed to act as a constable under provision made by virtue of section 16 of the Harbours Act 1964([48]);

(g) a designated customs official within the meaning of Part 1 of the Borders, Citizenship and Immigration Act 2009 (see section 14(6) of that Act)([49]);

(h) a designated NCA officer who is authorised by the Director General of the National Crime Agency (whether generally or specifically) to exercise the powers of a maritime enforcement officer under this Part.

(2) In this regulation, 'a designated NCA officer' means a National Crime Agency officer who is either or both of the following—

(a) an officer designated under section 10 of the Crime and Courts Act 2013([50]) as having the powers and privileges of a constable;

(b) an officer designated under that section as having the powers of a general customs official.

Power to stop, board, search etc.

91.—(1) This regulation applies if a maritime enforcement officer has reasonable grounds to suspect that a relevant ship is carrying prohibited goods or relevant goods.

(2) The officer may—

(a) stop the ship;

(b) board the ship;

(c) for the purpose of exercising a power conferred by paragraph (3) or regulation 92, require the ship to be taken to, and remain in, a port or anchorage in the United Kingdom or any other country willing to receive it.

(3) Where the officer boards a ship by virtue of this regulation, the officer may—

(a) stop any person found on the ship and search that person for—

(i) prohibited goods or relevant goods, or

(ii) any thing that might be used to cause physical injury or damage to property or to endanger the safety of any ship;

(b) search the ship, or any thing found on the ship (including cargo) for prohibited goods or relevant goods;

(4) The officer may—

(a) require a person found on a ship boarded by virtue of this regulation to provide information or produce documents;

(b) inspect and copy such information or documents.

---

[47] 2013 c.23.

[48] 1964 c.40. Section 16 was amended by; section 29(2) of the Wales Act 2017 (c.4); S.I. 1999/672; and S.I. 1970/1681.

[49] 2009 c.11. Designated customs officials are designated, as either a general customs official or a customs revenue official, under sections 8 and 11 of this Act respectively.

[50] 2013 c.22.

(5) The officer may exercise a power conferred by paragraph (3)(a)(i) or (b) only to the extent reasonably required for the purpose of discovering prohibited goods or relevant goods.

(6) The officer may exercise the power conferred by paragraph (3)(a)(ii) in relation to a person only where the officer has reasonable grounds to believe that the person might use a thing to cause physical injury or damage to property or to endanger the safety of any ship.

(7) The officer may use reasonable force, if necessary, in the exercise of any power conferred by this regulation.

Seizure power

92.—(1) This regulation applies if a maritime enforcement officer is lawfully on a relevant ship (whether in exercise of the powers conferred by regulation 91 or otherwise).

(2) The officer may seize any of the following which are found on the ship, in any thing found on the ship, or on any person found on the ship—

(a) goods which the officer has reasonable grounds to suspect are prohibited goods or relevant goods, or

(b) things within regulation 91(3)(a)(ii).

(3) The officer may use reasonable force, if necessary, in the exercise of any power conferred by this regulation.

Restrictions on exercise of maritime enforcement powers

93.—(1) The authority of the Secretary of State is required before any maritime enforcement power is exercised in reliance on regulation 89 in relation to—

(a) a British ship in foreign waters, or

(b) a foreign ship in international waters.

(2) In relation to a British ship in foreign waters other than the sea and other waters within the seaward limits of the territorial sea adjacent to any relevant British possession, the Secretary of State may give authority under paragraph (1) only if the State in whose waters the power would be exercised consents to the exercise of the power.

(3) The Secretary of State may give authority under paragraph (1) only if—

(a) the home state has requested the assistance of the United Kingdom for a purpose mentioned in regulation 89(2) or (3),

(b) the home state has authorised the United Kingdom to act for such a purpose, or

(c) the United Nations Convention on the Law of the Sea 1982 or a UN Security Council Resolution otherwise permits the exercise of the power in relation to the ship.

Interpretation of Part 9

94.—(1) Subject to paragraph (2), any expression used in this Part and in section 19 or 20 of the Act has the same meaning in this Part as it has in section 19 or (as the case may be) section 20 of the Act.

(2) For the purpose of interpreting any reference to 'prohibited goods' or 'relevant goods' in this Part, any reference in section 19 or 20 of the Act to a 'relevant prohibition or requirement' is to be read as a reference to any prohibition specified in regulation 89(2)(a) to (d).

PART 11
SUPPLEMENTARY AND FINAL PROVISION

Notices

95.—(1) This regulation applies in relation to a notice required by regulation 66 (licences: general provisions) to be given to a person.

(2) The notice may be given to an individual—

(a) by delivering it to the individual,

(b) by sending it to the individual by post addressed to the individual at his or her usual or last-known place of residence or business, or

(c) by leaving it for the individual at that place.

(3) The notice may be given to a person other than an individual—

(a) by sending it by post to the proper officer of the body at its principal office, or

(b) by addressing it to the proper officer of the body and leaving it at that office.

(4) The notice may be given to the person by other means, including by electronic means, with the person's consent.

(5) In this regulation, the reference in paragraph (3) to a 'principal office'—

(a) in relation to a registered company, is to be read as a reference to the company's registered office;

(b) in relation to a body incorporated or constituted under the law of a country other than the United Kingdom, includes a reference to the body's principal office in the United Kingdom (if any).

(6) In this regulation—

'proper officer'—

(a) in relation to a body other than a partnership, means the secretary or other executive officer charged with the conduct of the body's general affairs, and

(b) in relation to a partnership, means a partner or a person who has the control or management of the partnership business;

'registered company' means a company registered under the enactments relating to companies for the time being in force in the United Kingdom.

Article 20 of the Export Control Order 2008

96. Article 20 of the Export Control Order 2008 (embargoed destinations) is not to be taken to prohibit anything prohibited by Part 5 (Trade).

Trade: overlapping offences

97. A person is not to be taken to commit an offence under the Export Control Order 2008 if the person would, in the absence of this regulation, commit an offence under both—

(a) article 34, 35, 37 or 38 of that Order, and

(b) any provision of Part 5 (Trade) or regulation 68 (trade: licensing offences), 76(6) (general trade licences: records) or 77(5) (general trade licences: inspection of records).

Revocations of relevant retained EU law

98. The following are revoked—

(a) Council Regulation (EU) No 269/2014 of 17 March 2014 (concerning restrictive measures in respect of actions undermining or threatening the territorial integrity, sovereignty and independence of Ukraine)([51]);

(b) Council Regulation (EU) No 692/2014 of 23 June 2014 (concerning restrictive measures in response to the illegal annexation of Crimea and Sevastopol)([52]);

(c) Council Regulation (EU) No 833/2014 of 31 July 2014 (concerning restrictive measures in view of Russia's actions destabilising the situation in Ukraine)([53]).

Other revocations and amendments

99.—(1) The Ukraine Financial Sanctions Regulations are revoked.

(2) The Export Control (Russia, Crimea and Sevastopol Sanctions) Order 2014([54]) is revoked.

Transitional provision: Treasury licences

100.—(1) Paragraphs (2) to (4) apply to a licence which—

(a) was granted, or deemed to be granted, by the Treasury under the Ukraine Financial Sanctions Regulations,

(b) was in effect immediately before exit day, and

(c) authorises an act which would (on and after exit day, and in the absence of paragraphs (2) to (4)) be prohibited by Part 3 (Finance),

and such a licence is referred to in this regulation as 'an existing financial sanctions licence'.

(2) An existing financial sanctions licence has effect on and after exit day as if it had been issued by the Treasury under regulation 64(1) (Treasury licences).

(3) Any reference in an existing financial sanctions licence to the Ukraine Financial Sanctions Regulations is to be treated on and after exit day as a reference to these Regulations.

(4) Any reference in an existing financial sanctions licence to a prohibition in—

(a) the Ukraine Financial Sanctions Regulations, or

(b) the EU Russia Regulations,

is to be treated on and after exit day as a reference to the corresponding prohibition in Part 3 (Finance).

(5) Paragraph (6) applies where—

(a) an application for a licence, or for the variation of a licence, under the Ukraine Financial Sanctions Regulations was made before exit day,

(b) the application is for authorisation of acts which would (on and after exit day) be prohibited by Part 3, and

(c) a decision to grant or refuse the application has not been made before that date.

(6) The application is to be treated on and after exit day as an application for a licence, or for the variation of a licence (as the case may be), under regulation 64(1) (Treasury licences).

---

[51] OJ L 78, 17.3.2014, p. 6–15

[52] OJ L 183 24.6.2014, p. 9

[53] OJ L 229, 31.7.2014, p. 1–11

[54] S.I. 2014/2357, as amended by S.I. 2014/2932, S.I. 2015/97 and SI 2015/1933.

Transitional provision: trade licences

101.—(1) Paragraph (2) applies in relation to each licence or authorisation granted by the Secretary of State which—

(a) was in effect immediately before exit day, and

(b) authorises an act—

(i) which would otherwise be prohibited by any provision of the Export Control Order 2008 except article 20 of that Order (embargoed destinations), or which requires an authorisation under or pursuant to the Dual-Use Regulation, and

(ii) which would (on and after exit day, and in the absence of paragraph (2)) be prohibited by Part 5 (Trade),

and such a licence or authorisation is referred to in this regulation as 'an existing trade licence'.

(2) A licence is deemed to have been issued by the Secretary of State on exit day under regulation 65 (trade licences)—

(a) disapplying every provision of Part 5 (Trade) which would, in the absence of this paragraph, prohibit any act authorised by the existing trade licence, and

(b) otherwise in the same terms as the existing trade licence.

(3) Paragraphs (4) to (6) apply to a licence or authorisation granted by the Secretary of State which—

(a) was in effect immediately before exit day, and

(b) authorises an act—

(i) which would otherwise be prohibited by the EU Russia Regulations, and

(ii) which would (on or after exit day), and in the absence of Paragraphs (4) to (6), be prohibited by Part 5 (Trade),

and such a licence or authorisation is referred to in this regulation as 'an existing trade sanctions licence'.

(4) An existing trade sanctions licence has effect on and after exit day as if it were a licence which had been issued by the Secretary of State under regulation 65 (trade licences).

(5) Any reference in an existing trade sanctions licence to a provision of the Export Control (Russia, Crimea and Sevastopol Sanctions) Order 2014 or the Export Control Order 2008 is to be

treated on and after exit day as a reference to the corresponding provision of these Regulations (if any).

(6) Any reference in an existing trade sanctions licence to a prohibition in the EU Russia Regulations is to be treated on and after exit day as a reference to the corresponding prohibition in Part 5 (Trade).

Transitional provision: pending applications for trade licences

102.—(1) Paragraph (2) applies where—

(a) an application was made before exit day for a licence or authorisation under or pursuant to the Export Control Order 2008 or the Dual-Use Regulation,

(b) the application is for authorisation of an act prohibited by Part 5 (Trade), and

(c) a decision to grant or refuse the application has not been made before exit day.

(2) The application is to be treated on and after exit day as including an application for a licence under regulation 65 (trade licences).

(3) Paragraph (4) applies where—

(a) an application was made before exit day for a licence or authorisation under the Export Control (Russia, Crimea and Sevastopol Sanctions) Order 2014 or the EU Russia Regulations,

(b) the application is for authorisation of an act prohibited by Part 5 (Trade), and

(c) a decision to grant or refuse the application has not been made before exit day.

(4) The application is to be treated on and after exit day as an application for a licence under regulation 65 (trade licences).

Transitional provision: prior obligations

103.—(1) Where—

(a) a person was named in an Annex to the EU Russia Regulations immediately before exit day, and

(b) the person is a designated person immediately before exit day,

any reference in a provision mentioned in paragraph (2) to the date on which a person became a designated person is a reference to the date on which the person was named in an Annex to the EU Russia Regulations.

(2) The provisions referred to in paragraph (1) are—

(a) regulation 50(5) (finance: exceptions from prohibitions),

(b) paragraph 6 of Schedule 5 (pre-existing judicial decisions), and

(c) paragraph 8 of Schedule 5 (prior obligations).

(3) In this regulation, 'designated person' has the same meaning as it has in Chapter 1 of Part 3 (finance restrictions in relation to designated persons).

Alan Duncan
Minister of State
10th April 2019 Foreign and Commonwealth Office

SCHEDULES

SCHEDULE 1
REGULATIONS 7(3) AND 16(8)
RULES FOR INTERPRETATION OF REGULATIONS 7(2) AND 16(7)

Application of Schedule

1.—(1) The rules set out in the following paragraphs of this Schedule apply for the purpose of interpreting regulations 7(2) and 16(7).

(2) They also apply for the purpose of interpreting this Schedule.

Joint interests

2. If two or more persons each hold a share or right jointly, each of them is treated as holding that share or right.

Joint arrangements

3.—(1) If shares or rights held by a person and shares or rights held by another person are the subject of a joint arrangement between those persons, each of them is treated as holding the combined shares or rights of both of them.

(2) A 'joint arrangement' is an arrangement between the holders of shares or rights that they will exercise all or substantially all the rights conferred by their respective shares or rights jointly in a way that is pre-determined by the arrangement.

(3) 'Arrangement' has the meaning given by paragraph 12.

Calculating shareholdings

4.—(1) In relation to a person who has a share capital, a reference to holding 'more than 50% of the shares' in that person is to holding shares comprised in the issued share capital of that person of a nominal value exceeding (in aggregate) 50% of that share capital.

(2) In relation to a person who does not have a share capital—

(a) a reference to holding shares in that person is to holding a right or rights to share in the capital or, as the case may be, profits of that person;

(b) a reference to holding 'more than 50% of the shares' in that person is to holding a right or rights to share in more than 50% of the capital or, as the case may be, profits of that person.

Voting rights

5.—(1) A reference to the voting rights in a person is to the rights conferred on shareholders in respect of their shares (or, in the case of a person not having a share capital, on members) to vote at general meetings of the person on all or substantially all matters.

(2) In relation to a person that does not have general meetings at which matters are decided by the exercise of voting rights—

(a) a reference to holding voting rights in the person is to be read as a reference to holding rights in relation to the person that are equivalent to those of a person entitled to exercise voting rights in a company;

(b) a reference to holding 'more than 50% of the voting rights' in the person is to be read as a reference to holding the right under the constitution of the person to block changes to the overall policy of the person or to the terms of its constitution.

6. In applying regulations 7(2) and 16(7) and this Schedule, the voting rights in a person are to be reduced by any rights held by the person itself.

Rights to appoint or remove members of the board

7. A reference to the right to appoint or remove a majority of the board of directors of a person is to the right to appoint or remove directors holding a majority of the voting rights at meetings of the board on all or substantially all matters.

8. A reference to a board of directors, in the case of a person who does not have such a board, is to be read as a reference to the equivalent management body of that person.

Shares or rights held 'indirectly'

9.—(1) A person holds a share 'indirectly' if the person has a majority stake in another person and that other person—

(a) holds the share in question, or

(b) is part of a chain of persons—
(i) each of whom (other than the last) has a majority stake in the person immediately below it in the chain, and
(ii) the last of whom holds the share.

(2) A person holds a right 'indirectly' if the person has a majority stake in another person and that other person—
(a) holds that right, or
(b) is part of a chain of persons—
(i) each of whom (other than the last) has a majority stake in the person immediately below it in the chain, and
(ii) the last of whom holds that right.

(3) For these purposes, a person ('A') has a 'majority stake' in another person ('B') if—
(a) A holds a majority of the voting rights in B,
(b) A is a member of B and has the right to appoint or remove a majority of the board of directors of B,
(c) A is a member of B and controls alone, pursuant to an agreement with other shareholders or members, a majority of the voting rights in B, or
(d) A has the right to exercise, or actually exercises, dominant influence or control over B.

(4) In the application of this paragraph to the right to appoint or remove a majority of the board of directors, a person ('A') is to be treated as having the right to appoint a director if—
(a) any person's appointment as director follows necessarily from that person's appointment as director of A, or
(b) the directorship is held by A itself.

Shares held by nominees

10. A share held by a person as nominee for another is to be treated as held by the other (and not by the nominee).

Rights treated as held by person who controls their exercise

11.—(1) Where a person controls a right, the right is to be treated as held by that person (and not by the person who in fact holds the right, unless that person also controls it).

(2) A person 'controls' a right if, by virtue of any arrangement between that person and others, the right is exercisable only—
(a) by that person,
(b) in accordance with that person's directions or instructions, or
(c) with that person's consent or concurrence.

12. 'Arrangement' includes—
(a) any scheme, agreement or understanding, whether or not it is legally enforceable, and
(b) any convention, custom or practice of any kind.

Rights exercisable only in certain circumstances etc.

13.—(1) Rights that are exercisable only in certain circumstances are to be taken into account only—
(a) when the circumstances have arisen, and for so long as they continue to obtain, or
(b) when the circumstances are within the control of the person having the rights.

(2) But rights that are exercisable by an administrator or by creditors while a person is subject to relevant insolvency proceedings are not to be taken into account while the person is subject to those proceedings.

(3) 'Relevant insolvency proceedings' means—

(a) administration within the meaning of the Insolvency Act 1986([55])

(b) administration within the meaning of the Insolvency (Northern Ireland) Order 1989([56]), or

(c) proceedings under the insolvency law of another country during which a person's assets and affairs are subject to the control or supervision of a third party or creditor.

(4) Rights that are normally exercisable but are temporarily incapable of exercise are to continue to be taken into account.

Rights attached to shares held by way of security

14. Rights attached to shares held by way of security provided by a person are to be treated for the purposes of this Schedule as held by that person—

(a) where apart from the right to exercise them for the purpose of preserving the value of the security, or of realising it, the rights are exercisable only in accordance with that person's instructions, and

(b) where the shares are held in connection with the granting of loans as part of normal business activities and apart from the right to exercise them for the purpose of preserving the value of the security, or of realising it, the rights are exercisable only in that person's interests.

SCHEDULE 2
PERSONS NAMED IN RELATION TO FINANCIAL RESTRICTIONS

1. Sberbank
2. VTB bank
3. Gazprombank
4. Vnesheconombank (VEB)
5. Rosselkhozbank
6. OPK Oboronprom
7. United Aircraft Corporation
8. Uralvagonzavod
9. Rosneft
10. Transneft
11. Gazprom Neft

[55] 1986 c.45.
[56] S.I. 1989/2405 (N.I. 19).

SCHEDULE 3
ENERGY-RELATED GOODS AND INFRASTRUCTURE-RELATED GOODS
REGULATIONS 16, 17 AND 59

REGULATION 21

PART 1

General

Interpretation

1.—(1) For the purposes of this Schedule—

(a) a thing 'falls within' a commodity code if it is, or would be, classified under that commodity code, as set out in the Goods Classification Table;

(b) a thing 'falls within' a chapter if it is, or would be, classified under that chapter, as set out in the Goods Classification Table;

(c) where a commodity code or chapter is preceded by 'ex', the goods specified in this Schedule constitute only a part of the scope of the commodity code or chapter and must fall within both the description given to that code or chapter in this Schedule and the scope of the code or chapter in the Goods Classification Table.

(2) For the purposes of determining whether or not a thing is, or would be, 'classified' in accordance with sub-paragraph (1), the rules of interpretation contained in the following have effect—

(a) Part Two (Goods Classification Table Rules of Interpretation) of the Tariff of the United Kingdom;

(b) notes to a section or chapter of the Goods Classification Table.

(3) For the purposes of this paragraph—

'commodity code' includes a code denoting a heading or sub-heading;

'the Goods Classification Table' means the table so named in Annex # in Part Three of the Tariff of the United Kingdom;

'the Tariff of the United Kingdom' means the document containing the legal classification and import rate for products being imported into the United Kingdom, entitled 'The Tariff of the United Kingdom', as revised or re-issued from time to time([57]).

PART 2

Energy-related goods

2. Any thing falling within the following commodity codes— 7304 11 00
7304 19 10
7304 19 30
7304 19 90

[57] The Tariff of the United Kingdom, Version 1.0, is available electronically from: https://assets.publishing.service.gov.uk/government/uploads/system/uploads/attachment_data/file/785939/Tariff_Reference_Document_13_March_2019.pdf. A hard copy is available for inspection free of charge at the offices of HMRC at 100 Parliament Street, London, SW1A 2BQ.

7304 22 00
7304 23 00
7304 29 10
7304 29 30
7304 29 90
7305 11 00
7305 12 00
7305 19 00
7305 20 00
7306 11
7306 19
7306 21 00
7306 29 00
8207 13 00
8207 19 10
8413 82 00
8413 92 00
8430 49 00
8705 20 00
8905 20 00
8905 90 10

3. Any thing falling—
   (a) within a commodity code mentioned in column 1 of the following table; and
   (b) within the description in column 2 beside that code.

Code	*Description*
ex 8413 50	Reciprocating positive displacement pumps for liquids, power-driven with a maximum flow-rate greater than 18 m 3 /hour and a maximum outlet pressure greater than 40 bar, specially designed to pump drilling muds and/or cement into oil wells
ex 8413 60	Rotary positive displacement pumps for liquids, power-driven with a maximum flow-rate greater than 18 m 3 /hour and a maximum outlet pressure greater than 40 bar, specially designed to pump drilling muds and/or cement into oil wells
ex 8431 39 00	Parts suitable for use solely or principally with the oil field machinery of heading 8428
ex 8431 43 00	Parts suitable for use solely or principally with the oil field machinery of subheadings 8430 41 or 8430 49
ex 8431 49	Parts suitable for use solely or principally with the oil field machinery of heading 8426, 8429 and 8430

PART 3

INFRASTRUCTURE-RELATED GOODS

4. Any thing falling within the following chapters—
   (a) chapters 25 to 29;
   (b) chapters 72 to 76;
   (c) chapters 78 to 81;
   (d) chapter 86;
   (e) chapters 88 and 89; and
   (f) chapter 98.
5. Any thing falling within the following commodity codes— 3824
   3826 00
   8207 13 00
   8207 19 10
   8401 to 8418
   8420 to 8432
   8435 to 8437
   8439 to 8443
   8444 00
   8445
   8447
   8448
   8449 00 00
   8450
   8452 to 8468
   8470 to 8484
   8486
   8487
   8501 to 8505
   8507
   8511
   8514
   8515
   8525 to 8548
   8701
   8702
   8704
   8705
   8706 00
   8709
   8710 00 00
   8716
   7106 to 7112
   9013 to 9015
   9025 to 9033

SCHEDULE 4
PERSONS NAMED IN RELATION TO DUAL-USE ITEMS RESTRICTIONS

1. JSC Sirius
2. OJSC Stankoinstrument
3. OAO JSC Chemcomposite
4. JSC Kalashnikov
5. JSC Tula Arms Plant
6. NPK Technologii Maschinostrojenija
7. OAO Wysokototschnye Kompleksi
8. OAO Almaz Antey
9. OAO NPO Bazalt

SCHEDULE 5
TREASURY LICENCES: PURPOSES

PART 1

Asset-freeze etc.

Interpretation

1. In this Part of this Schedule—

'designated person' has the same meaning as it has in Chapter 1 of Part 3 (finance restrictions in relation to designated persons);

'frozen funds or economic resources' means funds or economic resources frozen by virtue of regulation 11, and any reference to a person's frozen funds or economic resources is to funds or economic resources frozen as a consequence of the designation of that person for the purpose of that regulation.

Basic needs

2.—(1) To enable the basic needs of a designated person, or (in the case of an individual) any dependent family member of such a person, to be met.

(2) In the case of an individual, in sub-paragraph (1) 'basic needs' includes—

(a) medical needs;

(b) needs for—

(i) food;

(ii) payments of insurance premiums;

(iii) payments of tax;

(iv) rent or mortgage payments;

(v) utility payments.

(3) In the case of a person other than an individual, in sub-paragraph (1) 'basic needs' includes needs for—

(a) payment of insurance premiums;

(b) payment of reasonable fees for the provision of property management services;

(c) payment of remuneration, allowances or pensions of employees;

(d) payment of tax;
(e) rent or mortgage payments;
(f) utility payments.

(4) In sub-paragraph (1)—
'dependent' means financially dependent;
'family member' includes—
(a) the wife or husband of the designated person;
(b) the civil partner of the designated person;
(c) any parent or other ascendant of the designated person;
(d) any child or other descendant of the designated person;
(e) any person who is a brother or sister of the designated person, or a child or other descendant of such a person.

Legal services

3. To enable the payment of—
(a) reasonable professional fees for the provision of legal services, or
(b) reasonable expenses associated with the provision of legal services.

Maintenance of frozen funds and economic resources

4. To enable the payment of—
(a) reasonable fees, or
(b) reasonable service charges,
arising from the routine holding or maintenance of frozen funds or economic resources.

Extraordinary expenses

5. To enable an extraordinary expense of a designated person to be met.

Pre-existing judicial decisions etc.

6. To enable, by the use of a designated person's frozen funds or economic resources, the implementation or satisfaction (in whole or in part) of a judicial, administrative or arbitral decision or lien, provided that—
(a) the funds or economic resources so used are the subject of the decision or lien,
(b) the decision or lien—
(i) was made or established before the date on which the person became a designated person, and
(ii) is enforceable in the United Kingdom, and
(c) the use of the frozen funds or economic resources does not directly or indirectly benefit any other designated person.

Extraordinary situation

7. To enable anything to be done to deal with an extraordinary situation.

Prior obligations

8. To enable, by the use of a designated person's frozen funds or economic resources, the satisfaction of an obligation of that person (whether arising under a contract, other agreement or otherwise), provided that—

(a) the obligation arose before the date on which the person became a designated person, and
(b) no payments are made to another designated person, whether directly or indirectly.

Consular posts

9.—(1) To enable anything to be done in order that the functions of a consular post in Crimea, or of an international organisation enjoying immunities in accordance with international law, may be carried out.

(2) In this paragraph, 'consular post' has the same meaning as in the Vienna Convention on Consular Relations done at Vienna on 24 April 1963([58]), and any reference to the functions of a consular post is to be read in accordance with that Convention.

PART 2

Investment in Crimea

Consular posts

10.—(1) To enable anything to be done in order that the functions of a consular post in Crimea, or of an international organisation enjoying immunities in accordance with international law, may be carried out.

(2) In this paragraph 'consular post' has the same meaning as in the Vienna Convention on Consular Relations done at Vienna on 24 April 1963, and any reference to the functions of a consular post is to be read in accordance with that Convention.

Medical and educational purposes

11. To enable the carrying out of projects exclusively in support of—
(a) hospitals, or other public health institutions providing medical services, or
(b) civilian education establishments, located in Crimea.

12. To enable anything to be done in relation to the provision or maintenance of appliances or equipment for medical use in Crimea.

Health and the environment

13. To enable anything to be done for the urgent prevention or mitigation of an event likely to have a serious and significant impact on human health or safety, infrastructure or the environment.

EXPLANATORY NOTE

(This note is not part of the Regulations)

These Regulations are made under the Sanctions and Anti-Money Laundering Act 2018 (c.13) to establish a sanctions regime under that Act in relation to Russia. These Regulations are made for the purpose of encouraging Russia to cease actions destabilising Ukraine or undermining or threatening the territorial integrity, sovereignty or independence of Ukraine. Following the UK's withdrawal from the European Union, these Regulations will replace the EU sanctions regimes in

[58] United Nations Treaty Series, vol. 596, p. 261.

relation to Russia. The EU sanctions regimes are currently implemented via EU Council Decisions and Regulations.

The Regulations confer a power on the Secretary of State to designate persons who are, or have been, involved in destabilising Ukraine or undermining or threatening the territorial integrity, sovereignty or independence of Ukraine. Designated persons may be excluded from the United Kingdom and may be made subject to financial sanctions, including having their funds or economic resources frozen.

These Regulations also impose restrictions on trade in military goods and technology, on certain dual-use and energy-related items, and impose restrictions on supplying infrastructure-related goods and technology to Crimea and on importing goods from Crimea. These Regulations also restrict the provision of services related to the trade in those items. The Regulations also restrict persons from dealing with certain financial instruments, restrict the provision of finance and funds, and restrict investment in relation to Crimea.

The Regulations provide for certain exceptions to this sanctions regime, including in relation to financial sanctions (for example to allow for frozen accounts to be credited with interest or other earnings), trade sanctions and also acts done for the purpose of national security or the prevention of serious crime. The Regulations also confer powers on the Secretary of State and the Treasury to issue licences in respect of activities that would otherwise be prohibited under the financial and trade sanctions imposed. Schedule 5 of these Regulations sets out the purposes pursuant to which the Treasury will issue such licences.

The Regulations make it a criminal offence to contravene, or circumvent, any of the prohibitions in these Regulations and prescribe the mode of trial and penalties that apply to such offences. The Regulations also confer powers on specified maritime enforcement officers to stop and search ships in international and foreign waters for the purpose of enforcing specified trade sanctions and to seize goods found on board ships which are being, or have been, dealt with in contravention, or deemed contravention, of those prohibitions. The Regulations prescribe powers for the provision and sharing of information to enable the effective implementation and enforcement of the sanctions regime.

The Regulations revoke the relevant EU Regulations relating to the existing EU Russia sanctions regimes, in so far as those Regulations would have had effect in the UK after exit day. The Regulations also revoke existing UK trade and financial sanctions regulations relating to the existing EU Russia sanctions regimes.

APPENDIX 5

Russia Guidance

Guidance for the financial and investment restrictions in Russia (Sanctions) (EU Exit) Regulations 2019

RUSSIA (SANCTIONS) (EU EXIT) REGULATIONS 2019

The Office of Financial Sanctions Implementation (OFSI), part of HM Treasury, is responsible for improving the understanding, implementation and enforcement of financial sanctions in the UK. We publish a list of individuals and organisations subject to financial sanctions as well as general guidance to help you comply. This is available on OFSI's gov.uk webpages—see back page of this guidance.

The Russia (Sanctions) (EU Exit) Regulations 2019 (the Regulations) impose financial, trade, transport and immigration sanctions to encourage Russia to cease actions which destabilise Ukraine, including actions undermining or threatening the territorial integrity, sovereignty and independence of Ukraine. The territorial extent of the Regulations is the whole of the UK, and it also applies to conduct by UK persons—both nationals and corporate bodies—outside the UK. The Regulations enter into force on 'exit day' and replace the EU sanctions regime relating to Russia's actions in the Ukraine.

The names of designated persons are not included in the Regulations, but instead will appear on the administrative list on gov.uk. This enables immediate publication following a decision to make or amend a designation, limiting the opportunity for designated persons to remove assets from the UK.

OFSI GUIDANCE ON RUSSIA REGULATIONS

While there are different sanctions outlined in the Regulations, this guidance produced by OFSI, expands specifically on financial and investment restrictions. In addition to asset freezes common among other sanctions regimes, these restrictions include unique measures that seek to prevent access to capital markets for Russian state-owned financial institutions.

They also detail restrictions on investments in relation to the Republic of Crimea and the city of Sevastopol.

Any exceptions related to each restriction, including instances where you may be able to apply for a licence from OFSI, are also outlined.

This guidance details instances involving both trade and financial sanctions separately, and also where they overlap. In addition, there is guidance available on the other restrictions detailed in the regulations, affecting transport, immigration, and trade sanctions in respect of Russia.

That additional guidance is published by other UK government departments including the Department for International Trade, Home Office and the Foreign and Commonwealth Office.

To achieve their purposes, the Regulations impose a number of prohibitions and obligations. The Regulations establish penalties and offences to enforce these, which are set out in detail in the corresponding report made under section 18 of the Sanctions and Anti-Money Laundering Act 2018 (SAMLA) which is available on gov.uk.

ASSET FREEZES

The Regulations detail financial prohibitions in relation to designated persons (DPs). DPs are persons (natural or legal) who are subject to financial sanctions. These sanctions include but are not limited to: asset freezes, restrictions on making funds and or economic resources available to, or for the benefit of, DPs, either directly or indirectly.

There are exceptions to some of the asset freezing provisions which apply within certain defined circumstances. Additionally, where a DP's assets have been frozen, the person or representative may apply for a licence from OFSI to be able to utilise their funds or economic resources in certain circumstances. For further information on asset freezes, see OFSI's General Guidance on Financial Sanctions.

FINANCIAL SERVICES—PROCESSING PAYMENTS

The Regulations set out how to prevent a DP benefitting from procuring financial services. Where the provision of financial services is prohibited, this includes the provision of processing payments. This comprises payment and money transmission services, including credit, charge and debit cards, travellers' cheques and bankers' drafts. This differs from the EU sanctions regime.

OTHER RESTRICTIONS: FINANCIAL SERVICES AND INVESTMENTS

Transferable securities or money-market instruments

The Regulations detail prohibitions on dealing in certain transferable securities and money market instruments. They prohibit dealing with, directly or indirectly, a transferable security or money market instrument if it has a maturity exceeding 30 days and was issued after 1 August 2014 by the following list in the box below:

- Sberbank
- VTB Bank
- Gazprombank
- Vnesheconombank (VEB)
- Rosselkhozbank
- An entity incorporated or constituted in a country other than the UK which is owned directly or indirectly by one or more of the banks listed above

The regulations also prohibit dealing, directly or indirectly, with a transferable security or money market instrument if it has a maturity exceeding 30 days and was issued after 12 September 2014 by the following again set out in the box below:

- OPK Oboronprom
- United Aircraft Corporation
- Uralvagonzavod
- Rosneft
- Transneft
- Gazprom Neft
- An entity incorporated or constituted in a country other than the UK which is owned, directly or indirectly, by one of these entities.

Prohibitions on dealing with certain transferable securities and money market instruments catch the securities of subsidiaries established in a country other than the UK and owned by the entities listed above (see Schedule 2 to the Regulations). This means that the securities of subsidiaries incorporated or established in the UK are not subject to these prohibitions. This differs from the EU sanctions regime.

There are no grounds under which a licence can be granted in relation to these prohibitions. There is an exception for acts done for the purposes of national security or the prevention of serious crime.

'Money-market instrument' means an instrument of a kind normally dealt in on the money market, such as treasury bills, certificates of deposit and commercial papers, excluding instruments of payment.

'Transferable security' is a security that's negotiable on the capital markets, including shares in companies and other securities equivalent to shares in companies, partnerships or other entities, and depositary receipts in respect of shares. It also includes bonds or other forms of securitised debt, including depositary receipts in respect of such securities.

Other securities that give the right to purchase or sell any security of a kind mentioned above are also covered by the term. However these do exclude instruments of payment.

LOAN AND CREDIT ARRANGEMENTS

You must not, directly or indirectly, grant, or enter into any arrangement to grant a new loan or credit with a maturity exceeding 30 days to:

- Sberbank
- VTB Bank
- Gazprombank
- Vnesheconombank (VEB)
- Rosselkhozbank
- OPK Oboronprom
- United Aircraft Corporation
- Uralvagonzavod
- Rosneft
- Transneft
- Gazprom Neft
- An entity incorporated or constituted in a country other than the UK which is owned, directly or indirectly, by one of the abovementioned entities.

The 11 entities listed immediately above, which appear in Schedule 2 to the Regulations, **are not subject to an asset freeze.**

Exceptions

The prohibitions outlined above in relation to loans and credit arrangements are not breached if any of the following are granted:

- A relevant loan which makes funds available for a non-restricted trade. 'Non-restricted trade' refers to any trade that is not prohibited under Part 5 of the Regulations.
- A relevant loan that makes emergency funds available to meet applicable solvency or liquidity criteria for a relevant subsidiary, as defined in the Regulations.
- A relevant loan consisting of a drawdown or disbursement made under an arrangement that was entered in to before 15th September 2014, as detailed in the Regulations.

The national security or prevention of serious crime exception applies to all prohibitions.

INVESTMENTS IN RELATION TO CRIMEA

Any reference to Crimea in the Regulations means the Autonomous Republic of Crimea and the city of Sevastopol.

Under the Regulations, it is prohibited to, directly or indirectly, extend a participation, or acquire any ownership interest, in land located in Crimea. The same restrictions also apply when it comes to acquiring any ownership interest in an entity which has a place of business located in Crimea (a 'relevant entity').

There is also a prohibition on granting any loan or credit to a relevant entity. This prohibition includes entering into any arrangement to grant a loan or credit, or otherwise provide funds, including equity capital, to a relevant entity, or for the purpose of financing any such entity.

It is prohibited to establish a joint venture in Crimea or with a relevant entity.

It is also prohibited to provide any investment services directly related to any of the activities listed above.

Exceptions

Provided that a person notifies HM Treasury no later than five working days before the day on which an act is carried out, no prohibition relating to investments in Crimea are contravened by a person meeting an obligation under a contract that was concluded before 20 December 2014. This includes an ancillary contract necessary to satisfy such a contract. Additionally, the prohibitions on investments in Crimea are not contravened by a person operating outside Crimea where the related investment is not destined for an entity in Crimea.

Additionally, where an activity would otherwise be prohibited in relation to investments in Crimea, a person or their representative may apply for a licence from OFSI to carry out those activities in certain circumstances. OFSI expects that legal and professional advisers will have fully considered the relevant law and formed a view about an application before approaching OFSI for guidance or submitting an application. All applications are assessed against the relevant regulations and are done so on a case by case basis.

CONTACTING OFSI

If you find out that a person or organisation you are dealing with is subject to the financial sanctions detailed in the Regulations, you must immediately:

- stop dealing with them
- freeze any assets you're holding for them
- inform OFSI as soon as possible by either emailing: ofsi@hmtreasury.gov.uk, or by calling the general enquiries line: +44 (0)20 7270 5454

FREQUENTLY ASKED QUESTIONS[1]

1) *If before 12 September 2014, a UK person extended a loan or credit to a targeted entity, can it then sell a part of or the whole claim with a maturity exceeding 30 days to another targeted entity?*
   In so far as the arrangement would not involve new loans or credit to either targeted entity, or any other restricted activity, such a resale would be allowed. A change of lenders, even if they are a targeted person, would not generally be prohibited by the Regulations, to the extent this does not constitute advancing new funds to a targeted entity.
2) *Are derivatives covered by the prohibitions in the regulations?*
   Derivatives which give the right to acquire or sell a transferable security or money market instrument covered by the regulations, such as options, futures, forwards or warrants, irrespective of how they are traded (on-exchange or over-the-counter (OTC)) are covered by prohibitions set out in the regulations. Certain other derivatives, such as interest rate swaps and cross currency swaps, are not covered by the prohibitions set out in the regulations, nor

[1] These FAQs reproduce relevant guidance from the 'European Commission guidance note on the implementation of certain provisions of regulation (EU) no 833/2014'

credit default swaps (except where these give the right to acquire or sell a transferable security). Derivatives used for hedging purposes in the energy market are also not covered.

3) *If a UK person extended a loan or credit with a maturity exceeding 30 days before or on 12 September 2014, could the UK person enter into an M&A transaction whereby a targeted entity assumes the role of the borrower of the debt arising from such loan after 12 September 2014?*

It would be prohibited for a UK entity to enter into any M&A transaction, whereby a targeted entity would assume the role of borrower of an existing loan or credit. The example above would effectively constitute making a new loan or credit available to a targeted entity after 12 September 2014 and would therefore be prohibited.

4) *A loan or credit with a maturity exceeding 30 days before or on 12 September 2014 had been extended by a UK person to a financial sanctions target. Can the UK person cancel or forgive debt arising from such a loan after 12 September 2014?*

The Regulations prohibit targeted entities from being extended credit or a new loan, as their purpose is to restrict access to capital, even in circumstances where the sums extended need to be reimbursed. Cancelation of the debt would provide access to capital in the same way as a loan but without a duty to reimburse or pay interest. It would therefore be prohibited.

5) *Can UK persons place term deposits with a maturity exceeding 30 days in a bank which is a targeted entity after 12 September 2014?*

While the prohibitions set out in the Regulations do not specifically target deposit services, where term deposits are used to circumvent the prohibition on new loans or credit, such deposits would be prohibited.

6) *With regards to loans made to a targeted entity, can UK persons provide payment or settlement services including in the context of correspondent banking?*

For the purposes of the Regulations, payment and settlement services, including through correspondent banking, would be construed as directly or indirectly 'making' or 'being part of an arrangement to make' a new loan or credit to a targeted entity. Any loans or credit made after exit day which are the subject of such payment or settlement services must comply with the 30-day maturity limit in order to avoid being caught by the restrictive measures.

7) *If a UK person has provided a good or service to a targeted entity, would payment terms/delayed payment for such a good or service exceeding 30 days constitute a new loan or credit?*

For the purposes of the Regulations, payment terms/delayed payment for goods or services are not considered loans or credit. The provision of payment terms/delayed payment may not be used, however, to circumvent the prohibition to provide new loans or credit.

8) *How should the rollover of debt obligations by targeted entities be treated?*

The prohibitions in the Regulations extend to the rollover (including cashless) of existing debt. Any rollovers must comply with the 30-day maturity limit imposed for new transactions made after 12 September 2014. However, multiple rollover agreements with a maturity of 30 days or less could amount to circumvention.

9) *Can a UK person provide funds to a non-targeted entity, which are channelled through a targeted entity, provided that the funds do not stay with the targeted entity for more than 30 days?*

Such an arrangement would not constitute providing a new loan or credit with a maturity exceeding 30 days to a targeted entity. It would therefore not fall within the prohibitions set out in the Regulations.

10) *Do the Regulations limit the ability of UK subsidiaries of targeted entities to monitor risks, including the evaluation of credit risk, for operations across the group?*

The purpose of the Regulations is to prevent access to capital markets for Russian state-owned financial institutions and to encourage Russia to cease actions destabilising Ukraine. While receiving information and undertaking risk management and monitoring is unaffected by the Regulations, such risk management would not be permitted if it amounted to circumvention of any of the financial sanctions.

11) *Can a modification be made to a transferable security entered into prior to 1 August 2014 or 12 September 2014 respectively?*

It is prohibited to adjust a transferable security entered into prior to 1 August 2014 or 12 September 2014 respectively where the change would result or potentially result in additional capital being made available to a targeted entity. While certain other changes may be permitted, a case by case assessment would be made of the effect and substance of any changes in order to determine whether or not such changes reasonably requires this to be considered a new instrument.

12) *Do promissory notes fall within the scope of prohibitions relating to transferable securities or money-market instruments?*

As a freely transferable debt instrument, promissory notes may be dealt in on the money markets and thus, to the extent that they are issued by a targeted entity, they would fall into the scope of the prohibitions.

If a targeted entity were to issue a non-negotiable promissory note as a means of payment for non-prohibited goods with UK persons, that would not be prohibited by the Regulations. This allows legitimate trade to continue while remaining consistent with the objectives of Regulation.

13) *Do bills of lading fall within the scope of prohibitions relating to transferable securities or money-market instruments?*

In so far as bills of lading document the carriage and receipt of goods and serve as proof of entitlement to such goods, they do not fall under the prohibitions.

In any negotiable form where bills can be traded for financing purposes, or any similar activity which could amount to circumvention, these instances would be prohibited by the Regulations.

14) *Can UK persons use repurchase agreements or securities lending agreements with a non-targeted entity using any transferable securities or money market instruments issued by a targeted entity as collateral?*

If transferable securities or money market instruments were issued between 1 August 2014 to 12 September 2014 with a maturity exceeding 30 days by entities 1-5 in Schedule 2 of the regulations, or after 12 September 2014 with a maturity exceeding 30 days by entities 6-11 in Schedule 2, UK persons are prohibited from entering into repurchase agreements or securities lending agreements where such transferable securities or money market-instruments, which are prohibited under the regulations, are used as collateral.

15) *Can UK persons enter into repurchase agreements or securities lending agreements with a targeted entity (bank), if non-prohibited instruments are used as collateral?*

Repurchase agreements or securities lending agreements are money market instruments as defined in Article 16 of the Regulations, as they are instruments normally dealt in on the money market. UK persons are therefore prohibited from entering into repurchase agreements or securities lending agreements with relevant targeted entities as outlined by the Regulations.

16) *Is the provision of financial research in relation to prohibited transferable securities allowed?*

In relation to 'dealing with transferable securities or money-market instruments', Article 16 states that it is prohibited to provide investment services, including the provision of investment advice, relating to the security or instrument. While the provision of research is formally different from the provision of advice, it may constitute indirect advice and in such case would tend to constitute a form of investment service and would thus be prohibited.

17) *What constitutes a letter of credit?*

A letter of credit is an undertaking by a bank to pay the beneficiary of the credit (or to accept and pay drafts drawn by the beneficiary) in accordance with, and upon satisfaction of the terms and conditions of the credit. it is no more than an undertaking from the bank (at the request of it's customer) to extend a credit, or make a payment, provided that the condition set out within the letter of credit itself are satisfied and the banks is provided with proof of this (usually by the provision of documents).

By way of example, a simple letter of credit in respect of a transaction to purchase oil, may provide that a bank 'B' will undertake to pay a sum of money (equal to the purchase price of the oil) to a third party oil provider, 'P', once a document is provided to B showing that the bank's customer, 'C' has received the oil.

Contact OFSI
Helpline:
0207 270 5454
Monday—Friday, 09.00–17.00
Email enquiries:
ofsi@hmtreasury.gov.uk
Visit OFSI's web pages:
https://www.gov.uk/government/organisations/office-of-financial-sanctions-implementation
OFSI's Financial Sanctions Guidance:
https://www.gov.uk/government/publications/financial-sanctions-faqs
Subscribe to OFSI's e-alert:
http://public.govdelivery.com/accounts/UKHMTRE AS/subscriber/new

APPENDIX 6

Extracts from the Policing and Crime Act 2017

PART 8
FINANCIAL SANCTIONS

Interpretation

143 Interpretation

(1) This section sets out definitions that apply for the purposes of this Part.

(2) 'EU financial sanctions Regulation' means an EU Regulation adopted under Article 215 of the Treaty on the Functioning of the European Union to the extent that the Regulation—
 (a) imposes prohibitions or obligations for one or more of the following purposes—
  (i) freezing funds or economic resources;
  (ii) preventing funds or economic resources being made available;
  (iii) prohibiting or restricting access to financial markets or financial services;
 (b) makes provision to supplement prohibitions or obligations of the kind mentioned in paragraph (a).

(3) 'UN financial sanctions Resolution' means a resolution adopted by the Security Council of the United Nations to the extent that the resolution provides under article 41 of the Charter of the United Nations for States to take measures that—
 (a) impose prohibitions or obligations for one or more of the following purposes—
  (i) freezing funds or economic resources;
  (ii) preventing funds or economic resources being made available;
  (iii) prohibiting or restricting access to financial markets or financial services;
 (b) make provision to supplement prohibitions or obligations of the kind mentioned in paragraph (a).

(4) 'Financial sanctions legislation' means—
 (a) an EU financial sanctions Regulation;
 (b) an instrument made under section 2(2) of the European Communities Act 1972 for the purpose of implementing, or otherwise in relation to, EU obligations created or arising by or under an EU financial sanctions Regulation;
 (c) a provision of an Act or of subordinate legislation (within the meaning of the Interpretation Act 1978) where the purpose of the provision is to implement a UN financial sanctions Resolution;
 (d) a freezing order under section 4 of the Anti-terrorism, Crime and Security Act 2001;
 (e) a direction under Schedule 7 to the Counter-Terrorism Act 2008 to the extent that it contains a requirement of a kind mentioned in paragraph 13 of that Schedule (limiting or ceasing business), paragraph 17 of that Schedule and Part 5 of that Schedule so far as it

relates to the enforcement of a requirement of a kind mentioned in paragraph 13 of that Schedule.

(5) The reference in subsection (2) to Article 215 of the Treaty on the Functioning of the European Union includes a reference to any of Articles 60, 301 and 308 of the Treaty establishing the European Community (as it had effect before 1 December 2009).

Enhanced maximum penalties

144 Powers to create offences under section 2(2) ECA 1972: maximum term of imprisonment

(1) Paragraph 1(1)(d) of Schedule 2 to the European Communities Act 1972 applies with the following modifications in relation to the exercise of the powers conferred by section 2(2) of that Act ('the section 2(2) powers') to make provision for the purposes of implementing, or otherwise in relation to, EU obligations created or arising by or under an EU financial sanctions Regulation.

(2) The prohibition arising under paragraph 1(1)(d) on the creation of offences punishable by imprisonment for more than a period specified in that paragraph does not apply to the exercise of the section 2(2) powers for those purposes.

(3) Instead, the section 2(2) powers may not be exercised for those purposes to create an offence punishable by imprisonment for a period exceeding—
  (a) in the case of conviction on indictment, 7 years;
  (b) in the case of summary conviction—
    (i) in relation to England and Wales, 12 months or, in relation to offences committed before section 154(1) of the Criminal Justice Act 2003 comes into force, 6 months;
    (ii) in relation to Scotland, 12 months;
    (iii) in relation to Northern Ireland, 6 months.

(4) Subsection (5) applies where, at any time before this section comes into force, the section 2(2) powers have been exercised for those purposes to create an offence punishable by imprisonment.

(5) The section 2(2) powers may (at any time after this section comes into force) be exercised for those purposes to vary the provision made for the maximum period of imprisonment by making any provision that could (by virtue of subsections (2) and (3)) be made if the offence were created after this section comes into force.

(6) A variation made in reliance on subsection (5) does not affect the penalty for an offence if any act or other event proof of which is required for conviction of the offence takes place before this section comes into force.

145 Other offences: maximum term of imprisonment

(1) Schedule 3 to the Anti-terrorism, Crime and Security Act 2001 (freezing orders) is amended in accordance with subsections (2) and (3).

(2) In paragraph 7 (offences), for sub-paragraph (6)(a) and (b) substitute—
  '(a) on summary conviction—
    (i) in England and Wales, to imprisonment for a term not exceeding 12 months (or, in relation to offences committed before section 154(1) of the Criminal Justice Act 2003 comes into force, 6 months) or to a fine, or to both;
    (ii) in Scotland, to imprisonment for a term not exceeding 12 months, or to a fine not exceeding the statutory maximum, or to both;

(iii) in Northern Ireland, to imprisonment for a term not exceeding 6 months, or to a fine not exceeding the statutory maximum, or to both;

(b) on conviction on indictment, to imprisonment for a term not exceeding 7 years or to a fine, or to both.'

(3) In that paragraph, in sub-paragraph (7), for the words from 'on summary conviction' to the end of the sub-paragraph substitute "—

(a) on summary conviction—

(i) in England and Wales, to imprisonment for a term not exceeding 12 months (or, in relation to offences committed before section 154(1) of the Criminal Justice Act 2003 comes into force, 6 months) or to a fine, or to both;

(ii) in Scotland, to imprisonment for a term not exceeding 12 months, or to a fine not exceeding the statutory maximum, or to both;

(iii) in Northern Ireland, to imprisonment for a term not exceeding 6 months, or to a fine not exceeding the statutory maximum, or to both;

(b) on conviction on indictment, to imprisonment for a term not exceeding 2 years or to a fine, or to both."

(4) Schedule 7 to the Counter-Terrorism Act 2008 (terrorist financing and money laundering) is amended in accordance with subsections (5) to (9).

(5) In paragraph 30 (offence of failure to comply with requirement imposed by direction), after sub-paragraph (4) insert—

"(4A) In a case where a person is guilty of an offence under this paragraph by failing to comply with a requirement of a kind mentioned in paragraph 13, the person is liable—

(a) on summary conviction—

(i) in England and Wales, to imprisonment for a term not exceeding 12 months (or, in relation to offences committed before section 154(1) of the Criminal Justice Act 2003 comes into force, 6 months) or to a fine, or to both;

(ii) in Scotland, to imprisonment for a term not exceeding 12 months, or to a fine not exceeding the statutory maximum, or to both;

(iii) in Northern Ireland, to imprisonment for a term not exceeding 6 months, or to a fine not exceeding the statutory maximum, or to both;

(b) on conviction on indictment, to imprisonment for a term not exceeding 7 years or to a fine, or to both."

(6) In sub-paragraph (5) of that paragraph, at the beginning insert 'In any other case,'.

(7) In paragraph 30A (offence of relevant person circumventing requirements), after sub-paragraph (1) insert—

"(1A) In a case where a person is guilty of an offence under this paragraph in relation to a requirement of a kind mentioned in paragraph 13, the person is liable—

(a) on summary conviction—

(i) in England and Wales, to imprisonment for a term not exceeding 12 months (or, in relation to offences committed before section 154(1) of the Criminal Justice Act 2003 comes into force, 6 months) or to a fine, or to both;

(ii) in Scotland, to imprisonment for a term not exceeding 12 months, or to a fine not exceeding the statutory maximum, or to both;

(iii) in Northern Ireland, to imprisonment for a term not exceeding 6 months, or to a fine not exceeding the statutory maximum, or to both;

(b) on conviction on indictment, to imprisonment for a term not exceeding 7 years or to a fine, or to both."

(8) In sub-paragraph (2) of that paragraph, at the beginning insert 'In any other case,'.

(9) In paragraph 31 (offences in connection with licences), in sub-paragraph (2), for the words from 'on conviction on indictment' to the end of the sub-paragraph substitute "—

(a) on summary conviction—

(i) in England and Wales, to imprisonment for a term not exceeding 12 months (or, in relation to offences committed before section 154(1) of the Criminal Justice Act 2003 comes into force, 6 months) or to a fine, or to both;

(ii) in Scotland, to imprisonment for a term not exceeding 12 months, or to a fine not exceeding the statutory maximum, or to both;

(iii) in Northern Ireland, to imprisonment for a term not exceeding 6 months, or to a fine not exceeding the statutory maximum, or to both;

(b) on conviction on indictment, to imprisonment for a term not exceeding 2 years or to a fine, or to both."

(10) The amendments made by this section do not affect the penalty for an offence if any act or other event proof of which is required for conviction of the offence takes place before this section comes into force.

Civil sanctions

146 Power to impose monetary penalties

(1) The Treasury may impose a monetary penalty on a person if it is satisfied, on the balance of probabilities, that—

(a) the person has breached a prohibition, or failed to comply with an obligation, that is imposed by or under financial sanctions legislation, and

(b) the person knew, or had reasonable cause to suspect, that the person was in breach of the prohibition or (as the case may be) had failed to comply with the obligation.

(2) The amount of the penalty is to be such amount as the Treasury may determine but it may not exceed the permitted maximum.

(3) In a case where the breach or failure relates to particular funds or economic resources and it is possible to estimate the value of the funds or economic resources, the permitted maximum is the greater of—

(a) £1,000,000, and

(b) 50% of the estimated value of the funds or resources.

(4) In any other case, the permitted maximum is £1,000,000.

(5) In subsection (3), 'funds' and 'economic resources' have the same meanings as they have in the financial sanctions legislation that contains the prohibition or obligation in respect of which the monetary penalty is imposed.

(6) The Treasury must keep the amount for the time being specified in subsection (3)(a) or (4) under review.

(7) The Treasury may by regulations made by statutory instrument amend subsection (3)

(a) or (4) so as to substitute another amount for the amount for the time being specified in it.

(8) Regulations under subsection (7) may include transitional provision.

(9) Before making regulations under subsection (7), the Treasury must consult such persons as it considers appropriate.

(10) A statutory instrument containing regulations under subsection (7) may not be made unless a draft of the instrument has been laid before and approved by a resolution of each House of Parliament.

(11) Any monetary penalty payable under this section is recoverable by the Treasury as a civil debt.

(12) Any monetary penalty received by the Treasury by virtue of this section must be paid into the Consolidated Fund.

(13) This section does not authorise the imposition of a monetary penalty on the Crown.

147 Monetary penalties: procedural rights

(1) Before imposing a monetary penalty on a person under section 146, the Treasury must inform the person of its intention to do so.

(2) The Treasury must also—
(a) explain the grounds for imposing the penalty,
(b) specify the amount of the penalty,
(c) explain that the person is entitled to make representations, and
(d) specify the period within which any such representations must be made.

(3) If (having considered any representations), the Treasury decides to impose the penalty, the Treasury must—
(a) inform the person of its decision,
(b) explain that the person is entitled to seek a review by a Minister of the Crown, and
(c) specify the period within which the person must inform the Treasury that the person wishes to seek such a review.

(4) If the person seeks a review, the Minister may—
(a) uphold the decision to impose the penalty and its amount,
(b) uphold the decision to impose the penalty but substitute a different amount, or
(c) cancel the decision to impose the penalty.

(5) A review under subsection (4) must be carried out by the Minister personally.

(6) If on a review under subsection (4) the Minister decides to uphold the Treasury's decision to impose the penalty and its amount, or to uphold the Treasury's decision to impose the penalty but to substitute a different amount, the person may appeal (on any ground) to the Upper Tribunal.

(7) On an appeal under subsection (6), the Upper Tribunal may quash the Minister's decision and if it does so may—
(a) quash the Treasury's decision to impose the penalty;
(b) uphold that decision but substitute a different amount for the amount determined by the Treasury (or, in a case where the Minister substituted a different amount, by the Minister).

(8) In this section, 'Minister of the Crown' means the holder of an office in Her Majesty's Government in the United Kingdom.

148 Monetary penalties: bodies corporate and unincorporated associations

(1) If a monetary penalty is payable under section 146 by a body, the Treasury may also impose a monetary penalty on an officer of the body if it is satisfied, on the balance of probabilities, that the breach or failure in respect of which the monetary penalty is payable by the body—
(a) took place with the consent or connivance of the officer, or
(b) was attributable to any neglect on the part of the officer.

(2) In subsection (1)—
'body' means a body corporate, a partnership or an unincorporated body other than a partnership;
'officer of a body' means—
(a) in relation to a body corporate, a director, manager, secretary or other similar officer of the body or a person purporting to act in any such capacity;
(b) in relation to a partnership, a partner or a person purporting to act as a partner;
(c) in relation to an unincorporated body other than a partnership, a person who is concerned in the management or control of the body or purports to act in the capacity of a person so concerned.

(3) Sections 146(2) to (5), (11) and (12) and 147 apply in relation to a monetary penalty that may be imposed under subsection (1) as they apply in relation to a monetary penalty that may be imposed under section 146(1).

149 Monetary penalties: supplementary

(1) The Treasury must issue guidance as to—
  (a) the circumstances in which it may consider it appropriate to impose a monetary penalty under section 146 or 148, and
  (b) how it will determine the amount of the penalty.

(2) The Treasury must, at such intervals as it considers appropriate, publish reports about the imposition of monetary penalties under section 146 or 148.

Other provisions about enforcement

150 Deferred prosecution agreements

In Part 2 of Schedule 17 to the Crime and Courts Act 2013 (which lists the offences in relation to which a deferred prosecution agreement may be entered into), after paragraph 26 insert—

'26A(1) An offence under an instrument made under section 2(2) of the European Communities Act 1972 for the purpose of implementing, or otherwise in relation to, EU obligations created or arising by or under an EU financial sanctions Regulation.

(2) An offence under an Act or under subordinate legislation where the offence was created for the purpose of implementing a UN financial sanctions Resolution.

(3) An offence under paragraph 7 of Schedule 3 to the Anti-terrorism, Crime and Security Act 2001 (freezing orders).

(4) An offence under paragraph 30 or 30A of Schedule 7 to the Counter-Terrorism Act 2008 where the offence relates to a requirement of the kind mentioned in paragraph 13 of that Schedule.

(5) An offence under paragraph 31 of Schedule 7 to the Counter-Terrorism Act 2008.

(6) In this paragraph—

'EU financial sanctions Regulation' and 'UN financial sanctions Resolution' have the same meanings as in Part 8 of the Policing and Crime Act 2017 (see section 143 of that Act);

'subordinate legislation' has the same meaning as in the Interpretation Act 1978."

151 Serious crime prevention orders

(1) Schedule 1 to the Serious Crime Act 2007 (which lists the offences in respect of which serious crime prevention orders may be made) is amended as follows.

(2) In Part 1 (England and Wales), after paragraph 13A insert—

'*Financial sanctions legislation*

13B (1) An offence under an instrument made under section 2(2) of the European Communities Act 1972 for the purpose of implementing, or otherwise in relation to, EU obligations created or arising by or under an EU financial sanctions Regulation.

(2) An offence under an Act or under subordinate legislation where the offence was created for the purpose of implementing a UN financial sanctions Resolution.

(3) An offence under paragraph 7 of Schedule 3 to the Anti-terrorism, Crime and Security Act 2001 (freezing orders).

(4) An offence under paragraph 30 or 30A of Schedule 7 to the Counter-Terrorism Act 2008 where the offence relates to a requirement of the kind mentioned in paragraph 13 of that Schedule.

(5) An offence under paragraph 31 of Schedule 7 to the Counter-Terrorism Act 2008.

(6) In this paragraph—

"EU financial sanctions Regulation' and 'UN financial sanctions Resolution' have the same meanings as in Part 8 of the Policing and Crime Act 2017 (see section 143 of that Act); 'subordinate legislation' has the same meaning as in the Interpretation Act 1978."

(3) In Part 1A (Scotland), after paragraph 16M —

'Financial sanctions legislation

16MA (1) An offence under an instrument made under section 2(2) of the European Communities Act 1972 for the purpose of implementing, or otherwise in relation to, EU obligations created or arising by or under an EU financial sanctions Regulation.

(2) An offence under an Act or under subordinate legislation where the offence was created for the purpose of implementing a UN financial sanctions Resolution.

(3) An offence under paragraph 7 of Schedule 3 to the Anti-terrorism, Crime and Security Act 2001 (freezing orders).

(4) An offence under paragraph 30 or 30A of Schedule 7 to the Counter-Terrorism Act 2008 where the offence relates to a requirement of the kind mentioned in paragraph 13 of that Schedule.

(5) An offence under paragraph 31 of Schedule 7 to the Counter-Terrorism Act 2008.

(6) In this paragraph—

'EU financial sanctions Regulation' and 'UN financial sanctions Resolution' have the same meanings as in Part 8 of the Policing and Crime Act 2017 (see section 143 of that Act); 'subordinate legislation' has the same meaning as in the Interpretation Act 1978."

(4) In Part 2 (Northern Ireland), after paragraph 29 insert—

"Financial sanctions legislation

29A (1) An offence under an instrument made under section 2(2) of the European Communities Act 1972 for the purpose of implementing, or otherwise in relation to, EU obligations created or arising by or under an EU financial sanctions Regulation.

(2) An offence under an Act or under subordinate legislation where the offence was created for the purpose of implementing a UN financial sanctions Resolution.

(3) An offence under paragraph 7 of Schedule 3 to the Anti-terrorism, Crime and Security Act 2001 (freezing orders).

(4) An offence under paragraph 30 or 30A of Schedule 7 to the Counter-Terrorism Act 2008 where the offence relates to a requirement of the kind mentioned in paragraph 13 of that Schedule.

(5) An offence under paragraph 31 of Schedule 7 to the Counter-Terrorism Act 2008.

(6) In this paragraph—

'EU financial sanctions Regulation' and 'UN financial sanctions Resolution' have the same meanings as in Part 8 of the Policing and Crime Act 2017 (see section 143 of that Act); 'subordinate legislation' has the same meaning as in the Interpretation Act 1978."

Avoidance of delay: temporary regulations

152 Implementation of UN financial sanctions Resolutions: temporary regulations

(1) Where a UN financial sanctions Resolution is adopted, the Treasury may by regulations made by statutory instrument make such provision as it considers appropriate for the implementation of the Resolution.

(2) Regulations under this section must provide for the regulations to cease to have effect at whichever of the following times first occurs—

(a) the time when an EU financial sanctions Regulation made for the purpose of implementing the UN financial sanctions Resolution enters into force;

(b) the end of a day specified in the regulations, which may not be a day that falls more than 30 days after the day on which the UN financial sanctions Resolution is adopted.

(3) At any time before the end of the day specified in the regulations under subsection (2)(b), the Treasury may amend the regulations (by making further regulations) so as to substitute for the day specified in the regulations in accordance with subsection (2)(b) a different day, which may not be a day that falls more than 60 days after the day on which the UN financial sanctions Resolution is adopted.

(4) The power conferred by subsection (3) may be exercised on only one occasion.

(5) Subsection (3) does not affect the power (by virtue of section 14 of the Interpretation Act 1978) to amend regulations under subsection (1) for a purpose other than that mentioned in subsection (3).

(6) A statutory instrument containing regulations under this section is subject to annulment in pursuance of a resolution of either House of Parliament.

(7) Section 153 makes further provision about regulations under this section.

153 Content of regulations under section 152

(1) Regulations under section 152 may impose prohibitions for such of the following purposes as are relevant to the UN financial sanctions Resolution that is being implemented by the regulations—

(a) freezing funds or economic resources owned, held or controlled by designated persons;

(b) preventing funds or economic resources being made available to, or for the benefit, of designated persons.

(2) In subsection (1), 'designated person' means a person who is specified in any of the following instruments as a person in relation to whom the measures required by the UN financial sanctions Resolution are to be taken—

(a) the UN financial sanctions Resolution or any other UN financial sanctions Resolution;

(b) an instrument made by an organ of the United Nations for the purpose of specifying the persons in relation to whom the measures required by the Resolution are to be taken.

For the purpose of this subsection, 'person' includes (in addition to an individual and a body of persons corporate or unincorporate) any organisation and any association or combination of persons.

(3) Regulations under section 152 must describe the designated persons to whom the prohibitions in the regulations relate but may do so by referring to any of the instruments mentioned in subsection (2) or in any other way; and, where the persons are described by referring to any of those instruments, the regulations may provide for the reference in the regulations to the instrument to have effect as a reference to the instrument as varied or supplemented from time to time.

(4) The regulations may create exceptions to any prohibitions included in the regulations by virtue of subsection (1), including provision for any of those prohibitions not to apply to anything done under the authority of a licence issued by the Treasury under the regulations.

(5) The regulations may make provision—

(a) for requiring a person who is subject to a prohibition, or any other person of a description specified in the regulations, to provide information to the Treasury;

(b) authorising or restricting the disclosure of information so provided.

(6) The regulations may make provision for the enforcement of any prohibitions or requirements set out in the regulations, including provision for preventing any prohibitions from being circumvented.
(7) The provision that may be made under subsection (6) includes—
(a) the creation of offences;
(b) provision corresponding or similar to sections 146 to 149 (civil sanctions).
(8) The regulations may not create an offence punishable by imprisonment for a period exceeding—
(a) in the case of conviction on indictment, 7 years;
(b) in the case of summary conviction—
(i) in relation to England and Wales, 12 months or, in relation to offences committed before section 154(1) of the Criminal Justice Act 2003 comes into force, 6 months;
(ii) in relation to Scotland, 12 months;
(iii) in relation to Northern Ireland, 6 months.
(9) The regulations may provide that a person is not to be subject to any form of liability in consequence of anything done by that person under the regulations.
(10) The regulations may bind the Crown but they may not—
(a) provide for the Crown to be criminally liable, or
(b) provide for the Crown to be liable to pay a monetary penalty.
(11) The regulations may include—
(a) incidental, supplementary or consequential provision;
(b) transitional or transitory provision.
(12) The regulations may—
(a) make different provision for different purposes;
(b) confer a discretion on any person.

Avoidance of delay: temporary listing

154 Linking of UN financial sanctions Resolutions with EU financial sanctions Regulations

(1) For the purposes of section 155, the Treasury may by regulations made by statutory instrument provide that a United Nations financial sanctions Resolution specified in the regulations is linked to an EU financial sanctions Regulation specified in the regulations.
(2) The regulations may provide for any reference in the regulations to a United Nations financial sanctions Resolution or to an EU financial sanctions Regulation to have effect as a reference to the United Nations financial sanctions Resolution or (as the case may be) to the EU financial sanctions Regulation as varied or supplemented from time to time.
(3) A statutory instrument containing regulations under subsection (1) is subject to annulment in pursuance of a resolution of either House of Parliament.

155 Implementation of UN financial sanctions Resolutions: temporary listing

(1) This section applies where—
(a) regulations under section 154 provide that a UN financial sanctions Resolution is linked to an EU financial sanctions Regulation,
(b) a person is designated for the purposes of the UN financial sanctions Resolution, and
(c) at the time the person is designated for those purposes, the person is not included in the list of persons, set out in the EU financial sanctions Regulation, to whom the prohibitions contained in the Regulation relate ('the EU list').

(2) The person is to be treated for a temporary period as if the person were included in the EU list (as well as being designated for the purposes of the UN financial sanctions Resolution).
(3) The temporary period referred to in subsection (2) begins at the time the person is designated for the purposes of the UN financial sanctions Regulation.
(4) The temporary period ends—
  (a) at the end of the day on which the person is (otherwise than under subsection (2)) included in the EU list;
  (b) if the person is not included in the EU list before the end of the period of 30 days beginning with the day after the day on which the person is designated for the purposes of the UN financial sanctions Resolution, at the end of that period of 30 days.
(5) For the purposes of this section, a person is designated for the purposes of a UN financial sanctions Resolution if the person is specified in any of the following instruments as a person in relation to whom the measures required by the UN financial sanctions Resolution are to be taken—
  (a) the UN financial sanctions Resolution or any other UN financial sanctions Resolution;
  (b) an instrument made by an organ of the United Nations for the purpose of specifying the persons in relation to whom the measures required by the Resolution are to be taken.

  For the purpose of this subsection, 'person' includes (in addition to an individual and a body corporate or unincorporate) any organisation and any association or combination of persons.
(6) This section applies where a person is designated for the purposes of the UN financial sanctions Resolution before this section comes into force (as well as where the person is designated after this section comes into force) but, in such a case, the temporary period begins on the day on which this section comes into force.

Power to extend to Bailiwick of Guernsey etc

156 Extension to the Bailiwick of Guernsey, Isle of Man and BOTs

(1) Her Majesty may by Order in Council provide for regulations under section 152(1) (whether made before or after the making of the Order in Council) to extend with or without modifications to—
  (a) the Bailiwick of Guernsey;
  (b) the Isle of Man;
  (c) any of the British overseas territories.
(2) Her Majesty may by Order in Council provide for section 143, regulations under section 154 (whether made before or after the making of the Order in Council) and section 155 to extend with or without modifications to—
  (a) the Bailiwick of Guernsey;
  (b) the Isle of Man;
  (c) any of the British overseas territories.
(3) The power conferred by subsection (1) or (2), so far as relating to regulations, includes power to provide for the regulations as amended from time to time to extend as mentioned in that subsection.
(4) The modifications that may be specified in an Order in Council under subsection (1) include a modification of any provision included in the regulations about the time at which the regulations are to cease to have effect.
(5) A modification included in an Order in Council by virtue of subsection (4)—

(a) may have the effect that the regulations (as extended by the Order in Council) continue to have effect after the time when the regulations have ceased to have effect under the law of England and Wales, Scotland and Northern Ireland, but

(b) must secure that the regulations (as so extended) cease to have effect on a day that falls no later than 120 days after the day on which the relevant UN financial sanctions Resolution is adopted.

(6) In subsection (5), 'the relevant UN financial sanctions Resolution' means the UN financial sanctions Resolution that is being implemented by the regulations.

APPENDIX 7

Guidance: How to prove and verify someone's identity

You should use this guidance if you need help deciding how to check the identity of a customer, employee, or someone acting on behalf of a business. You can check someone's identity:

- digitally
- over the phone
- by post
- by email
- face to face

You can also use this guidance if you:

- want to understand how another individual or organisation checks someone's identity
- are auditing and certifying identity products or services
- are comparing different identity checking processes, for example comparing schemes with the electronic identity and trust services (eIDAS) regulation

This guidance will not:

- tell you how to use accounts and passwords to give users access to something (also known as 'authentication')
- tell you how to assess your risk of identity fraud
- be relevant if you ask users for information about their identity but do not check it (also known as 'self-assertion')

WHAT IS IDENTITY

An identity is a combination of characteristics that identifies a person.

A single characteristic is not usually enough to tell one person apart from another, but a combination of characteristics might be.

When to check an identity

You should check someone's identity if you or your service:

- shows a user personal information about themselves, such as their driving licence or passport details
- gives the user something valuable, such as money or benefits

Users will not need to prove their identity to access some services. You might just need to ask them to create an account, for example if they need to sign in to your service more than once.

Why you should check an identity

By successfully checking someone's identity, you or your service can be confident that you'll give the right people access to the right things. If you do not do this, you or your service could be affected by identity fraud. This is when someone uses a 'synthetic' (made up) or stolen identity to pretend to be someone they're not.

The number of synthetic and stolen identities being used to commit identity fraud in the UK is growing every year. Some of the most common reasons people or criminal groups commit identity fraud are to:

- access services they're not entitled to
- get benefits they're not entitled to
- steal personal, medical or financial information from other identities
- enable organised crime, like human trafficking
- avoid being detected by the police and other authorities

If you follow this guidance, you or your service will check identities in a way that's consistent with other people or services that also follow this guidance.

This does not mean you have to check an identity in the exact same way as someone else. You can do different types of checks to another person or organisation, but achieve the same levels of overall trust in someone's identity.

Checking identities in a consistent way will reduce the chance that one person or service does less effective identity checks than others. This helps protect against identity fraud. It also means that there will be fewer people or services with less effective identity checks that could be targeted by identity fraud.

Consistent identity checks also make it easier for you to trust an identity that's been checked by someone else. Reusing identities will mean:

- people have to prove their identity less often
- organisations and services can share the cost of checking someone's identity

HOW TO CHECK SOMEONE'S IDENTITY

You'll need to know the 'claimed identity' of the person you're checking. A claimed identity is a combination of information (often someone's name, date of birth and address) that represents the characteristics of whoever a person is claiming to be.

When you have this, you can find out if the person is who they say they are. This process is known as 'identity checking' and is made up of 5 parts:

- get evidence of the claimed identity
- check the evidence is genuine or valid
- check the claimed identity has existed over time
- check if the claimed identity is at high risk of identity fraud
- check that the identity belongs to the person who's claiming it

Doing different parts of the identity checking process will help you build up confidence in an identity so that you can be sure someone is who they say they are.

You do not have to do all parts of the identity checking process at once. You can do them over any period of time and gradually build up your confidence in an identity.

You'll get a score for each part of the identity checking process you do.

How much confidence you'll have in an identity depends on:

- how many pieces of evidence you collect
- which parts of the identity checking process you do
- what scores you get for each part of the identity checking process

The different combinations of scores are known as 'identity profiles'.
Each identity profile relates to one of the following levels of confidence:

- low confidence
- medium confidence
- high confidence
- very high confidence

You should aim to get a higher level of confidence in someone's identity if you or your service are at high risk of identity-related crime.

How confident you are in a person's identity can increase over time if you do extra checks or collect more evidence.

Your confidence can also decrease over time, for example if you later find out that a piece of evidence you used might have been lost or stolen at the time you checked that person's identity.

You can also reuse identity checks done by another organisation if they do some or all parts of the identity checking process explained in this guidance.

AUTHORITATIVE SOURCES

You might need to check things with an 'authoritative' source. To be authoritative for a particular piece of information, the source must make sure:

- the integrity of the information is protected
- the information is up to date

The source must also do one of the following:

- issue evidence, for example the Driver and Vehicle Licensing Agency (DVLA) issues evidence such as driving licences
- get information from an organisation that issues evidence, for example credit reference agencies can have authoritative information about bank accounts
- get information from another authoritative source, for example from another identity scheme

GET EVIDENCE OF THE CLAIMED IDENTITY

Some pieces of evidence are 'stronger' than others, which means they will be harder to:

- forge (when an existing piece of evidence is changed to make it look like it belongs to someone else)
- counterfeit (when a piece of evidence is created from scratch)

You can check how strong a piece of evidence is by finding out:

- what security features are on it (for example a hologram or an electronic chip)
- what information it has
- how the person proved their identity to get the evidence

This is also known as a 'strength' check.

The stronger the evidence is, the higher its score will be. The highest score you can get for this part of the identity checking process is 4.

You must check and score one piece of evidence at a time. The evidence can be physical or digital.

To get evidence of a claimed identity, you can either:

- ask the person to provide evidence themselves, like a document (such as a passport) or account details (which they can show by giving you something like a bill or an account number)
- find some evidence of their identity yourself, for example by checking a database

The identity is sometimes shown as a synonym on different pieces of evidence. For example, it might say the person's name is Samantha on their passport, but Sam on their bank card. You can usually accept a synonym, unless you need to know the claimed identity's 'official name' (this is the name on any official documents they have, such as their passport).

The names might be different on different pieces of evidence. For example, someone's surname might have changed because they got married. If the names are different, you might need to collect other pieces of evidence or do other checks to make sure all the evidence belongs to the same person.

Sometimes other information might be different on different pieces of evidence. These are mistakes known as 'transposition errors'.

This can happen with:

- names that have multiple parts, for example 'Anna-Marie Jane' might appear as 'Anna Marie-Jane'
- days and months in dates, for example '08.10.1978' might appear as '10.08.1978'
- centuries in dates, for example '1998' might appear as '1898'
- addresses, for example 'Flat 1a, 29 Acacia Road' might appear as 'Flat 29a Acacia Road'

These mistakes will not usually affect how you do this part of the identity checking process.

Score 1

The evidence will have a score of 1 if it contains at least 2 of the following pieces of information:

- the claimed identity's name
- the claimed identity's date of birth
- the claimed identity's place of birth
- the claimed identity's address
- the claimed identity's biometric information (these are measurements of biological or behavioural characteristics, like an iris or fingerprint)
- a photo of the claimed identity
- a reference number

The evidence should come from an organisation that you know will:

- check the person's identity when they issue the evidence
- make sure its process for issuing the evidence will not be misused by anyone associated with the organisation

Some examples of evidence that will have a score of 1 include an email, PDF or letter from a local authority.

You may not be able to thoroughly check the validity of evidence that has a score of 1.

Score 2

The evidence will have a score of 2 if it has everything it needs to get a score of 1 and it includes information that's unique to either:

- the identity
- that piece of evidence

If the evidence includes a name, it must also show the person's full name instead of any pseudonyms, aliases or nicknames.

If the evidence is a physical document, it must be protected by physical security features. These features will stop it from being reproduced without specialist knowledge or information.

If the evidence includes digital information, it must either be protected by:

- cryptographic security features that correctly identify the person or organisation that issued it
- processes that make sure only authorised users can create, update and access it

Some examples of evidence that have a score of 2 include:

- a firearm certificate
- a Home Office travel document (convention travel document, stateless person's document, one-way document or certificate of travel)
- a birth or adoption certificate
- an older person's bus pass
- an education certificate from a regulated and recognised educational institution (such as an NVQ, SQA, GCSE, A level or degree certificate)
- a rental or purchase agreement for a residential property
- a proof of age card recognised under the Proof of Age Standards Scheme (PASS)
- a Freedom Pass
- a marriage or civil partnership certificate
- a building, contents or vehicle insurance policy
- a gas or electric account
- a 'substantial' electronic identity from a notified eIDAS scheme

Score 3

The evidence will have a score of 3 if it has everything it needs to get a score of 2 and:

- it includes information that's unique to both the identity and that piece of evidence
- the organisation that issued the evidence made sure it was received by the same person who applied for it

- the organisation that issued the evidence checked the person's identity in a way that follows the Money Laundering Regulations 2017

It must also:

- show the person's official name instead of their initials or synonyms, for example 'Julian' instead of 'Jules' (if the evidence includes a name)
- be protected by physical security features that stop it from being reproduced without specialist equipment (if the evidence is a physical document)

The evidence must also include one of the following:

- a photo of the person
- biometric information that uses cryptographic security features to protect its integrity
- cryptographic security features that can be used to identify the person who owns the evidence (this includes evidence with cryptographic chips and digital accounts that are protected by cryptographic methods)

Some examples of evidence that will have a score of 3 include:

- passports that meet the International Civil Aviation Organisation (ICAO) specifications for machine-readable travel documents
- identity cards from an EU or European Economic Area (EEA) country that follow the Council Regulation (EC) No 2252/2004 standards
- UK photocard driving licences
- EU or EEA driving licences that follow the European Directive 2006/126/EC
- a Northern Ireland electoral identity card
- a US passport card
- a bank, building society or credit union current account (which the claimed identity can show by giving you a bank card)
- a student loan account
- a credit account
- a mortgage account (including buy to let mortgage accounts)
- a digital tachograph driver smart card
- an armed forces identity card
- a proof of age card recognised under PASS with a unique reference number
- a loan account (including hire purchase accounts)
- a 'high' electronic identity from a notified eIDAS scheme

Score 4

The evidence will have a score of 4 if it has everything it needs to get a score of 3 and:

- it includes biometric information
- all digital information (including biometric information) is protected by cryptographic security features
- the cryptographic security features can prove which organisation issued the evidence
- the organisation that issued the evidence proved the person's identity by comparing and matching the person to an image of the claimed identity from an authoritative source

Some examples of evidence that will have a score of 4 include:

- biometric passports that meet the ICAO specifications for e-passports
- identity cards from an EU or EEA country that follow the Council Regulation (EC) No 2252/2004 standards and contain biometric information
- a UK biometric residence permit

CHECK THE EVIDENCE IS GENUINE OR VALID

To make sure you only accept a piece of evidence that's real, you can check if it:

- is genuine (not forged or counterfeit)
- is valid (this means you can find records that show the piece of evidence has been issued)
- has not expired
- has not been cancelled or reported as lost or stolen

This is also known as a 'validity' check.

You can check the evidence in person or remotely.

The highest score you can get for this part of the identity checking process is 4.

Only physical pieces of evidence can have a score of 1. A digital piece of evidence that includes data from an authoritative source will have at least a score of 2.

Score 1

The evidence will have a score of 1 if the physical features of the evidence appear to be genuine.

They'll appear to be genuine if the person checking the evidence can confirm:

- they're checking an original, certified copy or scan of the evidence
- there are no errors on the evidence, like wrong paper type, spelling mistakes, irregular use of fonts or missing pages
- the details, layout or alignment of the evidence look the way they should
- any logos look the way they should
- any references to information are the same across the evidence (for example if the body text of a letter references an address, this should match the address shown at the top of the letter)

Score 2

The evidence will have a score of 2 if you make sure it has not expired and do one of the following:

- confirm the evidence is valid
- confirm the visible security features are genuine (these are security features that can be seen without using specialist light sources)
- confirm the ultraviolet (UV) or infrared (IR) security features are genuine

Confirm the evidence is valid

The person or system doing the check can confirm the evidence is valid by making sure the details on it match those held by an authoritative source.

Confirm the visible security features are genuine

The person or system doing the check will need to make sure:

- the original evidence has been shown (this could be in person or remotely, for example by using an app)
- they do not accept scans, photos uploaded by a user, or photocopies of the evidence (this is because it can be difficult to tell if these are forgeries or counterfeits)
- the evidence was shared with the person or system in a way that protects it from being tampered with (for example it could be sent by secure delivery)
- the evidence (or the image or video of the evidence) is clear enough to be able to examine its security features

They should check this using non-specialist light sources such as natural sunlight, indoor lights or desk lamps.

The person or system will need to use official templates to check any of the following features on the evidence look the way they should:

- background printing
- fonts and alignment
- holograms and positioning
- the way it's been laminated
- designs printed with optical variable ink (and check they look the way they should at certain angles)
- the format of any 'compound identifiers', such as a DVLA driver number or a machine-readable zone (MRZ)
- the position of any photographs on the evidence (they should not have been replaced or edited)

Some places where you can find official templates are:

- the Public Register of Authentic travel and identity Documents Online (PRADO)
- the EU and EEA driving licence handbook
- EdisonTD

If the evidence is being checked by a person, they must:

- be trained in how to detect false documents by a specialist trainer, such as the Home Office, National Document Fraud Unit or Centre for the Protection of National Infrastructure (CPNI)
- refresh their training at least every 3 years

If the evidence is being checked by a system, it must:

- have been built following good practice, such as the Home Office's guidance on identification document validation technology
- update the templates it checks the evidence against at least every 3 years

Confirm the UV or IR security features are genuine

The person or system doing the check will need to use a UV or IR light to make sure:

- the paper the evidence is printed on looks the way it should
- the alignment of the evidence looks the way it should
- any fluorescent features (such as fluorescent inks or fibres) look the way they should
- the evidence has not been tampered with (for example a UV light will show where UV features have been covered by glue if something has been stuck on the evidence)

The person or system will need to use official templates to check any of the following features on the evidence look the way they should:

- background printing
- fonts and alignment
- holograms and positioning
- the way it's been laminated
- designs printed with optical variable ink (and check they look the way they should at certain angles)
- the format of any 'compound identifiers', such as a DVLA driver number or an MRZ
- the position of any photographs on the evidence (they should not have been replaced or edited)

Some places where you can find official templates are:

- PRADO
- the EU and EEA driving licence handbook
- EdisonTD

If the evidence is being checked by a person, they must:

- be trained in how to detect false documents by a specialist trainer, such as the Home Office, National Document Fraud Unit or CPNI
- refresh their training at least every 3 years

If the evidence is being checked by a system, it must:

- have been built following good practice, such as the Home Office's guidance on identification document validation technology
- update the templates it checks the evidence against at least every 3 years

Score 3

The evidence will have a score of 3 if you do all of the following:

- confirm the evidence is valid or check the evidence has not been cancelled, lost or stolen
- confirm the visible security features are genuine
- confirm the UV or IR security features are genuine
- check the evidence has not expired

Alternatively, you can check the cryptographic security features are genuine.

Confirm the evidence is valid

The person or system will need to do the same checks to confirm the evidence is valid that are needed at score 2.

Check the evidence has not been cancelled, lost or stolen

The person or system doing the check will need to make sure the evidence has not been:

- cancelled by the organisation that issued it
- reported as lost or stolen

They can do this by checking an authoritative database of cancelled evidence, for example Interpol for passports or a mobile phone operator for mobile phone contracts.

Confirm the visible security features are genuine

The person or system must do the same things needed at score 2 to confirm the visible security features are genuine.

They'll also need to:

- use evidence that has not been intercepted and reused (known as a 'replay attack')
- make sure any shadows or glare do not stop the security features on the evidence from being examined
- update any official templates that are used (such as those from PRADO) every year
- refresh their training in how to detect false documents every year (if the checks are being done by a person)

They must also confirm:

- designs printed using intaglio (raised) ink look the way they should
- designs that have been laser etched look the way they should
- features are consistent and correct across sections of the evidence

Example In a UK passport, there should be a passport number on the page with the person's details on it. You should check if this number is the same as the number punched on the other pages in the passport.

To check this, they must use one of the following:

- a magnification tool (such as a magnifier)
- other inspection equipment used to identify forged or counterfeit documents

Confirm the UV or IR security features are genuine

The person or system must do the same things needed at score 2 to confirm any UV or IR security features are genuine.

They'll also need to:

- use evidence that has not been intercepted and reused (known as a 'replay attack')
- make sure any shadows or glare do not stop the security features on the evidence from being examined
- update any official templates that are used every year
- refresh their training in how to detect false documents every year (if the checks are being done by a person)

Confirm the cryptographic security features are genuine

To make sure the cryptographic security features are genuine, the system that checks the evidence will need to:

- read the cryptographically protected information
- provide any required cryptographic keys
- check the evidence has not expired
- check the digital signature is correct

It will also need to check the signing key:

- belongs to the organisation that issued the evidence
- is the correct type for that evidence
- has not been revoked

Example Most debit or credit cards will have a cryptographic chip on them. You can check the chip is genuine by asking a user to make a zero balance payment using a card reader. If the transaction is successful you'll know the cryptographic chip and the bank account linked to it are genuine.

Score 4

The evidence will have a score of 4 if you do all of the following:

- confirm the visible security features are genuine
- confirm the UV or IR security features are genuine
- confirm the cryptographic security features on the evidence are genuine
- check the evidence has not been cancelled, lost or stolen
- check the evidence has not expired

Confirm the visible security features are genuine

The person or system must do the same things needed at score 3 to confirm the visible security features are genuine.

They'll also need to:

- be supervised when they capture and examine the evidence by someone who's also been trained by a specialist trainer, such as the Home Office, National Document Fraud Unit or CPNI
- examine the evidence under 'controlled' light conditions (which means the lighting in the room creates the best possible environment for examining the security features on the evidence)
- examine the evidence under 'controlled' security conditions (which means there are ways to prevent systems from being fooled or people from being manipulated)

They'll need to check the following features of the evidence look correct:

- watermarks
- security fibres
- consistency throughout the piece of evidence
- secondary background ('ghost') images

Example In the latest UK passport, there should be a ghost image of the person on the 'observations' page. You should check if the surname and date of birth in the image are the same as the person's details.

To check this, they must use one of the following:

- a magnification tool (such as a magnifier)
- a low angle ('oblique') light
- other inspection equipment to identify forged or counterfeit documents

Confirm the UV or IR security features are genuine

The person or system must do the same things needed at score 3 to confirm any UV or IR security features are genuine.

Confirm the cryptographic security features are genuine

The person or system must do the same things needed at score 3 to confirm the cryptographic security features are genuine.

Check the evidence has not been cancelled, lost or stolen

The person or system must do the same things needed at score 3 to confirm the evidence has not been cancelled, lost or stolen.

CHECK THE CLAIMED IDENTITY HAS EXISTED OVER TIME

To lower the risk of you accepting a synthetic identity or an identity that belongs to someone who's died, you can check the claimed identity has existed over time.

This is also known as an 'activity' check.

You do not need to do this part of the identity checking process to meet all the identity profiles.

The highest score you can get for this part of the identity checking process is 4.

You should check if the claimed identity has interacted with other organisations. Some examples of interactions are:

- credit card transactions
- student loan repayments
- mortgage payments
- gas or electricity account payments
- when someone signs in to an online bank or retail account

You can also check if the claimed identity has records that show it's been known by organisations over time. Some examples of these records are:

- health records
- employment records
- school records

How confident you can be that the claimed identity was involved in an interaction depends on if:

- the organisation the claimed identity interacted with checked their identity
- the claimed identity's interactions are what you'd expect them to be

You should expect some people's interactions to appear differently to others. What interactions you expect a claimed identity to have usually depends on the type of interaction they're doing and the type of person they are (like their age or financial situation).

Example You can expect someone who's been working for 20 years to have things like frequent financial transactions, but someone who's recently left school might not.

If you can't find interactions that happen in a way you'd expect for the claimed identity, you should find more interactions over a longer period of time.

Score 1

You'll get a score of 1 if you:

- have evidence of interactions between the claimed identity and an organisation
- know the organisation checked the claimed identity is who they say they are

These interactions need to have happened:

- over the last year
- in a way that you'd expect the claimed identity to behave

Example Over the last year you've seen posts on a social media website that you'd expect the owner of the account to make. This account appears to be linked to the claimed identity, but you cannot be sure they actually created it. This is because this social media website does not check users' identities when they sign up. However, you've used an authoritative source to make sure the email address or phone number associated with the account is linked to the claimed identity.

If the interactions do not happen in a way you'd expect the claimed identity to behave, you'll need to find interactions from over the last 3 years instead.

Score 2

You'll get a score of 2 if you:

- have evidence of interactions between the claimed identity and an organisation
- know the organisation used an authoritative source to check the claimed identity was who they said they were

These interactions need to have happened:

- over the last 6 months
- in a way that you'd expect the claimed identity to behave

Example Over the last 6 months you've seen payments to a post-pay electricity account that you'd expect the owner of the account to make. This electricity supplier checked the account owner's identity using a credit check. This means you know the claimed identity is linked to this account.

You've found evidence of these payments by looking at printed or online statements that you know belong to the claimed identity.

If the interactions do not happen in a way you'd expect the claimed identity to behave, you'll need to find interactions from over the last year instead.

Score 3

You'll get a score of 3 if you:

- have evidence of interactions between the claimed identity and an organisation
- know the organisation checked the claimed identity was who they said they were in a way that at least met the requirements of the Money Laundering Regulations 2017.

These interactions need to have happened:

- over the last 3 months
- in a way that you'd expect the claimed identity to behave

Example Over the last 3 months you've seen mortgage payments that you'd expect the mortgage owner to make. The mortgage provider checked the mortgage owner's identity when they applied for it in a way that follows the Money Laundering Regulations 2017.

You've found evidence of these payments by looking at printed or online statements that you know belong to the claimed identity.

If the interactions do not happen in a way you'd expect the claimed identity to behave, you'll need to find interactions from over the last 6 months instead.

Score 4

You'll get a score of 4 if you:

- have evidence of interactions between the claimed identity and an organisation
- know the organisation checked the claimed identity was who they said they were in a way that at least met the requirements of the Money Laundering Regulations 2017
- know the organisation compared the claimed identity to an image from an authoritative source

You'll need to find at least one interaction from the last 3 months.

Example You've seen that the claimed identity has been on an international flight in the last 3 months. You know their identity was checked when they crossed the border. They would've shown their passport to a border officer, who would've checked it was genuine. The border officer would also have checked the person matched the photo on their passport.

CHECK IF THE CLAIMED IDENTITY IS AT HIGH RISK OF IDENTITY FRAUD

You should make sure the claimed identity is not at a higher than usual risk of identity fraud or likely to be synthetic.

You can do this by checking the details of the claimed identity with authoritative counter-fraud data sources, such as a national fraud database.

This is also known as an 'identity fraud' check.

The highest score you can get for this part of the identity checking process is 3.

Score 1

You'll get a score of 1 if you use an authoritative source to check if the claimed identity has either:

- had its details stolen (even if those details have not been used fraudulently yet)
- been reported as stolen

If either of these things have happened, you must do extra verification checks.

You must also use an authoritative source to check if the claimed identity is a known synthetic identity.

If it is, you must reduce these risks by:

- doing additional verification checks
- collecting more evidence of the claimed identity

Score 2

To get a score of 2 you must do all the checks needed to get a score of 1. You must also use an authoritative source to check that the claimed identity:

- belongs to someone who's still alive
- is known by an organisation that should have a record of that person (for example an Electoral Registration Office in a local authority)
- is at a usual risk of being impersonated (for example, a 'politically exposed person' like a politician or judge is at a higher than usual risk of being impersonated)

You must do extra 'verification' checks if you get any information from the authoritative body that suggests these things are not true.

Score 3

You'll get a score of 3 if you use more than one authoritative source to do all the checks needed to get a score of 2.

The sources must also be 'independent', which means they're either:

- separate from the part of your organisation that checks the person's identity
- part of a different organisation

CHECK THAT THE IDENTITY BELONGS TO THE PERSON WHO'S CLAIMING IT

You must prove that the person who's going through your identity checking process is the claimed identity. You might let someone access your service using a claimed identity that belongs to someone else if you do not do this.

This is also known as a 'verification' check.

The highest score you can get for this part of the identity checking process is 4.

Score 1

The person will get a score of 1 if they can give you information that does not change over time ('static' information) that only the claimed identity should know.

You should check this by asking the person to answer questions or complete tasks. These are known as 'knowledge-based verification' (KBV) challenges.

Example You can ask the person to give you a customer reference number that was issued to them when they bought something from your organisation. You can make sure the number was issued to their claimed identity by checking it against your records. This reference number is static because it does not change over time.

How many KBV challenges you ask the person to do depends on if they're low, medium or high quality.

You should ask the person to do one of the following:

- 2 low quality KBV challenges
- 4 low quality multiple choice KBV challenges
- 1 medium quality KBV challenge
- 2 medium quality multiple choice KBV challenges
- 1 high quality KBV challenge

Quality rules for KBV challenges

KBV challenges should be specific enough to be able to prove that that person is who they say they are.

Someone who has stolen a claimed identity's wallet, purse or phone should not be able to complete all of the KBV challenges you ask them to do.

Low quality KBV challenges must be:

- about the claimed identity
- clear and simple so the person knows exactly what you're asking them
- about something the claimed identity can reasonably be expected to know
- from a source that maintains the integrity of the information the question is based on
- from a source that makes sure the information cannot be misused by the claimed identity (for example the claimed identity should not be able to create false records)

Low quality KBV challenges must not:

- be able to be answered with information that's available in the public domain (for example in an open dataset or on a website that anyone can access)
- be able to be answered using information the person has submitted at another point in the identity checking process
- be predictable (the questions and answers should change each time someone goes through your identity checking process)
- have answers that can be easily guessed if you're asking multiple choice questions
- include information that will give the person the answer to another question
- show personal information (unless the person has already submitted that at another point in the identity checking process)

Medium quality KBV challenges must meet all the requirements for low quality challenges, as well as:

- be based on information from a source that did its own identity checks on the claimed identity
- share codes, like a one-time password sent to the claimed identity's phone, in a way that means you can be sure they were given to the claimed identity (if you use them)

High quality KBV challenges must meet all the requirements for low and medium quality challenges. They must also be based on information:

- from a source that checked the claimed identity was who they said they were in a way that follows the Money Laundering Regulations 2017
- from a source that makes sure the information cannot be accessed, modified or created by its employees
- from a source that's separate from your organisation
- from a source that's regulated by a statutory or independent body
- that cannot be known or accessed by anyone apart from the claimed identity and their immediate family without breaking the law (for example you should not use information that you know is available on the dark web)

Score 2

The person will get a score of 2 if you do one of the following:

- make sure the person physically matches the photo on or associated with the strongest piece of genuine evidence you have of the claimed identity (you can do this in person or remotely)
- make sure the person's biometric information (such as their face or fingerprints) matches biometric information from (or associated with) the strongest piece of genuine evidence you have of the claimed identity
- ask the person to complete multiple 'dynamic' KBV challenges that only the claimed identity should be able to do

Make sure someone matches the photo in person

The person doing the match must have:

- been trained in how to detect impostors
- good enough eyesight (with or without prescription lenses) to effectively compare the person to the image

When doing the match, you must make sure:

- the person whose identity is being checked is present
- the light conditions are good enough to clearly see the person and the image on the evidence (for example there should be no glare or shadows)
- you are comparing the person to a photo from a genuine piece of evidence
- the photo has not been tampered with

The person whose identity is being checked must not:

- be wearing a head covering (unless it's for religious or medical reasons)
- have their eyes closed
- have anything covering their face or eyes (such as shadows or their hair)

Make sure someone matches the photo remotely

When doing the match, you must make sure:

- the person whose identity is being checked is present when their image or video is captured (you should not use a scan or an upload from a photo or video feed)
- the image or video has not been intercepted and reused ('replayed')
- you are comparing an image or video of the person to an image or video of a genuine piece of evidence
- the image or video has been shared in a way that prevents it from being tampered with (for example by using a 'man-in-the-middle' attack)

If a person is doing the match, they must have:

- been trained in how to detect impostors
- good enough eyesight (with or without prescription lenses) to effectively compare the person to the image

The image or video of the person must be:

- clear and in focus
- in colour

In the image or video, the person must:

- be in clear contrast to the background
- not have 'red eye'
- not wear a head covering (unless it's for religious or medical reasons)
- not have their eyes closed
- not have anything covering their face or eyes (such as shadows or their hair)

Make sure someone matches biometric information

When doing the biometric comparison, you must make sure:

- the number of 'false matches' and 'false non-matches' in your system are appropriate for your security and usability needs
- your system matches the person to biometric information that's known to belong to the claimed identity (this is known as 'one-to-one verification')
- the biometric information has not been tampered with (if it was taken from a piece of evidence)
- your system can identify if the person's biometric information has been intercepted and reused ('replayed')
- the biometric information has been shared in a way that prevents it from being tampered with
- your system can tell if someone's using an artefact to convince the system they're someone else (known as 'spoofing') - this could mean making sure they're not holding up a photo or playing a recording of someone's else's voice if you're checking a facial or vocal type ('modality') of biometric
- your system confirms that the person is real (known as a 'liveness' test)

Example If you're checking a fingerprint biometric modality, you can use heart rate sensors to make sure that the person who is providing their fingerprint is alive.

Asking the person to complete dynamic KBV challenges

To be 'dynamic', the answers to a KBV challenge must change over time. This will make it harder for impostors using information from things like data breaches to successfully complete the challenge.

The KBV challenges must follow the same quality rules that need to be followed to get a score of 1.

The KBV challenges must also not be based on information from a single source. An account and a mortgage from the same bank count as different sources if the claimed identity went through a different application process to get each one.

Example You can make a zero balance transaction into the claimed identity's bank account and attach a reference number (which is valid for a short period of time) to it. This will show up as a code on the claimed identity's bank statement.

The person will need to sign in to the claimed identity's account within the allowed time to get the code. If they give you the correct code, it will prove the person you're dealing with has control of and access to that account. Only the claimed identity should be able to do this.

How many KBV challenges you ask the person to complete depends on the quality of the questions. You should ask them to complete one of the following:

- 4 low quality KBV challenges
- 8 low quality multiple choice KBV challenges
- 2 medium quality KBV challenges
- 3 medium quality multiple choice KBV challenges
- 2 high quality KBV challenges
- 2 high quality multiple choice KBV challenges

Score 3

The person will get a score of 3 if you do either of the following in person or remotely:

- make sure they physically match the photo on (or associated with) the strongest piece of genuine evidence you have of the claimed identity
- make sure their biometric information matches biometric information from (or associated with) the strongest piece of genuine evidence you have of the claimed identity

Make sure someone matches a photo in person or remotely

The person doing the match must have all the skills and training needed to get a score of 2. They must refresh their training in how to detect impostors every year.

The person or system doing the match must do everything needed to check someone matches a photo (in person or remotely) at score 2. You must also make sure:

- your process has a way to identify if someone is wearing a mask, makeup or prosthetics to look like someone else
- their eyes are visible without any glare or reflections (if the person is wearing glasses)

Make sure someone matches biometric information

The system doing the match must do everything needed to check someone matches biometric information at score 2. You must also make sure:

- the number of 'false matches' and 'false non-matches' in your system are appropriate for your security and usability needs and are based on industry best practice (for example ISO/IEC TR 29156:2015)

- your system uses a biometric algorithm that's been proven to be effective against a recognised benchmark, like the National Institute of Standards and Technology's (NIST's) face recognition vendor test guidance
- the person's biometric information is captured under conditions that do not reduce the accuracy of the type of biometric check being used (things like light, noise, and humidity impact the success rates for different biometric modalities and should be adjusted if needed)
- your system can tell when someone is spoofing the system using an artefact that's taken time, money and effort to create, for example detecting if someone is changing the pitch and adding background noise to a recording of a vocal biometric
- your system uses multiple processes or measures to confirm that the person is real (known as an enhanced 'liveness' test)

Example If you're checking a facial biometric modality, you can ask the person to take a short video of themselves, during which they repeat a random sequence of words back to you. This helps you make sure there's a real person involved. You can also continually assess small movements of the person's head while the biometric measurement is taking place.

Score 4

The person will get a score of 4 if you make sure their biometric information matches biometric information from (or associated with) the strongest piece of genuine evidence you have.

The system doing the match must do everything needed to check someone matches biometric information at score 3.

It must also be able to identify when someone is spoofing the system using a sophisticated artefact that's taken a lot of time, money, effort or criminal activity to create. If you're checking a facial biometric modality, this could mean making sure the person is not showing a 3D animated avatar on a hijacked computer or device.

The biometric information on the evidence and the biometric information of the person must also be captured under 'controlled conditions'. This means:

- any equipment has been designed in a way that makes it difficult to be tampered with
- someone who was trained in how to compare people to their identity evidence by a specialist trainer (such as the Home Office, National Document Fraud Unit or CPNI) supervises how the biometric information is captured
- the supervisor refreshes their training every year
- the supervisor monitors the behaviour of the person whose biometric information is being captured to make sure it's not suspicious
- the area and equipment used to capture the biometric information has been designed in a way that reduces the likelihood of incorrect matches for the type of biometric information being used

Example Some facial recognition software will be less accurate in different light conditions. A facial biometric comparison should take place under the best light conditions for the biometric algorithm that's being used. This will reduce incorrect matches and false rejections.

The area where the check is being done should also be monitored by trained personnel who make sure people are not trying to fool the system.

IDENTITY PROFILES

Each part of the identity checking process will protect you or your service against different identity risks.

There are a number of ways to combine parts of the identity checking process to meet a level of confidence in an identity. These combinations are known as identity profiles.

Each identity profile will give you one of the following levels of confidence:

- low confidence
- medium confidence
- high confidence
- very high confidence

You can only meet a level of confidence if you meet an identity profile. The higher the level of confidence an identity profile meets, the more protection you or your service will have.

An identity profile is made up of scores for each part of the identity checking process. Your scores must be the same as, or higher than, the scores in each part to meet the profile. Do not add your scores up.

Example You need a validity score of 1 to meet an identity profile. The evidence from the person whose identity you're checking has a validity score of 2. You can use this score of 2 to meet the lower score requirements of the identity profile.

You can choose to meet any identity profile. The identity profile you choose might depend on:

- how confident you need to be in someone's identity
- what evidence your users are likely to have
- which parts of the identity checking process you can do
- how thoroughly you do each part of the identity checking process
- how many pieces of evidence you need

Meeting an identity profile and reaching a level of confidence will mean:

- you know how well your service is protected against identity risks
- your identity checking process can be understood and reused by other organisations or services

If you collect evidence from a user that does not include all the personal information you need, you will need to collect other evidence that does. You'll also need to link these pieces of evidence together to make sure they all relate to the claimed identity.

Example You need evidence of a person's name and address. A person gives you a bus pass that shows their photo and address but not their name. They also give you a genuine passport that shows their photo and their name. You check these photos match, so you know both pieces of evidence relate to the same claimed identity.

If you collect more than one piece of evidence, you must make sure the evidence has been issued by either:

- different organisations
- an organisation that used a different identity checking process to issue each piece of evidence you're using

Example You collect 3 pieces of evidence of a claimed identity from different organisations. One is a letter from a local authority, one is from a solicitor and one is from a gas company. They were all issued to the same claimed identity.

Low confidence in the person's identity

Compared to not doing any identity checks, having low confidence in the person's identity will lower the risk of you accepting either:

- synthetic identities
- impostors who are not close friends or family of the identity they're pretending to be

If you have 1 piece of evidence

There are 3 identity profiles you can meet if you collect 1 piece of evidence.

Low confidence, 1 piece of evidence, profile A (L1A)

Check	Score
Strength	2
Validity	2
Activity	Not needed
Identity fraud	2
Verification	1

By meeting this identity profile, you will:

- know that evidence of the claimed identity exists
- know if the evidence is genuine or valid
- have made sure you or your service have reduced the risks of any known identity fraud associated with the claimed identity
- be confident the person going through the identity checking process knows things that only the claimed identity should know

You do not need to do an activity check because you know the organisation that issued the evidence already did basic checks to make sure the claimed identity exists in the real world.

Low confidence, 1 piece of evidence, profile B (L1B)

Check	Score
Strength	3
Validity	2
Activity	Not needed
Identity fraud	Not needed
Verification	3

By meeting this identity profile, you will:

- know that strong evidence of the claimed identity exists
- know if the evidence is genuine or valid
- be confident the person matches either the photo or biometric information that's shown on the evidence

You do not need to do:

- an activity check because the organisation that issued the evidence did multiple checks to make sure the claimed identity exists in the real world
- an identity fraud check because the person going through the identity checking process has been matched to the claimed identity through a physical or biometric comparison

Low confidence, 1 piece of evidence, profile C (L1C)

Check	Score
Strength	3
Validity	3
Activity	Not needed
Identity fraud	1
Verification	2

By meeting this identity profile, you will:

- know that strong evidence of the claimed identity exists
- know the evidence is genuine and valid
- have made sure you or your service have reduced the risks of any known identity fraud associated with the claimed identity
- have checked the person going through the identity checking process matches the photo or biometric information that's shown on the evidence, or know they can complete challenges that only the claimed identity should be able to do

You do not need to do an activity check because you know the organisation that issued the evidence already did multiple checks to make sure the claimed identity exists in the real world.

If you have 3 pieces of evidence

There's only one identity profile you can meet if you collect 3 pieces of evidence.

Low confidence, 3 pieces of evidence, profile A (L3A)

Check	Score (first piece of evidence)	Score (second piece of evidence)	Score (third piece of evidence)
Strength	1	1	1
Validity	1	1	1

Check	Score
Activity	3
Identity fraud	2
Verification	2

By meeting this identity profile, you will:

- know each piece of evidence appears to be genuine
- be confident that the claimed identity exists in the real world
- have made sure you or your service have reduced the risks of any known identity fraud associated with the claimed identity
- have checked the person going through the identity checking process matches the photo or biometric information that's shown on the evidence, or know they can complete challenges that only the claimed identity should be able to do

You'll need to collect multiple pieces of evidence because the evidence you have does not have many security features that stop it being forged or counterfeit.

Medium confidence in the person's identity

Compared to low confidence, having medium confidence in the person's identity will lower the risk of you:

- accepting synthetic identities
- accepting impostors who are not close friends or family of the identity they're pretending to be
- accepting impostors who do not look like the identity they're pretending to be

Medium confidence also provides some protection against accepting impostors who are close friends or family of the identity they're pretending to be.

If you have 1 piece of evidence

There are 2 identity profiles you can meet if you collect 1 piece of evidence.

Medium confidence, 1 piece of evidence, profile A (M1A)

Check	Score
Strength	4
Validity	3
Activity	Not needed
Identity fraud	1
Verification	3

By meeting this identity profile, you will:

- know that very strong evidence of the claimed identity exists
- know the evidence is genuine and valid
- have checked the claimed identity exists in the real world

- have made sure you or your service have reduced the risks of any known identity fraud associated with the claimed identity
- be confident the person going through the identity checking process matches either the photo or biometric information that's shown on the evidence

You do not need to do an activity check because you know the organisation that issued the evidence already did multiple checks to make sure the claimed identity exists in the real world.

Medium confidence, 1 piece of evidence, profile B (M1B)

Check	Score
Strength	3
Validity	3
Activity	2
Identity fraud	1
Verification	3

By meeting this identity profile, you will:

- have strong evidence that shows the claimed identity exists
- know the evidence is genuine and valid
- have records that the claimed identity exists in the real world
- have made sure you or your service have reduced the risks of any known identity fraud associated with the claimed identity
- be confident the person going through the identity checking process matches either the photo or biometric information that's shown on the evidence

If you have 2 pieces of evidence

There are 4 identity profiles you can meet if you collect 2 pieces of evidence.

Medium confidence, 2 pieces of evidence, profile A (M2A)

Check	Score (first piece of evidence)	Score (second piece of evidence)
Strength	2	2
Validity	2	2

Check	Score
Activity	3
Identity fraud	1
Verification	3

By meeting this identity profile, you will:

- have more than one piece of evidence that shows the claimed identity exists
- know the evidence is genuine or valid

- be confident that the claimed identity exists in the real world
- have made sure you or your service have reduced the risks of any known identity fraud associated with the claimed identity
- be confident the person going through the identity checking process matches either the photo or biometric information on the evidence

Medium confidence, 2 pieces of evidence, profile B (M2B)

Check	Score (first piece of evidence)	Score (second piece of evidence)
Strength	3	2
Validity	3	2

Check	Score
Activity	2
Identity fraud	2
Verification	2

By meeting this identity profile, you will:

- have strong evidence that shows the claimed identity exists
- have another piece of evidence that shows the claimed identity exists
- know the evidence is genuine, valid or both
- have records that the claimed identity exists in the real world
- have made sure you or your service have reduced the risks of any known identity fraud associated with the claimed identity
- have checked the person going through the identity checking process matches the photo or biometric information that's shown on the evidence, or know they can complete challenges that only the claimed identity should be able to do

Medium confidence, 2 pieces of evidence, profile C (M2C)

Check	Score (first piece of evidence)	Score (second piece of evidence)
Strength	3	2
Validity	3	2

Check	Score
Activity	1
Identity fraud	1
Verification	3

By meeting this identity profile, you will:

- have strong evidence that shows the claimed identity exists
- have another piece of evidence that shows the claimed identity exists
- know the evidence is genuine, valid or both
- have checked the claimed identity exists in the real world
- have made sure you or your service have reduced the risks of any known identity fraud associated with the claimed identity
- be confident the person going through the identity checking process matches either the photo or biometric information that's shown on the evidence

Medium confidence, 2 pieces of evidence, profile D (M2D)

Check	Score (first piece of evidence)	Score (second piece of evidence)
Strength	4	2
Validity	3	2

Check	Score
Activity	Not needed
Identity fraud	2
Verification	2

By meeting this identity profile, you will:

- have very strong evidence that shows the claimed identity exists
- have another piece of evidence that shows the claimed identity exists
- know the evidence is genuine, valid or both
- have checked the claimed identity exists in the real world
- have made sure you or your service have reduced the risks of any known identity fraud associated with the claimed identity
- have checked the person going through the identity checking process matches the photo or biometric information that's shown on the evidence, or know they can complete challenges that only the claimed identity should be able to do

You do not need to do an activity check because you know the organisation that issued the evidence already did multiple checks to make sure the claimed identity exists in the real world.

If you have 3 pieces of evidence

There's only one identity profile you can meet if you collect 3 pieces of evidence.

Medium confidence, 3 pieces of evidence, profile A (M3A)

Check	Score (first piece of evidence)	Score (second piece of evidence)	Score (third piece of evidence)
Strength	2	2	2
Validity	2	2	2

Check	Score
Activity	2
Identity fraud	2
Verification	2

By meeting this identity profile, you will:

- have multiple pieces of evidence that show the claimed identity exists
- know each piece of evidence is genuine or valid
- have records that the claimed identity exists in the real world
- have made sure you or your service have reduced the risks of any known identity fraud associated with the claimed identity
- have checked the person going through the identity checking process matches the photo or biometric information that's shown on the evidence, or know they can complete challenges that only the claimed identity should be able to do

High confidence in the person's identity

Compared to medium confidence, having high confidence in the person's identity will lower the risk of you:

- accepting synthetic identities
- accepting impostors who know the identity (including close friends or family)
- accepting impostors who do not know the identity
- being targeted by people who do not look like the identity

If you have 1 piece of evidence

There are 2 identity profiles you can meet if the person gives you 1 piece of evidence.

High confidence, 1 piece of evidence, profile A (H1A)

Check	Score
Strength	4
Validity	3
Activity	Not needed
Identity fraud	3
Verification	3

By meeting this identity profile, you will:

- have very strong evidence that shows the claimed identity exists
- know the evidence is genuine and valid
- have made sure you or your service has reduced the risks of any known identity fraud associated with the claimed identity
- be confident the person matches either the photo or biometric information that's shown on the evidence

You do not need to do an activity check because you know the organisation that issued the evidence did multiple thorough checks to make sure the claimed identity exists in the real world.

High confidence, 1 piece of evidence, profile B (H1B)

Check	Score
Strength	4
Validity	4
Activity	Not needed
Identity fraud	Not needed
Verification	3

By meeting this identity profile, you will:

- have very strong evidence that shows the claimed identity exists
- know the evidence is genuine and valid
- be confident the person matches either the photo or biometric information that's shown on the evidence

You do not need to do:

- an identity fraud check as the person going through the identity checking process is unlikely to be someone else (you'll know this because they've been matched to the claimed identity through a physical or biometric comparison)
- an activity check because the organisation that issued the evidence did multiple thorough checks to make sure the claimed identity exists in the real world

If you have 2 pieces of evidence

There are 3 identity profiles you can meet if you collect 2 pieces of evidence.

High confidence, 2 pieces of evidence, profile A (H2A)

Check	Score (first piece of evidence)	Score (second piece of evidence)
Strength	3	3
Validity	3	3

Check	Score
Activity	3
Identity fraud	2
Verification	3

By meeting this identity profile, you will:

- have more than one piece of strong evidence that shows the claimed identity exists know both pieces of evidence are genuine and valid

- be confident that the claimed identity exists in the real world
- have made sure you or your service have reduced the risks of any known identity fraud associated with the claimed identity
- be confident the person matches either the photo or biometric information that's shown on the evidence

High confidence, 2 pieces of evidence, profile B (H2B)

Check	Score (first piece of evidence)	Score (second piece of evidence)
Strength	4	3
Validity	3	3

Check	Score
Activity	Not needed
Identity fraud	2
Verification	3

By meeting this identity profile, you will:

- have very strong evidence that shows the claimed identity exists
- have another piece of strong evidence that shows the claimed identity exists
- know both pieces of evidence are genuine and valid
- have made sure you or your service have reduced the risks of any known identity fraud associated with the claimed identity
- be confident the person matches either the photo or biometric information that's shown on the evidence

You will not need to do an activity check because the organisation that issued the evidence did multiple thorough checks to make sure the claimed identity exists in the real world.

High confidence, 2 pieces of evidence, profile C (H2C)

Check	Score (first piece of evidence)	Score (second piece of evidence)
Strength	4	2
Validity	3	2

Check	Score
Activity	2
Identity fraud	2
Verification	3

By meeting this identity profile, you will:

- have very strong evidence that shows the claimed identity exists
- have another piece of evidence that shows the claimed identity exists
- know the evidence is genuine, valid or both
- be confident that the claimed identity exists in the real world
- have made sure you or your service have reduced the risks of any known identity fraud associated with the claimed identity
- be confident the person matches either the photo or biometric information that's shown on the evidence

If you have 3 pieces of evidence

There's only one identity profile you can meet if you collect 3 pieces of evidence.

Check	Score (first piece of evidence)	Score (second piece of evidence)	Score (third piece of evidence)
Strength	3	2	2
Validity	3	2	2

Check	Score
Activity	3
Identity fraud	3
Verification	3

By meeting this identity profile, you will:

- have strong evidence that shows the claimed identity exists
- have more than one other piece of evidence that shows the claimed identity exists
- know the evidence is genuine, valid or both
- be confident that the claimed identity exists in the real world
- have made sure you or your service have reduced the risks of any known identity fraud associated with the claimed identity
- be confident the person matches either the photo or biometric information that's shown on the evidence

Very high confidence in the person's identity

Very high confidence makes it very difficult for someone to:

- use a synthetic identity
- impersonate someone without breaking the law

If you have 1 piece of evidence

There's only one identity profile you can meet if you collect 1 piece of evidence.

Very high confidence, 1 piece of evidence, profile A (V1A)

Check	Score
Strength	4
Validity	4

Check	Score
Activity	4
Identity fraud	3
Verification	4

By meeting this identity profile, you will:

- have very strong evidence that shows the claimed identity exists
- know the evidence is genuine and valid
- be very confident that the claimed identity exists in the real world
- have made sure you or your service have reduced the risks of any known identity fraud associated with the claimed identity
- be confident the person's biometric information matches what's shown on the evidence

You'll have been as thorough as possible with all parts of the identity checking process so you only need one piece of evidence.

If you have 2 pieces of evidence

There are 2 identity profiles you can meet if you collect 2 pieces of evidence.

Very high confidence, 2 pieces of evidence, profile A (V2A)

Check	Score (first piece of evidence)	Score (second piece of evidence)
Strength	4	4
Validity	4	4

Check	Score
Activity	Not needed
Identity fraud	2
Verification	4

By meeting this identity profile, you will:

- have more than one piece of very strong evidence that shows the claimed identity exists
- know the evidence is genuine and valid
- have made sure you or your service have reduced the risks of any known identity fraud associated with the claimed identity
- be confident the person's biometric information matches what's shown on the evidence

This means the organisation that issued the evidence did multiple thorough checks to make sure the claimed identity exists in the real world (so you do not need to do an activity check).

Very high confidence, 2 pieces of evidence, profile B (V2B)

Check	Score (first piece of evidence)	Score (second piece of evidence)
Strength	4	3
Validity	4	3

Check	Score
Activity	2
Identity fraud	3
Verification	4

By meeting this identity profile, you will:

- have very strong evidence that shows the claimed identity exists
- have another piece of strong evidence that shows the claimed identity exists
- know the evidence is genuine and valid
- have records that the claimed identity exists in the real world
- have made sure you or your service have reduced the risks of any known identity fraud associated with the claimed identity
- be confident the person's biometric information matches what's shown on the evidence

If you have 3 pieces of evidence

There's only one identity profile you can meet if you have 3 pieces of evidence.

Very high confidence, 3 pieces of evidence, profile A (V3A)

Check	Score (first piece of evidence)	Score (second piece of evidence)	Score (third piece of evidence)
Strength	4	3	3
Validity	4	3	3

Check	Score
Activity	1
Identity fraud	2
Verification	4

By meeting this identity profile, you will:

- have very strong evidence that shows the claimed identity exists
- have more than one other piece of strong evidence that shows the claimed identity exists

- know the evidence is genuine and valid
- have checked the claimed identity exists in the real world
- have made sure you or your service have reduced the risks of any known identity fraud associated with the claimed identity
- be confident the person's biometric information matches what's shown on the evidence

You can do weaker activity and identity fraud checks because you have multiple pieces of evidence that were issued by organisations that checked the claimed identity exists in the real world.

APPENDIX 8

Office of Financial Sanction Implementation FINANCIAL SANCTIONS Guidance January 2020

CHAPTER 5 YOUR REPORTING OBLIGATIONS TO OFSI

5.1 EU financial sanctions regimes

EU financial sanctions regimes have two reporting components to them. The first is a general obligation that applies to everyone. The second is a more targeted obligation that applies to specified businesses and professions.

5.1.1 General reporting requirement

EU regulations require natural and legal persons, entities and bodies to supply OFSI as soon as practicable with any information that would 'facilitate compliance' with the regulations. Any information provided will only be used for the purposes for which it was provided or received.

This requirement applies to natural and legal persons, entities and bodies in the UK or under UK jurisdiction and not just to credit or financial institutions or to individuals working for them.

Examples of the kind of information that will facilitate compliance can be found in Table 5.A.

If you are unsure of your reporting obligations, you should seek independent legal advice.

5.1.2 Relevant institution or relevant business or profession

UK regulations, which enforce EU regulations, set out specific reporting obligations for a 'relevant institution' and a 'relevant business or profession'. These include:

'Relevant institution'

- a person who has permission under Part 4A of the Financial Services and Markets Act 2000 (FSMA 2000) (permission to carry on regulated activities)
- a European Economic Area (EEA) credit institution authorised by its home state regulator and that has permission under FSMA 2000
- a business that operates a currency exchange office, transmits money (or any representations of monetary value) by any means, or cashes cheques which are made payable to customers

Table 5.A Examples of information to be reported

Reporting Area	Example
Person is a designated person	A customer or client of yours is a designated person or entity. As well as providing OFSI with any information you hold about the DP or entity by which they can be identified, if the DP is a customer or client you must also inform OFSI of the nature, amount, quantity of any funds or economic resources held on behalf of the customer or client, at the time this knowledge or suspicion arose.
Offences	Exact offences will depend on the relevant legislation, but can include: • making funds or economic resources available to a designated person (except where an exemption applies or under licence) • dealing with funds or economic resources that must be frozen (except where an exemption applies or under licence) • activities that circumvent an asset freeze • breaches of licensing conditions
Funds and economic resources[a]	You must include details of any funds and economic resources that you have frozen.
Credits to frozen accounts[b]	A relevant institution must inform OFSI without delay whenever it credits a frozen account with: • payments due under prior contracts • payments made under judicial decisions rendered in an EU member state • funds transferred to an account by a third party

[a] See Section 3.1.3 of this guide for a definition of what constitutes funds and economic resources.
[b] A relevant institution does not need to inform OFSI when it credits an account with interest or other earnings.

'Relevant business or profession'

- an auditor
- a casino
- a dealer in precious metals or stones
- an estate agent
- an external accountant
- an independent legal professional
- a tax adviser
- a trust or company service provider

Definitions of these businesses and professions can be found in the Schedules to the relevant UK regulation for each EU sanctions regime. See the European Union Financial Sanctions (Amendment of Information Provisions) Regulations 2017 which inserted these definitions into the Schedules:

http://www.legislation.gov.uk/uksi/2017/754/pdfs/uksi_20170754_en.pdf

5.1.3 What you must report

If you are a relevant institution or relevant business or profession you must report to OFSI as soon as practicable if you know or have reasonable cause to suspect that a person:

- is a designated person
- has committed an offence under the regulations

You are required to report this information, or any other matter on which your knowledge or suspicion is based, if it came to you in the course of carrying out your business.

When reporting to OFSI you must include:

- the information or other matter on which the knowledge or suspicion is based
- any information you hold about the person or designated person by which they can be identified

If you know or have reasonable cause to suspect that a person is a designated person and that person is a customer of your institution, you must also state the nature and amount or quantity of any funds or economic resources held by you for that customer.

Examples of the kind of information to be provided to OFSI can be found in Table 5.A.

If you are unsure of your reporting obligations, you should seek independent legal advice.

5.2 UK financial sanctions regimes

The UK's domestic regimes carry similar reporting obligations for relevant institutions to the EU regimes. However, you should note that there is no general obligation to report under the domestic regimes, and that they do not include 'relevant businesses or professions' as part of their reporting requirements.

In spite of this, the obligation to comply with financial sanctions still applies.

The reporting obligations under TAFA 2010 can be found in Chapter 3 of that Act. The reporting obligations under ATCSA 2001 can be found in the Schedule to the Orders made under that act. The Orders can be found on GOV.UK:

https://www.gov.uk/government/publications/financial-sanctions-uk-freezing-orders

Designations made under the domestic regimes can be found in the following sections of the consolidated list:

Terrorism and Terrorist Financing

- Which includes designations made under TAFA 2010 (and Council Regulation (EC) No. 2580/2001)

UK Freezing Orders

- Which includes designations made under ATCSA 2001

If you are unsure of your reporting obligations, you should seek independent legal advice.

Index

aircraft 6.01–6.08
Al Qaida 1.04, 1.15, 13.17
 Ombudsman to the ISIL and Al-Qaida Sanctions Committee 9.07
anti-money laundering (AML) measures
 assessment of UK policy 1.49
 in British Overseas Territories (BOTs) *see* British Overseas Territories (BOTs)
 broad UK AML scheme 1.19
 European Union (Withdrawal) Act 2018, effect 13.14
 Fifth Money Laundering Directive *see* Fifth Money Laundering Directive (5MLD)
 Financial Action Task Force (FATF) *see* Financial Action Task Force (FATF)
 Fourth Money Laundering Directive (4MLD) 1.09, 13.03, 13.08
 future divergence in 1.16
 'high-end' money laundering 1.50
 high-risk countries 13.77–13.78, 13.80
 implementation of 5MLD *see* Fifth Money Laundering Directive (5MLD)
 international assessment of UK schemes 1.45–1.54
 loss of EU mechanism following Brexit transition 1.08, 1.09
 Mossack Fonseca disclosures 13.10
 Panama Papers 13.10
 Paradise Papers 13.10
 post-Brexit powers 13.01–13.39
 pre-Brexit regime under EU law 13.05–13.11
 provisions under 2018 Act
  core power under Section 49 13.15–13.17
  impact in the UK 13.12–13.14
  new powers 1.75–1.77
  overview of amendments 13.01–13.04
 'red flag' transactions 13.73, 13.74
 repeal of European Communities Act 1972 13.14
 scope of activities 13.01
 'standalone' money laundering 1.50
 Third Money Laundering Directive (3MLD) 13.07
 topics on which further regulations may issue 13.18–13.39
  criminal offences/other penalties 13.33–13.35
  definitions 13.38
  future-proofing 13.37
  geographical scope 13.26
  policies and procedures 13.27
  potential expansion of the population subject to regulation 13.22–13.24
  prescribed measures 13.28–13.29
  risk assessments 13.25–13.26
  supervisory functions 13.32
appropriate Minister *see under* Ministers and ministerial reviews
arms embargoes, trade sanctions distinguished from 4.01–4.03
art dealers, 5MLD implementation 13.54
asset freezes
 before Brexit 3.21–3.30
 Consolidated List (OFSI) 3.04, 7.03
 crediting frozen accounts 10.15
 effects 3.04
 FATF on UK policy 1.47
 international human rights violators in the UK 1.59
 Landsbanki Freezing Order 2008 1.21
 Lugovoy (Andrey) and Dmitri Kovtun Freezing Order 1.21
 post-Brexit powers and 2018 Act 3.03–3.05, 3.31–3.35, 3.39–3.41
 Russian, financial sanctions against *see under* Russia, UK sanctions against (post-Brexit)
 terminology 3.31, 3.39–3.41

beneficial ownership (BO)
 Beneficial Owner, Officer or Manager (BOOM) 13.60, 13.61
 foreign companies 1.54
 information provision 1.51
 registers 1.53, 13.04, 13.45
Blocking Regulation, amending 1.13
BOTs *see* British Overseas Territories (BOTs)
Brexit
 AML regime prior to 13.05–13.11
 asset freezes prior to 3.21–3.30
 date of withdrawal, significance 1.36
 European Union (Withdrawal) Act 2018, effect 13.14
 immigration sanctions prior to 5.02
 pre-Brexit sanctions regime 1.01–1.02
 sanctions regime before 1.30–1.39
 sanctions regime following *see* designations (sanctions); financial sanctions; immigration sanctions; Office of Financial Sanctions Implementation (OFSI); OFSI Guidance; Russia, UK sanctions against (post-Brexit); Sanctions and Anti-Money Laundering Act 2018; trade sanctions
 scope of sanctions regime following 2.01

Brexit (*cont.*)
transition period 1.01–1.10
Withdrawal Agreement 1.18, 1.24
British Overseas Territories (BOTs)
anti-money laundering (AML) measures 13.40–13.47
Fifth Money Laundering Directive (5MLD) 13.31, 13.40
beneficial ownership (BO) registers 1.53, 13.04, 13.45
Commentary to 2018 Act 13.44–13.45
Consolidated List disseminated in 7.03
defining 13.43
financial sanctions 3.14
information sharing 12.08
mandate to create a public register 1.60
and passage of 2018 Act 1.61
British Virgin Islands 13.47

capital market restrictions, OFSI list 7.01, 7.09–7.10
Caribbean Financial Action Task Force (CFATF) 13.46
Cayman Islands
anti-money laundering (AML) measures, increased scope 13.23
Financial Reporting Authority 3.14
registers of beneficial ownership 13.45
see also British Overseas Territories (BOTs)
CFSP *see* Common Foreign and Security Policy (CFSP)
Charter of the United Nations 1.31, 2.08, 8.36
Civil Aviation Authority (CAA) 6.04, 6.08
closed material procedures (CMP) 9.16–9.20
Common Foreign and Security Policy (CFSP) 1.02, 1.22, 1.23
Companies House 1.52, 1.61, 13.72
Register 13.67
Consolidated List *see* Office of Financial Sanctions Implementation (OFSI)
core power under 2018 Act
additional requirements 2.25–2.29
additions to 2.02–2.06
appropriate Minister 2.07–2.09
categories of sanctions 2.15
furthering a policy objective 2.11
good governance 2.12
making of sanctions regulations 2.07–2.16
new sanctions, reasons for making 2.09
Council of the European Union 1.18
counter-terrorism
licences 10.41–10.42
pre-Brexit regime 1.31
regulations with counter-terrorism purpose 8.42–8.43
court review of decisions
Administrative Court 9.09, 9.21
Anns v Merton 9.26
appeal process 9.07
availability under 2018 Act 9.10–9.11
Bank Mellat I and II 9.24, 9.27
before Brexit 9.01
Civil Procedure Rules (CPR) 9.14, 9.17, 9.20, 9.21
closed material procedures (CMP) 9.16–9.20
Court of Appeal 9.09
damages 9.37–9.39
disclosure 9.21–9.24
following Brexit transition period 9.02
grounds for challenge (case law) 9.25–9.36
necessity 9.35
overview 9.01–9.09
preliminary matters 9.12–9.15
proportionality 9.28, 9.30, 9.31, 9.35
reasonable belief 9.34
Tariq v Home Office 9.27
Crimea
crediting frozen accounts 10.15
infrastructure related goods 3.45
prohibition of investments in 10.07
Russian annexation 10.06
trade sanctions 4.04
criminal offences 2.48
anti-money laundering (AML) 13.33–13.35
new 1.56, 1.57, 2.47, 4.23, 11.04
crypto-registration with FCA 13.84–13.85
Cuba 1.13
Customer Due Diligence (CDD) 13.62–13.65, 13.82

Da'esh 1.04, 1.15, 13.17
Ombudsman to the ISIL and Al-Qaida Sanctions Committee 9.07
dealing 3.37
Deferred Prosecution Agreements (DPAs) 11.05–11.07
Department of International Trade (DIT) 1.43
designations (sanctions)
designated persons
appropriate Minister, designated by 7.20, 7.24, 7.31–7.34, 8.01–8.37
defining 7.19
designation by description 7.20, 7.31–7.34
designation by name 7.06, 7.07, 7.20, 7.23–7.30
implementation of sanctions without delay 7.11–7.12
informing of their designation in timely manner 2.35
named by or under UN Security Council Resolutions 7.35
OFSI lists 7.01–7.16
potential infringements of due process 1.58
proscription under Terrorism Act 2000 7.13–7.16
publicly available lists 7.01–7.10
grounds for challenge (case law) 9.29

Mutual Evaluation Report (MER) 11.16
powers under 2018 Act
context/key provisions 7.17–7.22
designation of a person by description 7.20, 7.31–7.34
designation of a person by name 7.06, 7.07, 7.20, 7.23–7.30
regulations, power to vary or revoke under 8.04–8.06
sanctions review procedure 8.12–8.31
ships 6.12
variation or revocation
core right to request 8.07–8.11
power to vary or revoke 8.01–8.06
sanctions review procedure, new regulations 8.12–8.31
temporary EU lists, requests in relation to 8.32–8.35
UN-named person, right to request 8.36
see also Consolidated List *under* Office of Financial Sanctions Implementation (OFSI); Ministers and ministerial reviews
due diligence *see* Customer Due Diligence (CDD); Enhanced Due Diligence (EDD)

electronic identity verification (EIV) 13.65
enforcement
fines imposed by OFSI 11.01–11.02, 11.08, 11.09
HM Government departments and agencies with sanctions role 1.40–1.44
international assessment 11.14–11.16
level of penalties, expansion of 11.11
OFSI Guidance 11.08–11.13
overview of 2018 amendments 11.03–11.07
referral to law enforcement agencies 11.10
Enhanced Due Diligence (EDD), changes to 13.11, 13.73–13.80
European Convention on Human Rights 5.12, 5.15, 7.28
European Union
direct effect of laws 1.35
Directives on AML 1.09
pre-Brexit regime under EU law 13.05–13.11
sanctions *see* sanctions, EU
UK dependence on for discharging sanctions duties 1.01
exemptions
compliance, protection for 10.12–10.13
disapplying effect of sanctions 10.04
exceptions 10.04–10.07
frozen accounts, crediting 10.15
Guidance 10.14–10.42
immigration 5.05–5.11, 10.11
non-designated independent persons, protection for 10.16
ring-fencing 10.17
see also licences
Export Control Organisation (ECO) 1.43
export of goods, trade sanctions 4.08–4.10, 4.28
extra-territorial sanctions 1.28

FATF *see* Financial Action Task Force (FATF)
Fifth Money Laundering Directive (5MLD) 13.03
accounts and safe-deposit boxes 13.83
art dealers 13.54
British Overseas Territories (BOTs) 13.40–13.47
crypto-registration with FCA 13.84–13.85
Customer Due Diligence (CDD) 13.62–13.65
discrepancies on registers, dealing with 13.66–13.72
e-money thresholds for CDD 13.82
Enhanced Due Diligence (EDD) 13.11, 13.73–13.80
entry into force 13.09, 13.49
extension of scope 13.51–13.54
implementation 13.48–13.85
information requests, duty to respond to 13.83
information sharing 13.31
key amendments 13.11
letting agents 13.52
policies, controls and procedures 13.55–13.57
supervisors approving individuals 13.59–13.61
tax advisers 13.51
terrorist financing focus 13.09
training requirements 13.58
transposition 1.09
trust registration 13.81
virtual currencies, focus on 13.10
see also anti-money laundering (AML) measures
Financial Action Task Force (FATF)
anti-money laundering (AML)
assessment of schemes 1.45–1.48, 1.50–1.52
Recommendations 13.05, 13.06, 13.07, 13.14
role in relation to pre-Brexit regime 13.05
standards 13.02
and EU Directives 1.09, 13.03, 13.05
members 13.06
Mutual Evaluation Report (MER) 1.45–1.46, 11.14–11.16
virtual assets, supervision guidance 13.10
see also anti-money laundering (AML) measures; Fifth Money Laundering Directive (5MLD); Fourth Money Laundering Directive (4MLD); Third Money Laundering Directive (3MLD)
Financial Conduct Authority (FCA) 13.32, 13.84–13.85
financial sanctions
asset freezes (pre-Brexit) 3.21–3.30
banking and financial services 3.46
broad interpretation 3.18–3.20
Common Foreign and Security Policy (CFSP) 1.02
comparison of EU and UK 3.48
compliance, avoiding overly narrow approach to 3.50–3.51
dealing 3.37–3.38

financial sanctions (*cont.*)
definitions 3.36–3.49
economic resources 3.44
EU autonomous 1.34
FATF on UK policy 1.47
financial services and products 3.46–3.49
form of UK sanctions 3.07
freezing 3.03–3.05, 3.39–3.41
funds 3.42–3.43
goods *see* goods
implementation methods, new 3.01–3.10
information sharing 12.06
insurance-related 3.46
joint interests 3.58–3.59
minority interests 3.56–3.57
necessity 9.35
overview 3.01–3.30
ownership and control 3.50–3.59
publicly available lists 7.01–7.10
'reasonable cause to suspect' 3.23, 3.25
against Russia 3.06, 3.10
asset freezes 1.01, 3.29, 3.32, 3.34
comparison of EU and UK 3.48
dealing 3.37
ownership and control 3.54
services and products 3.48, 3.49
source of definitions 3.36
territorial application 3.11–3.17
types 3.01–3.10
unilateral, caution regarding 1.21
'wilful blindness' doctrine 3.24–3.26
see also sanctions, UK; sanctions regulations under 2018 Act
financial services and products 3.46–3.49
Foreign & Commonwealth Office (FCO) 1.41, 2.11, 7.12
Fourth Money Laundering Directive (4MLD) 1.09, 13.03, 13.05, 13.08, 13.27
freezing orders
interim 3.05
Landsbanki Freezing Order 2008 1.21
Lugovoy (Andrey) and Dmitri Kovtun Freezing Order 1.21
see also asset freezes; financial sanctions
'future-proofing' of sanctions scheme 2.49

Global Witness 1.61
goods
export of, trade sanctions 4.08–4.10, 4.28
financial sanctions 3.45
import of, trade sanctions 4.11–4.12, 4.28
origin 4.12
seized from ships 6.17–6.18

HM Revenue & Customs (HMRC)
and Beneficial Ownership 1.51
trade sanctions 1.43
HM Treasury (HMT) 1.42
Home Office (HO)/Home Secretary
exemptions to travel bans 5.10
Home Secretary regulations 5.16
proscription under Terrorism Act 2000 7.13, 7.15
travel bans 1.44, 5.01–5.04
human rights
designation powers 7.28
gross violation 2.18, 2.20
immigration sanctions 5.12, 5.15
Magnitsky clause 1.59, 2.01, 2.17–2.24
POCA 2002 provisions 2.23
torture 2.21
violations 1.24, 1.59, 2.17–2.24

immigration sanctions
appeals (Section 48) 5.12–5.16
European Convention on Human Rights 5.12, 5.15
exceptions 10.11
exemptions 5.05–5.11
extradition cases 8.08
post-Brexit 5.04
prior to Brexit 5.02
Refugee Convention 5.15
against Russia 5.09
travel bans 1.44, 5.01–5.04
implementation of sanctions
new methods, financial sanctions 3.01–3.10
without delay, by designated persons 7.11–7.12
see also Office of Financial Sanctions Implementation (OFSI); OFSI Guidance; sanctions, UK
import of goods, trade sanctions 4.11–4.12, 4.28
information sharing
accounts and safe-deposit boxes 13.83
anti-money laundering (AML) 13.30–13.31
duty to respond to 13.83
existing, overview 12.01–12.03
Section 16 of 2018 Act 12.04–12.08
sensitive information 9.16
see also reporting obligations
interim freezing orders 3.05
International Financial Centres Forum 1.61
Iran
negotiations with 1.16
sanctions against 1.04, 1.13, 1.15, 1.16, 1.25
Islamic State of Iraq and Syria (ISIS)/Islamic State of Iraq and the Levant (ISIL) *see* Da'esh

Joint Committee Plan of Action (JCPOA) 1.13, 1.16
joint interests, financial sanctions 3.58–3.59
judicial review
Administrative Court 9.21
availability under 2018 Act 9.11
financial sanctions 3.19
preliminary matters 9.12, 9.15
sufficient interest or standing 9.15
see also court review of decisions

Keatinge, Tom 1.27

Law Commission 2.47
Law Society of England and Wales 1.56
Legal Sector Affinity Group Guidance 13.57
Legislating for the Withdrawal Agreement between the United Kingdom and the European Union **(2018 White Paper)** 1.23, 13.14
letting agents, 5MLD implementation 13.52
licences 10.08–10.10
  applying for 10.34–10.37
  counter-terrorism regimes 10.41–10.42
  defining 10.01
  general 10.23–10.33
  grounds for sanctions 10.08
  humanitarian 5.07
  licensing grounds
    other domestic regimes 10.21–10.22
    UK regimes 10.20
  OFSI licensing review and non-retrospectivity 10.18–10.19
  provisions under 2018 Act 10.02
  submitting an application 10.38–10.41
  see also exemptions

Magnitsky **clause** 1.59, 2.01, 2.09, 2.10, 2.17–2.24
  see also human rights
Ministers and ministerial reviews
  aircraft 6.06
  appropriate Minister
    core power under 2018 Act 2.07–2.09
    designations by *see below*
    OFSI Guidance 2.45
    passage of Bill 2.04
    shipping 6.12, 6.17–6.22
    type of sanctions, amending 2.42
  designations 8.01–8.37
    by description 7.31–7.34
    discretion and judgement by Minister 7.34
    mechanism under 2018 Act 7.20, 8.01, 8.38–8.41
    by name 7.24
    periodic review of certain designations 8.37
    power to vary or revoke 8.01–8.06
    regulations *see below*
    reports on exercise of Section 1 power 8.44
    right of a UN-named person to request a review 8.36
    right to request variation or revocation 8.07–8.36
  regulations (derogations)
    with counter-terrorism purpose 8.42–8.43
    new, on sanctions review procedure 8.12–8.31
    Section 1 of 2018 Act 8.38–8.41, 8.44
  see also designations (sanctions); Foreign & Commonwealth Office (FCO); Home Office (HO)/Home Secretary; Secretary of State powers/directions
minority interests, financial sanctions 3.56–3.57
money laundering (ML) *see* anti-money laundering (AML) measures; Fifth Money Laundering Directive (5MLD); Financial Action Task Force (FATF); Fourth Money Laundering Directive (4MLD); Money Laundering Regulations (MLRs); Third Money Laundering Directive (3MLD)
Money Laundering Regulations (MLRs)
  comparison of 2017 MLRs with new system
    criminal offences 13.34
    future-proofing 13.37
    geographical scope 13.36
    information sharing 13.30
    policies and procedures 13.29
    potential expansion of the population subject to regulation 13.27
    risk assessments 13.25
  following Brexit transition period 1.03
  narrow focus compared with 2018 Act 13.23
  revision of UK's 2007 MLRs 1.09
  role of FATF 13.03
  see also anti-money laundering (AML) measures; Fifth Money Laundering Directive (5MLD); Financial Action Task Force (FATF); Fourth Money Laundering Directive (4MLD); Third Money Laundering Directive (3MLD)
money laundering/terrorist financing (ML/TF) risks 1.49, 1.51
Mutual Evaluation Report (MER), FATF 1.45–1.46, 11.14–11.16

National Crime Agency (NCA) 1.42
National Risk Assessment 1.50
necessity 4.26, 9.35, 10.15
North Korea, sanctions against 1.14, 1.15, 6.05
  weapons of mass destruction programmes 7.17

Office for Professional Body AML Supervision (OPBAS) 13.32
Office of Financial Sanctions Implementation (OFSI)
  access to capital markets, list on restrictions 7.01, 7.09–7.10
  Consolidated List 7.01–7.16
    asset freezes 3.04, 7.03
    Cayman sanctions 3.14
    delisted persons remaining on 7.05
    implementation of sanctions without delay 7.11–7.12
    proscription under Terrorism Act 2000 7.13–7.16
    publicly available 7.01–7.10
    regimes covered 1.15
    sanctions compliance, avoiding overly narrow approach to 3.50
    updating 7.02, 7.04

Office of Financial Sanctions Implementation (OFSI) (*cont.*)
creation 1.47
financial sanctions 3.04, 3.14, 3.18
fines imposed by 11.01–11.02, 11.08, 11.09
Guidance *see* OFSI Guidance
immigration sanctions 5.07
licensing review and non-retrospectivity 10.18–10.19
reporting obligations 1.42, 12.01
Russian citizens, focus on 1.01, 7.01
see also financial sanctions; Russia, UK sanctions against (post-Brexit); sanctions, UK
OFSI Guidance 2.44–2.46
enforcement 11.08–11.13
information sharing and reporting 12.09–12.10
Russia, UK sanctions against (post-Brexit) 1.07, 1.20, 2.44, 4.06, 7.30
AML powers 13.18, 13.29
designation powers 7.30, 7.32
exceptions 10.05, 10.10
financial sanctions 3.10, 3.20, 3.32, 3.34, 3.49, 3.52
trade sanctions 4.04, 4.06
transition period 1.07–1.08
see also financial sanctions; Office of Financial Sanctions Implementation (OFSI)
Ombudsman to the ISIL and Al-Qaida Sanctions Committee 9.07
Organization for Security and Co-operation in Europe (OSCE) 2.09
ownership and control (financial sanctions) 3.50–3.59
defining 3.52–3.55
joint interests 3.58–3.59
minority interests 3.56–3.57
sanctions compliance, avoiding overly narrow approach to 3.50–3.51

Panama Papers 13.10
Paradise Papers 13.10
People with Significant Control (PSC) 1.52
Register 13.66
policies, controls and procedures
implementation of 5MLD 13.55–13.57
Proceeds of Crime Act 2002 (POCA 2002)
asset freezes 3.05
human rights 2.23
proportionality
court review of decisions 9.28, 9.30, 9.31, 9.35
crediting frozen accounts 10.15
trade sanctions 4.25
training requirements, 5MLD implementation 13.58
Public Bill Committee 1.61

registers, discrepancies on
change to dealing with 13.66–13.72
reporting obligations 12.01–12.10
designations 8.44
information 12.09–12.10
ministerial reviews 8.44
offences, under the 2018 Act 2.47–2.48
to Office of Financial Sanctions Implementation (OFSI) 1.42, 12.01
OFSI Guidance 12.09–12.10
Suspicious Activity Report (SAR) 1.42, 12.10
see also information sharing
reviews *see* court review of decisions; Ministers and ministerial reviews
risk assessments
anti-money laundering (AML) 13.25–13.26
high-risk countries 13.77–13.78, 13.80
money laundering/terrorist financing (ML/TF) risks 1.49, 1.51
National Risk Assessments 1.50, 13.26
Risk-Based Approach (RBA) 1.09, 13.16
Russia, UK sanctions against (post-Brexit) 1.01, 1.04, 1.15, 1.20
and current UK trade sanctions 4.07, 6.09
designation powers 7.24, 7.30, 7.32
financial 3.06, 3.10
asset freezes 1.01, 3.29, 3.32, 3.34
comparison with the EU 1.01, 1.20, 3.48
dealing 3.37
ownership and control 3.54
services and products 3.48, 3.49
future divergence in 1.20
human rights abuses 2.17
immigration 5.09
information sharing 12.04, 12.07
licensing and exceptions 10.05, 10.10, 10.13
shipping 6.10
state-owned financial institutions 3.54
terrorist groups 1.04
trade sanctions 4.04, 4.07, 4.10
see also Crimea; OFSI Guidance; Ukraine, Russian destabilising action in

sanctions
conflicts between regimes 1.13
in the EU *see* sanctions, EU
extra-territorial 1.28
provisions in 2018 Act *see* Sanctions and Anti-Money Laundering Act 2018
shift in use 1.11
in the UK *see* sanctions, UK
sanctions, EU
adding or removing names from lists 2.31, 2.32
autonomous 1.34
comparison with the UK 1.01, 1.20, 3.48
financial 1.34, 3.48
temporary powers relating to existing lists 2.30–2.36
UK bound by in Brexit transition period 1.07
see also European Union
sanctions, UK
amending type 2.42–2.43
and comparative analysis 1.70–1.74

core power *see* core power under 2018 Act
current/pre-Brexit regime 1.04, 1.12, 1.30–1.39, 2.08
discretionary purposes 2.05–2.06, 2.25
drivers prior to Brexit 1.12
existing scale of 1.15
financial *see* financial sanctions
following EU withdrawal *see* Brexit
future divergence in 1.17–1.29
'future-proofing' of scheme 2.49
government departments and agencies with a sanctions role 1.40–1.44
immigration *see* immigration sanctions
international assessment 1.45–1.54
Landsbanki Freezing Order 2008 1.21
new, reasons for making 2.09
OFSI Guidance 2.44–2.46
purpose 1.11–1.16
reasonableness 2.26
recent controversy 1.11–1.16
reform of existing scheme 1.69
regulations *see* sanctions regulations under 2018 Act
against Russia *see* Russia, UK sanctions against (post-Brexit)
suspension period 2.38
targets 1.04
temporary EU lists, requests in relation to 1.05
trade *see* trade sanctions
see also anti-money laundering (AML) measures

Sanctions and Anti-Money Laundering Act 2018
aircraft 6.01–6.08
anti-money laundering (AML) measures
core power under Section 49 13.15–13.17
expansion of population subject to regulation 13.24
impact of 2018 Act in the UK 13.12–13.14
new powers 1.75–1.77
overview of amendments in relation to 13.01–13.04
see also anti-money laundering (AML) measures; Fifth Money Laundering Directive (5MLD); Fourth Money Laundering Directive (4MLD); Third Money Laundering Directive (3MLD)
asset freezes 3.03–3.05, 3.31–3.35, 3.39–3.41
context 1.30–1.80
core power *see* core power under 2018 Act
court review of decisions 9.03–9.06
designation powers 7.17–7.35
see also designations (sanctions)
enforcement under 11.01–11.13
fines, mechanism for imposing 11.01–11.02
OFSI Guidance 11.08–11.13
overview of amendments 11.03–11.07
Explanatory Note 1.12, 1.16, 2.19, 9.13
designations 8.05, 8.43, 8.44
'Henry VIII' powers 1.56
immigration appeals (Section 48) 5.12–5.16
legislative history 1.55–1.68
licences 10.02
Magnitsky clause 1.59, 2.17–2.24
overview 1.69
passage of Bill 2.02–2.06
and Public Bill Committee 1.61
purpose 1.06, 1.10
reform of existing sanctions scheme 1.69
regulations *see* sanctions regulations under 2018 Act
report stage 2.03
see also anti-money laundering (AML) measures; Office of Financial Sanctions Implementation (OFSI); OFSI Guidance; Russia, UK sanctions against (post-Brexit); sanctions, UK

sanctions regulations under 2018 Act
core power to make 2.07–2.16
derogation, power to vary or revoke 8.04–8.06
offences, reporting 2.47–2.48
revocation and amendment 2.39–2.41
suspension of prohibitions and requirements 2.37–2.38

Secretary of State powers/directions
aircraft 6.02, 6.04, 6.08
anti-money laundering (AML) 13.15, 13.42
counter-terrorism 8.43
designations, revocation or variation 1.69, 8.01
immigration sanctions 5.09, 5.12, 5.13, 5.15
ships 6.14, 6.16, 6.24, 6.25
terrorist groups 7.34

Security Council, UN *see* United Nations Security Council (UNSC)

Serious Crime Prevention Orders (SCPOs) 11.05, 11.07, 11.13

shipping
appropriate Minister 6.17–6.22
designated ships 6.12
disqualified ships 6.12
goods seized from, procedure for dealing with 6.17–6.18
movement of ships, controlling 6.09–6.16
revocation and review 6.19–6.25
Russia, UK sanctions against 6.09
specified ships 6.12
trade sanctions 4.02, 4.18, 4.22
UK Ship Register 6.15

supervision
Fifth Money Laundering Directive (5MLD) provisions 13.59–13.61
supervisory functions 13.32
virtual assets, FATF guidance 13.10

Suspicious Activity Report (SAR) 1.42, 12.10

Syria, sanctions against 1.14

targeted financial sanctions (TFS) 1.46, 1.47, 10.17, 11.14

tax advisers, 5MLD implementation 13.51

territorial application of financial sanctions 3.11–3.17

Terrorism Act 2000
proscription under 7.13–7.16
terrorist financing (TF) 1.76, 13.25
FATF assessment of UK policy 1.50
Fifth Money Laundering Directive (5MLD) 13.09, 13.56, 13.58
post-Brexit 13.02, 13.05, 13.06, 13.09, 13.14, 13.15, 13.17, 13.19, 13.22, 13.25
terrorist groups 1.04, 1.15
Third Money Laundering Directive (3MLD) 13.07
torture 2.21
trade sanctions
acquisition 4.15
aircraft 4.22
arms embargoes, distinguished from 4.01–4.03
and criminal law 4.24
definitions and concepts 4.13–4.22
exports 4.08–4.10, 4.28
imports 4.11–4.12, 4.28
making available 4.14
necessity 4.26
objects of cultural interest 4.19
and other UK laws 4.23–4.29
proportionality 4.25
purpose 4.04–4.07
Russia, UK sanctions against (post-Brexit) 4.04, 4.07, 4.10
scope 4.08–4.29
services provision 4.17
UK military list 4.01–4.03
vessels 4.02, 4.18, 4.22
training requirements, 5MLD implementation 13.58
transition period, Brexit 1.01–1.10
Transparency International UK 1.61
transport *see* aircraft; shipping
travel bans 1.44, 5.01–5.04
trust registration 13.81
Ukraine, Russian destabilising action in 1.72, 1.74
designated persons and powers 7.01, 7.24, 7.25, 7.32
territorial integrity, threats to 7.32
UN Security Council (UNSC)
choosing not to act 1.14
decisions binding on the UK 9.06
designated persons named under Resolutions 7.35
immigration sanctions 5.02
sanctions by 2.49
trade sanctions 4.22
Unexplained Wealth Order (UWO) 3.05
United Kingdom
alliances post-Brexit 1.26
AML powers post-Brexit 13.01–13.39
corporate transparency, promoting 1.51
HM Government departments and agencies with sanctions role 1.40–1.44
impact of 2018 Act on AML measures 13.12–13.14
licensing grounds 10.20
sanctions *see* sanctions, UK; Sanctions and Anti-Money Laundering Act 2018
signatory to the UN 1.01
statutory instruments 1.35
United Nations
Charter *see* Charter of the United Nations
immigration sanctions 5.10
listings publicized by the FCO 7.12
Security Council *see* UN Security Council (UNSC)
UK a signatory to 1.01
United States
Patriot Act 3.11
sanctions against Iran and Cuba 1.13, 1.16, 1.25

'wilful blindness' doctrine
financial sanctions 3.24–3.26